A History of Everyday Life in Scotland, 1600 to 1800

A History of Everyday Life in Scotland

SERIES EDITORS: CHRISTOPHER A. WHATLEY AND ELIZABETH FOYSTER

A History of Everyday Life in Scotland, 1600 to 1800

Edited by Elizabeth Foyster and Christopher A. Whatley

Edinburgh University Press

© editorial matter and organisation Elizabeth Foyster and Christopher A. Whatley, 2010
© the chapters their several authors, 2010

Edinburgh University Press Ltd
22 George Square, Edinburgh
www.euppublishing.com

Typeset in 10/12pt Goudy Old Style by
Servis Filmsetting Ltd, Stockport, Cheshire, and
printed and bound in Great Britain by
CPI Antony Rowe, Chippenham and Eastbourne

A CIP record for this book is available from the British Library

ISBN 978 0 7486 1964 1 (hardback)
ISBN 978 0 7486 1965 8 (paperback)

The right of the contributors to be identified as authors
of this work has been asserted in accordance with the
Copyright, Designs and Patents Act 1988

Published with the support of the Edinburgh University
Scholarly Publishing Initiatives Fund.

Contents

Tables

Figures

Acknowledgements

Preparing a book like this depends on the contributions of many people. The book, like the series of which it is part, has been a long time in gestation. It began with a tentative enquiry from John Davey, then of Edinburgh University Press, as to whether we would be interested in developing a series of books on everyday life in Scotland. Our response was positive, and we then entered into a dialogue with John and his advisers at Edinburgh University Press about content, themes and the time-frames to be covered by each of the four books in the series. The next step was to identify editors for each of the four volumes, who were not only experts in the social history of the periods identified, but who also had experience of, and some enthusiasm for, collaborative academic ventures. Happily, we were able to recruit: Professor Ted Cowan and Dr Lizanne Henderson (both University of Glasgow), Professor Graeme Morton (University of Guelph) and Dr Trevor Griffiths (University of Edinburgh) and Professor Lynn Abrams (University of Glasgow) and Professor Callum Brown (University of Dundee). In their turn, the editors have recruited teams of contributors – the authors of the individual chapters.

In order to get the project moving, we held a one-day conference in Dundee in 2004, at which methodological and other challenges surrounding the history of everyday life were discussed. For their invaluable contributions on this occasion we wish to thank Professor Anthony Cohen (Queen Margaret University) and Dr Stephen Wilson (University of East Anglia). For organising the conference, thanks are due to Sara Reid, formerly of the Department of History, University of Dundee. To provide an opportunity for the volume editors and their contributors to present their initial research findings to a critical but receptive audience, a two-day, multi-paper meeting was held in Dundee in September 2006. This was generously supported by the British Academy which awarded us with a Conference Grant to cover the costs of the event. Lynsey McIrvine, of the University of Dundee, made the necessary arrangements in her customary, highly efficient fashion. Lynne Elder, in the University of Dundee's College of Arts and Social Sciences office, assisted the editors by receiving, tidying up and storing the chapter files from the contributors as they arrived. The final version of the manuscript was prepared, for handover to the publishers, by Aileen Ross. To all these individuals and to everyone else who has played any part in the preparation of the series, we extend our sincere thanks.

Finally, but by no means least, we should thank Esmé Watson of Edinburgh University Press for her guidance, prompting and support over the past two years as we have sought to bring this and the other volumes to completion.

E.A.F.
C.A.W.

Series Editors' Foreword

Christopher A. Whatley and Elizabeth Foyster

The four books in this series examine the ordinary, routine, daily behaviour, experiences and beliefs of Scottish people from medieval times until the present day. Their focus is on the 'common people', that is, most of the population, the ordinary folk below the ranks of the aristocracy, substantial landowners, opulent merchants, major industrialists, bankers and financiers, even if it is true that people from relatively humble beginnings have managed periodically to haul themselves into the ranks of the nation's social elite. Contributors in each volume describe the landscapes and living spaces that formed the familiar contexts for daily life. The events and activities that determined how individuals spent their time are explored, including the experiences of work and leisure, and ranging in duration from those that affected the passage of a single day, through to those that impinged on peoples' lives according to the calendar or the seasons and weather, to those that were commonly experienced over the course of the life cycle. Scottish people made sense of their everyday lives, it is argued, through ritual and belief, by their interactions with others and by self-reflection.

As a whole, the series aims to provide a richer and more closely observed history of the social, economic and cultural lives of ordinary Scots than has been published previously. This is not to suggest that accounts and analyses of the everyday in Scotland have not been written. They have.[1] And this present series of four volumes overlaps with the publication of the fourteen volumes of the *Scottish Life and Society* series, sponsored by the European Ethnological Research Centre in Edinburgh, led by Alexander Fenton. The first volume in this series was published in 2000, with others following at intervals through to 2008. Unlike the series of which this volume is part, which is structured by chronological periods in which selected broad themes are studied, each of the books in the *Scottish Life and Society* series has been organised around a particular topic, including: farming and rural life; domestic life; boats, fishing and the sea; and religion.[2] They are substantial, multi-authored volumes and eclectic in the range of subjects and sub-topics covered, entirely befitting the series sub-title, *A Compendium of Scottish Ethnology*. It represents a monumental resource for future researchers.[3] Where appropriate, contributors to this series *A History of Everyday Life in Scotland* have drawn upon the *Scottish Life and Society* team's findings. Rather than clashing, however, or overlapping to the point of repetition, the two series complement each other, with ours concentrating more on continuities and change, and historical explanations for this, and written, mainly but not entirely, by professional historians. Together, both series offer readers a heady mix of historical information, and an array of approaches, analytical styles and depths and insights.

The everyday had a context, or contexts. At the individual level what was everyday altered across time and often differed according to class, gender, age, religion and ethnic group. It was also shaped by national and regional surroundings, and could vary between urban and rural environments, highland and lowland, inland and coastal settings, the northern and western islands.[4] Contributors pay attention to regional and local variations and peculiarities, especially with regard to language, dialect, practices and customs. The series reveals aspects of the everyday that were distinctively Scottish, but it also shows how the everyday lives of Scots were influenced by other cultures and nations. This resulted from travel, trading relations, or migration by Scots who lived and worked abroad, both temporarily and permanently. Indirectly, Scots read and learned of the shared or conflicting ideas and practices of everyday life in near and distant lands. Contributors to the series can point to inter-national differences and similarities because of the pioneering work on the everyday that has been conducted by historians on other countries across a range of periods. While relatively little has been published specifically on the everyday in Scotland, or even Britain, we are fortunate to be able to draw upon an extensive body of historical research for Europe and the Americas.[5]

The roots of this historical endeavour, and the approaches that this series takes, lie in a range of developments within the discipline. In Britain, the interest of social historians – often with a Marxist perspective – in writing 'history from below', has brought the lives of working-class people to centre stage.[6] In Scotland the study of 'new' social history was pioneered by T. C. Smout, with his seminal *History of the Scottish People, 1560–1830* (1969), although Smout's approach was liberal rather than leftist.[7] This was followed in subsequent decades by a surge of research on a range of topics, and a plethora of publications written by a small army of historians examining different historical periods, including the same author's *Century of the Scottish People, 1830–1950* (1986).[8] Furth of Scotland, *Annaliste* historians, such as Fernand Braudel, focused attention on the material culture of daily life, and a later generation of French and then Italian historians narrowed the scale of study to produce 'microhistories'. These examined in detail the history of one individual, village or incident in order to understand the wider *mentalité* of the societies of which they were a part.[9] Historians in Germany have addressed the issue of the everyday most directly, where the concept of *Alltagsgeschichte* ('the history of everyday life') was conceived, and continues to be the source of lively debate.[10] Preceding, running alongside and occasionally influencing historical work has been the study of everyday life by academics in other disciplines, including ethnology, sociology, social anthropology, geography, psychology and cultural theory.[11] Academics from these disciplines contribute to some of the volumes in this series.

What can the reader expect from this series, and how does the content of the books that comprise it differ from other social histories of Scotland?

First, by uncovering the everyday, we provide fresh insights into a diverse range of historical topics. Whereas much social history can focus on the structures, ideals or prescriptions that were intended to govern daily living, this series examines the practices and realities of life experience. Although not the primary purpose of the series, people's experiences of major change, like wars, famine and environmental disaster, are incorporated. The result is to demonstrate how the extraordinary affected the ordinary. But as Alexander Fenton correctly observed of Scottish rural society some years ago, broad trends, big ideas and eye-catching technologies can explain only so much; how they impacted on the everyday depended on local conditions and responses. As important for understanding the everyday lives of ordinary people, and the pace and nature of change, were, for example, how small-scale pieces of equipment were adopted and used, and how things were done in the home or barn or yard far from power centres that passed legislation, or from which sprang – as in the case of Edinburgh and east-central Scotland in the early eighteenth century – models for and aids to agrarian improvement. But on Orkney even in the later eighteenth century weighing machines – the pundlar and the pindlar – weights and measures, and the commonly used, one-stilt plough, had been in use since Viking times.[12] Change on the ground was invariably slow, piecemeal and indigenous rather than spectacular.[13]

Examples and case studies of aspects of everyday life in these volumes also enhance our understanding of some long-standing subjects of debate within Scottish history. Hence, readers will gain new insights about the role of the kirk in social and moral discipline, the impact of enclosure and the Clearances in the Lowlands as well as the Highlands, the struggles between popular and elite forms of culture, standards of living and the significance of 'public' and 'private' spaces in daily life. In addition, the exploration of the everyday has allowed our contributors to cover less familiar historical territory – some of which has posed considerable challenges. We discover how Scottish people's fears, anxieties and perceptions of danger changed over time, we learn about the importance of gestures as well as forms of verbal and written communication and we begin to recover how ordinary Scots experienced their sensory worlds of taste, sound, sight and touch. The everyday enables historians to engage with important emerging topics within the discipline of history, for example, the history of the Scottish landscape and the environment. Chapters in the books in the series explore the changing relationship with and impact of Scots upon their natural environment.[14] The series also demonstrates how women, whose lives were once considered too everyday and mundane to merit serious academic study, played a central part particularly in the negotiation and management of home and family daily life.[15] In addition, women could play an active role in everyday life beyond the domestic scene, as recent research has begun to reveal.[16] Scottish men's gendered identities were also constructed and experienced in the context of the everyday.

The contributors to this series have been able to write these histories not, on the whole, because they have discovered vast quantities of new evidence in the archives, although much original material has been uncovered. Rather, a new history has emerged because they have asked novel questions of material with which they were familiar, and have pieced together a wide range of what was often unused information from both primary and secondary sources. Undoubtedly, writing the history of the everyday presents unique problems of evidence for the historian. These problems can vary with historical period; those researching the everyday in medieval times can face a dearth of written sources, while it is easy to be overwhelmed by the mass of information available for the twentieth century. However, there are also more fundamental issues of evidence at stake that have to be faced by all historians of the everyday. As Braudel recognised, 'everyday life consists of the little things one hardly notices in time and space'.[17] Everyday life could be so banal, repetitive, tedious, boring, easily forgotten or taken for granted that our predecessors rarely bothered to record it. Sometimes this means we have to read 'against the grain' of the sources that do survive. In other words, examining the exceptional incident or object to deduce its opposite. For the most part, however, writing about the everyday necessitates the laborious sorting through and amalgamation of fragments of the past: written, visual and material. Contributors to this series have found evidence of the everyday in artefacts, archaeological sites, buildings, diaries, letters, autobiographies, polite and popular literature, trial records of church, burgh and state courts, estate papers, directories, prints, maps, photographs and oral testimony. It is the incidental comment, remark or observation, chance survival, brief glimpse or snapshot that often contains a clue to and even the core of the everyday. The historian's task is to put these details together, 'as in a jigsaw puzzle', so that we can present to readers a picture of the everyday.[18]

What the reader will not get from the series is a complete or comprehensive compendium of everyday life. This, as indicated earlier, is to be found elsewhere. It has not been our intention to list or describe all everyday objects and occurrences, even if this were practicably possible. Rather, our purpose is to explain and analyse the everyday as well as record it. The methodological tools used by contributors are diverse, and reflect their differing disciplinary backgrounds. This is especially the case in the twentieth century volume, where interdisciplinary approaches are most widely employed.

The second distinctive contribution of this series to our understanding of the Scottish past is concerned with what it reveals about historical change.

Across the series the reader can expect to find enduring continuities within everyday life, but also transformations, some rapid, but most long and drawn out. These can be observed by the historian; how far and in what ways they were experienced by ordinary people is harder to know. Yet, it is clear that over time changes did occur in everyday life, as new ways of working, forms of social organisation, products, sights and sounds expanded the experiences of ordinary Scots. Even the fundamentals that comprise everyday life – what people ate and drank, where they slept, what they wore, where they worked and how they travelled from A to B – were indisputably transformed. Even so, these volumes also present evidence of elements of everyday life stubbornly resistant to change. The consecutive volumes in this series do not signify a set of breaks with the last, or a turning point in all aspects of the everyday. Hence, to take some examples: Scots continued to trust self-administered and home-made cures for illness even as medicine became professionalised and institutionalised; oral culture continued to thrive long after literacy had become the norm; and families and their communities continued to mark birth, marriage and death as significant rites of passage. Ale is still widely drunk at the start of the twenty-first century; and walking and other earlier forms of transport, the use of the bicycle for example, are growing in popularity. The enduring qualities of everyday life have attracted comment. For the Marxist cultural theorist, Henri Lefebvre, the everyday in more recent times offered a glimmer of hope in capitalist societies, because it revealed 'a corrective to the spectacularizing discourse of modernity'. Despite industrial and technological change, the humdrum and main concerns of everyday life for many people remained little altered.[19] Historians have noted people's determination to maintain the routines of daily life in the face of dramatic change, such as during periods of crisis and conflict.[20] Our predecessors shared our need for food, drink and shelter, and our yearning for love and affection, but when other parts of their lives faced serious disruption, the relative importance of fulfilling these needs had to be adjusted. Scots could be proud of 'making do' in times of hardship, and of the fact that daily life 'went on' despite the havoc and destruction around them. This series looks more closely at why particular aspects of the everyday were so hard to disrupt.

By so doing, revealing perspective is provided upon the meaning for ordinary Scots of 'great events', such as wars, which traditionally have been seen as the key moments of change in Scottish – and other nations' – history. Arguably, it was in the context of the 'non-event-ness' of the everyday that the vast majority of Scots spent their lives.[21] Indeed, as Dorothee Wierling has observed, 'most persons have *nothing but* . . . ordinary everyday life'.[22] Studying the history of everyday life is about retrieving the history of what most people did most of the time.

The series demonstrates that the speed of change in everyday life could vary between that experienced within the space of a generation, to barely perceptible shifts across centuries. However, the series also offers some explanations for what brought about change when it occurred. More important is how change was accommodated within the everyday; this was a social process. The seeds for change in Scottish society were frequently contained within the everyday. The everyday was often 'political'. Studying the everyday allows us to see how ordinary people could exercise power over their lives to resist, counter, accommodate or adapt to the changes they encountered. As Ben Highmore has observed, everyday life often serves in helping people to cope with 'the shock of the new'. The everyday becomes the setting:

> for making the unfamiliar familiar; for getting accustomed to the disruption of custom; for struggling to incorporate the new; for adjusting to different ways of living. The everyday marks the success and failure of this process. It witnesses the absorption of the most revolutionary of inventions into the landscape of the mundane. Radical transformations in all walks of life become 'second nature'.[23]

In short, it is by examining the minutiae of people's daily lives that we can uncover the significance of historical change as this affected ordinary people.

Above all – and this is our third aim – the series aims to provide an accessible history that will interest, excite and engage with the reader. This should not be difficult to achieve given the degree of public interest in the everyday. From the popularity of 'reality' TV shows, where individuals are exposed to reconstructed life as their Iron Age ancestors might have lived it, for instance, to the fact that it is often the kitchens and servants' living quarters of stately homes which attract the most visitors and curiosity, it is clear that there is an appetite to find out more about the everyday. This is because the history of the everyday is one to which most people can relate, or at least with which we can empathise. It is the bread and butter of life in the past. This is not to suggest that the reader will find any straightforward or single narrative of everyday life in these volumes. The history of the everyday is complex in the extreme: the range of experience is immense, what evidence we do have is often contradictory and there are enormous black holes in our knowledge and understanding. The books in the series reflect all of this, but they have also identified patterns and processes that make some sense of the everyday life of the Scots over the centuries in all its diversity.

Notes

1. A classic in its time was H. G. Graham, *The Social Life of Scotland in the Eighteenth Century* (London, 1899), while Marjory Plant's *Domestic Life of Scotland in the Eighteenth Century* (Edinburgh, 1948) and Marion Lochhead's *The Scots Household in the Eighteenth Century* (Edinburgh, 1948) broke new ground in revealing much about everyday life in and around the home. It was Alexander (Sandy) Fenton,

however, who led the way in Scotland in modern exploration of the everyday, particularly that of rural society: see, for example, A. Fenton, *Scottish Country Life* (Edinburgh, 1976, 1977; East Linton, 1999) and *The Northern Isles: Orkney and Shetland* (Edinburgh, 1978; East Linton, 1997).

2. *Scottish Life and Society: A Compendium of Scottish Ethnology*, 14 vols (John Donald, in association with the European Ethnological Research Centre and the National Museums of Scotland).

3. Perhaps the most enduring research tool deriving from the project will be H. Holmes and F. Macdonald (eds), *Scottish Life and Society: Bibliography for Scottish Ethnology* (Edinburgh, 2003), vol. 14.

4. For a fine study of the impact of environmental factors and changing international conditions upon a locality and aspects of everyday life in the northern isles, see H. D. Smith, *Shetland Life and Trade, 1550–1914* (Edinburgh, 1984).

5. See, for example, C. Dyer, *Everyday Life in Medieval England* (London, 1994); S. Wilson, *The Magical Universe: Everyday Ritual and Magic in Pre-Modern Europe* (London, 2000); R. Sarti, *Europe at Home: Family and Material Culture 1500–1800* (New Haven, CT, 2002); R. Braun, *Industrialisation and Everyday Life*, trans. S. H. Tenison (Cambridge, 1990); S. Fitzpatrick, *Everyday Stalinism. Ordinary Life in Extraordinary Times: Soviet Russia in the 1930s* (Oxford, 1999); 'The Everyday Life in America series', edited by Richard Balkin; and M. Wasserman, *Everyday Life and Politics in Nineteenth-Century Mexico: Men, Women and War* (Albuquerque, 2000).

6. The work of E. P. Thompson was especially important in this regard, notably his seminal *The Making of the English Working Class* (London, 1965). See also the collection of his essays in *Customs in Common* (London, 1991). Thompson pays little attention to Scotland; more inclusive – and comparative – is Keith Wrightson's *Earthly Necessities: Economic Lives in Early Modern Britain* (New Haven, CT, 2000), which contains much on everyday lives and how these were affected by the emergence of the market economy.

7. Marxist analyses of Scottish society appeared later, for example, T. Dickson (ed.), *Scottish Capitalism: Class, State and Nation from before the Union to the Present* (London, 1980); Dickson also edited *Capital and Class in Scotland* (Edinburgh, 1982).

8. Some sense of what has been achieved over the past half century or so can be seen in the bibliographies that accompany each of the chapters in R. A. Houston and W. W. Knox's *New Penguin History of Scotland from the Earliest Times to the Present Day* (London, 2001).

9. See, for example, F. Braudel, *Civilization and Capitalism 15th–18th Century. Vol. I: The Structures of Everyday Life: The Limits of the Possible*, trans. S. Reynolds (London, 1981); E. Le Roy Ladurie, *Montaillou: Cathars and Catholics in a French Village 1294–1324*, trans. Barbara Bray (Harmondsworth, 1980); and C. Ginzburg, *The Cheese and the Worms: The Cosmos of a Sixteenth-Century Miller*, trans. J. and A. Tedeschi (Baltimore, 1980).

10. See, for example, A. Lüdtke (ed.), *The History of Everyday Life: Reconstructing Historical Experiences and Ways of Life*, trans. W. Templer (Princeton, NJ, 1995).

11. See, for example, A. J. Weigert, *Sociology of Everyday Life* (London, 1981); J. M. White, *Everyday Life of the North American Indian* (New York, 2003); T. Friberg, *Everyday Life: Women's Adaptive Strategies in Time and Space*, trans. M. Gray (Stockholm, 1993); G. M. Davies and R. H. Logie (eds), *Memory in Everyday Life* (Amsterdam, 1993); H. Lefebvre, *Critique of Everyday Life*, 2 vols (London, 1991 and 2002); Michel de Certeau, *The Practice of Everyday Life*, trans. S. Rendall (Berkeley, CA, 1984); and M. Certeau, L. Giard and P. Mayol, *The Practice of Everyday Life Volume 2: Living and Cooking*, trans. T. J. Tomasik (Minneapolis, MN, 1998).

12. W. S. Hewison (ed.), *The Diary of Patrick Fea of Stove, Orkney, 1766–96* (East Linton, 1997), pp. 21, 24.

13. Fenton, *Scottish Country Life*, p. v.

14. See T. C. Smout, *Nature Contested: Environmental History in Scotland and Northern England Since 1600* (Edinburgh, 2000); and for a study which looks more closely at the relationship between one element of the environment, trees, and aspects of everyday life, T. C. Smout (ed.), *People and Woods in Scotland: A History* (Edinburgh, 2003).

15. For discussion of the links between women and the everyday, see D. Wierling, 'The history of everyday life and gender relations: on historical and historio-graphical relationships', in Lüdtke, *History of Everyday Life*, pp. 149–68.

16. See, for example, E. Ewan and M. M. Meikle (eds), *Women in Scotland, c. 1100–c. 1750* (East Linton, 1999); L. Abrams, E. Gordon, D. Simonton and E. J. Yeo (eds), *Gender in Scottish History since 1700* (Edinburgh, 2006); W. W. Knox, *Lives of Scottish Women: Women and Scottish Society, 1800–1980* (Edinburgh, 2006). A pioneering if eccentric account of women's role in popular protest was J. D. Young's *Women and Popular Struggles: A History of Scottish and English Working-Class Women, 1500–1984* (Edinburgh, 1985).

17. Braudel, *Civilization and Capitalism*, p. 29.

18. Sarti, *Europe at Home*, p. 1.

19. J. Moran, 'History, memory and the everyday', *Rethinking History*, 8:1 (2004), 54–7.

20. See, for example, N. Longmate, *How We Lived Then: A History of Everyday Life During the Second World War* (London, 1971).

21. The concept of 'non-event-ness' is taken from B. Highmore, *Everyday Life and Cultural Theory* (London, 2002), p. 34.

22. Wierling, 'The history of everyday life', p. 151; the emphasis is in the original.

23. Highmore, *Everyday Life*, p. 2.

Introduction

Recovering the Everyday in Early Modern Scotland

Elizabeth Foyster and Christopher A. Whatley

> It must be remembered that life consists not of a series of illustrious actions, or elegant enjoyments; the greater part of our time passes in compliance with necessities, in the performance of daily duties, in the removal of small inconveniences, in the procurement of petty pleasures . . . The true state of every nation is the state of common life.[1]

In 1775 Samuel Johnson sat down to write an account of his journey around the western islands of Scotland, which he had undertaken two years before accompanied by James Boswell. His belief that it was the 'necessities', 'daily duties' and 'petty pleasures', that provided the greatest insights into the life of a nation, led him to write what was in effect a detailed account of everyday life in eighteenth-century Scotland, and earned him the gratitude of social historians ever since. Johnson was not alone in his attempt to capture the everyday. When the foundation stone of the bridewell on Calton Hill was laid in Edinburgh in 1791, it was decided to insert two glass bottles. One contained a list of names of the city magistrates and officers of the Grand Lodge; the other the *Edinburgh Almanack* and a copy of each of the city's four newspapers. It is certainly intriguing to ponder why these items were selected, and what contemporaries hoped future generations would learn by setting these representations of everyday city life into stone. It may well be that by the end of the eighteenth century there was a growing sense of change in everyday life. In the early modern period it is clear that everyday life could be, and was, affected by larger 'national' events. These, however, were sometimes transitory or temporary, leaving the underlying structures of everyday living more or less intact. These have to be identified. But there were also processes, developments and changes that, over time, altered aspects of the everyday, irrevocably. As this Introduction will outline, and the chapters that follow will demonstrate, population growth, urbanisation, changes to the rural economy and political and religious upheaval all had an impact on the daily patterns, rhythms and rituals of everyday life for ordinary Scots.

Changes to everyday life were often gradual, hard to discern and not unusually regional and even local in their impact. As the chapters of this volume will demonstrate, however, the historian of everyday life in the early modern period is aided considerably by the existence of a range of primary sources,

which are not available to those researching earlier times. Sir John Sinclair's
decision to compile a questionnaire sent to all parish ministers with some 160
queries about matters as diverse as population size, climate, disease, housing,
wages, household budgets, charity and the support of the poor has supplied
historians with a veritable mine of information about Scotland in the 1790s
– although Sinclair had his precursors dating back to Sir Robert Sibbald and
other early- and mid-eighteenth-century geographers whose local and parish
surveys contain valuable information about life 'on the ground'.[2] The eager-
ness of the post-Reformation kirk to regulate many aspects of daily life, and
the willingness of parishioners to report with remarkably close attention
to detail those who did not conform to the kirk's strict moral code, means
that we have access to records that give us otherwise hard to discern insights
into the details of everyday life for men and women across the social scale.
From church and other court minutes and papers that focus upon behaviour
that was deemed unacceptable, and probably exceptional, we can infer what
was normal and everyday. These same records can be especially valuable
as pointers to how people conducted their relationships, and occasionally
provide us with glimpses into our predecessor's most intimate moments.
Such occasions were unlikely to be otherwise recorded, yet early modern
historians are also fortunate that this was a period when literacy rates were
improving and more was recorded in ink and on paper. Burgh records and
estate papers – among both of which are frequently to be found volumi-
nous financial papers, including treasurers' and factors' and chamberlains'
accounts, invoices and memoranda – provide the raw material from which
we can construct an understanding of the lives of ordinary people as they
worked, traded, ate and drank and played. Diary keeping, too, became more
common, and even if they make for tedious reading at times, especially when
the writer's hand is crabbed and miniscule, can be remarkably revealing
about the everyday lives of particular individuals and their localities.[3] But life
could be dull and repetitive, with higher social standing offering no guaran-
tee of variety or fulfilment. The anguish of nineteen-year-old Janet Playfair,
daughter of a Forfarshire parish minister who allowed no book reading on
Sundays until after supper, resonates across the centuries with her reflection
at the turn of the new year in 1798 that another year had gone by, wasted: 'To
go for nothing', she wrote, 'to be contented with dressing, undressing, visiting or receiving visits, or trifling in household matters. It is too bad!'[4]

Across the early modern period Scotland attracted visitors from the
south, like Thomas Morer at the end of the seventeenth century and Daniel
Defoe in 1706–7 and again in the 1720s. Many recorded their impressions,
the best known being those of Johnson and Boswell, who were pioneers of
Highland travel, arriving just prior to the point at which such tours became
fashionable. Those embarking on such visits sought picturesque and sublime
landscapes, places associated with Ossian, historic spots like Bannockburn
and Culloden and modern marvels like David Dale's cotton mills at New

Lanark.[5] Visitors' accounts invariably betray certain prejudices, which were often unflattering as far as the Scots were concerned. But alongside much descriptive material there are observations and often incidental remarks that reveal aspects of Scotland and Scottish society that might otherwise be lost to posterity. At the same time we should guard against the very natural tendency of outsiders to record the exceptional, perhaps to startle or delight their readers. To be fair, the rapidly rising number of Scots who made exploratory forays into the land of their birth, could be equally guilty of making, and writing down, throwaway remarks about England and the English, but, fortunately for the historian, they often took note of farming practices, town life, the appearance of buildings, customs and practices that differed from those with which they had been familiar, thereby adding to our stock of knowledge of everyday Scotland.[6]

PEOPLING THE SCOTTISH LANDSCAPE

Everyday life for most Scots was lived on, or in some way closely connected with, the land. Consequently, whether for lairds or day labourers, each day's weather was of prime importance: upon the weather – whether fine, windy, freezing or wet – depended the tasks that could be carried out. Underlying the unpredictable day to day shifts in the weather, as Robert A. Dodgshon shows in Chapter 1, were the more or less regular rhythms of the seasons, which fixed an immutable pattern throughout the land: sowing in spring; harvesting in the late summer and autumn; breaking ground and ploughing; and a range of winter-time work.[7] Families, households and the able-bodied living alone maintained themselves by what the ground they tilled or herded could produce: that is, for their own personal or household use, or for their masters who might pay them either in money or kind for their services. For most of the period covered by this book, even those involved in manufacturing and mining – coal miners and their bearers, for instance – also worked on the land for some of the time, and certainly during sowing and harvest. Even by 1800, when unprecedented numbers of Scots were flocking to the expanding, mainly manufacturing towns like Paisley, Glasgow and Kilmarnock, two-thirds of the population lived in towns and villages of fewer than 2,500 inhabitants and in the countryside. Glasgow was not the grim, tightly-packed, upas tree of a city it would become in the nineteenth century. Rather it was a collection of villages such like Anderston, Bridgeton, Calton and Camlachie, each with distinct social and occupational characteristics, with fields and meadows in between, over which later in the eighteenth century and into the nineteenth, radical weavers and others would march, gathering supporters on their way.[8] Nor did everyone live in expanding towns: burghs such as Culross, Falkland, Lanark and St Andrews declined in the seventeenth and eighteenth centuries, while Dumfries was not much more populous in the 1790s than it had been in 1639.[9]

Across the countryside, too, Scotland's people were distributed more evenly than would be the case later. Until the middle of the eighteenth century half of the population may have lived north of an imaginary line stretching from the Tay to Dumbarton. More than a third was located in the Highlands and Islands. There were some densely populated districts, mainly in the more fertile lowlands along the rivers Forth and Tay, and in the lower Clyde valley, the Solway plain, central Ayrshire, the Merse and in the north-east around Aberdeen and the Moray Firth. But overall, population density was lower than most of the rest of Europe, including England and Wales and Ireland, although more than Scandinavia.[10] Nevertheless, by the first half of the eighteenth century the signs of future migration trends had been established, the main one being the flow of people to the western Lowlands, which experienced a bigger rise in numbers than any other region between the 1690s and 1755; over the course of the following half century there was a remarkable 82.7 per cent increase.[11] Indeed, it was internal movement and population redistribution that were more marked than a rise overall. What parish ministers were inclined to comment upon in the 1790s was the way in which some country districts were losing population, largely through the 'throwing together of farms' (whereby multiple tenancies were replaced by single tenants of larger holdings) and the attractions of the towns. It was relatively late in the eighteenth century that Scotland became noticeably more populous overall, and then only by just over a quarter, reaching around 1.6 million in 1801. This was a rate of growth considerably slower than Ireland's, but it represented a major change in that between the end of the 1690s – a decade during which famine slashed the population by between 5 and 20 per cent (in some districts) – and 1755, the date of the first census, the total increase may have been just 2.5 per cent, perhaps even less. It is doubtful whether the population of Scotland rose other than for short periods during the seventeenth century, given the frequency with which plagues and famines struck, but there are likely to have been surges in the first years of the century, and after the Restoration, to lift the number of inhabitants from something under 1 million at the end of the sixteenth century, to an estimated 1.2 million in 1691.

The process of urbanisation was substantial in its impact, but it was cumulative and drawn out. Scots had long been on the move: going abroad in search of employment as mercenaries, for instance, or as peddlers and the like and even as fairly substantial merchants.[12] As Alastair Durie illustrates in Chapter 10, internally there were streams of people in transit: young people travelling from country to town to take up apprenticeships and for marriage and of adults looking for work. Also on the roads and pathways were the aged, sick and infirm who were unable to support themselves or who had failed to secure regular charitable relief from their parishes or former employers. But there were limits to how many people could move and how far; for most ordinary people travel other than to the nearest town or village was unusual – and difficult to achieve given the demands of the agricultural calendar, reinforced on occasion by bans imposed by landlords and magistrates anxious to retain scarce labour.[13] Walking, Durie points out, is likely to have been the most common means of personal transportation when most everyday journeys were short distance. Yet, what might surprise the modern reader is how thick the press of wheeled, horse-drawn traffic could be at the end of the eighteenth century in the vicinity of the larger towns. The road from Paisley to Glasgow in 1796 was described as being encumbered with a 'multitude of carts & carriages'. Worse, or at least 'disagreeable', according to the same traveller (a Scot), were the roads around Ayr, where coal dust from the 'constant carriage' of carts had given the roads and hedges a 'gloomy hue'.[14]

Despite the number of Scots on the move, however, in the main, and until the later eighteenth century, the scale of migration was manageable and contained, in that individuals moving to a new parish were discouraged from settling unless they could provide a testimonial of their good behaviour from their place of origin. Even in Glasgow's sprawling Barony parish, at the turn of the eighteenth century the names of newcomers, whether from Ireland, the north-east of Scotland or much more often, the surrounding rural districts, were noted and their testimonials closely examined.[15]

The proportion of the population living in towns of 10,000-plus increased slowly during the seventeenth century, before rising sharply from 5.3 per cent in 1700 (less than half the figure for England and Wales and far less than in the Low Countries and Italy), through 9.2 per cent in 1750 to reach 17.3 per cent by 1801. This was not far short of the 20.3 per cent of England and Wales, and greater than most of the rest of Europe other than Belgium and the Netherlands. Life for newcomers to the capital, Edinburgh, and Glasgow, which overtook Edinburgh in size at the end of the eighteenth century, was radically different from what they had been familiar with in the countryside: for one thing there was the sheer volume of human beings. But there were other differences too. There were more opportunities to make a living through various kinds of casual work or even petty crime – and less risk of detection in what was a much more anonymous environment. Wages were usually higher too. For the fortunate few there were support systems in place (from fellow migrants drawn from the same parishes) and shelter was easier to find. There were the temptations of more numerous alehouses, easier sexual liaisons and of prostitutes, awe-inducing spectacles like companies of soldiers and town guards assembling and marching and loud, colourful civic celebrations to mark royal birthdays and naval and military victories (although these were also orchestrated in country parishes, where the exuberance of such events contrasted even more starkly with the humdrum of everyday living).[16] For the better-off arrivals from the middling and upper ranks, with money to spend and contacts, the transition was probably easier, but in addition they were able to join one or more of the multifarious voluntary associations, formal and informal – for musical performances, learned and lively discussion and debate, dancing and golf, for instance.

But in 1801 a slightly higher proportion of Scots were to be found in smaller towns – with populations between 2,500 and under 10,000; if we include villages and hamlets that might range upwards from a few hundred inhabitants the proportion would be even greater. It is with urban centres like this that most Scots in the early modern era were familiar, and became more so with the upsurge in the creation of new towns – mainly burghs of barony – in the seventeenth century, and planned villages in the eighteenth century. Albeit on a lesser scale, the more substantial of the towns housing fewer than 10,000 people – regional centres like Dumfries, for instance – were not without the attractions of the larger towns noted above. But the more important point is that many of the inhabitants of such places still retained a foothold in the countryside.

For more than a century after 1600 it was common for burgesses and others to grow crops and own and graze livestock either on their own plots or on common land, which was also a source of fuel, stone and turf (for building) for townspeople until these were either rented out by town councils or appropriated by neighbouring landowners who claimed ownership of them.[17] Throughout the period, fairs for the sale of agricultural produce and hiring workers, along with horse races and men's and women's foot races and other contests that paid prizes and facilitated betting, were regular features of urban life, especially in the smaller towns and in villages. As this suggests, country people and their produce were familiar sights in towns and villages; in places like Forfar and Montrose, and even Kirkwall in Orkney, the local gentry were regular visitors in the eighteenth century at assemblies and similar social events where dancing, dining, drinking and card games played for high stakes were on offer.[18]

CONDITIONS OF EVERYDAY LIFE

Inasmuch as everyday life is governed by the familiarity of places, physical structures and spaces, generations of Scots would have observed an urban landscape and participated in urban society that altered over two centuries, but not beyond recognition.

A feature of the period was greater social segregation according to wealth and status, with Edinburgh's better-off merchants and professionals favouring the old city centre, for instance. Middle-class women in Edinburgh seem to have been inclined to inhabit the churches, certain kinds of shops (notably those of milliners and perfumers) and the main streets – at certain times of the day.[19] Trades that were responsible for noxious smells or effluent, as Elizabeth Foyster describes in Chapter 8, were banished to remoter quarters, and particular districts became associated with the poor and poverty. Town gates were fewer, and in some places – Cupar in Fife, for instance – they had

been removed altogether by 1754.[20] Yet church towers continued to domi-
nate urban skylines, although not uniformly. Clear sight of the burghs on the
upper reaches of the Forth was obscured at times by the steam and smoke
from shore-side saltpans that operated more or less continuously through
the day and night (and throughout the 1600–1800 period), although they
were stopped for periods of weeks for repairs and for other reasons.[21] In the
vicinity of some Renfrewshire villages, clean-lined, three- and four-storey
mills rose up from the 1770s to dwarf the mainly single-storey dwellings
of craftspeople, handloom weavers and labourers of various descriptions.
More domestic housing was built of stone (although the move to stone was
already in place in the fifteenth century) and slated. As Charles McKean
shows in Chapter 2 much rebuilding took place. Glass windows became the
norm, and many of the outside stairs and other impediments that offended
local elites' perceptions of orderly improvement that became current in
the second half of the eighteenth century were removed from the frontages
of buildings, although the effect of this was not marked across the board
until the early nineteenth century. Townhouses were rebuilt and some were
built anew in new locations; market crosses, too, were moved, removed
and rebuilt. Some streets were widened and straightened, street lighting
became more common and greater attention was paid to cleanliness and
water supply. However, most burghs confined themselves to their medieval
limits until later in the eighteenth century when moves out to what became
their suburbs gathered pace. And while towards the end of the period
the town councils of several burghs authorised or sponsored new streets
and squares along the lines of Edinburgh's new towns – Edinburgh itself
extended its royalty in 1767 – older ground plans remained in place.[22] Yet,
the price of improvement and modernisation, McKean argues, was the loss
of individuality to uniformity, formality and new means of social control,
which together served to alter fundamentally the character of a town like
Edinburgh.[23]

There were also changes in rural lifestyles. By 1800 the degree of communal rural self-sufficiency had dropped dramatically, but by no means
had the old order been swept away. What had been set in train, however,
was a trend whereby rather than being sub-tenants or farm servants in the
thousands of clusters of ferm-towns of varying sizes that had been scattered
throughout the country, rural dwellers either joined the ranks of the more
prosperous single tenants of larger farms, of which there were relatively few,
or those of their paid employees – far and away the majority. Increasing
numbers now lived apart from their masters – and from their animals – in
rows of cottages, sometimes carefully located so that their occupants' movements, even during non-working time, could be observed by the farmer-
employer.[24] As Dodgshon's chapter argues, in the long term the impact of
these changes upon the social and economic relationships that structured
the Scottish countryside would be profound. But for a long time the pace

of change was slow and far from uniform. There were continuities too: if more affluent tenant farmers were now housed in substantial two-storey buildings, their workers' housing often carried forward old traditions: that is, largely single-storey, long and narrow.[25] In the northern Highlands much less had been done by 1800, even though agrarian capitalism had begun to break down the clan system and the culture dominated by clan chiefs in the seventeenth century. However, by the 1790s the revolution in social and economic relationships known as the Highland Clearances was under way, a process already well under way in the Lowlands. The move to commercial sheep farming would alter inexorably the everyday lives of those sub-tenants cleared from their upland holdings to marginal land by the coast.[26]

Elsewhere, seventeenth-century improvement – which largely took the form of enclosing fields, draining, and planting trees – was mainly confined to land close to and surrounding country houses, that is, essentially the mains farms. Farming methods altered little until well into the eighteenth century, although there were seventeenth-century experimenters and early eighteenth-century innovators, who used lime as a fertiliser and adopted new crop rotations. Runrig – a method of farming in strips allocated to tenants – predominated, along with a system in which there was a heavily manured, more or less continuously cultivated infield, and a separate outfield, for pastoral farming and oat production. Even during the so-called agricultural revolution in Scotland that can be dated from the 1760s, one estate might be in the vanguard of improvement, with neatly enclosed fields allocated to single tenant farmers governed by strict leases. But in close proximity there could be another where a less enterprising, poorer or a risk averse proprietor was not prepared to assume the costs associated with radical estate reorganisation and the rational management of land. Even on or in the vicinity of improved estates there were still small-holdings clustered in cot-towns that had existed for centuries. There were marked regional differences: advance was most apparent in the Lothians where most enclosing activity in the seventeenth century had taken place. By the early nineteenth century large farms of between 200 and 600 acres prevailed, each employing at least five full-time workers, who within a few decades would outnumber independent holders of land by ten to one. This was not new: in the early seventeenth century there were individuals and families in the countryside or in small industrial settlements – the textile workers, smiths, tailors, shoemakers, colliers, fisherfolk, day labourers and so on – who were dependent on money wages to buy grain or meal and other foodstuffs. Even so, in 1800 large numbers of labouring people still had some access to a plot of ground for their own use, made (and certainly repaired) some of their own clothing and furniture and survived by being able to turn their hand to any number of tasks. Recognition of the attachment that former rural dwellers had to the land, and of the cost advantages for employers in some circumstances of enabling workpeople to provide a proportion of their food requirements themselves, accounts for the widespread practice of allocating small plots of ground when new planned villages were laid out. Over two hundred such villages were founded in the eighteenth century, created to house clusters of country tradesmen and handloom weavers, and in some instances to establish fishing stations.[27]

But even the inhabitants of places of this sort had greater recourse to the market than their predecessors. Commercialism was in the driving seat; customary relations were being replaced by monetary ones, whether in the Lowlands or the far north. The same was true of towns, of course. In the older burghs change in this respect was slow, but it altered fundamentally their character and function. In some ways burgh living was less secure in 1800 than it had been two centuries earlier, as market forces impinged with greater impact. Such was Glasgow's pace of growth that from the 1720s grain had to be brought in from longer distances, rather than from farms nearby; as a consequence prices rose steeply at times when supplies were scarce and roads impassable.[28] Similarly, at the other end of the supply chain, the attraction of high prices encouraged farmers and merchants in counties such as Ayrshire and Dumfries to bypass local markets – the inhabitants of which in their turn experienced shortages and distress. Controls on prices – of bread, wine and ale, for example, and certain goods, such as candles – and the quality of produce, which had held burgh society together in the sixteenth century, were weakening. This is not to say that they had disappeared: forestalling and regrating, open dealing at market crosses and the quality and weight of bread continued after 1800, as in medieval times, to be matters with which town councils concerned themselves.[29] They still considered it their duty to purchase meal when it was scarce or unduly expensive in order to supply their inhabitants at a reasonable price.[30] And for good reason: where burgh magistrates failed, or were seen to fail, to uphold customary expectations that the town's market should be supplied with meal in sufficient quantity at a price that was acceptable to the consumer, rioting could result. This happened on numerous occasions in the eighteenth century; food riots, however, were never anything like everyday occurrences. What was ever present was the vigilance of the labouring poor – women in particular – at local food markets, ready to object if the price of a peck of meal rose by much more than a penny, to remind the authorities of their responsibilities and prepared if necessary to raise a mob.[31] In the sixteenth century there were no consumers' food riots in Scotland; only those of producers protesting that they were not being permitted to charge higher prices.[32]

Although too little is known for certain about the lives and experiences and particularly the mental world of those at the lower end of the spectrum of Scottish society – cottagers, crofters, rural tradesmen, day labourers and the like – there is little doubt that just getting by was intensely difficult, with most surviving just beyond the margins of subsistence. In the Lowlands life in this regard was tolerable, and by the end of the seventeenth century there was, in most years, an adequate supply of a narrow range of basic foodstuffs that offered little by way of stimulation for the ordinary Scot's taste buds. As Stana Nenadic shows in Chapter 5, oats and oatmeal were by far the most prominent constituents; the average adult male needed to consume some 37 ounces a day to do a day's work. Farinaceous foods accounted for at least half of the typical labouring family's expenditure, and became more rather than less important over the period 1600–1800. Oatmeal was supplemented with peas and beans and, when available, with some butter, cheese, milk and cabbage, but little meat. Fish was eaten by those living in coastal locations, when they could be caught, and in the northern isles were dried for winter use. But the everyday staple throughout, was oatmeal – and water, perhaps some milk and salt – eaten, variously, as porridge, brose, sowens and oat-cakes.[33] Potatoes were introduced as a supplement, and in some northern and western districts became the principal element in the diet of the labour-ing poor, as will be seen below. In the Lowlands they were resorted to as the principal source of calories in emergency. In favoured localities by the early 1790s, the diets of the labouring classes had become more varied, and might include milk and cheese, tea, wheaten bread and some meat. For many of the rest, however, diets were not only dull but they were probably also peri-odically deficient in terms of key nutrients – calcium and vitamins A and C, the last found in fresh vegetables, for example. It was the urban elites – the middle and upper classes – of towns like Edinburgh who enjoyed the benefits of fruit and vegetable consumption on a regular basis. Allowing for seasonal variations, of course, there was a continuously strong market for items like artichokes, herbs, radishes, strawberries, gooseberries, apricots, plums and peaches from the 1690s through to the 1760s, and occasional arrivals of luxury fruits such as lemons and oranges.[34] Imports of this kind, in chests holding up to 10,000 fruits – as well as olive oil, figs and wines – were not exclusive to Edinburgh, but were regular sights in port towns like Aberdeen, Dundee and Montrose.[35] Scotland's integration within the British empire in the eighteenth century, Nenadic tells us, brought the possibility of exotic imports of food and clothing, which were consumed with much pleasure and ostentation by, for example, the colonial merchants of Glasgow. For those fortunate enough to have sheltered, mainly walled gardens – lairds, tenant farmers, successful urban merchants with a suburban villa – a range of seasonal produce was available: lettuce, beetroot, parsnips and radishes, for instance, as well as apples, gooseberries and other fruit.

But in the Highlands and Islands of the north and west, where as much as half of the population was to be found prior to the middle of the eighteenth century, life was lived with the lingering spectre of crop failure in the most challenging of natural environments. For long spells, land and people were rain sodden and battered by severe winter winds; the region's geography and comparative isolation exacerbating the difficulties posed by an increas-ing dependence upon meal imported from the south in return for black cattle. Cold and dark winters necessitated long and laborious hours, days and weeks each year spent cutting and drying peat that would be needed to fuel fires (although peat usage was not confined to the Highlands and Islands; Aberdeen was primarily a peat-burning town until the later eighteenth century). But not every family had access to peat, in which case dried cow dung or seaweed was turned to for warmth.[36] Coal was mined only in parts of east Sutherland; that which was brought in by sea was expensive, prohibitively so for all but the very well off. Harsh enough everyday lives were punctuated by severe shortages of grain, and at worst, famine. Years of acute difficulty included 1604, 1623, 1650, 1671, 1680, 1688, 1695–1702, 1740–1, 1744–5, 1751, 1756, 1771–2, 1782–3, 1795–6 and the opening years of the nineteenth century. Some of these dates were excruciatingly hard in the Lowlands too, where, until it disappeared after the 1640s, plague was a periodic visitor to the towns. There were poor harvests in 1621 and 1622, which were followed by a sharp rise in mortality, and the second half of the 1690s saw a surge in mortality and famine-related drops in fertility and consequently births in many parishes south of the Highland line.[37] Before that, crop yields had begun to fall to dangerously low levels (that is below a seed–crop ratio of 1:3) even in relatively well-endowed districts in the eastern Lowlands.[38] But after this dislocating interlude few in the Lowlands had to resort to a desperate search for alternative foodstuffs, like seaweeds, edible land weeds and shellfish, a survival strategy embarked upon in many Highland communities. Other life-sustaining methods adopted included the use of raised 'lazy beds', where after around 1770s potatoes were grown on small plots of otherwise uncultivable ground prepared by the foot-driven *caschrom* and manured with liberal quantities of seaweed drawn from lochside shores.[39] There were periods of food shortage and extreme privation in the Lowlands in the eighteenth century – even as late as 1795–6 – which in some years led to restiveness and rioting as the inhabitants of grain-growing districts and port towns witnessed the shipment out of their means of subsistence as merchants sought the higher prices obtainable in the industrial areas. By this stage, however, there was nothing like the harvest failure of 1782–3 that hit the north-eastern Highlands particularly hard, and left an indelible stain in the memories of the people affected.

In the west and north Highlands and the western islands, where population rose particularly fast from the middle of the eighteenth century, it is unlikely that there was much, if any, improvement in conditions prior to 1800. They may even have deteriorated, although there was now the potato crop to fall back upon. Potato cultivation required less ground. Indeed, as long as smallholdings sufficient to grow a crop to support a family could be acquired, potatoes made for easier and early family formation, and may have increased population and pressure on scarce resources, thereby adding to the vulnerability of the region's people. Military service – perhaps as many as 85,000 Highlanders were so engaged between 1756 and 1815 – kelp harvesting and burning, the establishment of fishing stations, and hand-spinning of flax carried out for Lowland linen companies combined to relieve some of the pressures by generating money wages that that could be used to purchase meal and other essentials, temporarily at least.[40] In the southern and eastern Highlands by contrast, in closer proximity to the ports, towns and villages of the central belt, migration offered both long- and short-term opportunities for economic betterment. There was a strong, lasting, migrant stream from Argyll to Greenock, for example, the population of which was one-third Highland-born by 1791. Bleachfields, which spread in the Lowlands from the 1720s, were another new source of employment in rural locations – albeit largely seasonal – as were the flax and cotton mills that mushroomed from the 1770s and drew in young women and children not only from their hinterlands but also from the north. For fit Highland males, whether married or single, there was work to be had in hand-loom weaving – housed in workshops and weaving sheds – a trade the basics of which could be learned within a few weeks.

As this suggests, in the Lowlands the position was better, but not markedly so until the very end of the eighteenth century, and even then, as Christopher Whatley argues in Chapter 11, care has to be taken not to exaggerate the scale of improvement in living standards. Day labourers' wages, for instance, which rose at the very beginning of the seventeenth century, appear not have increased again until after 1760.[41] Thereafter real wages appear to have risen for thirty years or so, but there were enormous variations between and even within counties, although not unexpectedly, rates were higher in, and within the proximity of, towns and in rural districts where mixed rather than pastoral farming prevailed. But even in parts of Lowland Scotland the evidence that living standards were much higher in the 1790s than they had been fifty years earlier is at best ambiguous; from some places there were reports of deterioration and greater poverty, but also increased whisky drinking. The numbers drawn into hand-loom weaving may have been growing, but in some fabrics – muslins, for instance – the cost of oatmeal rose faster than weekly wages during the 1790s, while in the same decade there were four serious recessions in the cotton industry, throwing thousands out of work for lengthy periods.[42] From 1793 the picture is considerably gloomier for most workers, and for some, bleak in the extreme.[43] Even with the higher wages that were being paid by the 1790s, as in the preceding centuries, much depended on the life cycle stage of the individual or a household. A single male – a labourer – with no dependants would have fared reasonably well, at least if he lived and worked in a village or town. He might even have been able to save a portion of his summer earnings to tide him over periods of unemployment in winter. There would have been times when he was hungry and cold – and winters were increasingly harsh towards the end of the decade – but he would not starve.[44] A skilled urban craftsman would have been able to support his family – provided that he was able to find more or less year-round employment and, if in a rural village, the family had access to a plot of ground on which to raise produce both for consumption and sale. Yet it is unlikely that a married labourer would have been in such a favoured position. His earnings would have been considerably below what was required to feed, clothe and house a family of two or three children (roughly the Scottish average for the eighteenth century), even when such a household had possession of a smallholding on which to grow some potatoes and kale and keep a milk cow.

With the onset of industrialisation, however, the demand for labour intensified and, as noted above, wage rates did rise in some parts of the Lowlands at least. The common people in two types of locality benefited more than others, and were able to enjoy occasional portions of meat, drink tea and wear better quality clothing, purchased rather than self-made. Rural areas that were close to growing towns were one. The other was the manufacturing towns and villages that were flourishing in Angus, Fife and Perthshire and, in the west, Ayrshire, Lanarkshire and Renfrewshire. New openings for paid work appeared too. Vital in this regard were increasing opportunities for women (and to a lesser degree children), whose economic contributions to the households have been described as 'pivotal'.[45] Such earnings could come from any number of activities, from selling dairy produce, to wet nursing through laundry work (in the towns), but increasingly commonly, by part-time, domestic employment in textiles. Pay rates for virtually all kinds of women's work were lower than for males. Nevertheless, they were sufficient in countless cases to lift families out of absolute poverty and into a situation where by living frugally there was enough money for food, additional clothing (so that apparel could be changed and washed with soap) and warm shelter – and perhaps to pay for a period of schooling for their children. Some workers and households managed to generate small surpluses with which to buy haberdashery, combs, knives, night-caps and trinkets from travelling hawkers and at fairs, and perhaps a clock, but the abyss of poverty was never far distant and Scottish wage rates lagged behind those of England.[46] By and large it seems that it was those in skilled trades, and even then masters rather than journeymen, as well as professionals and merchants – the rising middle class – who on their deaths left behind them goods and gear of any value. With their larger, five-, six- and seven-roomed houses they could accommodate the dining tables that after *c.* 1750 overtook beds as the most expensive item of furniture in the middle-class home, and had the wall space upon which could be hung gilt-framed pictures and mirrors.[47]

The belated improvement in working-class living standards, and possibly inoculation against smallpox which started in the mid-eighteenth century, may be reflected in two key demographic variables: an apparent fall in infant mortality and an increase in adult life expectancy. Death was a frequent visitor in early modern Scotland and, although hardly an everyday occurrence, Deborah Symonds argues in Chapter 3 that it can rarely have been far from the minds of parents of new-born babies and infants. Survival beyond infancy required constant attention to individual health. As Helen Dingwall makes clear in Chapter 4, ill-health had no respect for social status and, although the elite may have had access to professional medical practitioners, their fears about illness, disease and pain were shared across the social spectrum, and cures were based on common medical knowledge. At first sight, she argues, there may appear to have been significant change in the experiences of illness and pain, and there were important developments in medical theory. But an examination of everyday practice reveals how little changed in the early modern period. There was a noticeable time lag before advances in medical knowledge affected professional and institutional medical care. Belief in the power of prayer continued to be held as the surest cure to illness. Folk-healing and magic remained common practices, argue both Dingwall and Joyce Miller (Chapter 9), and carried on well into the nineteenth century and even beyond.[48] Death though, when it came, was accompanied by rituals that changed little over two centuries: the body of the deceased was laid out and watched during the wake until burial, at which time a bellman called solemnly for neighbours and friends (those closest acted as pallbearers) to attend at the graveside. The attendance of ministers was rare, as were funeral sermons and prayers.[49]

Once into adulthood, the normal expectation was that an individual could safely reach his or her fifties, and there are numerous accounts of cases of exceptional longevity. Much else remained more or less the same. As far as can be ascertained, the birth rate in Scotland – around thirty-five per 1,000 – was more or less constant throughout the eighteenth century, and perhaps even prior to that, although falls had occurred periodically in the seventeenth century. Plague was one cause in 1606 and also between 1644 and 1647. The other precipitating factor was the more serious food shortages, and famine. As has been seen, serious food shortages were experienced fairly often in the seventeenth century, although in the Lowlands these were rare in the following century. The effect of the famine of the second half of the 1690s, however, was severe and long lasting. Although baptisms are not a measure of births, they are a useful substitute. In each of the main Scottish regions, baptisms fell below the average for 1691–4 and failed to recover to these levels until after the early 1700s.[50]

The age of first marriage in Scotland also appears to have remained relatively constant, at around twenty-six or twenty-seven years – higher than in England in the eighteenth century but not out of line with much of the rest of Europe.[51] Celibacy rates were high too, at around 20 per cent, twice the English level in the eighteenth century. Other than in the west and the adjoining islands, there appear to have been insufficient inducements to draw young women in Scotland to the marriage bed early – or at all in some cases, as just noted – and certainly not before they had had some experience of independent living, in a hefty proportion of cases as domestic or farm servants. In the towns things might have been different, with the employ-ment opportunities there probably making it possible to set up independent households slightly earlier, something that was difficult in the Lowland coun-tryside, where sub-division of land was rare and contrary to the trend of large farm formation. There was a relatively high level of bastardy though – more apparent after around 1760 than earlier – with some striking consequences of sexual misdemeanour in the south-west, in parts of the north and in rapidly growing manufacturing places like Cathcart in Renfrewshire, where the rate was 8 per cent in the 1770s and 1780s.[52] Scottish adults, however, were living longer, at least seven years more in the 1790s than in 1755, at which point adults in England could anticipate living up to ten years longer. By the 1790s Scottish adults at birth, like their English counterparts, could expect to reach their late thirties – just – although not in the western Lowlands, where life expectancy was only thirty-six years.[53]

EVERYDAY POLITICAL CULTURE

For Scotland, the two centuries between 1600 and 1800 were a time of profound political and constitutional significance and much upheaval and change. Nevertheless, with the absence of a uniform system of justice a notable exception, even by the start of the period, at least in outline, there were in place some of the structures associated with a relatively well ordered, if somewhat penurious, early modern state. In 1603, following the death of England's Queen Elizabeth I, a Scot, Mary Queen of Scots' son, James, added the English throne to the one he had inherited as a minor in Scotland. Thenceforth the two nations – as well as Wales and Ireland – were bound together in what proved from the Scottish perspective to be a highly unsatis-factory regal union. Scotland under James fared reasonably well. Under his successor, Charles I, however, a period of major dislocation ensued. There was revolution in 1637, followed by civil war – through the three kingdoms – and ultimately, in 1651, conquest of Scotland under Oliver Cromwell. Although English hostility had put paid to James's dreams of a peaceful federal union between Scotland and England, under Cromwell Scotland was forcibly pulled into an incorporating union, on England's terms, with token representation at Westminster. The arrangement lasted less than a decade, but the issue of Scotland's constitutional relationship with England contin-ued to be a running sore until the union of the parliaments was implemented in 1707. The settlement, which was deeply unpopular in Scotland, not least because the promises of economic gain made by the proponents of incorpo-ration failed to materialise, was finally secured after yet another bout of civil division, with the defeat of the Jacobite army on the battlefield of Culloden in 1746 and the subsequent campaign on the part of the Hanoverian state to extirpate its enemies.[54]

James VI and I's departure from Edinburgh had removed the royal court

from Scotland. Scottish intellectuals, writers and poets, however, continued to engage with their counterparts elsewhere in Europe, links that were
maintained by the practice of writing and reading in Latin.[55] Yet there was a
dip in cultural achievement, with court-sponsored drama in particular being
all but silenced by the disapproving Presbyterian kirk. Immoral behaviour
and even failure to uphold the sanctity of the Sabbath had been matters of
concern for parliament before 1560, but in the wake of the Reformation,
church and state exerted a tighter grip over public and private morality and
imposed Presbyterian rule in large parts of Lowland Scotland as well as
Argyll to the west.[56] Or at least they tried to. An exception was the north-
east, where episcopalianism continued to flourish, and there were areas like
the Borders where Catholic nobles did their best to resist the Reformation;
the pre-Reformation calendar of holy days that included Christmas, and the
associated customs and practices were hard to eradicate on the ground.[57]
There was something of a return to the much-missed joyfulness associated
with the Stuart court at the time of the Restoration of Charles II – and the re-
emergence of some Catholic practices in and around Aberdeen. A resurgence
of sponsorship of the arts and learning followed the residence in Edinburgh
from 1679 of the king's brother, the duke of York (the future James VII and
II). Royal, aristocratic and Episcopalian culture, which stretched back to the
Jacobean court, was revived. Despite the Whig revolution of 1688–9, and the
appearance of the Protestant Hanoverians in the shape of George I in 1713,
the tradition remained strong enough to sustain major Jacobite risings in the
first half of the following century and a nostalgic but, none the less, potent
strain of Jacobitism thereafter.[58]

Nevertheless, the eyes of ambitious Scottish aristocrats and those from
the upper echelons of landed society were increasingly drawn to London,
now the main locus of royal patronage. Although they were by no means
alone in the crush, the sight of Scots clamouring for royal favour was not a
pretty one, even for Scots themselves. Regardless, several of them journeyed
south again at the end of 1688 to greet William of Orange on his arrival
from the Dutch republic; by January 1689 there was a veritable scrum of
Scottish noblemen and gentlemen in London ready to offer William and his
wife, Mary, the Scottish crown.[59] The successful passage of the 1707 Union
through the parliaments in London and Edinburgh presaged yet another
unseemly charge south by virtually any Scottish politician who thought he
had any chance of catching Queen Anne's attention, and securing from her
some kind of government post.[60] Unfortunately, some who did –serving
Scottish ministers – were ordered back to Edinburgh to keep the peace, but
at least in Scotland they could afford to live in some comfort; down-at-heel
Scotsmen stood out in London.

At elite level, too, elements of Anglicisation can be discerned – with
some families moving to England, increased inter-marriage as Scottish peers
sought English wives and the growing use of English for writing.[61] There was

also a belief in some quarters in the idea of a Britain in which the Scots would be equal partners; some Scotsmen going as far as styling themselves Scoto-Britons, proud citizens of a united Protestant state, a beacon of the Counter-Reformation.[62] In the light of the English failure to reciprocate, the tendency of what can be regarded as naive self-imaging became more noticeable after 1707 when the term North Britain came into play. Nevertheless, the patriotic impulse remained strong, and contrary forces were at work too, in defence of Scottish customs, institutions and practices – as well as of Scottish history and language; paradoxically, the 1707 Union produced a new-found interest in balladry and a surge of vernacular writing, found in the poetry of Allan Ramsay, Robert Fergusson and Robert Burns.

It is a mistake to assume that the 'people below', the great majority of Scots – day labourers, domestic and agricultural servants, cottars, small tenant farmers and rural and urban tradesmen – were divorced from what at first sight appear to be simply high-level developments and incidents, or from the cultural changes that were under way. Take the move to English: this was the language of the pulpit, and preaching, and in which the Bible was read. Few Scots outside the *Gaidhealtachd* heartlands prior to the middle of the eighteenth century would have avoided the aural moralising of their parish minister, nor, indeed, the sound of the bells that demanded their attendance. But we should not exaggerate the speed of the kirk's move to English. English was the language of print, but not uniformly, at least not before the Westminster Assembly of 1643–8, when a series of important documents relating to church worship and teaching in England and Scotland were produced – in English. Yet many ministers, and especially those from humble backgrounds, used Scots in their preaching and prayers, and most would have spoken English with Scots pronunciation.[63]

However, so pervasive had English become by the early nineteenth century that even ordinary Scots had difficulty in understanding Burns' poems written in the vernacular. It is worth noting, too, that such was the power of regional and local dialect that Burns' Ayrshire-located verse was something of a bar to his being understood in the Lothians and Borders.[64] Increasingly, as Bob Harris argues in Chapter 6, language and accent became markers of age, social position, area and region; it was the lower orders in the north-east who in 1796 the Revd James Macdonald thought looked 'clownish' in their dress, were 'lumpish & dull' and whose dialect was 'truly grating'. The higher ranks in towns like Peterhead, he was convinced, 'were people inferior in no respect to those of any part of Britain'.[65] Chapbooks – cheap and enormously popular works of prose, poems and song that were printed and bought in their thousands by the labouring classes in the eighteenth century – ensured the survival of Scots as a vigorous medium, although much of the material in these was also written in English.[66]

Pulpits were places where news was broadcast and proclamations made on matters local and national.[67] Ministers were not the only people from the middling ranks within Scottish society who had a good sense of what was going on in the world around them, locally as well as nationally and internationally. Other professionals such as merchants, lawyers, surgeons and apothecaries were also well-informed, as were lairds and the relatively few better off tenant farmers there were in Lowland Scotland (in the Highlands their equivalent, the clan gentry, were the *fine*). There were good reasons for keeping one's ear to the ground. Overseas merchants needed to be aware of potential trouble spots for their shipping and goods, or conversely of new opportunities that might arise as a result of conflicts between states – for third parties, trade wars were welcome. Lawyers had to be alert to changes in criminal and civil law and were aided in this ambition by the creation of the Advocates Library in Edinburgh in 1682; landed proprietors and their agents and principal tenants made it their business to know of the powers permitted by the growing number of statutes relating to agriculture in seventeenth-century Scotland that favoured their interests. Much justice was exercised at estate level, through the barony courts that the powerful Scottish aristocracy managed to hold on to until the abolition or at least a reduction in the authority of the heritable jurisdictions in 1747.[68] It was people from the middling and upper ranks who were the more avid readers of newspapers (the *Edinburgh Gazette* was published twice weekly from 1699), almanacs, broadsheets, prints and pamphlets. Newspapers could be read in inns and the increasingly numerous coffee houses, whereas almanacs, which circulated widely even before they were first printed in Scotland around 1632, could be bought cheaply. Books, too, became more readily available through the seventeenth and eighteenth centuries. Private libraries increased the readership of books further, and made them accessible to those from the artisan classes. Throughout much of the Lowlands there was a lively trade in reading materials, distributed by itinerant chapmen – hawkers – booksellers, the postal service and private carriers.

For the middling ranks there were grammar schools and, indeed, Scotland's four universities (England had only two). Facilitated by a proliferation of burgh and parish schools as well as private provision in various guises, literacy levels in Scotland were on a par with the rest of Europe, and in the burghs particularly so. Edinburgh led the way with a 95 per cent literacy rate among craftsmen in the early eighteenth century, close to the figure for London.[69] But in large parts of the relatively isolated, poorer, Highlands male craftsmen and tenant farmers – and virtually everyone else – were some way behind their Lowland counterparts. Yet in the Lowlands and in parts of the Gaelic-speaking Highlands too, the popularity of the chapbooks and their writers – Dougal Graham (1724–79), is judged to have made an impact on 'hundreds of thousands' of readers – is indicative of a hunger for the written word.[70]

Fewer women would have read these than men, however. The illiteracy rate for females was over 90 per cent in the mid-seventeenth century and around 81 per cent over the following century. But this is if the ability to sign one's name is the measure used. At the elite level this was hardly an issue: despite discrimination against them, women higher up the social scale did have access to both formal and informal education, and letter writing between them was fairly common. Women of this rank also participated in person and as correspondents in the Union debate, the Jacobite movement and the Scottish Enlightenment, for example.[71] Below them, however, there were women teachers and traders; women were clearly skilled dealers in the market place who could count and calculate, and played a crucial role in maintaining an oral culture through ballad composition and recital. This was increasingly important in the Highlands – with the eighteenth-century winter *ceilidh* in part replacing the clan chiefs' bards.[72] But older songs were also preserved and transmitted in print, issued as broadsides in the early eighteenth century and increasingly in chapbooks.[73]

That decisions taken by government impacted upon society generally is relatively easily demonstrated. Taxation, and in particular the land tax, which rose steeply under Charles I, was resented by landowners and merchants and feared by tenants alarmed that rents would increase. Wars, too, had direct effects in making demands upon men for military service, while peace also had ramifications, with discharged soldiers posing problems for the authorities as they sought to return home, sometimes causing minor havoc in the communities through which they passed, in search of accommodation and sustenance. The 1707 Union brought in its wake new and additional taxes, and much more efficient and intrusive systems for collecting the same. As Whatley shows in Chapter 7, this created yelps of protest from brewers and their customers across the country, along with virtually anyone importing excise-able goods to Scotland. The old Scottish coinage was taken in and re-issued.[74] English weights and measures were introduced to replace the array of local and customary usage that had developed prior to Union (not without some success in achieving greater standardisation), although the replacements were usually adopted reluctantly, patchily and over a long period of time that stretched into the nineteenth century.[75] Given the prominence of ordinary men, women and even children in risings, riots and disturbances, it is clear that religious affiliation, dynastic loyalties and the fate of the Scottish nation itself mattered for many thousands of Scots throughout the early modern period – as was the case elsewhere in Europe as rulers and the ruled negotiated not only the particulars of government policy but also the limits of sovereignty.[76]

Monarchs in Scotland from at least the time of the Reformation had been aware of the 'dangers' of democracy, as embodied by Presbyterian theologians and ministers, and were condemned in forceful treatises penned by James VI and I in his defences of kingly divine right. Parliament too, especially after the Revolution of 1688–9 – and until 1707 – was forced to recognise that public opinion was something to be cognisant of, and that, unchecked, it could be dangerous. There were occasions – periods of days, weeks and even months – when big political issues became part of everyday discourse, spilling over into song and balladry, and sometimes, more forceful participation.[77] One such event was the Scottish Revolution, 1637–41, which was led by noblemen, but with merchant involvement too. Mass support, however, came from ordinary people who, by signing and defending with their lives the National Covenant, demonstrated their opposition to Charles I's religious innovations and their antipathy to the pope – the antichrist – and the Church of Rome.[78] These were mortal enemies which would continue to arouse fierce and sometimes ugly passions that erupted into open violence through to the end of the period with which this volume is concerned and well into the twentieth century. It is striking that during the winter of 1706–7, as the terms of the incorporating Union were being finalised inside Edinburgh's Parliament Hall, the issue that appears to have most enraged the minds of the people milling outside was a rumour that the honours of Scotland, the regalia that comprised the royal crown and the sword and sceptre of state, were to be removed to England. Although anxieties were heightened by panic-mongering on the part of opposition politicians, what is undeniable is the strong sense that these venerable symbols of Scottish nationhood and sovereignty were the property of the Scots and should remain in Scotland, a visible reminder that the nation had not been conquered by incorporation. What has also become clear is the extent to which Jacobitism depended on widespread popular support in Lowland Scotland, most notably in 1715 but in 1745 too, although on the first occasion in particular, anti-unionism appears to have been as a powerful a motivating force on the rebel side as strength of commitment to the cause of the exiled Stuarts.[79] Coins, medals, glasses, portraits, miniatures, song, verse and a palpable emotional commitment created a cult of Jacobitism that remained part of the nation's everyday political culture long after Culloden.[80] But Hanoverian monarchs and the Protestant British state had their adherents too, to the extent that demonstrations of popular loyalism, which had taken place as early as the 1720s, became increasingly common in Presbyterian strongholds like Glasgow in the later eighteenth century, but also in smaller places and rural parishes.[81]

The early modern period was one of expanding political horizons, when the view of ordinary Scots could extend well beyond the British Isles. It was at the urban elites that newspaper advertisements early in the eighteenth century were directed when offering for sale, 'a pair of new Globs' along with 'Large Mapps of the Seats of War in all the different places in Europe'. Yet there was also a drive to learn more about these new worlds that was reflected in the curricula of some burgh schools, where geography lessons began to be taught in Irvine and St Andrews from around 1728, followed thereafter in Ayr, Perth, Edinburgh and other places.[82] Over time, what appear to have been relatively minor decisions – as in June 1796 when the minister of

Auchterhouse near Dundee purchased for the local schoolmaster two globes from Edinburgh[83] – could have lasting consequences, in this case the fresh knowledge of the world opened up to the schoolchildren concerned.

CONCLUSION

This volume emphasises the centrality of the everyday for our understanding the dynamics of early modern Scotland. Everyday objects, such as food and clothing, could take on a political meaning in this society where visual symbols could have as much potency as the written word. Tartan, plaid, glasses, medallions, fans and feathers allowed Scots to display their political loyalties and allegiances, as in different ways did songs, broadsheets and books. Banners, other forms of decoration in paint and stone fulfilled similar functions: as means of displaying individual, family or group identities. In both urban and rural communities the everyday bore considerable significance for the demonstration, negotiation and contest of social power. As the chapters that follow show, social position and wealth were revealed by the way in which Scots spoke, dressed, ate and even smelt, and they determined access to land, housing and transport. But while the everyday could highlight the differences between Scots, it could also reveal their similarities. This was a period when the fear of illness was shared by all and the shadow of death loomed large. For many – perhaps the majority, regardless of rank – religion, despite confessional differences and splits within presbyterianism after 1733, was a source of solace and also a guide to good, or godly, behaviour.

The contributions to the study of everyday life in this volume show that much remained the same or little changed over the course of the seventeenth and eighteenth centuries. Scots were acutely aware of the seasons – and the weather – as they impacted upon the availability of work, food and fuel. In large measure, the seasons affected the pace and rhythms of daily life. Many tasks continued to depend upon physical strength, and working life, as much as other aspects of everyday life, continued to be differentiated along gender lines. But this is not the same as saying that nothing changed: from the seventeenth century to the nineteenth century in large swathes of the Scottish countryside there was a radical role reversal. With the near-universal sickle, women cut the harvest; with the introduction at different times and places of the heavier scythe, men did the cutting while women 'lifters' gathered the cut corn.[84]

While the church played a key role in guiding, disciplining and controlling the lives of ordinary Scots, there remained a considerable degree of low level disorder. And try as the kirk might to eradicate magic and suspicion, many people managed to combine church attendance with a belief in the supernatural. Traditional practices and rituals continued and gained their strength in part from a thriving oral culture, which endured despite rising levels of literacy and the availability of cheap print.

There is consensus in this volume that when change did occur, it was mainly during the eighteenth century. It was at this time that there was a breakdown of the customary practices of the Scottish countryside; improvement and modernisation of domestic architecture; an increase in the quantity and range of available food and clothing; a marked decline in the numbers of those who spoke Gaelic; advances in transport and greater numbers travelling for leisure as well as work; an increase in the range of occupations and full-time waged labour; and the beginnings of the institutionalisation of the mentally ill. Yet it is acknowledged that there were some geographical areas that were immune from much of this. Those living in the far north and north-west of Scotland and many of its islands remained isolated, and little touched by change, holding on to many of traditional ways of life and beliefs as before. Thus, it was also in the eighteenth century that we have clearest evidence of the importance of place and locality to everyday life in Scotland.

Notes

1. S. Johnson, *A Journey to the Western Isles of Scotland*, J. D. Fleeman (ed.) (Oxford [1775] 1985), p. 16.
2. C. W. J. Withers, *Geography, Science and National Identity: Scotland Since 1520* (Cambridge, 2001), pp. 142–57.
3. See, for example, P. Cadell, 'The Reverend John Brand and the Bo'ness of the 1690s', in G. Cruickshank (ed.), *A Sense of Place: Studies in Scottish Local History* (Edinburgh, 1988), pp. 5–14.
4. USA, Playfair Collection, PLFR/1B/1, Journal of Janet Playfair, p. 9.
5. P. Hume Brown (ed.), *Early Travellers in Scotland* (Edinburgh, 1973 edn); T. C. Smout, 'Tours in the Scottish Highlands from the eighteenth to the twentieth centuries', *Northern Scotland*, 5:2 (1983), 99–121; A. J. Durie, *Scotland for the Holidays: Tourism in Scotland, c. 1780–1939* (East Linton, 2003), pp. 21–43.
6. See, for example, University of St Andrews [USA], Special Collections, Playfair Collection, PLFR/1A/1, Journal of the Revd James Macdonald, 1796.
7. For a telling example, see A. Fenton (ed.), *The Diary of Patrick Fea of Stove, Orkney, 1766–96* (East Linton, 1997).
8. C. A. Whatley, *Scottish Society, 1707–1830: Beyond Jacobitism, Towards Industrialisation* (Manchester, 2000), p. 310.
9. R. A. Houston, *Scottish Literacy and the Scottish Identity* (Cambridge, 1985), p. 43; I. D. Whyte, 'Scottish and Irish urbanisation in the seventeenth and eighteenth centuries: a comparative perspective', in S. Connolly, R. A. Houston and R. J. Morris (eds), *Conflict, Identity and Economic Development: Scotland and Ireland, 1600–1939* (Preston, 1995), p. 24.
10. I. D. Whyte, *Agriculture and Society in Seventeenth-Century Scotland* (Edinburgh, 1979), pp. 8–9.
11. R. E. Tyson, 'Contrasting regimes: population growth in Ireland and Scotland during the eighteenth century', in Connolly, Houston and Morris, *Conflict*, p. 66.

12. See T. M. Devine, *Scotland's Empire, 1600–1815* (London, 2003), pp. 1–25.
13. Whyte, *Agriculture*, pp. 12–13.
14. USA, Journal of Revd James Macdonald, pp. 43, 49.
15. National Archives of Scotland, CH2/173/2, Barony parish, kirk session minutes, 1699–1727.
16. R. A. Houston, *Social Change in the Age of Enlightenment: Edinburgh, 1660–1760* (Oxford, 1994), pp. 147–233; USA, Journal of Janet Playfair, entries for 1797.
17. Whatley, *Scottish Society*, pp. 153–5.
18. Bob Harris, 'Towns, improvement and cultural change in Georgian Scotland: the evidence of the Angus burghs, c. 1760–1820', *Urban History*, 33:2 (2006), 195–212; Fenton, *Diary of Patrick Fea* , p. 41.
19. Houston, *Social Change*, pp. 132–44.
20. P. Martin, 'Cupar, Fife, 1700–c. 1820: A Small Scottish Town in an Era of Change', unpublished Ph.D. (University of Dundee, 2000), pp. 154, 162.
21. C. A. Whatley, *The Scottish Salt Industry, 1570–1850: An Economic and Social History* (Aberdeen, 1987), pp. 9–32.
22. M. Lynch, 'Introduction: Scottish towns, 1500–1700', in M. Lynch (ed.), *The Early Modern Town in Scotland* (London, 1987), p. 27.
23. Houston, *Social Change*, pp. 11–12.
24. M. Gray, 'The social impact of agrarian change in the rural Lowlands', in T. M. Devine and R. Mitchison (eds), *People and Society in Scotland, Volume I, 1760–1830* (Edinburgh, 1988), pp. 59–62.
25. R. J. Naismyth, *Buildings of the Scottish Countryside* (London, 1989), p. 30.
26. M. Bangor-Jones, 'Sheep farming in Sutherland in the eighteenth century', *Agricultural History Review*, 50:II (2002), 181–202; E. Richards, *Debating the Highland Clearances* (Edinburgh, 2007), pp. 36–50.
27. D. G. Lockhart, 'Planned village development in Scotland and Ireland, 1700–1850', in T. M. Devine and D. Dickson (eds), *Ireland and Scotland, 1600–1850* (Edinburgh, 1983), pp. 132–9.
28. A. J. S. Gibson and T. C. Smout, 'Regional prices and market regions: the evolution of the early modern Scottish grain market', *Economic History Review*, XLVIII:2 (May 1995), 279.
29. I. Blanchard, E. Gemmill, N. Mayhew and I. D. Whyte, 'The economy: town and country', in E. P. Dennison, D. Ditchburn and M. Lynch (eds), *Aberdeen before 1800: A New History* (East Linton, 2002), p. 150.
30. See Whatley, *Scottish Society*, pp. 206–8.
31. C. A. Whatley, 'Roots of 1790s radicalism: reviewing the economic and social background', in Bob Harris (ed.), *Scotland in the Age of the French Revolution* (Edinburgh, 2005), pp. 30–6.
32. Lynch, 'Introduction', p. 26.
33. A. J. S. Gibson and T. C. Smout, *Prices, Food and Wages in Scotland, 1550–1780* (Cambridge, 1995), pp. 225–60.
34. R. A. Houston, 'The economy of Edinburgh 1694–1763: the evidence of the common good', in Connolly, Houston and Morris, *Conflict*, pp. 59–60.
35. D. G. Adams, 'Trade in the eighteenth and nineteenth centuries', in G. Jackson and S. G. E. Lythe (eds), *The Port of Montrose* (Tayport, 1993), p. 129.

36. Fenton, *Diary of Patrick Fea*, p. 15.
37. T. C. Smout, 'Famine and famine-relief in Scotland', in L. M. Cullen and T. C. Smout (eds), *Comparative Aspects of Scottish and Irish Economic and Social History, 1600–1900* (Edinburgh, 1979), pp. 22–3.
38. K. J. Cullen, C. A. Whatley and M. Young, 'King William's Ill Years: new evidence on the impact of scarcity and harvest failure during the crisis of the 1690s on Tayside', *Scottish Historical Review*, LXXXV:2 (October 2006), 256–61.
39. A. I. Macinnes, 'Scottish Gaeldom: the first phase of clearance', in Devine and Mitchison, *People and Society*, p. 75.
40. Richards, *Debating the Highland Clearances*, pp. 32–6.
41. J. Teble, 'The standard of living of the working classes', in Devine and Mitchison, *People and Society*, pp. 194–200.
42. N. Murray, *The Scottish Hand Loom Weavers: A Social History* (Edinburgh, 1978), pp. 40–2.
43. Treble, 'Standard of living', pp. 200–3.
44. Whatley, 'Roots of 1790s radicalism', p. 26.
45. Gibson and Smout, *Prices*, pp. 347–8, 350.
46. Whatley, *Scottish Society*, p. 223; 'Roots of 1790s radicalism', p. 27.
47. S. Nenadic, 'The rise of the urban middle class', in Devine and Mitchison, *People and Society*, pp. 109–26; Martin, 'Cupar', pp. 195–251.
48. See D. Buchan (ed.), *Folk Tradition and Folk Medicine in Scotland: The Writings of David Rorie* (Edinburgh, 1994).
49. D. Stevenson, 'The travels of Richard James in Scotland, c. 1615', *Northern Scotland*, 7:2 (1987), 116; H. R. Sefton, 'Occasions in the Reformed Church', in C. MacLean and K. Veitch (eds), *Scottish Life and Society: A Compendium of Scottish Ethnology: Religion* (Edinburgh, 2006), pp. 476–8.
50. K. J. Cullen, 'Famine in Scotland in the 1690s: causes and consequences', unpublished Ph.D. thesis (University of Dundee, 2004), pp. 221–32.
51. M. W. Flinn, *The European Demographic System, 1500–1820* (Baltimore, MD, 1981), pp. 26–9.
52. R. A. Houston, 'The demographic regime', in Devine and Mitchison, *People and Society*, pp. 12–20.
53. M. W. Flinn (ed.), *Scottish Population History from the Seventeenth Century to the 1930s* (Cambridge, 1977), pp. 260–70.
54. For two splendid surveys which offer reasonably comprehensive coverage of the periods they cover, see K. M. Brown, 'Reformation to Union, 1560–1707', and B. P. Lenman, 'From the Union to the Franchise Reform of 1832', in R. A. Houston and W. W. Knox (eds), *The New Penguin History of Scotland From the Earliest Times to the Present Day* (London, 2001).
55. R. Crawford, *Scotland's Books: The Penguin History of Scottish Literature* (London, 2007), pp. 181–9.
56. F. Lyall, 'The impact of the Reformation in relation to church, state and individual', in MacLean and Veitch, *Religion*, pp. 103–23.
57. M. Lynch, G. DesBrisay and M. G. H. Pittock, 'The faith of the people', in Dennison, Ditchburn and Lynch, *Aberdeen*, pp. 289–303.

58. See A. Hook (ed.), *The History of Scottish Literature, Volume 2, 1660–1800* (Aberdeen, 1987).

59. D. J. Patrick, 'Unconventional procedure: Scottish electoral politics after the Revolution', in K. B. Brown and A. J. Mann (eds), *Parliament and Politics in Scotland, 1567–1707* (Edinburgh, 2005), pp. 211, 242–44.

60. C. A. Whatley, *The Scots and the Union* (Edinburgh, 2007 edn), pp. 7–8.

61. K. M. Brown, *Kingdom or Province? Scotland and the Regal Union, 1603–1715* (Basingstoke, 1992), pp. 45–7.

62. Crawford, *Scotland's Books*, pp. 163–7; C. Kidd, 'Protestantism, constitutionalism and British identity under the later Stuarts', in B. Bradshaw and P. Roberts (eds), *British Consciousness and Identity: the Making of Britain, 1533–1707* (Cambridge, 1998), pp. 321–42.

63. G. Tulloch, 'The English and Scots languages in Scottish religious life', in MacLean and Veitch, *Religion*, pp. 339–49.

64. J. Carswell (ed.), *The Autobiography of a Working Man by Alexander Somerville* (London, 1951 edn), pp. 42–5.

65. USA, Journal of Revd James Macdonald, p. 105.

66. E. J. Cowan and M. Paterson, *Folk in Print: Scotland's Chapbook Heritage, 1750–1850* (Edinburgh, 2007), p. 18.

67. See, for example, W. M. Inglis, *Annals of an Angus Parish* (Dundee, 1888).

68. A. E. Whetstone, *Scottish County Government in the Eighteenth and Nineteenth Centuries* (Edinburgh, 1981), pp. 1–5.

69. The main work on this subject is R. A. Houston, *Scottish Literacy and the Scottish Identity* (Cambridge, 1985).

70. Cowan and Paterson, *Folk in Print*, pp. 24–7.

71. L. Abrams, E. Gordon, D. Simonton and E. J. Yeo (eds), *Gender in Scottish History* (Edinburgh, 2006), pp. 47–50.

72. R. Black (ed.), *An Lasair: Anthology of 18th Century Scottish Gaelic Verse* (Edinburgh, 2001), pp. xii–xiv.

73. Cowan and Paterson, *Folk in Print*, p. 39.

74. Whatley, *Scots and the Union*, pp. 323–46.

75. A. D. Morrison-Low (ed.), *Weights and Measures in Scotland: A European Perspective* (East Linton, 2004), pp. 356–96.

76. W. T. Brake, *Shaping History: Ordinary People in European Politics, 1500–1700* (Berkeley, CA, 1998), pp. 187–8.

77. See K. Bowie, *Scottish Public Opinion and the Anglo-Scottish Union, 1699–1707* (Woodbridge, 2007).

78. D. Stevenson, 'Charles I, the Covenants and Cromwell: 1625–1660', in Bob Harris and A. R. Macdonald (eds), *Scotland: The Making and Unmaking of the Nation, c. 1100–1707* (Dundee, 2007), p. 43.

79. M. G. H. Pittock, *The Myth of the Jacobite Clans* (Edinburgh, 1997); D. Szechi, *1715: The Great Jacobite Rebellion* (New Haven CT, 2006).

80. H. Cheape, 'The culture and material culture of Jacobitism', in M. Lynch (ed.), *Jacobitism and the '45* (London, 1995), pp. 32–48.

81. Whatley, *Scottish Society*, pp. 305–6; see also, for example, A. B. Barty, *The History of Dunblane* (Stirling, [1944] 1994), p. 209.

82. See Withers, *Geography, Science and National Identity*, pp. 134–5.
83. Dundee Archive and Record Centre, CH 2/23/2, Auchterhouse Session Minutes, 1740–1804, 23 June 1746.
84. A. Fenton, *Scottish Country Life* (East Linton, 1999 edn), pp. 53–66.

Chapter 1

Everyday Structures, Rhythms and Spaces of the Scottish Countryside

Robert A. Dodgshon

By its very nature, the everyday or mundane is not what is generally recorded. For this reason, its historical recovery is not straightforward for those who depend on what is written down. In attempting to recover it in relation to life in the Scottish countryside from 1600 to 1800, I want to organise what I say around three themes, all of which are an established part of the everyday debate: *structures*, *rhythms* and *spaces*. The everyday *structures* of the country-side involved a weave of relationships, some threaded vertically through the rural community and others horizontally. As the warp and weft of the everyday, these were not equal threads. Top-down relationships penetrated into the everyday periodically but powerfully, leaving a greater archival residue, whereas those acting horizontally, while locally more prescribed, served to energise the everyday in a regular, ongoing way, but left less documentary trace. As with any community, the *rhythms* of the countryside imparted order and shape to lives. Whether these rhythms involved those engaged in working the land or those involved in the processing of its produce, they invariably had a seasonal and consensual character. Their seasonality was driven by the need to fit in with a natural cycle of output that not only determined when particular farm tasks had to be done but when other less seasonally-sensitive tasks like spinning and weaving could be squeezed into the schedule. Their consensual character was driven by the extent to which so much work in the countryside was organised around the farming town-ship, or toun, a landholding unit based on a number of occupiers who shared the arable and pasture resources of the toun. In such communities, when and how work was carried out depended on enduring collective agreements that provided a customary basis to the routines of the everyday. Of course, the everyday was also played out across *spaces* as well as seasons, spaces that were differentiated in terms of ownership, accessibility, function, symbolic value and gendering. Recovering these different spaces is far from easy, even after detailed surveys became available during the eighteenth century, but their recognition adds a dimension that matters fundamentally to the everyday.

Adding to the challenge of establishing these structures, rhythms and spaces of the everyday is the fact that the seventeenth and eighteenth centu-ries were a time of change in the countryside, a change that slowly gathered momentum during the seventeenth and early eighteenth century, but which became markedly more dramatic, more revolutionary, from the mid-eighteenth century onwards. We may start off with an everyday rooted in long-standing, customary forms, but the overall story of the period is about their transformation, a breaking down of the cake of custom.

STRUCTURING THE EVERYDAY: THE RURAL COMMUNITY

The structures through which everyday life in the countryside was played out can be seen in different ways, but two aspects stand out: first, the character of rural communities and, secondly, the extent to which they were closed or self-sufficient with their history from 1600 to 1800 being about their gradual integration into a wider world.

Taking the first of these, most people in the Scottish countryside lived in small farming communities known by contemporaries as touns, or fermtouns, prior to the spread of the improving movement. The vast majority of these touns were part of large estates and typically comprised a mix of tenants, under-tenants, crofters, cottars, labourers, tradesmen and their families (Figure 1.1). While there is much documentation for these tenanted touns in the form of rentals and tacks, understanding their character is not straightforward. This is because such sources invariably list the chief tenant(s), that is, those who held directly from the estate, together with those who held service crofts (for example, millers), but they do not normally specify the welter of under-tenants, crofters, cottars, grassmen and hirds who might hold land or grazing rights from the main tenant(s), nor the landless who might be present. There is an iceberg effect, with more being concealed than revealed as we try to work down through the different levels of tenure to that at which land was actually farmed (Figure 1.1). For this reason, the paper communities seemingly brought together in such sources cannot be taken as capturing the working communities around which everyday life was organised in a complete way.

These part-hidden hierarchies were a feature of both Highland and Lowland touns but in different ways. In the Highlands, it was common for touns along the western seaboard and in the Hebrides to be set to a tacksman, who performed an economic role on behalf of the estate, having 'full power . . . to out putt and in putt tennants grant Receipts and Discharges of the Rents',[1] as well as a political role, ensuring the loyalty of those under them.[2] While some held a sizeable cluster of touns, others held only a single toun. Among the latter, some farmed most of the toun themselves, letting out 'the skirts' to 'cottars,[3] but a significant number sub-let more substantial parts. When we analyse rentals across the Highlands over the seventeenth and first half of the eighteenth century, as much as one half of all touns appear in the hands of single tenants or tacksmen, the remainder being set directly to multiple tenants (Table 1.1). Of course, a significant proportion of those set to

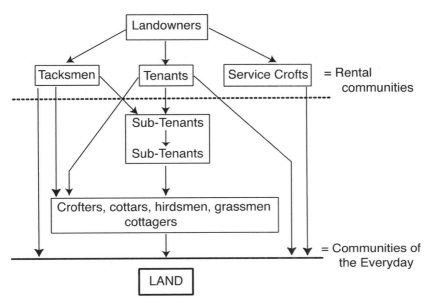

Figure 1.1   *The toun community, showing the distinction between the paper communities depicted in rentals and the on-the-ground working communities of the everyday.*

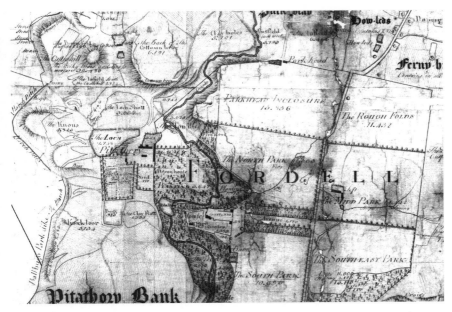

Figure 1.2   *The landscape around Fordell Castle, Fife, with the irregular forms of old pre-improvement farms standing in marked contrast to the regular lines of the new enclosures, shelter belts and plantations that came with improvement.*

Table 1.1   *Balance between single and multiple tenancies. Source: Based on data from T. Devine,* Transformation of Rural Scotland *(Edinburgh, 1994), p. 10; R. A. Dodgshon,* From Chiefs to Landlords *(Edinburgh, 1998), p. 128.*

	Number of touns with single tenants	Number of touns with multiple tenants
Islay (1686)	148	85
Breadalbane (1688)	68	85
Netherlorn (1709	10	24
Kintail (1718)	30	5
Arisaig (1699)	9	5
Lochalsh (1718)	37	7
Lewis (1718)	44	28
North Uist (1718)	21	15
South Uist (1718)	13	17
Trotterness (1718)	63	36
Renfrewshire (1690s)	536	360
Lowland Aberdeenshire (1690s)	299	93
Selkirkshire (1690s)	21	32
Berwickshire (1690s)	63	28
Midlothian (1690s)	86	46
West Lothian (1690s)	116	85

tacksmen would also have been sub-let in their entirety or in part to multiple under-tenants, but only in exceptional circumstances do rentals inform us about such under-tenants.[4] By the second quarter of the eighteenth century, criticism of the role played by tacksmen led estates like the Argyll estate to act against them, setting land directly 'in tenendry' rather than to tacksmen.[5] Yet sub-letting proved to be a stubborn practice. Even on the Argyll estate, a 1771 report could still refer to the 'unrestrained liberty of sublet' on the estate.[6] Analysis of late seventeenth- and early eighteenth-century rental data for the Lowlands also shows that around a half of all touns were in the hands of single tenants, the rest being set directly to multiple tenants (Table 1.1). As with their Highland counterparts, some of these single tenants also sub-let to under-tenants but – compared with the Highlands – a much higher proportion farmed their touns as single holdings, using cottars and different forms of hired labour.

Whatever the balance between the two, recovering a complete picture of those who formed the community of the everyday clearly requires us to go beyond those recorded in rentals. For parts of the Highlands, some listings recognise this, variously recording the number of inhabitants, families or cottars as well as tenants. Those listing the number of cottars present suggest that over a half of all touns had a handful present (Table 1.2). An analysis

Table 1.2 *Who lived in touns? Source: R. J. Adam (ed.), Home's Survey of Assynt, Scottish Historical Society, 3rd series, vol. lii (Edinburgh, 1960), pp. 68–88; Dodgshon, From Chiefs to Landlords, p. 140; Inveraray Castle, Argyll papers, V65, 'Contents of the Different Farms of Tiree', by James Turnbull, 1768; A. Murray of Stanhope, True Interest of Great Britain, Ireland and Our Plantations (London, 1740), appendix a; V. Wills (ed.), Statistics of the Annexed Estates, 1755–1756, Scottish Record Office (Edinburgh, 1973), pp. 30–75.*

	Touns	Tenants	Cottars	Families	Total inhabitants	Inhabitants per toun	Families per toun	Cottars per toun
Arran (late 1700s)	22			186	898	36.3	8.4	7.5
Tiree (1768)	34	236	170		1676	49.29		5.6
Lorn (1730)	24	92	49					2.04
Ardnamurchan (1723)	32			101	957	28.1	3.06	
Sunart (1723)	18			67	395	19.75	3.72	
Coigach (1755)	28			167	896	32	5.96	
Assynt (1766)	44			339	1718	39	7.7	
Barrisdale (1755–6)	19			39	249	13.1	2.05	
Stratherrick (1755–6)	31			156	896	29.9	5.03	
Strathpeffer (1755–6)	19			175	790	41.5	9.21	
Lovat (1755–6)	27			114	630	23.3	4.22	
Slisgarrow (1755–6)	10	63	48	111	516	51.6	11.1	4.8
Kinloch/Murlaggan (1755–6)	10	40	13	53	211	21.1	5.3	1.3
Fernan (1755–6)	9	40	22	62	286	31.7	6.88	2.4
Glenerochie (1755–6)	11	37	15	52	214	19.4	4.72	1.36
Lix (1755–6)	4	17	11	28	128	32	7	2.75
Balquidder (1755–6)	8	23	45	68	257	32.1	8.5	5.6
Comrie (1755–6)	21	89	93	182	891	42.4	8.66	4.4
Muthill (1755–6)	80	269	122	391	1638	20.4	4.88	1.5
Auchterarder (1755–6)	13	32	30	62	261	20	4.76	2.3
Kinbuck (1755–6)	7	20	13	33	194	27.7	4.71	1.85
Strathgartney (1755–6)	14	16	84	100	414	29.5	7.14	6
Stobhall (1755–6)	27	105	103	208	990	36.6	7.7	3.8

of poll tax returns (1694–6) for Lowland areas concluded that there, too, between a half and two-thirds of touns had cottars present, with lower than average figures for Renfrewshire and upland Aberdeenshire, but higher than average figures for coastal Aberdeenshire, Midlothian and Berwickshire.[7] Where sources are specific, cottars come across as a diverse group. A detailed listing of cottars occupying cot-houses 'within [the] farm called the Plewlands' in Inverdovart, Fife, 1714, records as many as fifteen present, some having a house, yard and one or two acres, others an acre without a house or yard, and some an acre or two acres 'Laboured'.[8] Likewise, a 1739 rental for the Scott of Harden estate in Berwickshire recorded fourteen 'Coate Houses' at Mertoun, holding between one and three acres.[9] Such arable land formed part of that held by the tenant to whom a cottar was attached.[10] Likewise, any right to graze a cow or few sheep would have come out of the tenant's soum. For others, their stake in land amounted to no more than a garden or kailyard, though some might also be given meal and clothing as part of their contract. As a source of labour, cottars carried out a variety of work, including basic tasks like ploughing and herding, while some also carried out the labour services and carriages that tenants were still burdened with down to the mid-eighteenth century.

The different ways in which these tacksmen, tenants, sub-tenants, crofters and cottars came together make it difficult to squeeze the size and composition of the pre-improvement community into a standard form. However, what is clear is that for most people in the Scottish countryside, the everyday was shaped around small communities embracing a number of families. Few families lived alone, though we can find some one-family 'touns'.[11] At the very least, the typical community comprised a small handful of tenants, their cottars and their respective families, or a single tenant plus a few cottars and their families, with the largest having ten or more families and some, many more. For some Highland areas, if not for Lowland areas, we can actually quantify their overall size, though the aggregate data presented in Table 1.2 conceals much local variability. What is also clear is that few pre-improvement Highland or Lowland touns could have formed a community entirely of equals, made up solely of tenants holding the same amount of land. Instead, most brought together people with different degrees of resource entitlement, with ample low-order rungs on the farming ladder for those cottars and lesser tenants with initiative and enterprise to better themselves.

Yet establishing the scale and composition of touns in this way may still not be the last word on who exactly came together in everyday routines. This is because what we find recorded in rentals and listings as forming a 'toun' need not necessarily have been the *working* unit around which communities organised their everyday. Some touns may, in actuality, have been informally sub-divided by their occupiers into smaller working sub-touns.[12] Two factors encouraged this practice. First, many had arable sectors sprawled discontinuously over fairly large areas, often with their settlement broken down into clusters that matched the spread of arable land. Arranging such arable land into smaller working units enabled tenants to work it more efficiently. The desire to create smaller, more manageable units was the reason for a comprehensive reorganisation of touns into smaller units in Strathavon during the early seventeenth century.[13] Secondly, many pre-improvement touns were held by multiple tenants. In the majority of cases, formally dividing out the holding of each tenant would have been a regular occurrence owing to the prevalence of short tenures prior to the improving movement.[14] While dividing such shares into runrig was a widespread choice, it was not one mandated by agreements. It can be no surprise that some opted to have their shares as separate holdings, a decision that had a far-reaching impact on their everyday.[15] What adds extra interest to this last point is that many touns across east-central Scotland involved large units of assessment (that is, the ploughgate or davach), whose organisation into working touns could involve a complex internal division into ploughs, halves, quarters, etc. When we look at the interlocking pyramid of shares that could exist, such as with the 'sixth part of the lands of Nethir Fornocht called the west half of the middle third part of the lands of Nethir Fornocht', 1623,[16] it becomes difficult to decide at what level such shares were laid out as runrig shares or as separate touns, but each level must, at some point, have involved an active decision over the preferred size of the everyday working community.

Whether the typical pre-improvement toun was flexible over how it organised itself raises questions about whether we can identify factors that bound communities together in their everyday and others that fostered division. Where odal tenure still existed in the northern isles, the successive partition of holdings between co-heirs tended to map the close ties of kinship into local landholding, creating 'township estates' bonded through the ties of a single family, such as the Corrigalls of Corrigall or the Ibisters of Ibister.[17] These township estates relied on a continuity of occupation by particular families combined with the partible inheritance of land. Such continuity can be found elsewhere, but the absence of partible inheritance meant kinship mattered to the bonding of communities only when other factors were at work. Thus, just as landowners in the west Highlands tended to appoint tacksmen who were affiliated to them, so also could tacksmen look after their kin when sub-letting land.[18] Yet we must not overstate the extent to which working communities were forged through kin ties. Part of the reason for this is that when we look at Highland toun communities through rentals, they do not come across as socially stable. The temporariness of tenure for many Highland tenants fostered a regular turnover of occupants.[19] Subsistence crises were also disruptive.[20] The majority of Highlanders may have lived out their lives in the same district but not necessarily in the same toun, so that what constituted the everyday for most was subject to continuous renegotiation. Leading tacksmen were an exception to this generalisation, reinforcing their position with claims of a *duthchas* or the hereditary right to their possession,[21] or by holding a wadset of their land as security for a loan made to the landowner.[22] In the Lowlands, some tenants also claimed an hereditary possession of their land on the basis of kindly tenure.[23] While, where it existed, feuing also brought a stability to landholding.[24] Yet among ordinary tenants, continuity of occupation by particular families was more likely within the same estate or barony than within the same toun, as work on the Panmure estate has shown.[25]

Just as some factors worked to bind communities together, others cut across them creating tensions and even cleavages. Within some, the position of those who held crofts may have been ambivalent. Most formed a physically and tenurially discrete unit, some even being set down as a private enclave in the midst of a toun's runrig arable land. While they were very much involved in the day-to-day activities of touns, there must have been a sense in which they were also outside it. This applied particularly to the service crofts set to millers, brewers and the like. The commonest form was the mill croft, which were widespread in the Lowlands and across the eastern and southern Highlands, but thinned as one moved north-westwards, where the small horizontal or ladle mill and the hand-operated rotary quern took its place. Where mills existed, touns in the district immediately around it were thirled to it or compelled to have their grain ground there, the miller taking a share or multure as payment.[26] For tenants, this imposed relationship led to endless friction with millers over the quality of the service and its cost.[27] Such tension was probably present wherever thirlage existed, but it must have been a particular problem along the dividing line between those areas that had vertical mills and those areas that avoided paying multures by relying on more do-it-yourself forms like the smaller horizontal mill or quern. In the transitional zone between the two, the inevitable tension is well captured by bylaws ordering the confiscation of querns.[28]

So-called brew-seats, ailhouses or changehouses were also a focus for a great deal of tension owing to the way in which some tenants were bound by their tacks to have their barley converted to malt at those controlled by estates.[29] It also arose from the growing involvement of estates in the suppression of illicit distilling.[30] There was a degree of self-interest here, for many estates derived rental income from the brew-seats or ailhouses established on their land.[31] As at Snizort on Skye, such brew-seats or ailhouses had the privilege 'of brewing, malting, vending and Distilling all sorts of legal spirits and liquers therein',[32] and were the logical precursor for the inns that spread across the region over the eighteenth century;[33] places where the outside world and travellers like Johnson and Boswell touched the local.

Even over the seventeenth century, the structure of the everyday community was changing, with tenant numbers in Lowland touns being slowly reduced.[34] This creation of larger holdings was probably bound up with a shift toward a more commercial orientation of the toun economy, with many single tenants in fertile areas like the Lothians keeping all the toun in their own hands and farming it using cottars.[35] It has been argued that this trend toward larger holdings amounted to a gradual revolution in landholding, one that paved the way for the investment and husbandry changes of the improving movement.[36] Precisely because of this connection, those touns that still carried multiple tenants found themselves subject to a rapid catch-up once the improving movement got under way in the mid-eighteenth century, their tenant numbers being reduced over one or two leases or, in some cases, over night.[37] In fact, contemporary comments on this surge in tenant reduction compare with what was later said about the Highland Clearances.[38] However, not all landowners saw profit in reducing tenant numbers so as to create large working units. Where cattle rearing was important, such as in parts of Aberdeenshire and Ayrshire, landholding was reorganised out of runrig in a way that preserved the size of holdings that had existed under runrig.[39] Instead of being part of a larger runrig community, these newly divided farms were now independent farms based largely around family labour. In the Highlands, too, some single tenants possessing large tacks by the 1720s functioned not as tacksmen but as commercial cattle farmers. By the 1750s though, it was the spread of sheep that started to drive tenant reduction, runrig touns being cleared to make way for sheep farmers.[40] Initially, the touns affected by the clearances were relatively small, as were the sheep farms that replaced them, but as the process reached north of the Great Glen, and especially as it spread into Sutherland by the 1790s, we find single sheep farms displacing a number of runrig touns and whole communities replaced by a single shepherd and his family.[41]

Given the extent of social dislocation associated with the Sutherland clearances especially, the scale of public reaction generated by them is not surprising. However, we must not lose sight of the fact that a great deal of runrig in the Lowlands was also removed by tenant reduction. When we ask how this reduction changed the social basis of everyday life for the farm community, three specific changes stand out. First, in many areas, it led to larger working units held by fewer tenants, with the farming ladder being simplified by the removal of its lower rungs. Secondly, while the new husbandries that spread across the Lowlands from the mid-eighteenth century onwards required significant amounts of hired labour, the overall size of communities shrank in the transition from runrig toun to farm. Part of this loss was due to the reduction in tenant numbers, but some contemporary reports also make it clear that the number of cottars also shrank noticeably.[42] Thirdly, in some areas, the contraction of numbers was more a relocation than a disappearance, with the growth of planned villages being sustained by labourers who 'lived in rural villages while still working on the land',[43] and by the fact that many farmsteads were relocated to sites more appropriate to their newly laid out farms.

STRUCTURING THE EVERYDAY: THE RURAL ECONOMY

Traditional peasant societies have been described as made up of part societies, comprising an indigenous cultural base overlain with what was imposed on them by the linkages and demands of a wider world. The pre-improvement rural community of early modern Scotland fits easily into this model. Yet we still need to ask how far such wider linkages and demands intruded downwards into the everyday life of the ordinary toun-dweller? I want to consider this question from one particular but vital perspective: was the world of the ordinary farming community open or closed economically?

The typical fermtoun of the early seventeenth century had a non-specialised farm economy, geared as much to the production of grain as to livestock and livestock produce. When we take into account the other ways in which many farmers answered their own needs – as their own weaver, ploughwright and even house builder – it raises the question of whether the typical toun subsisted in a relatively self-sufficient world at this point and whether the progressive loss of economic insularity and opening up to the market provides us with an over-arching theme for the period from 1600 to 1800? We can answer yes to this question, but it needs to be heavily qualified.

Many Lowland touns were already engaged in marketing by the seventeenth century. However, a significant part of what reached markets, probably the predominant share during most of the seventeenth century, comprised grain received by landowners as part payment of rents in kind.[44] Such payments meant many farm communities had an involvement with marketing, with some, such as those on the Mar and Kellie estate in Aberdeenshire,[45] even being required to deliver their grain rents to nearby markets or ports, but it was not yet an involvement driven by a marketing mentality among farmers. That said, alongside what they marketed through landlords, many ordinary tenants must have had a small, more direct involvement that addressed their own needs In some cases, it was the need to raise money for the cash component of their rents. In other cases, it was to balance deficiencies in their farm economy. In the more marginal areas of the Highlands, grain deficiencies were endemic, so that communities routinely traded what they had in abundance (for example, cheese) for that in which they were deficient (for example, meal). Such marketing was about correcting imbalances in the farm economy, a trade in use not exchange values.

The distinction being drawn here between the large-scale marketing of food rents by landlords, a sector probably infused from the outset with a search for exchange value, and the petty marketing engaged in by ordinary farmers, a sector infused as much with a search for use as for exchange value, survived for most of the seventeenth century. The increased volumes of grain that were marketed over the seventeenth century were, in the first instance, sustained by that marketed by landlords.[46] The increased flow came not just from landlocked Lowland touns close to the major urban markets but also from touns set at a much greater distance that had easy access to the coast, including areas as far north as Caithness, Orkney and Shetland.[47] The extent to which this trade reconfigured the everyday life of toun is underlined by the extent to which toun economies in some areas, like the Lothians, had become specialised and market-oriented by the end of the seventeenth century. By this point though, a key change had started to unfold as some landlords began to convert their rents in kind into cash, shifting the burden of marketing on to the ordinary farmer.[48] Farms in parts of the south-west and southern uplands also became more specialised by the late seventeenth century, the former feeding steady numbers of cattle into cross-border droves and the latter supplying sheep.[49] In both cases, their early shift toward specialisation was socially disruptive of communities. In the south-west, tenant numbers were reduced and large cattle enclosures established in response to the growing market opportunities for stock, the pioneer or 'chiefe' enclosure being at Baldoon in Galloway.[50] In time, attempts to level such enclosures became a focus of opposition to the loss of tenancies.[51] To the east, in the southern uplands, touns were being converted into more specialised sheep farms as early as the 1670s and 1680s. Out of 148 hill farms on the Buccleuch estate, twenty had over 1,000 sheep and forty-seven over 500 by this point.[52] Again, it was a shift underpinned by a contraction in tenant numbers.[53]

Even in the Highlands, it would be difficult to support claims that farmers had a wholly self-sufficient economy prior to the spread of sheep. In terms of its basic grain needs, the region mixed areas of surplus with areas of scarcity, so that most found themselves drawn into the market process, directly or indirectly. Remarkably, isolated areas, like the fringe of small islands around the southern and western edge of Harris, such as Killegray and Pabbay, can be seen handing over substantial payments of grain to MacLeod of MacLeod in late seventeenth-century rentals.[54] By contrast, mainland areas like Glengarry[55] and Knoydart,[56] routinely imported grain, offsetting its cost by marketing livestock products such as butter, cheese, hides and wool. The vast bulk of such marketing probably involved low value goods traded at low thresholds. Thus, farmers from Knoydart, most of whom had barely an acre or two of arable land, regularly sold cheese at markets like Inverness so as to buy grain. Some were probably among the traders seen at Inverness market in the 1720s whose marketable goods appeared:

> of a most contemptible Value, such as these; viz. – two or three cheeses, of about three or four Pounds weight a piece; a kid sold for sixpence or Eight pence at most; a small Quantity of Butter, in something that looks like a Bladder, and is sometimes set down upon the dirt in the street; three or four Goat skins; a Piece of Wood for an Axeltree to one of the little Carts, &c.[57]

Most of these transactions would have amounted to an exchange of use values, with individuals trading in one basic item of necessity so as to immediately purchase another, often bartering one against the other. Indeed, given the scarcity of money in the Highlands, bartering would have been an important form of everyday interaction for farmers and cottars. The rise of the cattle droving trade from the early seventeenth century onwards did not escape this problem. Outwardly, it served the purpose of providing a source of cash at a time when landowners were converting rents in kind into cash. However, when we probe into how droving was organised, we find that a great deal was organised by estates themselves, working through their agents or professional drovers. Further, though rents were set in cash, tenants were often allowed to set cattle against this cash so that responsibility for the drove passed to the estate.[58]

RHYTHMS OF EVERYDAY LIFE

As with all traditional rural communities, everyday life in the Scottish countryside from 1600 to 1800 was shaped around the rhythms of the seasonal calendar and the basic routines of resource exploitation. Three types of evidence enable us to recover these rhythms. First, there are the calendars of work disclosed by farm diaries and day books. Secondly, there are the bylaws passed by local barony or birlaw courts that detail when and how particular routines should be carried out. Thirdly, there is the documentation, again in court records, of the disputes that arose over particular routines.

If we look at year-round activities drawn from day books, like that for the Nethermains of the Monymusk estate in Aberdeenshire, 1749, and for the Marchmont home farm in Berwickshire, 1758–9, we find some basic routines spread across the calendar (Table 1.3). Before seeing this year-round spread as a feature of all touns, we should note that many home farms had started to acquire enclosed parks, plantations, new roads and open ditch drainage by the mid-eighteenth century, so there were tasks to fill the slack times of year. Further, home farms used not just hired labour but also the labour obligations burdened on tenants, such as ploughing and shearing, so their calendar of work may reflect a need to work around the commitment that tenants had to their own holdings. Finally, the Monymusk and Marchmont estates were in areas where pre-improvement cropping involved winter sown crops so that we would expect more signs of year-round activity.

If we could reconstruct the seasonal rhythms in fermtouns elsewhere, we would probably find that pre-improvement labour routines were more seasonally uneven when compared with the husbandries ushered in by the improving movement. There are three reasons why this would be so. First, the narrower range of crops sown (mostly bere and oats) and the dependence on spring ploughing and sowing meant that, for most communities, the basic routines of husbandry were seasonally confined, concentrated into the months between March and May, with harvest lasting from late August through to late October for oats. Secondly, stock were notoriously under-managed in winter, being allowed to forage across different touns over

Table 1.3 *Calendar of work: Monymusk, 1749, and Marchmont, 1758–9. Source: H. Hamilton (ed.),* Life and Labour on an Aberdeenshire Estate 1735–1750, *Third Spalding Club (Aberdeen, 1946), pp. 80–130; NAS, Marchmont Muniments, GD1/651/17.*

	Monymusk 1749
January:	Ploughing, Threshing, Taking Down Fold Dykes, Building Fold Dykes, Attending Cattle and Sheep, Threshing, Taking Malt to Miller, Cutting Broom, Driving Burnet Clay, Making Ropes
February:	Ploughing, Threshing, Harrowing, Drawing and Spreading Clay, Casting Outfield Dykes, Building Tathfolds, Digging, Attending Sheep and Cattle, Sowing, Trenching, Cleaning Houses
March:	Ploughing, Sowing, Threshing, Filling Crown of Rigs
April:	Ploughing, Threshing, Harrowing, Rolling, Dunging, Sowing, Ditching, Gathering Stones, Cleaning Houses and Byres
May:	Ploughing, Harrowing, Sowing, Dunging, Mending Dykes inc. Fold Dykes, Managing Cattle, Carting Hay, Mending Horse Graith, Making Gates, Making Bridge
June:	Ploughing, Harrowing, Dunging, Bleeding Cattle, Smiddie Work, Mending Graith, Mending Folds, Sowing, Drawing Stones
July:	Ploughing, Harrowing, Dunging, Pulling Thistles, Drawing Stones, Carting Peats, Preparing Folds
August:	Ploughing, Pulling Thistles, Hoeing, Weeding, Mending Stable and Byre, Filling Holes, Attending Market, Drawing Stones, Cutting Peats, Casting Feal, Building Byre
September:	Ploughing, Drawing Peat, Shearing, Making Ropes and Horse Graith, Threshing, Attending Market, Drawing Divots
October:	Ploughing, Threshing, Stacking, Making Ropes, Drawing Stone, Attending Market, Pulling Turnips, Drawing Divots, Cleaning Houses
November:	Ploughing, Threshing, Cutting Broom, Cleaning Houses, Drawing Dung, Harrowing, Fold Dykes
December:	Ploughing, Threshing, Drawing Dung, Spreading Dung, Taking Down Previous Year's Fold Dykes, Mending Graith, Dressing and Carting Bear
	Marchmont 1758–9
January:	Ploughing, Leading Divots and earth, Leading Hay, Felling Timber, Levelling Dykes, Leading Broom
February:	Ploughing, Levelling Old Dykes, Leading Hay, Leading Timber, Leading Lime
March:	Ploughing, Levelling, Leading Timber, Leading Lime,

Table 1.3   (continued)

April:	Ploughing, Sowing, Cutting Up Trees, Rolling Marl, Levelling Dykes
May:	Ploughing, Sowing, Carting and Spreading Marl, Levelling, Leading Dung, Rolling
June:	Ploughing, Leading Dung, Grinding Malt, Drawing Stones, Making Drains, Hoeing
July:	Ploughing, Hoeing, Mowing, Leading Hay, Levelling
August:	Ploughing, Mowing, Shearing, Leading Hay, Making Ropes, Spreading Lime
September:	Ploughing, Threshing, Leading Stones, Setting Up Corn, Spreading Lime, Leading Stones, Leading Timber
October:	Ploughing, Setting Up Corn, Spreading Lime
November:	Ploughing, Leading Corn, Threshing, Road Making, Lime Spreading, Clearing Stones
December:	Ploughing, Road Making and Maintenance

winter without close grazing management, a neglect addressed by the 1686 Act anent winter herding.[59] Thirdly, the typical toun faced a summer growing season that was crowded with vital routines, each competing for labour at one and the same time. Admittedly, some tasks, like weeding, had little place in pre-improvement husbandry, despite the fact that its arable land was notoriously weed infested.[60] Indeed, some communities would have seen the presence of arable weeds as a positive advantage, because of their role as famine foods[61] or because, as with the barley crop of Galloway,[62] they added flavour to beer. However, in addition to the standard routines of husbandry, some pre-improvement communities faced heavy summer labour demands from the cutting of peat and turf, the harvesting of hay and the gathering of seaweed and ferns. Where touns had access to summer shielings, then the transfer of stock to them – along with the herding of stock, milking and the making of cheese – was a further demand on labour at this time of year. Differences in labour demand also existed as regards the processing of grain. In the more fertile, grain-abundant touns, the annual routines of harvesting and threshing were onerous but, once complete, the burden passed to the miller, albeit at a cost. By comparison, when we look to north-west Highlands and across the Hebrides, areas whose ecology favoured the hand quern, considerable amounts of labour, invariably female, were required to grind corn. On Tiree, it was said to consume the work of 100 women for an entire year.[63] Squeezed in around such tasks were other demands, such as spinning, weaving and house maintenance. Where the last-mentioned involved perishable raw materials, like wattle, turf, peat, ferns and heather, then the labour involved in their regular maintenance would have been significant.

Another way of approaching the rhythms of the pre-improvement toun is through bylaws enacted by local barony courts. Those rhythms that were most critical to the smooth running of the toun, and which required an in-step approach between occupiers, were those most likely to be under-pinned by such bylaws. To some extent, the need for farmers to work together, to synchronise their routines of husbandry, was secured by general acts of good neighbourhood.[64] In addition to these generic acts, more specific acts targeted a range of practices from stock control to peat cutting. Those enacted over stock control were usually designed to regulate the movements of stock. There were three basic expectations: setting the date when stock had to be moved (that is, beyond the head dyke, to the shielings, or to the tath-folds on outfield), binding tenants to move stock in step with the common herd or flock, and binding them to maintain folds and dykes so as to make the regulations over stock movements effective and secure.[65] Mundane activ-ities like the cutting of peat were also regulated through bylaws, some courts issuing acts that bound farmers to cut their peats progressively along a single face and to replace the turf cover.[66] Bylaws were also used to give protection to those resources over which estates sought to exercise a more exclusive control, such as deer, game birds and blackfish, or over which they sought closer regulation, such as timber.[67] The careful definition of who had right to what is shown by the regulations issued over roof timbers and doors and whether tenants were allowed to remove them at the end of their tacks.[68]

Bylaws can be revealing, but what fills the court record most is not their enactment but the evidence for their infringement. Such references high-light the conflicts that could erupt around the mundane aspects of everyday routines. In runrig touns especially, the potential for disruption was ever present. As one late-eighteenth-century source for Netherlone put it:

> if man's dispositions were nearly equal & if they considered their neighbours good at all times as nearly connected with their own, such a method of carrying on the works of a farm might do very well, but the Contrary is a fatal mistake . . . often more time is spent in contending, not only what work is first to be done, than would actually carry the double into execution, and that none may do less than his neighbour.[69]

Falling out over basic routines caused many a toun to descend into a chaos of the everyday, though courts did act to restate obligations of good neighbour-hood, as at Lude, where, in 1627, it was restated that 'none within the said ground pertaining to the said Alexr Robertson brak nytborheid to uthers efter they have streikit ane pleuche togither'.[70] Invariably, those who were most disruptive tended to be disruptive in every way. A Sutherland court entry for 1782 described a Katherine Gun in Achincoull as 'Guilty of every sort of bad Neighbourhood in so far as that, she declines assisting in any thing that belongs to the Welfare of the place.'[71] Failure to control stock, especially stock that could cause damage like goats and swine, was a peren-nial problem, as when, in 1730, a complaint was made that the possessors of

Moy More 'have for the season bypast kept Great Droves or herds of Swine and allowed the same to pasture up & down the Severall Towns of the neighbourhood without any kind of tethering or Binding'.[72]

How did the improving movement from the mid-eighteenth century onwards change the basic rhythms of the countryside? Three probable areas of change can be noted. First, the introduction of winter fodders like turnips and sown grasses, the wider use of winter sown grains in the Lowlands, the need to fit in a range of activities like marling, liming, ditching, the laying of drains, hedge laying, stone clearing and rig straightening, led to farming rhythms spread more evenly across the year. Secondly, as regional farm economies became more specialised toward the end of the century, everyday rhythms of farm life probably became regionally more specific. Thirdly, the specialisation of farm output was matched by a growing specialisation of roles within the rural community, the labour force acquiring some of the gradations that were to characterise it during the nineteenth century.[73] There were now more full-time craftsmen and tradesmen, some living in the planned villages that landowners laid out as a focus for such services.[74]

THE SPACES OF EVERYDAY LIFE

The spaces through which traditional society played out its daily rhythms were an intrinsic part of how it experienced the everyday. Different kinds of space need to be recognised. First and foremost were the functional spaces around which everyday life was organised. The most telling point to be made here is that there appears to be a remarkable degree of uniformity about how rural communities divided their functional spaces. Distinctions like infield, outfield, common pasture and shielings were widespread across the mainland. Only in the Hebrides and northern isles was it simplified into townland arable, common pasture and shieling.[75] The way in which parts of the south-west Highlands referred to infield as wintertoun,[76] in contrast to the summer spaces of outfield or tathing ground, common pasture and shieling grounds reminds us that these spaces were imbued with a time–space character. In addition to these broad categorisations of space, there also existed a welter of other work or activity spaces, such as kailyards, penfolds, tathfolds, cot-touns, crofts, as well as buildings in which key activities were focused, like the house itself, the byre, grain barns or girnals, hay barns, drying and malting kilns, mills and shielings. These activity spaces were found widely, although some were confined in their distribution, like the small garden-like enclosure known as a *planticrue* that was used for growing vegetables, but especially cabbages, in Shetland.[77] Such spaces were usually linked to specific uses, often at particular times of the year and, to judge from some contemporary comments, there may have been a gender bias as to who used them: thus, while all took part in shearing, threshing was a men-only task, on the other hand where the quern was used, grinding was a woman's task.[78]

Being a feature of most touns, functional spaces did not provide touns with individuality. This came only from the identity which they constructed out of the spaces that they occupied, an identity founded on the bounded-ness which they imposed on the world around them and on toponymic naming. Though we find ample references to communities perambulating their bounds, and to boys being beaten at key points along the way so as to imprint the memory indelibly in their mind as well as on the ground, such rituals can give the impression that bounds were always simple and abso-lute.[79] The head dyke, the point where what was exclusive to a toun gave way to its common grazings, was patently an unambiguous boundary, one that each toun was obliged to maintain.[80] Beyond, a toun might have some exclusive right to grazing and to resources like peat and turf, but often these rights overlapped or merged with those of adjacent touns. We need only take note of the disputes over grazing that frequently erupted between adjacent touns within the same estate and, more seriously, between touns on adjacent estates to realise that the outer reach of touns, the bounds of its use rights, could be fuzzy.[81] Identities were also constructed through naming, though this could inflect a range of meanings. At the level of the toun itself, there was a marked conservatism that is well shown by the way in which names persisted despite change. In the case of the eastern Grampians, old davach names continued to be used as a generic form of identity despite the fact many were sub-divided into a cluster of small touns. In effect, the identity of such touns had a genealogy to it. At a finer scale, most touns also named their fields and pastures, though these are not routinely recorded by eighteenth-century surveys. The typical farm community did not live its everyday in a bland world of rigs, shotts and meadows, but in one that was richly differ-entiated and valued through the close naming of arable plots, furlongs and grazing areas, names that display a strong regional patterning in terms of the place elements used.[82] Yet, just as the improving movement of the mid- to late eighteenth century saw a simplification of ecological differences through its programmes of land improvement, drainage and reseeding, so also did it see the loss of some of these fine-scaled identities, as farms were comprehen-sively realigned into wholly new and larger fields.[83]

The way in which traditional communities constructed their everyday space symbolically provides a third kind of space. This symbolic meaning is not easily documented from the sources available but there are clues. Many touns in eastern Scotland were divided out into runrig shares, or split into wholly separate and discrete touns, using customary methods of land divi-sion, including one based on sunny and shadow shares.[84] Early Scottish law books explain what was involved: divisions started on the east side of touns at dawn and worked their way round it in a sun-wise direction, giving out rigs to each landholder, finishing in the east by evening. Landholders who held the sunny portion of the toun were always given the strips that lay to the east or south in each sequence of allocation and those holding the shadow portion receiving those that lay to the west or north.[85] Such a system used a natural ordering of time–space so as to frame a division process that was similarly enacted through time–space. At first sight, it might be thought that this was simply a convenient method of land division, with no carry-over for communities once the division was complete. However, some evidence suggests otherwise. First, some sources refer to sunny/shadow or easter/wester *ploughs*, as if the symbolic ordering implicit in such divisions was carried over into the routines of husbandry and the way land was ploughed.[86] Secondly, early legal descriptions of such divisions depict the terms sunny/shadow as synonymous or interchangeable with forms like east/west, upper/lower, fore/back and *more/beag*. We can appreciate the implications of this only when we take into account the fact that some touns carried over this potential ambiguity of identity into their day-to-day world, so that we find touns named as Easter Herrocks in one source but as Little Herrocks in another, or Over Lethnot in one and as West Lethnot in another.[87] Thirdly, a 1715 entry for Fintray barony court in Aberdeenshire referred to the appointment of birlawmen for 'foreside' of the estate and others for the 'backside'. Any doubt as to what this meant is removed by a later 1717 entry which compelled tenants in 'ye forside viz. the two ploughs in Woodhead, two in Cowstones, two in Woodhead . . .', etc., to bring in lime when required.[88] Each toun had a further two ploughs comprising the backside. Clearly, the symbolic order embodied in land divisions appears part of a *mentalitié* that was carried over into everyday routines.

A further indication of how communities may have symbolised the world around them is provided by evidence drawn from pre-improvement estate plans for north-east Scotland. In a number of cases they show touns as having an arable field called *The Lost*, usually close to their settlement or core.[89] Though its occurrence was concentrated in the Strathavon and Glenlivet area, there are also signs that it may also have been used elsewhere, such as on the Uists.[90] As a field name, *The Lost* does not have an obvious derivation. It may be linked with the Gaelic word for fire but it may also be connected to *losaid*, meaning bread basket, and denote a particularly fertile part of the toun. The areas where the field name *The Lost* occurs are also those where kirk sessions records document the practice of fire rituals by local communities: significantly, these were focused on one particular field, along with the dwellings, byres and barns of the toun, the farm community reportedly taking a lighted torch in a sun-wise manner around them.[91] *The Lost* may have been the focus for this ritual based on fire. In other words, it was not just a fertile field but one which communities charged with all the symbolism that was thought to underpin fertility and renewal.

A fourth and final way in which we can characterise the spaces of the early modern countryside is through their form in the landscape. When we look at pre-improvement estate plans and their depiction of settlement, arable, meadow, pasture and major markers, like head dykes, we find a landscape whose shapes and forms fitted in with the natural ecology of environmental opportunity. Arable land comprised small, irregular patches that were often broken by numerous small areas of poor drainage, even in the more fertile parts of the Lowlands. In the Highlands, rock outcrops broke up the arable land still further. Pasture, too, was not the uniform, improved pasture that we see today, but highly variegated in character thanks to local variations in groundwater conditions and ecology. Contemporaries talked about spouty land, a reference to the numerous eruptions of water and flushes that existed prior to the use of effective under-drainage. The sum effect was a variegated, discontinuous and uneven landscape. Along with its adoption of new farming systems, the improving movement witnessed the transformation of such landscapes, with extensive programmes of field realignment, enclosure, land improvement and stone clearance. There were two components to this transformation. A landscape that had hardly known a straight line, in which natural ecology always had the upper hand in shaping farm layout, was now covered with the uncompromisingly regular shapes and lines of the surveyor, with new fields, roads and plantations turning parts of the landscape into an exercise in geometry, a statement of how improvement was about taming the wild. The process began around estate policies in the 1720s and 1730s, before becoming more general from the 1750s and 1760s onwards.[92] A second feature of the improving movement's transformation of space stemmed from its heavy programmes of land improvement, marling, liming, stone clearance, drainage and reseeding. The weeds that had so enhanced the species richness of arable land in the pre-improvement landscape, and which had made the difference between arable and pasture a matter of degree, were now systematically weeded out. The variety that had characterised the farming ecologies of the pre-improvement landscape were slowly reduced, though not removed, as its more variable ecology slowly gave way to the simpler ecology of the improved farm. For those who lived through the improving movement, the way it transformed the landscapes of their everyday in this way would have been among its more obvious visible effects.

CONCLUSION

Except for some communities in the far north and north-west, those living in the Scottish countryside would have had a fundamentally different experience of everyday life in 1800 compared with what it had been in 1600. The social structures in which they lived and worked, and through which they played out their everyday, the very nature of the rural community itself, had been transformed. The new husbandries and systems of farming that were adopted over the second half of the eighteenth century initiated a transformation in the basic rhythms of the everyday, not least through the emergence of more year-round cycles of husbandry and a shift toward more specialised farm economies. Finally, the everyday was now increasingly played out across a different kind of space, a managed space made up of regular enclosures, roads and shelter belts, one whose ecologies had been simplified through land improvement, drainage, stone clearance and reseeding. If we had to reduce such changes to a single overarching experience, then it would be to see the everyday as having begun the period from 1600 to 1800 mostly, if not exclusively, energised and framed by local needs and horizons, but then gradually opened out to the demands of a much wider world, one in which market opportunities at a national scale played an increasing role in shaping its character.

Notes

1. Dunvegan Castle, Macleod of MacLeod Papers, 2/10.
2. E. Cregeen, 'Tacksmen and their successors: a study of tenurial reorganisations in Mull, Morvern and Tiree in the early eighteenth century', *Scottish Studies*, 13 (1969), 93–144.
3. MacLeod Papers, 4/294.
4. Typical was National Archives of Scotland, Gordon Castle Muniments, GD44/51/732/1, which recorded Moy and Keillisoss as held by John Macdonald 'but that the hail of it is possest be the Subtenants'; Cregeen, 'Tacksmen and their successors', p. 101.
5. Cregeen, 'Tacksmen and their successors', pp. 93–144; Armadale Castle, Clan Donald Trust, GD221/3695/2.
6. Inveraray Castle, Argyll Papers, vol. 65, 1771.
7. T. M. Devine, *Transformation of Rural Scotland: Social Change and the Agrarian Economy 1660–1815* (Edinburgh, 1994), p. 13 and appendices 2–5.
8. Devine, *Transformation of Rural Scotland*, p. 12.
9. NAS, Polwarth Papers, GD157/1030 and 1031.
10. As illustration, NAS, Clerk of Penicuik, GD18/722, has a 1694 entry for Lasswade saying 'those 5 houses abovementioned are cottars to me & not to David McKall'.
11. For example, NAS, Breadalbane Muniments, GHD112/16/13/3/1 lists the number of families in Glenorchy touns, 1730 and shows a number where only one family was present.
12. NAS, Airlie Muniments, GD16/30/11; A. Geddes, 'Conjoint tenants and tacksmen on the isle of Lewis, 1715–26', *Economic History Review*, 2nd series, 1 (1948–9), 54–60.
13. A. Mitchell (ed.), *Geographical Collections Relating to Scotland by W. Macfarlane*, ii, Scottish Historical Society, vol. 52 (Edinburgh, 1907), pp. 270, 463–4. For a mid-eighteenth-century example, see NAS, Breadalbane Muniments, GD112/12/1/2/14.
14. Occasionally, agreements refer to the need to divide shares, such as that dealing with the just and equal half of Little Formestoun, NAS, Huntly Muniments, GD312/30/3.
15. For example, NAS, Lindsay of Dowhill, GD254/78, Contract between Laurence

Mercer, James Lyndsey and Robert Douglas, 1611, records the division of Culcairny, Fife, which had been 'occupit be the tennentis and labororis thairof be Rin Rig quhilk hes oftymes movit and raisit cummer and trubull amangis thames'.

16. NAS, Airlie Muniments, GD16/5/148.
17. J. Storer Clouston, *The Orkney Parishes* (Kirkwall, 1927), p. 146; F. J. Shaw, *The Northern and Western Islands of Scotland: Their Economy and Society in the Seventeenth Century* (Edinburgh, 1980), pp. 35–42; W. P. L. Thompson, *The New History of Orkney* (Edinburgh, 2001), pp. 311–14.
18. Dunvegan Castle, MacLeod of MacLeod papers, 1/382; Armadale Castle, Clan Donald Trust, GD221/3695/2; GD221/4284, No. 11/2.
19. For example, in Netherlorn, comparison shows only 91 out of 123 tenants listed in 1692 as being in the same toun a year later, NAS, Breadalbane Muniments, GD112/9/1/4/1–2; *Ibid.*, GD112/9/1/3/5.
20. G. S. Keith, *A General View of the Agriculture of Aberdeenshire* (Aberdeen, 1811), pp. 143, 151–4,
21. C. Withers, *Gaelic Scotland. The Transformation of a Culture Region* (London, 1988), pp. 77–8, 318–22.
22. A.I. MacInnes, *Clanship, Commerce and the House of Stuart 1603–1766* (East Linton, 1996), p. 144; Armadale Castle, Clan Donald Trust, GD221/3695/2.
23. M. H. B. Sanderson, *Scottish Rural Society in the 16th Century* (Edinburgh, 1982), pp. 56–63.
24. Sanderson, *Scottish Rural Society*, pp. 77–123; I. D. Whyte, *Agriculture and Society in Seventeenth Century Scotland*, (Edinburgh, 1979), pp. 161–2.
25. Whyte, *Agriculture and Society*, p. 162; I. D. Whyte and K. A. Whyte, 'Continuity and change in a seventeenth century Scottish farming community', *Agricultural History Review*, 32 (1984), 162–3, 167.
26. For example, NAS, Abercairny Muniments, GD24/1/32.
27. NLS, Sutherland Papers, 313/982/37.
28. For example, Inveraray Castle, Argyll Papers, Bundle 663; NAS, Macgregor Collection, GD50/159, 9 December, 1740.
29. Macgregor Collection, 1 November 1723; NAS, Campbell of Jura Papers, GD64/1/86/7.
30. Inveraray Castle, Argyll Papers, Bundle 2530, 1761.
31. *Miscellany of the Spalding Club*, vol. 4 (Aberdeen, 1849), pp. 261–319; G. Smith, *The Book of Islay* (Glasgow, 1895), p. 483 lists seventeen 'official' or rented changehouses on Islay.
32. Dunvegan Castle, MacLeod of MacLeod Papers, 2/20.
33. Examples included the inn at Tyndrum, NAS, Breadalbane Muniments, GD112/16/25, and at Minginish, 1792, Dunvegan Castle, MacLeod of MacLeod Papers, 2/485/59.
34. R. A. Dodgshon, 'The removal of runrig in Roxburghshire and Berwickshire, 1680–1766', *Scottish Studies*, 16 (1972), 121–37; Devine, *Transformation of Rural Scotland*, pp. 24–9.
35. Devine, *Transformation of Rural Scotland*, p. 27.

36. Devine, *Transformation of Rural Scotland*, pp. 28–9.
37. Devine, *Transformation of Rural Scotland*, pp. 21–9. For analysis of the process in the Borders, see Dodgshon, 'The removal of runrig in Roxburghshire and Berwickshire, 1680–1766', pp. 121–37.
38. *Old Statistical Account*, 1791–99, i, pp. 101–2; viii, pp. 112 and 310, x, p. 166; xi, pp. 376 and 416.
39. NAS, Breadalbane Muniments, GD112/16/4/2/22.
40. E. Richards, *A History of the Highland Clearances: Agrarian Transformations and the Evictions, 1746–1886* (London, 1982).
41. M. Bangor-Jones, 'Sheep farming in Sutherland in the eighteenth century', *Agricultural History Review*, 50 (2002), 181–202.
42. *Old Statistical Account*, 1791–99, viii, pp. 112 and 310, x, p. 166; xi, pp. 376 and 416.
43. Devine, *Transformation of Rural Scotland*, p. 151.
44. Whyte, *Agriculture and Society*, pp. 224–6.
45. NAS, Mar and Kellie, GD124/17/130/1 and 6.
46. A. Fenton and T. C. Smout, 'Scottish agriculture before the improvers – an Exploration', *Agricultural History Review*, 13 (1965), 73–93.
47. Whyte, *Agriculture and Society*, pp. 223–4 and 230.
48. Devine, *Transformation of Rural Scotland*, p. 23.
49. Devine, *Transformation of Rural Scotland*, p. 236.
50. A. Mitchell (ed.) *Macfarlane's Geographical Collections* (Edinburgh, 1907) p. 107; Whyte, *Agriculture and Society*, pp. 124–5.
51. I. D. Whyte, *Scotland's Society and Economy in Transition, c. 1500–c. 1760* (Basingstoke, 1997), p. 92.
52. R. A. Dodgshon, 'Agricultural change and its social consequences in the southern uplands of Scotland, 1660–1780', in T. M. Devine and D. Dickson (eds), *Ireland and Scotland, 1600–1850* (Edinburgh, 1983), pp. 49–52.
53. Dodgshon, 'Agricultural change', pp. 53–4.
54. Dunvegan Castle, MacLeod of MacLeod Papers, 2/487/14; *ibid.*, 2/487/14.
55. NAS, Breadalbane Muniments, GD112/16/13/4/1–2.
56. NAS, Forfeited Estates, E788/42; see also, E745/59.
57. *Burt's Letters from a Gentleman in the North of Scotland to His Friend in London*, ed. R. Jamieson (Edinburgh, [1754] 1876), vol. ii, p. 83.
58. C. Innes (ed.), *The Book of the Thanes of Cawdor*, Spalding Club (Edinburgh, 1859), p. 378; NLS, Sutherland Papers, 313/918.
59. Acts of Parliament of Scotland, viii, p. 595.
60. Forbes's report is reprinted in *Report of the Commissioners of Inquiry into the Conditions of the Crofters and Cottars in the Highlands and Islands* (Edinburgh, 1884), p. 389.
61. R. A. Dodgshon, 'Coping with risk: subsistence crises in the Scottish Highlands and islands, 1600–1800', *Rural History*, 15 (2004), 1–25.
62. Mitchell (ed.), *Macfarlane's Geographical Collections*, i, vol. 51, p. 103 says bear mixed with darnel or roseager had a 'narcotick' effect on ale.
63. Inveraray Castle, Argyll Papers, vol. 65, 1788.

64. J. M. Thomson (ed.), 'The Forbes baron Court Book 1659–78', *Miscellany of Scottish Hist Society*, Scottish History Society, 2nd series, vol. 19 (Edinburgh, 1919), pp. 239 and 292.

65. Typical is NAS, John Macgregor Collection, GD50/136/1, 11/12 July 1660, 'All tenants to goe to the sheills with ther goods, the tenth day of May everie yeir.'

66. NAS, Gordon Castle Muniments, GD44/25/2/76; NAS, Breadalbane Muniments, GD112/1/7/3.

67. NAS, Breadalbane Muniments, GD112/17/5, August, 1625; GD112/17/6, May, 1628.

68. Inveraray Castle, Argyll Papers, Bundle 2531, September/October 1747; NAS, GD50/136/1.

69. NAS, Breadalbane Muniments, GD112/12/1/2/14. See also, NAS, GD112/14/12/7/8.

70. NAS, John Macgregor Collection, GD50/159 Barony Court Book of Lude 1621–1806, 1627. See also, Thomson , 'The Forbes baron Court Book 1659–78', p. 318.

71. NLS, Sutherland Papers, 313/982, Miscellanous Papers on estate Management, No. 29, Petition the Tenants of Achintoull to Lt Col. Sutherland, Dunrobin, 1782.

72. NAS, Mackintosh Muniments, GD176/760; C. B. Gunn (ed.), *Records of the Baron Court of Stitchill*, Scottish History Society, vol. 50 (Edinburgh, 1905), p. 2.

73. I. Carter, *Farm Life in Northeast Scotland 1840–1914* (Edinburgh, 1979), pp. 138–42.

74 T. C. Smout, 'The landowner and the planned village in Scotland, 1730–1830', in N. T. Phillipson and R. Mitchison (eds), *Scotland in the Age of Improvement* (Edinburgh, 1970), pp. 73–106.

75. R. A. Dodgshon, 'Strategies of farming in the western Highlands and Islands of Scotland prior to crofting and the clearances', *Economic History Review*, xlvi (1993), 679–701; Thompson, *The New History of Orkney*, pp. 323–6.

76. NAS, Breadalbane Muniments, GD112/14/12/7/8.

77. A. Fenton, *The Northern Isles: Orkney and Shetland* (Edinburgh, 1978), pp. 101–5.

78. Mitchell (ed.), *Macfarlane's Geographical Collections*, iii, vol. 53, pp. 224, 324; M. Martin, *A Description of the Western Islands of Scotland* (London, 1716 edn), p. 286.

79. Martin, *Description of the Western Isles*, p. 114; 'Corshill Baron Court Book', in *Archaeological and Historical Collections relating to the Counties of Ayr and Wigton*, 1884, vol. 1v, p. 72.

80. Typical is NAS, John Macgregor Collection, GD50/159, 6 June 1622.

81. A good example is provided by NAS, Macpherson of Cluny Papers, GD80/384/12–26; NAS, Breadalbane Muniments, GD112/5/9/59.

82. The Grampian region possessed the most regionally distinctive field elements, see, for example, NAS, RHP 6586/1–8, RHP 1846 and 1847.

83. B. M. W. Third, 'The significance of Scottish estate plans and associated documents', *Scottish Studies*, 1 (1957), 39–64.

84. R. A. Dodgshon, 'Scandinavian solskifte and the sunwise division of land in eastern Scotland', *Scottish Studies*, xix (1975), 1–14.

85. J. Baillie (ed.), *Sir Thomas Craig's Jus Feudale* (1603) (Edinburgh, 1732 edn), p. 425.

86. Examples occur in NAS, Dalhousie Muniments, GD45/16/1544.

87. NAS, GD248/248/31; NAS, Airlie Muniments, GD16/13.

88. J. Cruickshank, 'Court Book of the Barony of Fintray 1711–26', in *Miscellany of the Spalding Club*, vol. I, Third Spalding Club (Aberdeen, 1935), pp. 28 and 33.

89. Examples occur in NAS, RHP 1746; RHP 1747; RHP 1752; RHP 1754; RHP 3964/2, 4, 6, 8 and 24.

90. J. L. Campbell (ed.), *Gaelic Words and Expressions from South Uist and Eriskay, Collected by Rev. Fr. Allan McDonald* (Dublin, 1958), p. 158.

91. NAS, CH2/191/vol. 2, Kirk Session of Inveravine, reported how farmers 'goe about yr. folds & cornes with kindled Torches of ffirr, superstitiouslie & Idolouslie ascribing ye power to the fire of santifieing yr Cornes & cattell', 1703.

92. Third, 'The significance of Scottish estate', pp. 39–64.

Chapter 2

Improvement and Modernisation in Everyday Enlightenment Scotland

Charles McKean

INTRODUCTION

In this chapter, the concept of everyday building is taken to imply virtually any structure that did not have a primary ceremonial purpose. However, given the disparate array of other structures then in use for craft, trade or industry, the focus is primarily upon the home.

There are four themes to this chapter. The first addresses rank – how Scots at almost all levels had a keen appreciation of rank, which was reflected in their dwellings. The second addresses self-provision – what people did when they had to fend for themselves by constructing their own vernacular buildings. There were two distinct phases to this. The first comprised building according to a vernacular tradition of self-shelter to an inherited evolving pattern; the second, emerging in the later eighteenth century, took the form of the occupier or self-builder having to conform to externally enforced rules according to an imposed 'improvement' model set by, for example, the feu superior, the landlord or the founder of the new town or village in which they lived. Throughout the period, however, there remained an absolute distinction between the lesser rural buildings in Lowland Scotland and those beyond the Highland line.[1]

Self-provision was almost entirely a rural phenomenon. Once the very earliest phases of urban settlement were passed, self-provision became almost impossible in Scots towns. The Scottish form of feu tenure led landlords to maximise the income from their burgage plots, with the consequence that they built upwards; and such structures needed skilled erectors. Thus, urban buildings in the larger town centres comprised increasingly tall blocks of tenement or apartment flats – eventually rising to six or more storeys in Edinburgh and Dundee – with the result that self- provision was restricted to the aristocracy or the very rich. Everyday urban life was much more a matter of adapting, refurbishing or customising existing apartments.

The third theme is that of decay and abandonment. Although most of the evidence comes from travellers and commentators imbued with the modernising Enlightenment spirit, it seems impossible to avoid the fact that a good number of Scots burghs – Nairn, Selkirk and Renfrew are good examples

– had fallen into severe decay in the eighteenth century. Robert Southey found Hamilton, for example, 'a dirty old town with a good many thatched houses in the street implying either poverty or great disregard of danger from fires'.[2] A significant proportion of the country's Renaissance country seats were in similar trouble. They had been abandoned as being too unfashionable for the Enlightenment world, so when Dorothy Wordsworth passed through Dumfriesshire in 1803, she observed many of the 'gentlemen's houses which we have passed have an air of neglect and even of desolation'.[3] Conditions in many vernacular rural cottages had become such as to inspire the most evangelical moderniser. Wordsworth again: 'The hut was after the Highland fashion, but without anything beautiful save its situation; the floor was rough and wet with the rain that came in at the door . . . The windows were open' [that is, no frame, shutter or glass].[4] By the end of the eighteenth century, decay was also infecting the ancient urban centres as higher status apartments, abandoned by their inhabitants for the new towns, slid down the social ladder.

The overriding theme, however, is the influence of the Enlightenment and the impulse of modernity. Its desire to create a new civil society, free from the arbitrary rule of the past, was characterised by a new sense of ordered community. In order to forge a modern Scotland, it condemned the history, culture and architecture of its past – particularly that of the Stuart monarchs. Thus, Robert Heron in 1799: 'The improvement, the industry and the riches, lately introduced into Scotland, form a striking contrast with the barbarity, the indolence and the poverty of former times.'[5] The expression of modernity lay in the planning or construction of almost 500 new towns, elite suburbs or grid-iron manufacturing villages.[6] For the most part, the power of ordinary country folk below the Highland line to build for themselves where and how they wished was replaced by a requirement to conform to the new agenda of regular rectangular modernity, more or less as a moral imperative.

RANK

In his manuscript maps, prepared *c.* 1585–1608, Timothy Pont distinguished up to nine scales of rural building, the top four of which appear to be depictions of different ranks of country seats.[7] The remainder vary from individual buildings to strings of what look like cottages with chimneys indicating cottowns, kirktowns and similar rural settlements. His maps also appear to indicate other rural structures, such as windmills, mills, kilns and tide mills.[8] If this interpretation is correct, visible hierarchy in buildings was intentional.

In the west Highlands, for example, the manse (where the laird had been prepared to pay for new one) might stand out, but the principal middle ranking building, the tacksman's house, would be considerably grander. In

Figure 2.1   *View of Dunvegan, Skye from the east, drawn for Captain Francis Grose's* Antiquities of Scotland, *Vol. II (London, 1797). Note the black house (right foreground) as compared with modern slated cottages (left background) and the fact that the oldest part of the stronghold lies in ruins.*

general form, the tacksman's house was a rather larger and more elaborate version of the ubiquitous middle ranking building of Lowland Scotland – the 'Improvement' farmhouse – a sturdy, usually harled, three-bay house, occasionally double-pile (that is, two rooms deep) adjacent to the improved steading. A 1790 engraving of Dunvegan, Isle of Skye by Tom Cocking undertaken for Captain Francis Grose (Figure 2.1) shows two houses in the neighbourhood of the semi-ruined castle: the one in the foreground is a long, thatched roof 'black house', a building type that escaped total obliteration only because its walls were of stone (see later), in contrast to another in the background: regularly built, presumably new stone cottages with that particular symbol of modernism the pitched slated roof. The drawing itself conveyed its own value judgement.[9]

Changes in the fortunes or rank of the occupier would be marked on the exterior of even the humblest homes: at its simplest being carved initials on a door lintel, or a pedimented or otherwise elaborated doorway. Many single-storey cottages were initially extended into the attic space then formalised with further storeys added on top. The joints and junctions that evidenced this progression were never intended to be visible: they would have been obscured by the building's harled overcoat, thus giving the desired impression of being wholly newly built. The ruse would be spotted only if the building fell foul of the 'rubblemania'[10] fashion causing the harling to be cloured off in the early nineteenth century. Only the very smartest village houses might be graced with a new façade of expensive squared stone (ashlar).

Rank was equally important in towns. In Scotland's largest Renaissance towns – notably Dundee and Edinburgh[11] – occupiers of all apartments shared a common stair – an 'upright street' as the Enlightenment condemned it[12] – even though the rank of those who occupied each storey differed considerably. The street level, accessed separately, was occupied by merchants' booths and storage, usually screened by arcades of loggias, of which the best surviving examples are to be found in Elgin and at Gladstone's' Land, Edinburgh.[13] In 1835, Leith Ritchie interpreted the already historic living pattern of upper tenement floors for Walter Scott's English readers: 'The floor nearest heaven, called the garrets, has the greatest number of subdivisions; and here roost the families of the poor. As we descend, the inmates increase in wealth or rank; each family possessing an "outer door".'[14] The primary apartment was on the *piano nobile* or principal floor, occupied by persons of the highest rank of those who lived in such properties.[15]

Being generally undefended and walled for burgh control and customs purposes only,[16] Scottish towns had evolved without the centrifugal defensive plan with multiple squares and plazas normal in European walled cities, but had instead spread out in a linear manner. Their urban 'outdoor rooms' were restricted to two: the high gait or market place, from which the wind was as far as possible excluded; and the service centre with its urban stench (in Edinburgh the Grassmarket, and in Dundee the Fishmarket) through which the wind was welcome.[17] The highest value merchant apartments were those nearest to the market place,[18] the centre of urban life. In 1560, Dundee rearranged its public buildings – a new tolbooth, fleshmarket, grammar school and public weighhouse – to form a self-conscious new axis between the market place and the harbour. In both Edinburgh and Dundee, the catchpull (Scots for tennis court) lay on one edge of the town toward one of the gates.

The extent to which Scots towns shared the European pattern of identifiable craft districts is not yet clear. In the early nineteenth century hammermen, for example, were concentrated in Edinburgh's West Bow where the noise was ferocious: it 'was one of the most noisy quarters of the city – the clinking of coppersmiths' hammers, the bawling of street criers, ballad singers and vendors of street merchandise'.[19] Alexander Campbell observed of Perth in 1800:

> Different streets and lanes appear to have been very early allotted to different craftsmen who, with few exceptions, still inhabit the same quarters. The skinners, for instance, live in one street, the weavers in a second, the hammermen in a third,

the shopkeepers or, as they are generally called in Scotland, the merchants, in a fourth, and so on.[20]

But such a strong identification of a craft with a particular part of the city has been much more difficult to establish in Scotland than in Europe. A recent survey of occupations in a section of Edinburgh's High Street has revealed that crafts were scattered rather than concentrated; although the dirtier or noisier activities were located away from the High Street and stables were down in the Cowgate.[21] It has likewise proved extraordinarily difficult to assess the pattern in Dundee, although its cordiners or shoemakers appear to have been clustered around the West Port, its bucklemakers by the Wellgate and its bakers and brewers near, naturally, to the town's mills.[22]

Rank in later Renaissance Scotland was a pliable concept, and there were, perhaps, more opportunities for an ambitious person to change rank than during the Enlightenment – particularly if they were involved in construction. James Murray, time-served wright and son of a wright, rose to become the royal architect and died as a landed gentleman: Sir James Murray of Kilbaberton.[23] Some decades later, Andrew Wright, a rural joiner from the village of Glamis who worked for the earl of Strathmore at his ancient paternal seat, was paid by the latter in the form of a grant of the lands of Rochilhill, which he renamed Wrightsfield, took the name Wright of Wrightsfield[24] and died a minor laird.

VERNACULAR ARCHITECTURE

Vernacular architecture, taken literally, means 'untutored', and refers to buildings erected by non-professionals, using materials available to hand and following structural precedents handed down over the generations. It has been suggested that materials for a truly vernacular building would have been obtained within 100 metres of the site,[25] but there is some evidence of scarce timber being carried greater distances. Materials for smaller urban houses such as stone and divots – and perhaps occasionally timber – may well have been obtained from the burgh's common lands, which was the usual source of fuel. The limits on sourcing materials would be transformed where sites were close to waterborne transport. Even the mode of using an identical material differed locality to locality,[26] and it is from this close association between vernacular architecture and its locality – the form, shape, texture and colour of the materials used to construct the vernacular architecture – that regional and local identity derives (Figure 2.2). It was very regionally specific. Thomas Pennant noted how the cottages in Breadalbane, for example, were roofed with broom,[27] as compared with the heather, straw, turves or reeds he saw elsewhere.

Although short pieces of timber were in widespread use for the roof structures of rural houses, particularly near great forests such as Rothiemurchus,

Figure 2.2 *Vernacular houses near the shore at Lamlash Bay, Arran, drawn by J.C. and published in* Views in Scotland *(London, 1791). These fairly substantial buildings appear to have been timber-framed and thatched, and their upper storeys reached by external stairs.*

Scotland was very short of long-span structural timber, which it tended to import from Norway through the principal ports of Leith and Dundee. It is in those towns, therefore, that there is the greatest evidence for the use of significant structural timber in urban construction.[28] Otherwise, by the mid-fifteenth century the predominant Scottish structure had become that of stone, and the predominant building craft that of the mason.[29] Some locations retained an alternative technology. In the Carse of Gowrie and Garmouth (Moray), for example, there was sufficient clay for ordinary people to construct walls of clay bool,[30] a process recorded by Pennant:

> The houses in this country [Moray] are built with clay: after dressing with clay, and working it up with water, the labourers place it on a large stratum of straw which is trampled into it and made small by horses; then more is added until it arrives at a proper consistency, when it is used as a plaister, and makes the houses very warm.[31]

People developed a natural sense of appropriate location for rural cottages and built in the manner of their ancestors; in constructing vernacular cottages they sought comfort, warmth and shelter, dryness, adjacent cultivatable land, with shelter for beasts. It is likely that most were built by the householder, his friends, relatives and neighbours. The consequence is that the structure had to be simple and the techniques easily understood. Cottages were orientated to maximise light within, set near water and, where possible, dug deep into a slope for protection against the wind. Improvement came only gradually and innovation almost never. The pursuit of comfort naturally extended to the interior and its furnishings and may explain the cane hood of the Orkney chair as a protection against draughts in those windswept islands.

There appears to have been a fundamental divide between the quality of cottages on either side of the Highland line. Even making allowances for the inevitable distortion caused by a post-Enlightenment perspective, the constantly reiterated contrast between the interior of Lowland cottages – plastered or painted, with glazed windows, perhaps with rooms or chambers within, and a well-tended garden attached – and the virtually single-chambered unplastered, unpainted and miry earthen-floored Highland black house, shared with its sprawling livestock, cannot be ignored. The scientist Thomas Garnett recorded of Port Sonachan:

> These cottages are in general miserable habitations. They are built of round stones without any cement, thatched with sods and sometimes heath; they are generally, though not always, divided by a wicker partition into two apartments, in the larger of which the family reside; it serves likewise as a sleeping room for them all . . . The other apartment is reserved for cattle and poultry when the last do not choose to mess and lodge with the family.[32] (See Figure 2.3)

Given that, it is scarcely believable that he found even worse conditions in cottages at Torosay, Mull where 'the mud floors were in general damp, and in wet weather quite miry'.[33] When arriving in Luss, Dorothy Wordsworth observed: 'Here we first saw houses without windows, the smoke coming out of the open window places'; and of a later inn she added:

> The walls of the whole house were unplastered. It consisted of three apartments – the cow house at one end, the kitchen or house in the middle, and the spence at the other end . . . The rooms were divided not up to the rigging, but only to the beginning of the roof, so there was a free passage of light and smoke from one end of the house to the other.[34]

Nor was it just the black house. The King's House inn in Glencoe had 'naked walls': 'Never did I see such a miserable, such a wretched place.'[35] Generally, these eye witness accounts have been supported by later research – particularly by Bruce Walker and Alexander Fenton, and by the publications of the Scottish Vernacular Buildings Working Group.[36]

ANCILLARY BUILDINGS OF THE COUNTRY SEAT

Until the urban expansion of the mid-eighteenth century, the country seat remained both the centre of the rural economy and the focus of the majority of Scots. Enfolding the 'main house' of the country seat, therefore, were the buildings of the everyday support services required for maintenance of both household and estate. In addition to guest lodgings, the gallery, library

Figure 2.3 *The interior of a cottage on Islay, drawn in 1772, probably by Moses Griffiths for Thomas Pennant's* Tour in Scotland. *A single central space, a fire without a chimney, window without frame or glass, with a box bed behind, and chicken on the roof trusses.*

and offices there were also the woman house, the dairy, brewery, gill house, bakehouse, coal house, bottle house, laundry, gardener's house, apple houses, hen houses, barns and many others.[37] Probably reflecting the crucial role played by the need for self-sufficiency in the country seat, the gardener was nearly always provided with a purpose-designed house, frequently built into the walls of the kitchen garden.[38] Within the house itself, the most important day-to-day role in the early eighteenth century was played by the housekeeper – the chief executive of the hotel, as it were – and that was reflected in the much larger suite of rooms she occupied than those of the butler,[39] whose emergence as the principal figure of the household appears to date only from the early nineteenth century.

If you could afford to, you would pay others to construct your buildings rather than build them yourself. It was customary to approach craftsmen on a 'separate trades' contract, whereby each craft contracted separately with the client, usually leaving the client with significant duties in terms of providing the materials, scaffolding, food and accommodation for the workers.[40] However, there is some evidence that by the late seventeenth century, some of the more powerful craftsmen were emerging as what we would now call 'main contractors'. James Bain, for example, king's master wright, was acting not just as a wright in the houses of Glamis and Panmure, but as a timber supplier and contractor employing all the other wrights, masons, plasterers and painters.[41] The penalty for acting in what we would regard as a 'modern' manner was duly visited upon him when his aristocratic clients disputed his bills and refused to pay. Since he had already paid his sub-contractors, Bain went bust.[42]

From the later seventeenth century, the maze of high-walled enclosures that enfolded the Renaissance country seat, providing the microclimates necessary for cultivation, began to be removed. The outer entrance court of barns, stables and coal house was replaced by a back court invisible to visitors, and the principal farm became the main farm or mains, banished out of sight with its barnyards. Back courts were, in turn, replaced in the later eighteenth century when country estates were remodelled according to the dictates of the Picturesque. The country seat now appeared proudly as a free-standing monument in the landscape and stables or farm squares were carefully placed as picturesque objects to be glimpsed from the entrance drive. The capital was made available by the provisions of the 1770 Entail Improvement Act, which permitted landowners to pass on the cost of estate improvements to their descendants.

A good number of estates, however, remained unimproved. Contemporary illustrations of abandoned country houses reveal derelict demesnes in semi or total abandonment, occupied in a makeshift manner – and only by the poorest (Figure 2.4). At New Tarbat, 'once the magnificent seat of an unhappy nobleman who plunged into a most ungrateful rebellion', Pennant observed, 'the tenants, who seem to inhabit it *gratis* are forced to shelter themselves from the weather in the very lowest apartments, while swallows make their nests in the bold stucco of some of the upper'.[43]

URBAN FORTUNES

A number of Scots towns fared so badly in the eighteenth century that rescue by a new turnpike road or growth in the herring fishery had been their only means of survival. They had either been in the wrong place – as Renfrew was overwhelmed by its aggressive near-neighbour Paisley,[44] or else geographically bypassed – like Selkirk, Nairn and Tain. Whithorn, for example, had prospered greatly as a pilgrimage centre before the Reformation, but was in a state of collapse by the seventeenth century. By the mid-eighteenth century, most houses in the upper end of town had mouldered into ruin, their plots then subdivided into two narrow weavers' cottages (Figure 2.5). When a measure of prosperity returned, however, some of those plots were reassembled to make larger houses to the former scale, so rendering urban archaeology extremely challenging. A turnpike road, however, might bring

Figure 2.4 *Goldieland Tower, Borders, drawn by T. Clennell in 1814 for Scott's* Border Antiquities. *The tower is probably used for storage (hence the ladder), whereas the once noble buildings of the inner court appear to have been cut down and squatted by shepherds.*

inns and stables, followed by banks and in some cases – Tain being a good example – by an academy for the education of the regional gentry.

A preoccupation with neo-classical suburbs and grid-iron new towns is a distorting prism through which to study Scottish burghs. There were many more with a largely unchanged street pattern, dominated by thatched houses – like Melrose or Jedburgh or, occasionally punctuated by the taller, slate-roofed, dressed-stone townhouses of local gentry, such as the majestic Balhaldie Lodging in Dunblane[45] (Figure 2.6), than there were towns that had undergone a modernist makeover. The fictional burghs of Gudetown and Dalmailing portrayed in John Galt's two novels, *Annals of the Parish* (1821) (thought to be Irvine) and *The Provost* (1822), are quite probably accurate in their depiction of small town life in Scotland, preoccupied more with paving the streets, lighting them, maintaining civic order and keeping tabs on emigrants and immigrants rather than with grandiose schemes. Moreover, there was also substantial 'unplanned' urban colonisation. In the Scouringburn,

Figure 2.5 *The upper part of the Main Street of Whithorn. The view downhill to the central ceremonial space of the town, and further to the service end of the town, would have been blocked by a large tolbooth on the site of the palm trees. This upper part was probably the gathering point of pilgrims. The houses were once grander, became ruined and were subdivided, and then enlarged again in the early nineteenth century. Source: C. A. McKean.*

Figure 2.6 *Dunblane from the south, painted by Captain Francis Grose in the 1780s. The burgh is very quiet – almost rural – and most houses are harled and thatched. The exception is the tall, ashlar (and presumably slate-roofed) townhouse of Drummond of Balhaldie. Reproduced by permission of the National Galleries of Scotland.*

outside Dundee, a village of jumbled cottages grew up in the 1780s and 1790s whose householders were entirely artisans and labourers.[46] Likewise, the former islands of Netherhaugh and Overhaugh in the valley of the Gala Water at Galashiels had been colonised by random cottages and unplanned streets in the later eighteenth century, to the extent that the Scotts of Gala felt compelled to lay out a more formal High Street on new ground to the north-west, to ensure that the expanding lower town had the requisite dignity.[47] Dorothy Wordsworth, predictably, much preferred the pictur-esque thatched cottages to the new plainly elegant, two-storeyed, whinstone-built High Street houses which she found 'ugly'.[48]

As in cities throughout Europe, control of fire and sanitation were the two principal causes of civic intervention. In most Scots burghs, the dean of guild had the duty of overseeing construction and condemning decayed buildings. A maximum height for buildings facing Edinburgh's High Street, for example, had initially been set at twenty feet, based upon the height of the fire ladder. Fearful of the continual fires, it banned the use of thatch as a roof covering in the early seventeenth century. After a disastrous fire fanned by timber foregalleries in 1651, Glasgow rebuilt its four principal streets in four-storeyed ashlar upon arcaded ground floors for the merchants' booths. The resulting urbanism attracted the admiration of all visitors.[49] A century later, in the 1760s, in explicit pursuit of modernism, but none the less prompted by the need for fire control, Dundee swept away its street-fronting timber galleries, leaving the much plainer stone substructures behind. At the same time, it removed the arcades that formerly ran in front of the merchants' booths at ground floor level. Although Perth still retained a few 'wooden houses in the old style', magistrates prohibited their rebuilding in such fashion.[50]

Scotland's sewage regulations had not kept up with the increasing height of urban tenements. Whereas Antwerp, for example, had introduced down-pipes to carry sewage from upper storeys to street level sewers in the early 1500s, it was a standing reproach to Edinburgh that two hundred years later it still had not done so – earning opprobrium from Jonathan Swift and Samuel Johnson alike. Edmund Burt left a particularly vividly revolting description of what happened in 1734, when the nightly 10 pm curfew permitted a uni-versal slop-out from upper storey windows.[51] Edinburgh lagged behind even Dundee in tackling the problem, and did not address it until the late 1760s.

Most aristocrats and country gentlemen maintained townhouses in their regional urban centres, and some magnates had townhouses in several: the earls and marquesses of Huntly, for example, had townhouses or villas in at least Inverness, Fortrose, Aberdeen and Edinburgh. In a burgh like Wigtown, the principal structures, apart from tolbooth and church, would have been the townhouses of the regional gentry: Ahannays, Stewarts, Vaus, McLellans, McCullochs, Dunbars, Agnews, Gordons and Kennedies.[52] The most prominent house in a smaller burgh might well be the townhouse of a local laird, such as the Errol lodging in Turriff and the Glencairn lodging in Dumbarton. In larger towns, they often took the French pattern of a court-yard *hotel*, such as the Gowrie lodging in Perth's Watergate, the Strathmartine lodging in Dundee's Vault, the Argyll lodging in Stirling's Castle Wynd and Moray House in Edinburgh's Canongate.

Until the later eighteenth century, burgh society was heavily dependent upon the gentry occupying their townhouses during the season, thus enrich-ing its social life. As Edinburgh and then London proved to be the bigger draw, the growing absence of their elites from small town life became a problem. In 1799, *Philetas* lamented of Dundee that the country squires had 'for the present, quitted the town. Like Cincinnatus, they have returned to the ploughshares and to their seats and have thus become *burgh seceders*.'[53] The economy of its concerts, theatres and bookshops might depend upon them, and their departure threatened the continuing health of its 'society'.

Part of the changing urban agenda was the growing fashion for privacy. Aristocrats had often chosen a site away from the market place when con-structing a townhouse, preferring – like the marquess of Tweeddale's or Lady's Stair's lodgings – a location at the bottom end of a close. Perhaps that was the only available plot of empty land; but it also detached them from the noise of the High Street and the air was probably cleaner. The first developer (in modern parlance) to provide privacy in Edinburgh was Robert Mylne, who constructed two large courtyards or squares of apartments: Mylne's Court and Miln's Square. Set back from the High Street, they had a shared but otherwise private court, organised refuse collection and an exclusive social life of routs and balls. One can infer pressure for more of this from the construction by James Brown of James Square, to the north of the High Street in 1725. Home to people such as James Boswell (for it was to here that he brought Dr Johnson back for tea), James Square provided substantial apartments with outstanding views to the north. For all that, such apart-ments still did not provide the public social life that the suburban 'houses in the English manner'[54] were expected to do. For breakfast with companions, Boswell, for example, would normally go out from James Court to the coffee houses in the courtyard of the Royal Exchange when he was not suffering from a hangover.

When the Revd John Sime altered his middle ranking apartment in the Lawnmarket, the agenda was one of privacy. Apartments like his contained, in terms of descending size, a large bedroom, kitchen, a 12-foot square parlour, a narrow hall, two closets and a windowless bedroom the size of the bed. Sime altered that to form a formal hall, a much larger parlour and a grander bedroom, squeezing the kitchen and reducing the other bedrooms to miniature bed closets. The parlour presumably was for the reception of guests who, one suspects, would no longer be allowed to penetrate else-where.[55] The public and private parts of the apartment were separated. Thus, polite society in the apartments of Edinburgh's High Street itself was becoming more formal, irrespective of significant changes emerging else-where in the city.

IMPROVEMENT AND MODERNISATION

The Enlightenment retrospective perspective has distorted our perception of the evolution of Scotland's urban centres, and the processes of improve-ment upon which they were all embarked. They were driven by the desire to improve efficiency, enhance trade and ennoble the burgh. A useful distinction to help understand the diverging agendas can be made between 'improvement', that is, the bettering of what already existed, and 'moderni-sation', that is, the importation and imposition of an *a priori* concept or idea. Pre-eminently, new towns embodied the latter.

Improvement, which had begun before the '45, proceeded swiftly after it. Traffic impediments had to go, so in the 1750s, Glasgow, Dundee, Edinburgh and smaller towns like Irvine all removed their town ports (gates), and the latter two also relocated their mercat crosses. Towns then reorganised them-selves around the arrival of the turnpike roads (Tay Street in Dundee and Union Street in Aberdeen, for example). Improvement also encompassed street lighting, better paving of the streets, and – eventually – the establish-ment of a police force with greater effectiveness than the city guards of Edinburgh and Dundee or the night watch of Glasgow.[56]

The original '*Proposals*' for Edinburgh of 1752 contained as many sugges-tions for *improving* the existing city – the addition of a Royal Exchange, the construction of access bridges and the construction of a new building for the records of Scotland (not to say the rebuilding of the university) – as they did for *modernising* it through the addition of a new town.[57] Moreover, the latter was explicitly restricted to 'people of certain rank and fortune only'. This exclusive aristocratic suburb would flourish in a creative partnership with the existing High Street in which all professionals, merchants, commerce and places of entertainment were expected to remain. A vivid illustration of the contrast between the two urban lifestyles, according to Robert Chambers, was that the New Town's urban parade of George Street was so sublimely grand as to make the very respectable people who had previously managed to cut a dash in the High Street feel outclassed and embarrassed.[58]

Disliking the promiscuous mixing of ranks exemplified by all classes using the same staircase,[59] the devisors of this new civil society preferred people to be ordered, categorised and classified. Streets were intended to be occupied by people of a similar rank; and separate streets were provided for those of different rank. That applied equally to the small plantation towns on moors in the north-east, whose principal, central street usually contained houses altogether more substantial than the cottages in back streets. In pursuit of the sublimation of the individual to the collective, feu conditions would ensure that all houses in the same street were identical in scale and virtually in appearance. The new towns would express order through a rational rectangular plan with well-built houses to a standard design. Non-conforming uses were rigorously excluded. At the peak of the 'new town' boom in the 1820s, even minuscule communities such as Langholm, Nairn and Banff proposed to embellish themselves with a new town far beyond their purse, as an essential symbol of forward thinking.

In 1745, the *Gentleman's Magazine* had commented on how fashionable living was beginning to emerge on Edinburgh's 'Society Green [where] they have lately begun to build new houses there after the fashion of London, every house being designed for only one family'.[60] These houses after the English manner, 'inhabited', as Forsyth put it, 'by a single family from top to bottom',[61] became Argyll and Brown Squares. Pennant approved of the 'small but commodious houses in the English fashion' being built on the twenty-seven acres of George Square to the south,[62] and praised the new houses 'in the modern style' in St Andrew Square because they were 'free from *the inconveniences attending the old city*' (emphasis added).[63] (See Figure 2.7.). The strong implication, reiterated by much later historiography, is that there was a pent up demand from Edinburgh citizens to move from antique tenements to more modern houses.[64] The facts, however, do not support it. It took until 1823 – or over half a century – before the first New Town was complete.[65] No Enlightenment Club met in the New Town. Their preferred location remained the large, vaulted, windowless taverns like Johnny Dowie's tavern near the foot of Carrubber's Close in the Old Town. It was not until *c.* 1795, almost thirty years after Edinburgh's New Town project was begun, and ten years after isolation had been ended by the opening of the Earthen Mound, that the first New Town began to move to completion. Scotland's ancient capital city began to be regarded as an 'Old Town' only after the turn of the century (Figure 2.8).

The Enlightenment model adopted in Edinburgh, Aberdeen, Perth and most of Scotland was that of low terraced houses in an exclusive residential suburb.[66] However, when Lisbon rebuilt itself after the earthquake in the later 1750s with all the regularity and rectangularity of Enlightenment thinking, it did so with five- and six-storeyed blocks of apartments with commercial premises at street level – appropriate for a European commercial city centre. The dwellings of Glasgow's first new town (now the Merchant City) around Wilson Street were likewise apartments above an arcaded commercial ground floor; and when Robert and James Adam designed a series of street blocks for George Square, Ingram Street and Stirling's Square, that is what they designed (Figure 2.9). The apartments in Dundee's town centre had been refitted with panelling, plasterwork and Adam fireplaces so lavishly during the eighteenth century[67] that moving to new houses on the 'new town' plots of Castle and South Tay Streets proved simply to be not attractive enough. The stances remained unbuilt. Dundee and Glasgow were *improving* where Edinburgh and Aberdeen were *modernising*.

Figure 2.7 *Liberton's Wynd (now under George IV Bridge), Edinburgh, drawn in 1821 by Walter Geikie. This affectionate record of the close that housed the celebrated Johnny Dowie's tavern (and its Enlightenment Clubs) emphasises the density and mixed nature that the Enlightenment was so anxious to rationalise.*

Moreover, even in Edinburgh's Princes Street, things were not what they seemed. In 1781, the mason Alexander Reid built what looked like a new house on his first stance: in fact, it was four spacious apartments in a block designed to resemble a house.[68] That became the norm in the cross streets: a group of Scottish traditional apartments wholly disguised as a classical villa (Sir Walter Scott's house at 39 Castle Street being an excellent example).

Towns and landlords alike sought to ensure that the character of their new settlements was rigidly enforced through feu conditions governing use, appearance and scale. Purchasers were forbidden from constructing brickworks or carrying out any other industry in the garden.[69] The number of storeys of the houses was prescribed, together with their facing material (usually ashlar) and a slated roof (dormer windows were expressly forbidden in Edinburgh's first new town). The width of streets was fixed – Dundee's were unusually narrow at 40 feet (c. 13 metres) – and houses

Figure 2.8 *Edinburgh by John Elphinstone. Edinburgh on its rock (right), drawn by John Elphinstone in picturesque darkness and variegated roof-line in contrast to the white regularity of the houses of the New Town then inching slowly westward from St Andrew Square. The Nor' Loch has been completely drained, but the Mound has not yet begun (completed 1787). It was an exemplification of the rational order of the new civil society in contrast to the arbitrariness of the old.*

were forbidden to encroach upon the pavement. Within these restrictions, design was left open:[70] broad homogeneity and elegance was sufficient. It was only when Edinburgh was feuing out Charlotte Square in the 1790s that developers were made to follow a pre-ordained design; and the fact that it took until 1823 for Charlotte Square to be completed implies that the cost of Robert Adam's design (as well as having to stump up for the maintenance of the square gardens), depressed the market and pushed purchasers toward the more economical designs of the second new town downhill to the north.

As the new suburbs were occupied, older burgh centres were progressively abandoned. Robert Chambers recorded that the last persons of quality to live in Edinburgh's Old Town – Governor Ferguson of Pitfour and his brother – quit the Lawnmarket with a great party in 1817 (almost exactly fifty years after the new town was initiated).[71] Judging from John Strang's *Glasgow and its Clubs*, the wealthy of Glasgow had by then long since quit its High Street for the three 'new towns' that had been constructed to the west.[72] By the end of the eighteenth century, therefore, formerly elite apartments were declining in status, occupied by lesser ranks, then by poorer people, inevitably to become multi-occupied by the destitute, with the squalor so vividly recorded by the new medical officers of health in the 1840s.

Figure 2.9 *Glassford Street, Glasgow, drawn by John Knox in 1828 for Glasgow and its Environs. When the Trades House on the right was designed by Robert and James Adam in 1791, it was flanked originally by plain blocks of handsome apartments above arcaded commercial premises (as can still be seen on the right). That was urban living in the old Scoto/European manner in contrast to the terraces of individual houses soon to emerge in Glasgow's later new towns.*

RURAL CHANGE

To a large degree, the modernisation of rural Scotland was led by government institutions: the Forfeited Estates Commissioners and the Fisheries Society. The Forfeited Estates had been responsible for the orderly laying out of cottages for the settlement of veteran soldiers as part of its pacification strategy. Pennant admired the 'neat small houses inhabited by veteran soldiers settled here in 1748' which he saw at Tummel, although he observed mordantly 'in some few places this plan succeeded, but they did not relish an industrial life and, as soon as the money was spent, left their tenements to be possessed by the next comer'.[73] The Board of Manufactures was preoccupied with processes and subsidies to foster improved industrial skills, but was probably not directly involved in dwelling construction, although it may well have influenced it. By contrast, the Fisheries Society was responsible for new fishing towns ranging from Ullapool to Wick and Tobermory, and promoted standardised house designs for simple, symmetrical cottages which largely presaged the humbler rural house of nineteenth-century Scotland.

Figure 2.10 *Burgh of Barony, Dumfriesshire. A small burgh (presumably a burgh of barony) in Dumfriesshire drawn in the 1780s either by Francis Grose or his friend the antiquarian, Robert Riddell. That it is a burgh of barony is indicated by its market cross and the date 1692 (the high point of founding burghs of barony). Houses are thatched, and there is no sign of a church or tolbooth. This community probably vanished during the improvement era. Source: Riddell Manuscript collection. Reproduced courtesy of the Society of the Antiquaries of Scotland/National Museums of Scotland.*

In contrast to these sturdy incomers, the humblest of self-built cottages could indeed be regarded as temporary, formed, as they were of soluble materials like turf, divots and timber. Pennant found Scotland a country of civilised people living in uncivilised conditions (Figure 2.10). The inhabitants of the cottages in Dollar roofed with sods were 'extremely civil, and never failed to offer brandy or whey'.[74] He regarded the dwellings in the soon-to-be-cleared burgh of Fochabers as wretched, and was equally unimpressed with the 'very miserable' peasant houses of Morayshire, constructed entirely of turf. That he was evaluating condition rather than type is indicated by his praise for some cottages in Angus built of 'red clay or sods, prettily thatched and bound by straw ropes',[75] whereas barely twenty miles away in Braemar, he found 'the houses of the common people in these parts shocking to humanity, formed of loose stones and covered with clods which they call *devots*, or with heath, boom or branches of fir; they look, from a distance, like so many black mole hills'.[76] Fifty years later, the poet laureate, Robert Southey, travelling through Scotland with Thomas Telford, was appalled when he reached Ross: 'I have never, not even in Galicia, seen any human habitations as bad as the Highland *black-houses* . . . The worst . . . are the *bothies* – made of very large turfs, from four to six feet long, fastened with wooden pins to a rude wooden frame.'[77]

Enlightenment commentators found the black house offensive not just because of the conditions within. It affronted their sense of decorum. However, the anthropologist Helen MacDougall, writing from a Highland perspective, has warned of the danger of confusing the condemnation of poor conditions with the condemnation of a cultural type of building. Referring specifically to Garnett's descriptions, she wrote:

> such a superficial view of passing travellers was not unusual at the time – especially if they had not been privileged to experience the very real quality to be found in the homes of the fine type of Highlander who met hardship and poverty with dignity. Nor would they appreciate the beauty of the traditional building materials which blended with the landscape from which they were drawn.[78]

That she was correct is indicated by the fact that the black house remained a dwelling type of choice in the Highlands until the twentieth century.

The most common category of rural house in the later eighteenth century was the improved model cottage. Since most of the surviving smaller rural houses in Scotland date from the nineteenth century, records for earlier types of dwellings are much more scarce, hence the dependence in this chapter on eye-witness accounts. It is also difficult to generalise about rural Scotland since practice varied throughout the country. That view differs from Naismith in *Buildings of the Scottish Countryside*.[79] Focusing exclusively upon post-1750s cottages, Naismith concluded that there was a remarkable homogeneity, since he discovered standardised proportions 'in every county in Scotland'. Some generalised proportions, and standardisation in, for example, doors and windows, might have been expected from the plethora of improvement books. From the early eighteenth century onward, burgeoning agricultural societies had discussed the improved agricultural building at length,[80] and county surveys of agricultural improvement contained prototypes, supplemented by pattern books, such as *The Rudiments of Architecture*.[81] George Robertson's *General View of Agriculture in the County of Midlothian*[82] is much more specific. It contains a delightful drawing of the recommended improved farmhouse and steading; and its resemblance to the farmhouses in Kinross described by Forsyth cannot be purely coincidental. There was an accepted way of doing things, but differences were greater than similarities. There is a clear inference from Naismith's research (although he himself did not make it) that districts with higher land values had narrower and taller cottages to reduce their footprint, and that location, weather and shelter still mattered.

It is not always clear who undertook the construction of the new houses in this modernising world. Sometimes, new farms were built by the landlord, a rent being charged according to size (in the Highlands, they were assessed by their roof structure or number of timber couples); sometimes the landlord expected the tenant to build for himself. George Dempster, the improving landlord of Skibo, left construction to the tenants: 'Mr Dempster . . . encouraged the tenants to improve their little spots of land, and to build houses for themselves of more durable materials.'[83] Most of the houses in mid-eighteenth-century Kerrera 'were put up by the family who occupied them, and repaired and rethatched as required'. But the arrival on the island of the professional builder, John MacMartine, was regarded as a harbinger of significant change to come.[84] If the occupier had been left to himself, his house would have been a vernacular structure; if built or instructed by the landlord, it would have followed the fashion of the time for the appropriate rank of building. As Helen MacDougall has put it, 'buildings, made from materials at hand in the landscape by people who were going to use them, have been succeeded by buildings partly or wholly constructed of imported materials by men whose profession was building'.[85]

Forsyth found that improvement, modernisation and thereby wealth were unevenly distributed throughout Scotland. Whereas farmhouses in Clackmannanshire were single storey with a garret, generally thatched or covered in pantiles,[86] those in Kinrossshire were two storey, 'substantially built, covered with slate, neatly finished, and with every necessary convenience for the accommodation of the farmer's family'. Even Kinross's cottages were now well lit, built of stone and lime, covered with thatch and 16 feet wide.[87] By contrast, the farmhouses and offices of Cromarty remained 'mean and wretched hovels' (from the description, it appears that they were black houses), anathema to improving Lowland eyes.[88] Even post-Improvement cottages for poorer tenants and mechanics could be fairly miserable: for every occasion Forsyth praised cottages built of stone and clay, lime harled, with a small window or two even with panes of glass instead of the former opening, there were others, as down in Tweeddale, that were just 'miserable hutts' – single storey, ill built and thatched.[89] Interior furnishings remained sparse.[90]

The worst conditions could be found in Argyll. As late as 1807, Forsyth's typical Argyllshire farmhouse was:

> a parcel of stones up to the height of five or six feet without mortar, or with only mud instead of it; and these walls, burdened with a heavy and clumsy roof, need to be renewed with almost every lease; and the roof generally so flat at top that one might securely sleep on it, is seldom water tight . . . The cottages here are for the most part mean and wretched hovels, except where a tradesman here and there may have found proper encouragement to build for himself a commodious habitation.[91]

That was indeed the rub. People needed encouragement and the initiative had to lie with the landlord. Forsyth was particularly impressed by the gentlemen of Ross who had devised various means of inducing Highlanders to improve: 'Some give them wood for building a house, a pick and a spade, with what seed they require for the first year; to sow on any new ground that they bring into culture; and they are allowed to remain for the first seven years without paying any consideration except one fowl and twenty eggs.'[92] But in his survey of the entire country, that remained his sole example of that kind of action.

Most surviving estate structures will post-date the Entail Improvement Act. The simplest cottages were single storey, with a central entrance, a communal room, including the kitchen, on the one side and a bedchamber, often with multiple box beds, on the other. Sometimes there might be a coal store or a privy projecting to the rear. The distinction between this and earlier practice was that there was no pretence that any part of these houses should contain livestock. Slightly grander cottages would have a central staircase up to storage space or further rooms in the attics – and thus exponentially for houses of higher rankings. However, appearance was sometimes all they were. For example, Dorothy Wordsworth observed with disdain a new cottage built for the Ballachulish quarry blacksmith: 'the shell of an English cottage left unfinished, without plaster and with a floor of mud'.[93] A decade later, a similar comparison crossed Southey's mind as he approached Loch Venachar in the Trossachs: 'We saw the skeletons of several Highland cabins in decay, where the ribs rested on the mud. What new ones had been erected were better built and of better materials, having stone walls and slate roofs, like decent English cottages.'[94]

THE PLANNED ENVIRONMENT

The most striking exemplars of rural modernisation, however, lay not in the fermtouns, but in the new towns – that is to say, new plantation villages laid out to a grid-iron pattern. The great boom in such villages was between 1770 and 1830, and they often sprouted – like Cuminestown, New Pitsligo, Tomintoul and Aberchirder – upon unforgiving moorland. Excellent examples of the north-eastern new towns may be seen at Fochabers and Cullen on the Moray Firth. The dukes of Gordon and earls of Seafield, respectively, had substantial ancient burghs at the entrance to their policies, both with narrow streets opening out into a market place at the centre with tolbooth and parish kirk.[95] Few had much good to say about old Cullen. Forsyth found its houses 'in general mean and ill-built', with streets of an 'irregular and dirty appearance'.[96] Fochabers was surveyed in 1766–72 and a new grid-iron town planned more distant from Gordon Castle (Figure 2.11); and fifty years later that pattern was replicated at Cullen. In both cases, the new town straddled the main road from Banff to Elgin in a rectilinear manner, although in the case of Fochabers the road was realigned to accord with the new town's main street. A square at the centre would be adorned with the laird's inn (the Gordon Arms and the Seafield Arms), the church (save in Cullen's

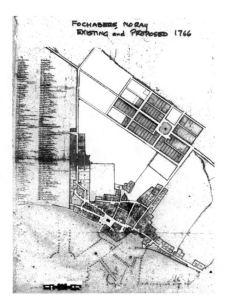

Figure 2.11   *Old Fochabers (NAS RHP 2358) by Thomas Milne. 'Town plan of old Fochabers', Moray, surveyed by Thomas Milne in 1773, who noted the inhabitant of each house. The tolbooth lay in the central square, and the black mass at the bottom represented the recently rebuilt Gordon Castle. The plan proposed the re-alignment of the Elgin–Aberdeen road and the laying out of the grid-iron new town on its axis. The old town was duly excised and its inhabitants relocated to the new. Reproduced by permission of the National Archives of Scotland.*

case since the medieval parish church was retained within the Cullen House policies) and the factor's office. The principal street was of regular two-storey houses, with parallel back streets of lesser cottages. The Lowland equivalent occurred where small-holdings in central Scotland were cleared to allow for agricultural improvement, the former occupiers forced into new towns such as Blackburn and Whitburn. A similar impulse lay behind the formation of Tomintoul, Glenlivet, by the duke of Gordon. There was often a mismatch between the grandiose town plan and the small scale of the cottages that provided the urban enclosure of these new communities. Stewartfield and New Pitsligo, both in Buchan, exemplify where such new towns wholly failed to create the 'weather-protected spaces' so typical of the ancient burghs – and wind remains their dominating characteristic.

Feu conditions generally ensured a well ordered, regulated and homogeneous settlement (Figure 2.12). Too ordered, perhaps. Dorothy Wordsworth disliked the appearance of the village of Springfield, built by Sir William Maxwell: 'a dull uniformity in the houses as is usual when all built at one time, and belonging to one individual, each just big enough for one or two people to live in, and in which a family . . . is crammed'.[97] As part of the inducement for

Figure 2.12 *Helmsdale, Sutherland. A new town established by the Sutherland estate partly, at least, for families cleared from inland and Strathnaver. It is an excellent example of the austere nature of these settlements – of regimented, usually harled houses and wide grid-iron streets that took no account of the climate. Source: C. A. McKean.*

urbanites to settle on a barren moor, each plot was graced with a garden almost large enough to offer self-sufficiency, and there were usually rights to free peat (that is, fuel) and to use the local river for both power and bleaching linen. In the case of New Pitsligo, it seems probable that Sir William Forbes of Pitsligo permitted his feuars to plunder the Renaissance palace of Pitsligo for materials, to judge by contemporary reports of internal furnishings and box beds being made of its finely carved timberwork.[98] It is not clear whether the laird took responsibility for providing that key marker of improvement – slates – or even timbers – for a roof in the 'improved' manner – but it is difficult to see how an ordinary occupier in a location as remote as Tomintoul could otherwise have had access to slates and timber. George Dempster went further when founding his planned village of Letham in Angus. He established an independent committee of feuars whom he made responsible for running his new town.

Far fewer new towns were constructed than were planned; and some barely started. Many others never achieved their full potential. Forsyth concluded that the inducements to ambitious people – particularly in the small amount of land allotted to each incomer – were insufficient to be really attractive.[99] The grandiose New Leeds, by Kininmonth, Buchan, remains just a deserted church and a straggle of cottages, its English rival remaining contentedly unchallenged.

None the less, a certain type of settlement could now be deemed modern,

Figure 2.13 *View of Inveraray in 1791 drawn by J.C. for* Views in Scotland. *It shows the newly built castle, with the old seat and church behind, not yet removed; and the shore lined with cottages, with herring boats drawn up on the shingle. The letter press states that the new town remained unfinished. Source: C. A. McKean.*

Figure 2.14 *Inveraray High Street. A view up the high street of the new town, designed principally by John Adam in the 1750s, axially focused upon the town's churches. The town's magnificent Celtic Cross has been placed on that axis, indicating its fundamental cultural confusion. Source: C. A. McKean.*

Figure 2.15 *Bon Accord Square, Aberdeen. The new civil society: a vision of order, regularity and the suppression of individuality. The regimented houses of Bon Accord Square, Aberdeen, designed by Archibald Simpson in 1823, combining to create a sense of ordered opulence. Source: C. A. McKean.*

Figure 2.16 *Perth in the early nineteenth century, drawn to emphasise the classical ambience created by Rose Terrace forming the western edge of North Inch. Perth Academy forms its centrepiece, with Atholl Terrace lying to the left. The old town of Perth lies out of sight to the left. Source: C. A. McKean.*

whereas an old one – no matter how improved – could be condemned as antique or rude. Where both survived for a time side-by-side, as in the case of Inveraray, the contrast was easier. Thomas Garnett happily characterised the original burgh as 'a dirty ill-built village' by contrast with the new town 'built with uniformity . . . commodious well-built and covered with slate'.[100] The newly built houses of Aberfeldy suggested to Alexander Campbell an 'air of business and even of consequence'.[101] Thus, by the opening of the nineteenth century, Scotland had not just modernised; the mindset of its intellectuals had been revolutionised. Neither the urban nor the rural built culture of the past was acceptable any longer.

CONCLUSION

Between 1600 and 1800, everyday buildings in Scotland underwent more a significant cultural shift rather than a gradual evolution. Whereas evolution was generally represented by the concept of 'improvement', modernisation implied cultural shift. Even though most parts of Scotland had been improved considerably over the eighteenth century, that was not deemed to be sufficient. Possibly inspired by government institutions and their planned soldier resettlements and fishery colonies,[102] but firmly within Enlightenment ideology, Scotland had begun on the route of wholesale modernisation.

Since so few pre-1800 everyday houses survive in Scotland, it is not as straightforward to arrive at an unbiased view of their condition as it might seem. Allowing for the fact that most of the evidence may be skewed by the Enlightenment's modernist perspective, conditions in parts of rural Scotland in the early eighteenth century must have been very poor, with decaying towns and abandoned country estates. By 1800, such problems were on the way to being solved – albeit modernisation was taking longer to reach the remoter parts. The houses were better built. Moreover, whereas there may have been an increasing consumption of space by those who could afford it in the larger new towns, that was probably not the case beyond the Highland line where multi-functional communal spaces were still preferred to single purpose chambers. Modernisers failed to understand the separate and valid culture of the Highlands, and condemned it accordingly.

The principal outcome of the eighteenth century was the physical expression of the Enlightenment's new civil society: much greater social formality, with discrete spaces allotted to different ranks of society, each to its own place. There were both new social chambers within these new houses and greater opportunities for privacy. The middling suburbs, however, also exemplified a marked suppression of individuality in order to emphasise the homogeneity of their occupiers. Even that great admirer of progress, Robert Southey, expressed reservations about the new, highly controlled landscape and townscape which he visited, lamenting the 'mournful uniformity' of Rothes, evidence of its having been 'planted as a colony';[103] just as Robert

Mudie, five years later, would condemn the New Town of Edinburgh as 'a cold eternity of stone and lime'.[104]

Overall, by 1800, Scotland was well on the way to constructing an extraordinarily well-ordered built environment, perhaps to act as both a lure to those seeking a more ordered civil society and as a means of controlling those who did not.

Notes

1. Highland cottages or 'hutts' of the 'black house' (that is, Highland) form were found in rural Aberdeenshire, Moray and Nairn, throughout much of Perthshire and also as close to the capital as Stirlingshire.
2. Robert Southey, *Journal of a Tour through Scotland in 1819*, C. H. Herford (ed.) (London, 1929), p. 258.
3. Dorothy Wordsworth, *Recollections of a Tour made in Scotland AD 1803*, J. C. Sharp (ed.) (Edinburgh, 1974), p.9.
4. D. Wordsworth, *Recollections of a Tour*, p. 109.
5. R. Heron, *Scotland Delineated 1799* (Edinburgh, 1975 edn), p. 16.
6. D. Lockhart, 'The evolution of the planned villages of north-east Scotland: studies in settlement geography, c. 1700–c. 1900', unpublished Ph.D. (University of Dundee, 1978).
7. C. McKean, 'Timothy Pont's building drawings', in I. Cunninghame (ed.), *The Nation Survey'd* (Edinburgh, 2001), ch. 7.
8. I am very grateful to Dr Mary Young for this information.
9. F. Grose, *The Antiquities of Scotland, Vol. 2* (London, 1797), p. 128.
10. R. MacInnes, '"Rubblemania": ethic and aesthetic in Scottish architectural history', in *Journal of Design History*, 9:3 (1996), 137–51.
11. The two largest burghs of sixteenth-century Scotland, with the tallest urban blocks.
12. *PROPOSALS for carrying on certain PUBLIC WORKS in the CITY of EDINBURGH* (Edinburgh, 1751), p. 8.
13. There were arcaded buildings also in Aberdeen, Portsoy, Dunfermline, Linlithgow, Leith and Dundee. In 1652 Glasgow rebuilt itself after a fire with four streets of elegant regular ashlar-fronted tenements sitting on arcades at a standard 11-foot (c. 3.3 metres) deep.
14. L. Ritchie, *Scott and Scotland* (Edinburgh, 1835), p. 153.
15. J. Gilhooley, *A Directory of Edinburgh in 1752* (Edinburgh, 1988). Because the Edinburgh buildings were built against the edge of the escarpment, there could be a number of storeys to the back lower than the High Street. These tended to be occupied by the underclass, the 'broken men of war' of the sixteenth century, and some crafts people. It was in these lower storeys – in taverns such as Johnny Dowie's in Liberton Wynd – that many of the Enlightenment Clubs deliberated in the later eighteenth century.
16. That was the contemporary perception. See C. McKean, *The Scottish Chateau* (Stroud, 2001), pp. 45–6.

17. See C. McKean, 'The evolution of the European weather-protected city', in P. Dennison (ed.), *Conservation and Change in Historic Towns* (York, 2000).

18. For more information about tenements see F. Worsdall, *The Glasgow Tenement* (Glasgow, 1979), particularly chs 1 and 2.

19. J. Ballantine, *The Gaberlunzie's Wallet* (Edinburgh, 1843), p. 98.

20. A. Campbell, *Journey from Edinburgh through Parts of North Britain, Vol. 1* (London, 1803), p. 99.

21. A. A. Allen, 'Occupational mapping of 1635 Edinburgh', *Proceedings of the Society of Antiquaries of Scotland*, 136 (Edinburgh, 2006), pp. 278–94.

22. C. McKean, 'What kind of town was Renaissance Dundee?', in C. McKean, B. Harris, and C. A. Whatley (eds), *Dundee 1500–1800* (forthcoming).

23. A McKechnie, 'Scots court architecture of the early 17th century', unpublished Ph.D. (University of Edinburgh, 1993).

24. D. M. Gauld (ed.), *The Book of Record* (Glamis, 2004), p. 97.

25. Ben Tindall, personal communication.

26. Historic Scotland, Technical Advice Note, TAN 4 Thatch, 'Thatches and thatching techniques: a guide to conserving Scottish thatching traditions', (Edinburgh, 1996).

27. Thomas Pennant, *Tours in Scotland, 1769*, p. 94

28. K. Newland, 'Norwegian timber and the Scottish great house', *Architectural Heritage*, XVIII (Edinburgh, 2007).

29. This is disputed by B. Walker, who has suggested that a history of timber construction in Scotland has been suppressed by those favouring masonry. See B. Walker 'The use of vertical timber cladding in conjunction with the platform frame in urban Scotland during the sixteenth century', *Transactions of the Ancient Monuments Society* (London, 2006). While there was certainly some timber construction, most timberwork in towns took the form of timber galleries and superstructures extending forward from a stone structure rather than being wholly timber-framed, which was very rare.

30. Clay bool is a construction where clay and rounded stones – and sometimes straw – was packed between shuttering, and then finished with a weather-protecting coat of limewash or harl.

31. Pennant, *Tour, 1769*, p. 146.

32. T. Garnett, *Tour through The Highlands, Vol. 1* (London, 1800), p. 12.

33. Garnett, *Tour through the Highlands*, pp. 159–60.

34. Wordsworth, *Recollections of a Tour*, p. 104.

35. Wordsworth, *Recollections of a Tour*, p. 176.

36. B. Walker and A. Fenton, *The Rural Architecture of Scotland* (Edinburgh, 1981), chs 5 and 6, and 'Scottish Vernacular Building', *Bibliography*, 2 (Edinburgh, 1987).

37. See C. McKean, 'Galleries, girnals and the woman house', *Review of Scottish Culture* (2004); C. McKean, 'The laird and his guests', *Architectural Heritage*, XIII (Edinburgh, 2002); C. McKean 'The Scottish Renaissance country seat in its setting', *Garden History* (London, 2004).

38. Good examples are the gardener's houses at Glamis, Culloden, Culzean and Tyninghame.

39. Plans of Haddo House in J. Simpson (ed.), *Vitruvius Scoticus*, (Edinburgh, 1980); S. Lammie, 'Separate worlds? The changing nature of the country house in eighteenth-century Scotland', unpublished M.Phil dissertation (University of Dundee, 2006).
40. Newland, 'Norwegian timber and the Scottish great house', p. 40.
41. Glamis Papers MSS 255/7.
42. I am indebted to Charles Wemyss for this information.
43. Pennant, *Tour, 1769*, p. 186.
44. E. Reid, 'Renfrew 1650–1850', unpublished M.Phil (University of Dundee, 2006).
45. Watercolour of Dunblane by Francis Grose, National Galleries of Scotland Prints and Drawings.
46. C. McKean, 'Not even the trivial grace of a straight line', in L. Miskell, B. Harris and C. A. Whatley (eds), *Victorian Dundee – Image and Realities* (East Linton, 1999), p. 22.
47. NAS, Plan of the lands and barony of Galashiels . . . belonging to Hugh Scott of Gala, 1796.
48. Wordsworth, *Recollections of a Tour*, p. 255.
49. C. A. McKean, F. A. Walker and D. Walker, *Central Glasgow* (Edinburgh, 1993), p. 24.
50. Pennant, *Tour, 1769*, p. 87.
51. Edmund Burt, *Letters from the North of Scotland*, R. Jamieson (ed.), (Edinburgh, 1974), vol. 1, pp. 20–1.
52. R. D. Oram, T. Neighbour, P. de C. Martin and C. McKean, *Historic Wigtown* (Historic Scotland, forthcoming).
53. Philetas, *Dundee Magazine*, 1799, cited in R. Mudie, *Dundee Delineated* (Dundee, 1822), p. 187.
54. 'The greatest part of the New Town is built after the manner of the English, and the houses are what they call here "Houses to Themselves"', E. Topham, *Letters from Edinburgh in 1774 and 1775* (Edinburgh, 2003 edn), p. 6.
55. RCAHMS, Sketchbook of the Revd John Sime.
56. See D. G. Barrie, 'Urban order in Georgian Dundee', in C. McKean and Bob Harris (eds), *Dundee 1500–1800* (forthcoming).
57. *PROPOSALS for carrying on certain PUBLIC WORKS in the CITY of EDINBURGH* (Edinburgh, 1751).
58. R. Chambers, *Traditions of Edinburgh, Vol. I* (Edinburgh, 1825), pp. 49–52.
59. Chambers, *Traditions of Edinburgh*, p. 8. They classified the turnpike stairs as 'constantly dark and dirty'.
60. F. C. Mears and J. Russell, *BOEC*, XX1 (Edinburgh, 1939), p. 169.
61. Robert Forsyth, *Beauties of Scotland*, vol. III, p. 191.
62. Pennant, *Tour, 1769*, p. 68.
63. Pennant, *Tour, 1769*, p. 69.
64. A. Youngson, *The Making of Classical Edinburgh* (Edinburgh, 1966), ch. 1 and Introduction, ch. 2.
65. See C. McKean, 'Twinning cities – the old and new towns of Edinburgh',

in B. Edwards and G. Jenkins (eds), *Edinburgh – the Making of a Capital City* (Edinburgh, 2005).

66. McKean, 'Twinning cities', p. 48.
67. Dundee Central Library, Lawson Collection.
68. Register of Sasines, Midlothian, PR247140, 17.5.71; PR 17177, 19.1.81.
69. 'Copy Restrictions as to buildings in the New town of Glasgow', held in Aberdeen, New Street Trustees NSET/4/12. Undated, but c. 1780s. Prohibited activities (which Dundee forgot to include in its feuing of South Tay Street) were tanning of leather, making of candle soap or glues, preparing vitriol, erecting glueworks, distilleries, sugar houses, foundries, smelting houses of brass, lead or other metals, or forges, etc.
70. Act of Town Council of Edinburgh, 24 February 1768.
71. Chambers, *Traditions of Edinburgh*, vol. I, p. 312.
72. J. Strang, *Glasgow and its Clubs* (London, 1856).
73. Pennant, *Tour, 1769*, p. 116. Pennant saw much the same on the military road to Crieff, and came to the same conclusions, *Tour 1772*, vol. II (London, 1776), p. 91.
74. Pennant, *Tour, 1769*, p. 83.
75. Pennant, *Tour, 1772*, vol. II, p. 155.
76. Pennant, *Tour, 1769*, p. 131.
77. Southey, *Journal of a Tour*, p. 136.
78. H. MacDougall of MacDougall, *Island of Kerrera – Mirror of History* (Oban, 1979), p. 25.
79. R. J. Naismyth, *Buildings of the Scottish Countryside* (London, 1985), p. 143.
80. See, *inter alia*, H. Holmes, 'The circulation of Scottish agricultural books during the eighteenth century', *Agricultural History Review*, 54:1 (2006), and C. W. Withers, 'William Cullen's agricultural lectures and the development of agricultural science in eighteenth-century Scotland', *Agricultural History Review*, 37:2 (1989). I am grateful to Sue Hewer for these references.
81. *The Rudiments of Architecture* (Edinburgh, 1778).
82. G. Robertson, *General View of Agriculture in the County of Midlothian* (Edinburgh, 1795), facing p. 40.
83. Forsyth, *Beauties*, vol. V, p. 206.
84. MacDougall, *Kerrera*, p. 24.
85. MacDougall, *Kerrera*, p.20.
86. Forsyth, *Beauties*, vol. IV, pp. 1–2.
87. Forsyth, *Beauties*, vol. IV, pp. 61–3.
88. Forsyth, *Beauties*, vol. II, p. 522.
89. Forsyth, *Beauties*, vol. II, pp. 455 and 177.
90. See D. Jones, 'Living in one of two Rooms in the country', in A. Carruthers (ed.), *The Scottish Home* (Edinburgh, 1996).
91. Forsyth, *Beauties*, vol. V, p. 420.
92. Forsyth, *Beauties*, vol. V, p. 222.
93. Wordsworth, *Recollections of a Tour*, p. 167.
94. Southey, *Journal of a Tour*, p. 34.

95. Captain Francis Grose painted old Cullen's main street when passing through to study the palace of Boyne for his *Antiquities of Scotland*. The drawing is in the Prints Collection of the National Gallery of Scotland.
96. Forsyth, *Beauties*, vol. IV, p. 461.
97. Wordsworth, *Recollections of a Tour*, p. 4.
98. D. Fraser (ed.), *The Christian Watt Papers* (Edinburgh, 1983), pp. 8–13.
99. Forsyth, *Beauties*, vol. V, pp. 202–3.
100. Garnett, *Tour through the Highlands*, p. 86.
101. Campbell, *Tour I*, p. 239.
102. Chris Whatley has argued that it was the consequence of a shared ideology in the Hanoverian state. See C. A. Whatley, *Scottish Society, 1707–1830* (Manchester, 2000), pp. 96ff.
103. Southey, *Journal of a Tour*, p. 93.
104. R. Mudie, *Modern Athens* (London, 1824), p. 319.

Chapter 3

Death, Birth and Marriage in Early Modern Scotland

Deborah A. Symonds

INTRODUCTION

In August of 1757 John Callendar of 'powfout bridge' had 'been for a long time past labouring under a dropsy and other distempers'. In June, 'he was not able to go the length of his own door', and in late August he 'continue[d] in the same weak condition'. We know this because a surgeon in Falkirk, George Dennistoun, recorded it for him in a note written to secure him some money from his parish's funds for the poor. Too many John Callendars were born in Falkirk in the late seventeenth and early eighteenth centuries to make this man identifiable, but the rigours of old age, presuming that he was old, and the pinch of poverty were not unusual.[1] If he was nearing death, he was doing so in a familiar manner, one that would have been recognisable to him and his friends and neighbours. By the 1790s, 150 persons in Falkirk were on the 'poors' roll' according to the *Statistical Account* (OSA), out of a current population of 4,128, and many of the 150 were probably old and unfit for work. But Callendar's access to money for the poor and to a surgeon were relatively recent developments in the early modern period.[2] The common image evoked by John Callendar, unable 'to go the length of his own door', probably worn by many years of labour, or disease, and reduced to living on handouts from the poor box, should stand as an example to us of the experience of dying and death at this time. Early modern Scots found death in many places, in their beds, on the scaffold, on the battlefield, by the roadside or behind a barn. In particular, pregnancy and birth took its toll on women, as did the witch hunts; political and religious strife took men as well as a few women; and children died in droves from disease, starvation and occasionally infanticide.[3]

In the face of those relentless early modern horsemen of the Malthusian apocalypse, war, famine and disease, stood physicians, apothecaries, surgeons, traditional healers and a smattering of rough-and ready means of relief in famine.[4] Those means encompassed a few responsive landlords, the kirk's collection of poor law money and the occasional attempts of local and national government to raise funds and buy grain. But we must remember that growing numbers of surgeons like Dennistoun, along with the regular collection and disbursement of funds for the poor, were elements of eighteenth-century life, and had not been common before. As Michael Flinn and others have pointed out, mortality crises, brought on by those three horsemen, were dissipated by moral force, as the obligation to aid the starving was taken more seriously by heritors and burgh authorities between 1690 and 1740. Such intervention was eased by better transportation and the availability of grain and meal at prices that lairds, councils and the kirk could afford.[5] By the end of the early modern period, belief in the three horsemen must have been eroded, if not by Malthus, then by mathematics and the sale of meal at prices subsidised by the better-off during periods of hardship, and by the provision in a few places – Edinburgh, Glasgow, Forfar, for example – of soup kitchens.

The study of demographic history has given us a great deal of information about ordinary Scots like John Callendar, at least in outline. From this, we know when and where disease and famine struck, and coupled with the history of internal conflicts and rebellions in the seventeenth and eighteenth centuries this provides us with a good sense of the variety and frequency of calamities faced by those generations. But as these causes of hardship abated in the eighteenth century, we are left with an important question: was life for the majority of Scots in tenant farms, villages, small burghs and the bigger towns, better, or did they merely find themselves assailed by new problems? What we know of births and deaths suggests that life improved, but there is little evidence that the age of marriage fell (other than in the towns), or that household formation increased; this and slow population growth suggest that other challenges were being confronted by those who lived in a Scotland increasingly free of famine, warfare, and certain types of killer disease.[6]

BIRTH, DEATH AND COUNTING

Death and birth presented as unequivocal mathematical data bring us to the eighteenth-century's interest in population. Their interest was no accident, for the early modern world had changed and death was, to paraphrase Harold Perkin, beginning to be held at bay, almost undoubtedly by better farming, perhaps by better weather.[7] Disease abated and births could more directly influence population growth. The exact timing of this so-called 'demographic transition' is notoriously hard to pinpoint, given the nature and survival of records, especially those of ordinary folk. For Scotland, Michael Flinn acknowledged, given the cycles of erratically harsh and then better conditions of the seventeenth century, 'we cannot . . . be sure that the population of Scotland was, say, less in 1690 than it was in 1755, as is commonly assumed'. It had recovered by the later date, and in second half of the eighteenth century the population was growing, but slowly.[8]

In Scotland Alexander Webster attempted a census in 1755, and in May 1790 Sir John Sinclair sent out a questionnaire to every parish minister in Scotland, inviting a wide variety of reliable, erratic and sometimes odd

Figure 3.1   'William Wilson', taken from John Kay, A Series of Original Portraits and Caricature Etchings (Edinburgh, 1837–8). William Wilson was probably older than John Callander or the surgeon would have remarked on Callendar's age; if Wilson was 107 in 1815, Kay's interest suggests that this was as remarkable then as now. But scantily and ill-recorded documentation makes exact age a matter of local memory and tales for someone possibly born in 1708.

information about the state of the parishes, including population data. The carefully edited results, known as the OSA, are both more and less than a census.[9] In Comrie, Perthshire, for example, under the heading climate and diseases, we find that 'The small pox were formerly very destructive; but, about seven years ago, the people were prevailed upon to allow their children to be inoculated; and ever since the practice has been general, and very successful.' This was not unique to Comrie, for inoculation spread across the Highlands in the later eighteenth century, decreasing childhood mortality significantly wherever it was accepted.[10] The OSA abounds in information like this, touching on the social measures that fostered and eroded population growth. The entry for Comrie also records that when the estates of the dukes of Perth, amounting to about a third of the parish, were forfeited in 1746:

> and put under the management of commissioners, several farms, formerly possessed by many tenants, were given to one person. This lessened the number of inhabitants considerably. The village indeed has increased very much of late; but, by comparing what the large farms have lost of tenants and cottagers, with what the village has gained, the population does not appear to be on the increase.[11]

Agricultural improvement, for such was the goal of the commissioners of the forfeited estates, promised increased productivity, but at some human cost, as farms were stripped of tenants and their labour replaced by that of seasonal wage workers. If more stable supplies of food supported healthier populations, a shrinking supply of tenancies for young couples thwarted marriages, or forced couples to search for work in other parishes.

Birth and death, and implicitly marriage, were perhaps the most basic of all parameters of everyday life, but the populating and depopulating of Scotland was also dependent on the institutions of the early modern agricultural economy, replete with landlords, their agents, tenants and sub-tenants, varying by region. And while disease and famine sometimes drove away, through emigration, those they did not kill, alterations in the farming economy, especially through the enclosure or engrossment of multiple-tenancy farms also drove many out, or impeded marriage. Emigration in the early modern world was a dark number that affected village life, marriage and consequently birth and death. The population of Comrie, the ministers of Comrie and Monzievaird thought, was decreasing; but whether the people had gone to a neighbouring parish, a nearby town or Maryland, we do not know.[12] While counting people was only one aspect of the broader spirit of rational enquiry that led to the re-ordering of Scottish society, this activity was emblematic, like Da Vinci's Vitruvian Man, of the growing centrality of human life to Western thinking in the seventeenth and eighteenth centuries.[13]

What we know of birth and death in Scotland in quantifiable form comes from Webster's census of 1755, the OSA of the 1790s, irregularly surviving parish registers and, even more rare, bills of mortality from some towns and cities before statistical techniques developed that allow reconstitutions from other sources. What this means is that our knowledge of Scotland's population through aggregate statistics is approximate, but necessary and useful. But this approximation may be a blessing, because the aggregate picture that emerges can and should be contrasted with the surviving parochial records and descriptions of certain localities suggesting tremendous regional variation, even from parish to parish.[14]

HUMAN LIFE AS DEMOGRAPHY

Across Western Europe, the demographic history of the early modern period was simple: plague struck in the fourteenth century, populations struggled with recurrences together with smallpox and famines, which, in turn, generated new outbreaks of disease among weakened populations, to re-establish and then surpass pre-plague levels by 1750 or 1800. Wars, migrations and feuds (local wars) abetted the mortality crises. Villagers and towns-people must have seen old age as a desirable but not always usual end to life. In Scotland population was the measure of success of a predominantly agricultural society in the face of disease, adverse weather and inadequate technology. War was a vile event, bringing depredation, disorder and infection.

Famine, more commonly known as dearth, struck fiercely in the seventeenth century. Coming in the 1620s, 1640s and 1690s, Scots were subjected not only to famine, but also to marching armies and the diseases they carried. In July 1695, in the face of a promising harvest, exports were encouraged, but by August much of the crop was ruined and several years of difficulty, sometimes severe, followed. Much of this was documented by those loyal to the covenanted field preachers of earlier decades, for they saw the hand of God at work in the last great national famine – that in some people's minds seemed to follow from the political settlement of 1688; for others it was indicative of the extent to which the Scots – God's chosen people – had strayed from the path of righteousness.[15] Crops failed again in 1709 and 1740. During the second of these years, 'the populace of Edinburgh attacked the mills, certain granaries in Leith, and sundry meal-shops, and possessed themselves of several hundred bolls of grain, the military forces being too limited to prevent them'.[16] Fighting between the mob and the military continued and demonstrates a distinct change of attitude, for the famine of the 1690s was met with proclamations requiring prayer and fasting from a sinful population, and government measures to allow for the importation of grain. Crowds demanding immediate redress were relatively few.[17] By 1740, high prices for meal, and hunger, were experienced as remediable. In 1709 it is questionable if there was a real shortage, or just an excess of speculation in the grain market.[18] If sin brought dearth and famine in the 1690s, by 1740 exporters and the town councils were blamed. The prospect of privation and hunger was not accepted as quietly as it had been in 1698, when, perhaps owing to the sheer scale and longevity in some districts of the suffering, those afflicted had little energy to protest against their fate:

> I have seen some walking about at sunsetting, and next day, at six o'clock in the summer morning, found dead in their houses, without making any stir at their death, their head lying upon their hand, with as great a smell as if they had been four days dead; the mice or rats having eaten a great part of their hands and arms.[19]

But this is one person's view; the truth is that we know very little about how ordinary Scots at this time faced and dealt with death. Thereafter a minister or elder might offer a prayer. Burials for the majority were simple affairs – deliberately so after the Reformation – conducted without a minister present, although the wake and funeral might be accompanied in the north and west by a dirge on the pipes, and everywhere, where it could be afforded, by drinking, reflection and some festivity (too much according to some churchmen).[20] Transported to the grave-side in mortcloths, unlike the Netherlands, corpses were generally buried in the kirkyard, rather than in the church itself.[21]

PEACE AND LOCAL RECORDS

When in 1755 Alexander Webster made a serious attempt at estimating Scotland's population, there are faint signs that material conditions were improving.[22] After an interval in the early modern period in Scotland in which religion dominated intellectual and social life, civil wars in which religion played a major part sapped the nation's resources and famines recurred every ten years or so, the larger British political settlement of 1688 brought something like peace. But not immediately. The massacre at Glencoe and the Jacobite risings that followed posed serious challenges for the post-Revolution state. Nevertheless, the new central government under Hanover held, and sections of the population, many of whom were modestly educated by the kirk, tired of religious disputation, or marshalled their religious beliefs in the cause of material advancement.[23] As the long drama begun by Mary Stewart and John Knox faded, capitalism eroded clan and feudal ties, stable and improving supplies of food ended the cycles of famine and disease and the people began to emerge and be counted, often more assiduously than the old parish clerks and registers had recorded their baptisms, marriages and deaths.

Local officials, however, were not always rigorous in the execution of their duties. The session clerk of Crieff, Perthshire wrote what he chose for several years, including imaginary baptisms:

> The Minister and two Elders met according to appointment and revising the Baptisms find that in the register a great many Childrens Names are left blank, and also some parents names are left out. There are also some parents in it quite altered from what they should be; He has also insert in the Register three Sons to Patrick McCawlay . . . and yet the Said Patrick McCawlay never had any sons preceeding the date thereof except Thomas.

He made up for the extra sons by recording no marriages at all for several years, and when called before the session in 1747, he was too drunk to explain.[24] This is more than a foible, but it is still a useful reminder of the problems inherent in any local collection of data, past or present.[25]

PUBLIC AND PRIVATE DEATHS

Death, registered or not, was no abstraction either before or during the new interest in population. In a nation of small communities in the countryside and numerous small burghs, every death was at least a small rent in the social fabric. And there were many important deaths, deaths that directly or indirectly affected many others: Mary Stewart at Fotheringhay, Fletcher of Saltoun at London, David Hume at Edinburgh, and perhaps marking the very last moment of the early modern period for Scotland, Walter Scott at Abbotsford. But commoners also died notably and far from their beds: in the second category were Covenanters, Jacobites and indentured servants who were shipped to New World plantations. On 26 January 1681, Isabel Alison and Marion Harvey were hanged in Edinburgh for adhering to the Solemn League and Covenant, as were the field preachers Richard Cameron and Donald Cargill. Both women were in their twenties, probably servants, possibly literate, and standing on the scaffold they sang psalms, read or recited from the Bible, prayed with some vehemence and sang to drown out the words of the appointed curate who prayed for them and the five women who were hanged with them for child murder. They saw themselves as martyrs, as did the friends who 'attended' them as they walked from the tol-booth to the scaffold in the Grassmarket. Their deaths were public performances. Both left 'dying testimonies' written shortly before their executions, perhaps written for them, no doubt to be circulated outside Edinburgh for those who could not attend. Marion Harvey's began:

> Christian friends and acquaintances – I being to lay down my life on Wednesday next, January 26, I thought fit to let it be known to the world wherefore I lay down my life, and to let it be seen that I die not as a fool, or an evil-doer, or a busy-body, in other men's matters. No; it is for adhering to the truths of Jesus Christ, and avowing him to be king in Zion, and head of his church; and the testimony against the ungodly laws of men, and their robbing Christ of his rights, and usurping his prerogative royal, which I durst not but testify against.

Whether a servant girl from Bo'ness wrote this or not, one should not under-estimate the religious voice in early modern Scotland, especially in confronting death, and in this case an elective death. Alison and Harvey were ordinary women when compared with Mary Stewart, but ordinary people, too, could turn their dying into something of a spectacle, demonstrating that queens and villagers might all entertain similar notions of what made a good death.[26]

Almost one hundred years later, David Hume died quietly at home, sur-rounded by domestic tranquillity. None the less, in frequent letters that are self-conscious and carefully composed, Hume made his deathbed public. Writing to Adam Smith two days before his death, he calmly complained about his tedious illness, and wished for a speedier resolution:

> I am obliged to make use of my nephew's hand in writing to you, as I do not rise today . . . I go very fast to decline, and last night had a small fever, which I hoped might put a quicker period to this tedious illness, but unluckily it has, in a great measure, gone off. I cannot submit to your coming over here on my account, as it is possible for me to see you so small a part of the day, but Doctor Black can better inform you concerning the degree of strength which may from time to time remain with me. Adieu.[27]

Three days later, Doctor Joseph Black, the noted chemist and medical doctor, wrote that:

> Yesterday about four o'clock afternoon, Mr. Hume expired . . . He continued
> to the last perfectly sensible, and free from much pain or feelings of distress. He
> never dropped the smallest expression of impatience; but when he had occasion
> to speak to the people about him, always did it with affection and tenderness . . .
> When he became very weak, it cost him an effort to speak, and he died in such a
> happy composure of mind, that nothing could exceed it.

While this was far more private than the execution of Harvey and Alison,
the record Hume left of his last days suggests a self-conscious control com-
parable to their public performance.[28] But dying, even in one's own bed,
would rarely have been quite so private, for in 1776 most Scots were accommodated in quarters that were far simpler in form – and open to the gaze of
their neighbours.[29]

LEGACIES AND SOCIAL TIES

Dying was rarely private in the early modern world, and people often died
among relatives, friends and enemies.[30] If religion and philosophy framed
what Marion Harvey or David Hume said before dying, property was not
forgotten. As Adam Smith described the death of Hume to a mutual friend,
he noted that he had asked Hume 'if you have at least the satisfaction of
leaving all your friends, your brother's family in particular, in great prosperity. He said that he felt that satisfaction.'[31] Death with its legacies and
testaments, and birth with the attendant naming of godparents placed one
squarely in the midst of society, not at the margin. Even Christian Gellan, a
poor cottager at Monymusk, Aberdeenshire, knew and kept her place in her
community, leaving her few possessions to pay for coffin, shroud, candles
and the services of a man who invited guests for gin and honey.[32] Andrew
Fletcher of Saltoun left £200 to Scots taken captive in the failed Jacobite
rising of 1715, reportedly exclaiming 'my poor country' as he died.[33]

One final example of a good death, with social ties intact, is that of
Grisell Hume Baillie of Jerviswood, a heroine to Covenanters during the
Restoration. She died in London in 1746 with her family around her, sug-
gesting they read 'the last chapter of Proverbs', and giving her daughter, Lady
Murray, detailed directions about where, 'in a black purse in my cabinet,
you will find money sufficient' to convey her body back to the family burial
plot on the estate of Mellerstain in Berwickshire. She was 'conveyed from
London to Scotland; and on Christmas day, December 25, which was her
birth-day, was laid to rest by the side of her husband in the monument at
Mellerstain. She was buried in the same manner in which, according to his
own orders, she herself had directed *his* funeral – near relations, near neighbours, and her own tenants, only, being present.'[34] It is worth remembering
that on the estates outside the burghs, the deaths of the social elite were the
business not only of their peers, but also of their tenants. Apparently Grisell

showed some restraint in limiting the guests, which gives us some sense of the extent of the family's community.

A WORLD FULL OF CHILDREN

Birth in a world where so many children died before the age of five could not have been an unequivocally happy event, since it marked the beginning of what must sometimes have been a struggle to keep the child alive. Small children, especially those of sub-tenants and cottagers, are often invisible in the historical record. Registration of births and deaths by parish clerks, and tombstones, cost money, and early modern kirkyards reflect the lives and monuments of the most substantial members of the parish, not the poor, or the children of the poor. A stone in Auchindoir Old Kirkyard reads: 'In memory of Kattie Henderson aged 3 y. 6 mths', but it is undated, and nearby stones are from the late eighteenth and nineteenth centuries, so it is unlikely to be early modern.[35] At the time of the OSA, Auchindoir, in Aberdeenshire, contained 572 inhabitants, of whom almost exactly half were under the age of thirty, 104 were under the age of ten and relatively few were over sixty. The minister remarked that there were more baptisms per year in 1694 than later, with only a handful from 1697 to 1702, and then a stable but lower number through the eighteenth century.[36]

This reflects a high birth rate marred by the last great famine of the late 1690s, and is a reasonably representative picture of population structure in the period, with large numbers of children and young people, and few over the age of sixty, although there were always some who lived to a great age and reaching ninety or more was possible. In a world that was chiefly rural, agricultural and organized through tenant farms, what we are often seeing through this lens of age structure is a society of young agricultural servants moving on to marriage and tenancy as the generation ahead of them failed, declined, took small cottages or died in their late fifties and sixties.[37] In Edinburgh in 1722 a Dr Blair reckoned that about 20 per cent of the population would be children, which is very roughly the same proportion as in Auchendoir; the figure also argues a certain consistency in the environment in stable periods, for disease, food and weather, stretching across town, hamlet and country.[38]

UNWANTED CHILDREN

Beyond disease, weather and the hardships of childbirth, children faced the dangers of a complex society in which, despite the local authority of the kirk, fornication, adultery and thus, the likelihood of illegitimacy were rarely absent. Unusually, for only a brief interlude in the later 1590s, was the parish 'kirk by law established' in St Andrews able to eliminate almost completely by a regime of terror sexual misdemeanours among their charges.[39] In normal circumstances, where controls were less severe, or ignored, and illegitimate births resulted, there existed the possibility of infanticide.[40] In Argyll between 1664 and 1742, six illegitimate children were murdered at birth by their mothers, or in one case by a grandmother. In 1679 Mary M'Millan, daughter of a tenant farmer in Ardlarich, guilty of fornication with Donald M'Onlea, son of another tenant in Ardlarich, gave birth to their child near a burn. She admitted hiding the child under the straw of her bed, and 'thereafter delivering his corpses [sic] to her brother to be buried'.[41] In 1681 Finvall N'Cannill was indicted for giving birth to a child conceived in an adulterous relationship. The child was born in her father's house in Knockhanti 'in the end of the said house where she ordinarily sat at her weaving and hidd the chyld under a turff'. Because this had happened four years before, there was no means of proving the murder, and she was found guilty of 'ignominious burying of her said chyld', and was sentenced to a public whipping at the market cross of 'Campbeltoun'.[42] Ten years later in Drumseynie, Catharin N'Inturnor was indicted for the murder of her daughter's child, conceived in adultery. N'Inturnor was charged with making a hole in the child's head and 'being examined anent the said murder . . . she acknowledged that after the midwife had given over all hopes she found the said hole in the chylds head before he was fully borne but cunningly would lay the cryme to the midwifes charge by which it appeard that she was actor'.[43] She was found not guilty, possibly because the men on the jury had little way of knowing, between the mother, grandmother and midwife, who, if anyone, was to blame.

But in 1705, Margaret Campbell, alias Guinich, pregnant by her master's son James Montgomrie, and questioned according to the evidentiary demands of the 1690 statute against child murder, was found guilty and hanged. According to Argyll Justiciary Records:

> she at length confessed before the [Kilmichael-Glassary] Kirk session upon the threttieth day of March last . . . that the said James Montgomerie had gotten her with chyld in summer last that she concealed all alongst her being with chyld during the whole space in all the places and to all the persones above mentined and to all others albeit frequentlie channenged thereupon except the said James Mongomry [sic] whom she gave up as the father to the chyld and also confessed she was delivered of the said man chyld in ane obscure place in Barnagadd all alone in the night tyme and that she buried or hidd the said man child [sic] so brought forth by her in the same place and covered him with fogg and stone having wrapped him in a little linnin cloath.[44]

While Campbell never admitted killing the child, she had been wandering over Argyll, leaving her master's in Ballimeanoch and staying in Kilberry, Leckuary, Downan and finally Barnagadd, where she was visibly pregnant. In response to questions from women in each house or village, she denied any pregnancy, and moved on, until she gave birth in Barnagadd. Both her death and that of the children mentioned above demonstrate the variety of ways in which one might unexpectedly die, without famine, war or disease. But Campbell's trial and execution also remind us of the kirk's role in the formal oversight of both birth and death, through recording, interrogating and finally burying villagers great and small.

Most children did not face such beginnings, and we know about these exceptional and miserable instances of cruelty, self-interest and desperation precisely because tenants, villagers and townspeople, often acting through the kirk, kept a watchful eye on those who might be sexually active outside marriage, or pregnant. Many more children died of smallpox, according to the parish ministers who compiled the OSA, although inoculation in the later eighteenth century was effective in lowering death rates in many parishes. The minister in Kilmichael-Glassary, the parish where Margaret Campbell was forced to confess, commented roughly eighty years later that children had often died from smallpox in the past, but as inoculation was now practised, it was rarely fatal. At the time he wrote, he calculated that 44 per cent of the population of Glassary was under the age of twenty-one, few were over fifty, and 26 per cent were aged ten or less. For all the risks of childhood, there were always many children to be seen, probably because the rigours of age were worse. Glassary boasted seventeen persons between the ages of fifty and seventy, forty-four between eighty and ninety, and five between the ages of ninety and one hundred. This gives us a parish in which those we would consider the elderly were less than 3 per cent of the population.[45]

CHILDBIRTH EXPERIENCES

One of the eighteenth-century ballads of Anna Gordon Brown, all of which show the hallmarks of oral composition and traditional transmission by word-of-mouth, allows us to glimpse one birth, however atypical.[46] The ballad is 'Child Waters', in which Ellen proves herself worthy of 'Lord John' by her strength, culminating in bearing their child alone, in a barn:

> She's leaned her back against the wa;
> Strong travail seizd her on;
> An even amo the great horse feet
> Burd Ellen brought forth her son.
> Lord John'[s] mither intill her bowr
> Was sitting all alone,
> Whan, I the silence o the night,
> She heard fair Ellen's moan.
>
> 'Won up, won up, my son,' she says,
> 'Go se how a' does fare;

For I think I hear a woman's graosn,
An a bairn greeting sair.'

O hastily he gat him up,
Stayd neither for hose nor shoone,
An he's doen him to the stable-door,
Wi the clear light o the moon.

He strack the door hard wi his foot,
An sae has he wi his knee,
An iron locks and iron bars
Into the door flung he:
'Be not afraid, Burd Ellen,' he says,
'Ther's nane come in but me.'

Up he has taen his bonny young son,
An gard wash him wi the milk;
An up he has taen his fair lady,
Gard row her in the silk.[47]

In fact few children were born in stables, or 'in ane obscure place in Barnagadd all alone in the night tyme' unless they were illegitimate. The more common birth would have been in a bed, however humble or stately, attended by women midwives that the village could provide, or the family afford. Male midwives, or obstetricians, were rare in Scotland until the mid- to later eighteenth century. The great Scottish anatomist, surgeon and male midwife, William Hunter, practised in London, not Edinburgh, in the late eighteenth century, although in the Scottish capital men had been appointed to instruct female midwives from at least as early as 1726.[48]

Most children, with a little luck, and no great degree of isolation, would have come into the world attended by one or more older women, not professionally trained, but accustomed to childbirth. These women learned their expertise and established their reputations much as those in other trades, by first assisting others with more experience, and then attending when neighbours called for help. When a young woman in Terregles, near Dumfries, was suspected of infanticide in 1762, four local women were called to examine her and the child's corpse. The first midwife sent for by the minister was Marion Jardine, an eighty-year-old widow who lived nearby. The second, Elizabeth Patterson, was fifty-one, the wife of a tenant farmer in another parish and referred to midwifery as her 'trade'. The third was Janet Irving, another fifty-year-old tenant farmer, who she said she was not a midwife, but had had thirteen children. The fourth woman did not testify, but presumably was also seen as adept in childbirth by her community. All four were called by men determining if a murder had been committed, so what they had to say was taken seriously, used in court and probably reflected the villagers' belief that any one of them would be helpful at a birth. Terregles was a small parish, with a population of between 400 and 500 people in 1762, so the ease with which the minister was able to summon two practising midwives and two women who would have made good assistants for them suggests that midwives were available, and commonly called. No surgeons, much less male midwives were sought, strongly suggesting that they simply were not available, and possibly not yet seen as authoritative, even near a thriving town like Dumfries.[49] Yet training was extending into towns other than Edinburgh, where there was an unknown number of professional female midwives who could demand decent fees from their upper- and middle-class clients, enough certainly to provide them with a living.[50] It seems likely that infant mortality was falling in the later eighteenth century before the advent of the male midwife, and that greater attention to childhood followed in the wake of children's improving chances of survival.[51] A glimpse of the nursery furnishings of the Drummonds of Stobhall in 1717 shows a stark 'Nur[s]ery – an Ovell Table 5s 2 Old Trunks 3s A Cane Chear 2s a furnishd. Bed with Green hangings £2 a furnishd. Box bed £1[.]' If this sounds bare, it is a useful reminder of the simplicity of life, even for the greater nobility.[52] Contrary to most of the examples given above, the great majority of children born were legitimate, and birth brings us to the social institution governing births and consequently deaths, marriage.

MARRIAGE AND SURVIVAL

Marriage was shaped by custom, law, the kirk and, to a lesser extent, by the nature of the local economy, with perhaps some room for personal preference. For Scots marriage was, under the kirk and by law, a simple contract made by mutual declaration, in either present or future tense, of the intent to marry.[53] Whatever there was of courtship, love and ceremony, in a broader view marriage represented household formation, with households representing the basic building blocks of the early modern economic and social structure. But ceremonial and celebration, with all the implications of alliances and community ties, cannot be overlooked. The following record of an important wedding early in the eighteenth century makes clear just how public, raucous and expensive such occasions were:

> Sir James Stewart's marrige with President Delrimple's [sic] second Daughter brought together a number of people related to both familys. At the signing of the eldest Miss Delrimple's Contract the year before there was an entire hogshead of wine drunk that night, and the number of people at Sir James Stewart's was little less.
>
> The marrige was in the President's house, with as many of the relations as it would hold. The Brides favours was all sowed [sic] on her gown from tope to bottom and round the neck and sleeves. The moment the ceremony was performed, the whole company run to her and pulled off the favours: in an instant she was stripd of all of them.[54]

The Evening Walk

Figure 3.2 *'The Evening Walk', taken from John Kay, A Series of Original Portraits and Caricature Etchings (Edinburgh, 1837–8). Courtship, as shown here in Captain Justice's walk with a friend, was a matter for much speculation in novels and ballads, and probably in everyday conversation. It was an important building block of the early modern society.*

The account includes descriptions of successive suppers and balls, at both family homes, and then at those of friends and extended family, including a Sunday parade by twenty-three couples in 'high dress' to church. Such a public performance, lasting for many days was clearly extraordinary, but it made clear that weddings served to cement bonds among families, generating alliances of political, social and economic significance. For those lower down the social scale there was the penny wedding, often attended by large numbers of paying guests, their shillings contributing to the cost of the festivities, and perhaps leaving something left over for the couple. The ubiquity of these ceremonials is underlined by the repeated attempts of the church at both national level and in the parishes to ban them by restricting numbers and forbidding the presence of musicians and dancing.[55]

Much has been written about the relationship between marriage, childbirth, famine and death rates, and the sequence is not surprising. As noted earlier, for much of the early modern age, mortality crises struck with some regularity, and in the seventeenth century these regulated the size of Scotland's population with grim reliability. In the wake of each crisis, young couples would take advantage of tenancies fallen vacant and marry; widows

Figure 3.3 *'Sabbath School', taken from John Kay, A Series of Original Portraits and Caricature Etchings (Edinburgh, 1837–8). Moderates, breaking with the rigour and control of the old church, dominated the Church of Scotland in the late eighteenth century. If the moderates matched Enlightenment principles, the self-importance of this minister, compounded by his disconnection from the lives of these very young parishioners, highlights the disintegration of the old communities and families.*

and widowers would reconstitute new families from the survivors; and surviving couples conceived as amenorrhoea dissipated.[56] But such demographic determinism, which is integral to studies of weather, crops and epidemics, tells only part of the story of what was happening in the early modern world. Human agency may never be more apparent in history than it is in marriage and procreation, carried on in defiance of plague, smallpox, war and famine. For most of the early modern period, those marrying and repopulating their villages and towns succeeded in replacing lives lost in mortality crises, and in making bearable lives for themselves and their children.

Between 1649 and the later 1700s, the great diseases waned. Plague disappeared in Scotland after 1649, and smallpox was controlled by 1770. The Poor Law Act of 1649 mandated that the poor should not be left to starve, although they still would from time to time; the earlier Poor Law of 1574 was relatively ineffective, given Scotland's weak central authority. Consequently, the poor relied on the traditional means of survival: begging; theft on occasion; meagre support from parishes; scraps from the tables of those with a bit left over; and handouts from guilds, great houses and other establishments with which they had some pre-existing connection.[57] From 1651 to 1674, and again from 1700 to 1739, there were no national harvest failures. The process of agricultural improvement, while patchy and regional, began to increase productivity even as it limited access to that produce in the eighteenth century as landlords, tenant farmers and merchants sought the best price. And the potato mitigated some of the worst depredations of nature and landlords. Thus, marriage and the bearing of children, always a basic constituent of social order, but previously vulnerable to weather, famine and disease, was about to emerge as a far more important institution as families were no longer broken so frequently by death.[58]

Human agency, not to mention lust, greed and advantageous family alliances were always at work in the formation of marriages, both ordinary and noble, although the degree to which the various elements mattered varied with each union. At the margins, marriage was a fluid and tenuous arrangement. Marriages not broken by early death could be broken by divorce and separation, and while the numbers seem to have been low, the possibility was recognised, and ordinary people, not the gentry or nobility, brought most cases before the Commissary Court in Edinburgh. Marriage in Scotland was amenable to individual will at entry and exit, since marriage rested on consent, followed by sexual intercourse. The kirk added one requirement, that of public declaration in the form of banns, or announcements read from the pulpit some weeks before a marriage, with the intention of finding out bigamists, or of otherwise guaranteeing the legitimacy of a marriage. But retaining such an old consensual definition of marriage forced the kirk into a long-running battle to control other forms of marriage, from hand-fasting to those blessed by rival faiths.[59]

MARRIAGE ECONOMIC, MARRIAGE ROMANTIC

Marriage, clearly confirmed as an economic institution for most past centuries, seems to have been changing, and one might argue that post-Reformation, choice in a marriage partner became a significant new form of freedom and independence.[60] But we should not exaggerate: for many thousands of ordinary people, marriage was an economic necessity, especially for women, who were lower paid and more likely to be in part-time and casual employment. Spinsterhood, other than for the daughters of the aristocracy and gentry, and perhaps better-off merchants, was a bleak proposition, and single women could find themselves hounded by the authorities who feared that they would engage in immoral activities. Worse was widowhood, other than for those women fortunate enough to be able to support an independent existence. The case of Ann Smith, self-confessedly a 'poor Disconsolate Widow', speaks for many women in similar circumstances: two months previously the wife of a burgess brewer in Arbroath, but semi-anonymous and

ISOBEL TAYLOR Aged 105 widow of JOHN ALICE
She was Born in the parish of Crieff County of Perth the 4 of March 1713.
and died in Edin' the 23 of April 1818.

Figure 3.4 *'Isobel Taylor', taken from John Kay, A Series of Original Portraits and Caricature Etchings (Edinburgh, 1837–8). John Kay was equally interested in the existence of old women. Of course, given the recording of births, or absence thereof in the period, Isobel Taylor's age is somewhat subjective.*

in lodgings in Dundee, in March 1739 she made a second plea to a former provost of Arbroath that he might intervene and obtain something for her from the brewers' poor fund to relieve her 'very mean' circumstances.[61] There were occupations which demanded the different skills and attributes of a man and his wife and children: coal mining, for example, where males cut coal and their wives and children acted as bearers; and in farming in the Lothians, where agricultural servants – hinds – were required to have their wives to engage in harvest work and other laborious tasks.[62] There are countless other cases where wives made critical contributions to the household economy.

If cruelty and failure to support a wife had often figured – and would continue as claims made in suits for separation and divorce – emotional disappointment or dissatisfaction would matter more as people lived longer. Although we know too little about the expectations and realities of married life among the lower classes, there are tantalising hints that love was an important ingredient.[63] For the upper ranks, romantic love as a factor in marriage appears to have been rare, but not unknown, and certainly fondness and deep affection were much in evidence even in a society which was both

paternal and hierarchical.[64] As Elizabeth Mure, writing in 1790, recalled of
her grandfather's lifetime, 'Every master was revered by his family, honour'd
by his tenants, and aweful to his domestics.' She also noted about the same
generation 'that while that reverence and Awe remain'd on the minds of
man for masters, Fathers, and heads of Clans, it was then that the Awe and
dread of Deity was most powerful'.[65] But in the eighteenth century, despite
the political contentions of the first half of the century, sentiment vied with
reason in popular representations of courtship; for the middling sorts love
and matrimony were promulgated as a desirable combination alongside the
Enlightenment's advocacy of reason.[66] Henry Mackenzie published *The Man
of Feeling* in 1771, and began chapter thirteen with this description of a young
woman:

> She had been ushered into life (as that word is used in the dialect of St. James's)
> at seventeen, her father being then in parliament, and living in London: at seven-
> teen, therefore, she had been a universal toast; her health, now she was four-and-
> twenty, was only drank by those who knew her face at least. Her complexion was
> mellowed into a paleness, which certainly took from her beauty; but agreed, at
> least Harley used to say so, with the pensive softness of her mind. Her eyes were
> of that gentle hazel colour which is rather mild than piercing; and, except when
> they were lighted up by good-humour, which was frequently the case, were sup-
> posed by the fine gentlemen to want fire. Her air and manner were elegant in the
> highest degree, and were as sure of commanding respect as their mistress was far
> from demanding it.[67]

Mackenzie's sensibilities marked a change from that older literature of
courtship, the Scottish traditional ballads, where one would find in the
ballad 'Lord Thomas and Fair Annet' these stanzas describing a young man's
ruminations on possible brides:

'O rede, O rede, mither,' he says,
   'A gude rede gie to mee;
O sall I tak the nut-browne bride,
   And let Faire Annet bee?'

'The nut-browne bride haes gowd and gear,
   Fair Annet she has gat nane;
And the little bauty Fair Annet haes
   O it wull soon be gane.'

And he has till his brother gane:
   'Now, brother, rede ye me;
A, sall I marrie the nut-browne bride,
   And let Fair Annet bee?'

'The nut-browne bride has oxen, brother,
   The nut-browne bride has kye;

I wad hae ye marrie the nut-browne bride,
   And cast Fair Annet bye.'

'Her oxen may dye i the house, billie,
   And her kye into the byre,
And I sall hae nothing to mysell
   Bot a fat fadge by the fyre.'[68]

Lord Thomas is then advised by his sister to take Fair Annet, but he insists that he will take his mother's advice and marry the nut-brown bride. With this decision, Thomas, Annet and the anonymous nut-brown bride are doomed. Annet appears at the wedding in stunning array, the nut-brown bride stabs her, Thomas stabs the bride and then kills himself. The conflict between family interest and property, on the one hand, and making a right choice, a choice ordained in the ballad by romantic love, honour and values older than wealth, on the other hand, is quite clear in this text. This version of the ballad was published in 1765, probably after transmission through several generations of singers. Traditional singers, familiar with its formulaic phrasing, also understood that they were expressing a very conservative view: breaking old ties and old contracts lead to death, if not always of persons, then of a society built on those obligations. This is a far cry from Mackenzie's man of feeling, and of the motif of feeling as a newly important aspect of personality. In ballads love is akin to loyalty and obligation; in novels it was opposed to the calculations on which marriages had been constructed by the friends, to use an eighteenth-century word, of the couple. Marriage was at the centre of many novels in the eighteenth century, and by the end of the century, two Scots novels, among many in Britain, catalogued the new ideas of marriage: Susan Ferrier's *Marriage*, and Sir Walter Scott's *The Heart of Mid-Lothian*.[69] Like the classic, and slightly earlier British novel that redefined marriage, Maria Edgeworth's *Belinda*, the new marriage emerged as companionate, domestic, egalitarian and, compared with the violence, risk and passion of the ballads, the new marriages were reasonable, loving and tame – a domesticity based on domestication and mutual affection.

The Scots traditional ballads collected in the eighteenth and early nineteenth centuries provide very late early modern examples of the difficulties of marriage and family life. The ballad found in more variations than any other by late-eighteenth- and early-nineteenth-century collectors was 'Mary Hamilton', which is about infanticide.[70] Others examine murder, jealousy, betrayal, incest and parental violence. If we assume that ballads had remained popular for several generations, up to the time of their collection and publication, because they offered valuable counsel until a more urbane, bourgeois population turned to novels and fashionable sermons for advice, we have a variety of quite gruesome accounts of courtship still circulating among eighteenth-century Scots, suggesting the memory of a society structured by force, threat, alliance and compliance with the wishes of others – a

Figure 3.5 *'Saut Wife'*, taken from John Kay, A Series of Original Portraits and Caricature Etchings *(Edinburgh, 1837–8). Salt wives, fish wives and many other peddlers supplied city households with food and other necessities, highlighting both the growing demand and the growing populations of the late eighteenth century.*

world in which everyone was bound to someone, and 'nobody in those times thought of pleasing themselves'. As Mure reflected, 'The established rule was to please your company[.]'[71]

CONCLUSION

Throughout the early modern period, the adult life cycle of marrying, giving birth and dying in Scotland was usually accomplished within a network of social ties that formed the basis of the political and economic state, for the most part lived and experienced at parish level. In the eighteenth century conditions improved: famine abated; child mortality declined; and after Culloden the kind of military action that resulted in large numbers of fatalities relocated from Scotland to North America and India. The weather began to release its grip, or at least its worst effects could usually be overcome, although the threat to human life and the suffering that wet, wind and cold could exert on families and individuals by no means disappeared. Yet, paradoxically, as nature relented in the eighteenth century and as other demographic challenges receded, the essential foodstuffs that might have made conception and childbirth easier and more frequent, and prolonged life, may for the poorer sections of society have become harder to acquire as the market economy in agricultural produce strengthened. Vagrancy and the presence of the poor continued to pose problems for the authorities in town and country, especially during periods of food shortage. The sanctity of marriage continued to be eroded by fornication for some, while others delayed entry to the matrimonial state.[72] The erratic and regionally variable illegitimacy figures that may have marked the degrees to which ordinary people had hoped for or given up on marriage were joined after 1690 by prosecutions for infanticide.[73] Infanticide has never been absent from any society, but it had to be visible to be prosecuted. The spectre of the single woman murdering her infant was surely a sign of a new kind of despair.[74] None the less, the population slowly increased. Life found a way, amid the new difficulties that replaced the old horrors catalogued by Malthus, and perhaps John Callendar got to die in his bed, an old man.

Notes

1. For John Callendar, see CS299/4 in National Archives of Scotland (NAS), West Register House (WRH), Edinburgh. A search of digitised birth records, available at: www.scotlandspeople.gov.uk shows twenty-nine John Callanders or Callandars born in Falkirk between 1671 and 1723, or twenty-nine in fifty-two years.

2. For the *Statistical Account* (OSA) for Falkirk, see the Edina site, available at: http://stat-acc-scot.edina.ac.uk/link/1791-99/Stirling/Falkirk/. Surgeons had risen in status and training by the early eighteenth century; see Helen M. Dingwall, *Physicians, Surgeons and Apothecaries. Medical Practice in Seventeenth-Century Edinburgh* (East Linton, 1995), pp. 72–9; and on the rise of the Old Poor Law, see Rosalind Mitchison, *The Old Poor Law in Scotland. The Experience of Poverty, 1574–1845* (Edinburgh, 2000), pp. 3–43; and on the moral obligation to help, see Michael Flinn (ed.), *Scottish Population History* (Cambridge, 1977), pp. 10–12.

3. On children, whose high death rate was perhaps the most obvious and familiar form of death, see T. C. Smout, *A History of the Scottish People 1560–1830* (London, 1985), pp. 252–3; and 'The population problem', ch. XI, pp. 240–60.

4. On the physicians, see Helen M. Dingwall, *A History of Scottish Medicine* (Edinburgh, 2003), pp. 72–4; for traditional healers, see pp. 95–102; and also Dingwall, *Physicians, Surgeons and Apothecaries*.

5. Flinn, *Scottish Population History*, pp. 11–12.

6. On population growth, see R. E. Tyson, 'Contrasting regimes: population growth in Ireland and Scotland during the eighteenth century', in S. J. Connolly, R. A. Houston and R. J. Morris (eds), *Conflict, Identity, and Economic Development: Ireland and Scotland, 1600–1939* (Preston, 1995), pp. 64–76.

7. See Harold Perkin, *The Origins of Modern English Society* (London, 1969).

8. Flinn, *Scottish Population History*, p. 4; his suspicion of slow growth or even a decline in population has been confirmed, see Tyson, 'Contrasting regimes', pp. 64–7.

9. See descriptive material, available at: http://edina.ac.uk/stat-acc-scot/access/sub-service.html.

10. OSA on line, available at: http://stat-acc-scot.edina.ac.uk/link/1791-99/Perth/Comrie/11/180.

11. OSA on line, available at: http://stat-acc-scot.edina.ac.uk/link/1791-99/Perth/Comrie/11/183.

12. OSA on line, available at: http://stat-acc-scot.edina.ac.uk/link/1791-99/Perth/Comrie/11/178.

13. On the Scottish Enlightenment, see, among innumerable works, primary and secondary: Jane Rendall, *The Origins of the Scottish Enlightenment 1707–1776* (New York, 1978); Karl Miller, *Cockburn's Millennium* (Cambridge, MA, 1976); William Ferguson, *Scotland 1689 to the Present* (Edinburgh, 1968), pp. 198–233; and the recent readable overview by James Buchan, *Crowded with Genius* (New York, 2003).

14. See Flinn, *Scottish Population*, pp. 3–4, 45–51; James Gray Kyd (ed.), *Scottish Population Statistics including Webster's Analysis of Population 1755* (Edinburgh, 1975), pp. 7–81.

15. Robert Chambers, *Domestic Annals of Scotland, from the Revolution to the Rebellion of 1745* (Edinburgh, 1861), pp. 136–7, 195–9.

16. Chambers, *Domestic Annals*, p. 606.

17. Chambers, *Domestic Annals*, p. 196 – Chambers is colourful; for recent scholarship on famine in Aberdeenshire, and riots in particular, see Karen J. Cullen, Christopher A. Whatley and Mary Young, 'King William's ill years: new evidence on the impact of scarcity and harvest failure during the crisis of 1690s on Tayside', *The Scottish Historical Review*, LXXXV (October 2006), 272–3.

18. Chambers, *Domestic Annals*, p. 348.

19. Chambers, *Domestic Annals*, p. 197.

20. Revd J. L. Buchanan, *Travels in the Western Hebrides from 1782 to 1790* (Waternish, 1997 edn.), pp. 73–4; R. M. Inglis, *Annals of an Angus Parish* (Dundee, 1888), p. 144.

21. A. Spicer, 'Rest of their bones: fear of death and Reformed burial practices', in W. G. Naphy and P. Roberts (eds), *Fear in Early Modern Society* (Manchester, 1997), pp. 167–83.

22. For Alexander Webster and his 1755 census, see A. J. Youngson, 'Alexander Webster and his "Account of the Number of People in Scotland in the Year 1755"', *Population Studies*, 15:2 (November, 1961), 198–200; and Kyd, *Scottish Population Statistics*, pp. 7–81.

23. See, for example, G. Marshall, *Presbyteries and Profits: Calvinism and the Development of Capitalism in Scotland, 1560–1707* (Edinburgh, 1980).

24. For the clerk, see NAS, CH2/545/3/7, for October and November 1747. The old parish registers, or OPRs, have survived sketchily; see the online resource, available at: www.scotlandspeople.gov.uk/content/help/index.aspx?r=554&405.

25. On erratic records of baptisms, see Cullen, Whatley and Young, 'King William's ill years', p. 265; on the nature of Scottish records, and demography (although most data is, due to the scarcity of records, from the late eighteenth century

to 1861), see R. A. Houston, 'The demographic regime', in T. M. Devine and Rosalind Mitchison (eds), *People and Society in Scotland, Vol. I, 1760–1830* (Edinburgh, 1988), pp. 9–26.

26. For Alison and Harvey, see Revd James Anderson, *The Ladies of the Covenant, Memoirs of Distinguished Female Characters, Embracing the Period of the Covenant and Persecution* (New York, 1880), pp. 272–99.

27. See the letter of Adam Smith to William Strahan, 9 November 1776, in Ernest Campbell Mossner and Ian Simpson Ross (eds), *The Correspondence of Adam Smith*, vol. VI (Indianapolis, IN, 1987), p. 217.

28. Letter, Adam Smith to William Strahan, 9 November 1776, in Mossner and Ross, *Correspondence of Adam Smith*, p. 217.

29. Smout, *A History of the Scottish People*, pp. 283–7 on housing.

30. Philippe Aries, *Western Attitudes Towards Death: From the Middle Ages to the Present* (Baltimore, MD, 1974); and by the same author, *The Hour of Our Death* (New York, 1981).

31. Adam Smith to William Strahan, 9 November 1776, in Mossner and Ross, *Correspondence of Adam Smith*, p. 217.

32. Henry Hamilton (ed.), *Selections from the Monymusk Papers* (Scottish History Society, Edinburgh, 1945), pp. 15–17.

33. W. C. Mackenzie, *Andrew Fletcher of Saltoun His Life and Times* (Edinburgh, 1935), p. 310.

34. For Lady Baillie, see Anderson, *Ladies of the Covenant*, p. 457.

35. See Sheila M. Spiers, *The Kirkyard of Auchindoir Old & New* (Aberdeen, 1987), p. 15.

36. See the OSA for Auchindoir, available at: http://stat-accscot.edina.ac.uk/link/1791-99/Aberdeen/Auchindoir; on the OSA generally, see Maisie Steven, *Parish Life in Eighteenth-century Scotland: A Review of the Statistical Account (OSA)* (Aberdeen, 1995). The absence of births between 1697 and 1702 probably reflects the impact of the great famine: see Cullen, Whatley and Young, 'King William's ill years', pp. 250–76.

37. On the movement of female servants, see Ian D. Whyte and Kathleen Whyte, 'The geographical mobility of women in early modern Scotland', in Leah Leneman (ed.), *Perspectives in Scottish Social History* (Aberdeen, 1988), pp. 83–106.

38. Or it may be coincidence; see the OSA for Edinburgh, available at: http://stat-acc-scot.edina.ac.uk/link/1791-99/Edinburgh/Edinburgh/6/561.

39. G. Parker, 'The "Kirk by Law Established" and the origins of the "taming of Scotland": St Andrews, 1559–1600', in Leneman, *Perspectives*, pp.17–18.

40. On the extent of and patterns for illegitimate births, see Leah Leneman and Rosalind Mitchison, 'Scottish illegitimacy ratios in the early modern period', *Economic History Review*, 2nd series, XL: I (1987), 50; this is a brief introduction to their work, see also their *Girls in Trouble* (Edinburgh, 1998) and *Sexuality and Social Control: Scotland 1660–1780* (London, 1989).

41. For Mary M'Millan see John Cameron (ed.), *The Justiciary Records of Argyll and the Isles*, vol. I (Edinburgh, 1949), pp. 110–12.

42. Cameron, *Justiciary Records*, pp. 124–5.

43. Cameron, *Justiciary Records*, pp. 133–4.

44. Cameron, *Justiciary Records*, pp. 196–98.

45. See the OSA for Glassary, or Kilmichael-Glassary, available at: http://stat-acc-scot.edina.ac.uk/link/1791-99/Argyle/Glassary/13/658.

46. Oral composition and transmission were first identified in the Homeric epics by Albert B. Lord, *Singer of Tales* (Cambridge, MA, 1960), and later demonstrated among a large group of Scots ballads by David Buchan, *The Ballad and the Folk* (London, 1972).

47. For the B text of 'Child Waters', stanzas 30–35, from the singing of Anna Gordon Brown, collected in Aberdeenshire in 1800, see Francis James Child, *The English and Scottish Popular Ballads*, vol. II (New York, 1965), pp. 87–9.

48. E. Sanderson, *Women and Work in Eighteenth-Century Edinburgh* (London, 1996), p. 53.

49. For the midwives, see the South Circuit court records, NAS JC12/11, October 1762, case of Agnes Walker; for William Hunter, and further commentary on Agnes Walker, the young woman suspected of infanticide, see Deborah A. Symonds, *Weep Not for Me: Women, Ballads, and Infanticide in Early Modern Scotland* (University Park, PA, 1997) pp. 73–83, 143–50.

50. Sanderson, *Women and Work*, pp. 60–4.

51. On infant mortality and birth rates, see Tyson, 'Contrasting regimes: population growth', pp. 70–1.

52. See papers of the Forfeited Estates Commission, NAS E 626/17/1, 2. The absence of a grate, common to other rooms in this inventory, suggests the room was unused at the time.

53. See Mitchison and Leneman, *Girls in Trouble*, pp. 40–52; and Kenneth M. Boyd, *Scottish Church Attitudes to Sex, Marriage and the Family, 1850–1914* (Edinburgh, 1980), pp. 46–50.

54. Elizabeth Mure, 'Some remarks on the change of manners in my own time. 1700–1790', in William Mure (ed.), *Selections from the Family Papers preserved at Caldwell; 1696–1853* (Glasgow, 1854), pp. 263–4.

55. See, for example, A. B. Barty, *The History of Dunblane* (Stirling, 1994), p. 85.

56. Flinn, *Scottish Population*, p. 7.

57. Mitchison, *Old Poor Law*, pp. 3–19.

58. On the Poor Law Act, see Mitchison, *Old Poor Law*, pp. 22–44. For the other demographic data, see Flinn, *Scottish Population*, pp. 1–11.

59. On divorce and separation in Scotland, see Leah Leneman, *Alienated Affections: The Scottish Experience of Divorce and Separation, 1684–1830* (Edinburgh, 1998); for England, see Elizabeth Foyster, *Marital Violence: An English Family History, 1660–1857* (Cambridge, 2005). Divorce came to Scotland with the Reformation, and was possible for both adultery and desertion by 1573; see Boyd, *Scottish Church Attitudes*, pp. 47–9; and on handfasting, see A. E. Anton, '"Handfasting" in Scotland', *The Scottish Historical Review* 37: 124 (October 1958), pp. 89–102.

60. In the online dictionary of the Scots Language, available at: www.dsl.ac.uk, hand-fasting also has an economic connotation, in reaching an agreement to employ

someone; see too R. Mitchison, *Lordship to Patronage: Scotland, 1603–1745* (London, 1983), p. 9.

61. Angus Archives, Abroath Brewers Guild, MS 444/5/71, Ann Smith to John Auchterlony, 25 March 1739.

62. R. A. Houston, 'Women in the economy and society of Scotland, 1500–1800', in R. A. Houston and I. D. Whyte (eds), *Scottish Society 1500–1800* (Cambridge, 1989), pp.120–1.

63. Houston, 'Women', pp. 142–3.

64. On feelings in one marriage that crossed the seventeenth and eighteenth centuries, see Lady Murray of Stanhope, *Memoirs of the Lives and Characters of the Right Honourable George Baillie of Jerviswood and of Lady Grisell Baillie* (Edinburgh, 1824), pp.83–5. See, too, H. and K. Kelsall, *Scottish Lifestyle 300 Years Ago* (Edinburgh, 1986).

65. Mure, 'Some remarks', pp. 260, 266.

66. J. Dwyer, *The Age of Passions: An Interpretation of Adam Smith and Scottish Enlightenment Culture* (East Linton, 1998), pp. 101–39.

67. Henry Mackenzie, *The Man of Feeling*, Project Gutenberg text online, available at: www.gutenberg.org/dirs/etext04/mnfl10h.htm, third paragraph in chapter thirteen.

68. Child, *English and Scottish Popular Ballads*, vol. II, ballad number 73, A text, stanzas 4–8, p. 182. There are seven texts of this ballad in Child; the A text was first printed in 1765 in Bishop Thomas Percy's *Reliques of Ancient English Poetry*; see Child, vol. II, p. 179.

69. *Marriage* and *The Heart of Mid-Lothian* both appeared in 1818; they can be usefully compared with Maria Edgeworth's *Belinda* (1802), and Hannah More's *Coelebs in Search of a Wife* (1810).

70. Symonds, *Weep Not*, pp. 56–67.

71. Mure, 'Some remarks', p. 268.

72. Population growth was slow in Scotland in the later eighteenth century, which is consistent with rising age at first marriage in some areas, migration and skewed sex ratios; see T. M. Devine, *The Scottish Nation* (New York, 1999), p. 151, on population growth.

73. On illegitimacy, briefly, see Leneman and Mitchison, 'Scottish illegitimacy ratios', pp. 41–63; the authors rely on the role of the kirk locally to explain illegitimacy, rather than economic factors.

74. See Symonds, *Weep Not*, pp. 127–78 on the 1690–1820 period; and on the second half of the century in the south-west, see Kilday, 'Maternal monsters'.

Chapter 4

Illness, Disease and Pain

Helen M. Dingwall

INTRODUCTION

In the early modern period, illness and pain were considerable social levellers. Status could not prevent the onset of disease, and treatment was centred on the same basic principles, whether prescribed by the most eminent physician in the land, or a wise woman in a remote Highland village. Few escaped illness or injury, and it is this area which illustrates commonalities among social groups perhaps more than any other aspect of everyday life. In the area of health and disease, the everyday experience was in many ways common to all, regardless of social status.

Historians of medicine in recent times have tried to analyse medicine 'from below', in terms of the experiences and perspectives of the patients, rather than assessing the role of 'great doctors' or of institutions, and this has helped to bring new perspectives to the topic.[1] Health was an unavoidable concern for everyone, and the social construction of 'un-health' was multi-faceted, manifesting itself in ways which varied widely, but which also shared common features throughout society. The social construction of illness was shaped by many factors, including demography, social status, religion, superstition and tradition.

Change over time is a key element in any aspect of the historical process, but continuity is equally important. Toward the end of the eighteenth century, body structures were explained more scientifically and some towns had hospitals in which to treat the sick, but these developments affected most people indirectly, and often not at all. Despite new knowledge, there was a considerable delay in its application to new treatments. Complex surgery was not possible until the advent of anaesthetics and antiseptics in the mid-nineteenth century. Other factors which had a major impact on everyday health and disease included the state of war or peace, the vagaries of the economy and the occurrence of epidemic disease.

The main factor dominating the sphere of health for almost the entire period was that medicine was based on the classical, humoral philosophy which had been articulated by Hippocrates and Galen in the heyday of ancient Greece and Rome, and added to by Arabic medicine. These composite influences produced what is termed 'western medicine'.[2] This took a strongly holistic view of life, health and disease, and the state of the individual was very much related to the rhythm of the seasons, astrology and the balance of bodily humors.

Religion had long been at the root of medical treatment, but also – and quite naturally – alongside a complex array of other beliefs, including witchcraft and the supernatural. Early modern Scots were perhaps more sophisticated in their ability to embrace beliefs which nowadays might be seen as mutually exclusive in a much more compartmentalised society. This meant that Christian faith could be combined easily with incantations or rituals derived from pagan times or from white witchcraft. The witchcraft prosecutions of the late sixteenth and seventeenth centuries did not detract from belief in the supernatural process, good as well as evil. Examples are found easily in the relatively sparse records which survive from the earlier part of the period, such as a cure for migraine:

> Take foure penny wecht of the root of pellitory of Spayne [nettle family, often grown in physic gardens], and half penny wecht of spyngard and grynd thame and boyle them in gude vynegar, and quhen it is cauld put into an sponefull of hony and ane saucer of mustarde, and medle them weill togither and hauld theirof in thy mouth ane sponefull at once as long as ane man may say two creeds[3]

Watches were not widely available, but everyone knew how long it took to say a creed. In most cases involving drugs (often referred to as Galenicals because of their derivation from the works of Galen), the ingredients were similar, whether dispensed by a professional physician or a lay healer. This was partly because of the common philosophical outlook on the causes of disease and its treatment (which included a significant degree of fatalistic acceptance), and partly because the ingredients used in cures were mainly organic and seasonal, including herbs, other plants, snails and beetles, and only occasional items produced by anything recognisable as a laboratory process. (Mercury was an exception, being prescribed for a wide variety of conditions well into the mid-nineteenth century, though its particularly vicious side-effects were well known long before that time. Antimony was also used in various forms as an emetic or purgative.) More complex drugs contained exotic, imported items such as saffron. Most treatments depended on location, season and weather as much as on the medical condition of the patient. Perhaps a significant contrast between rural areas and large towns was that there was often more in the way of attendant ritual involved with the administration of Galenical remedies in the remoter parts. An incantation or superstitious action was often prescribed in conjunction with recipes, and this was less likely to happen when the same remedies were prescribed by a qualified physician. The main point, though, is that in terms of everyday cures, the materials were similar at all levels of society and in most areas. Among the vast array of plants used were betony (nerve tonic), dandelion (diuretic, tonic, stimulant), foxglove (heart complaints, scrofula, epilepsy, mental disorders), fumitory (liver and skin problems, leprosy), rue (coughs, jaundice, rickets, kidney stones) and sorrel (poultices).[4]

Care must be taken with the word 'drug', though, as modern connotations are rather different. What were prescribed were tonics, emollients, poultices or concoctions designed to restore humoral balance. They were general in application, as conditions were believed to originate from general causes, though they could manifest themselves in local pathology or symptoms. Systemic treatments were the norm, even for circumscribed, local pathology.

A key point to emphasise is the considerable time-lag between new knowledge and its practical application to the extent that everyday life might be affected. In the broader world of science, the seventeenth century was the period of Kepler, Bacon, Galileo, Descartes, Boyle, Newton, Hooke and, of course, William Harvey, whose De Motu Cordis et Sanguinis in Animalibus (1628) revolutionised medicine – but not immediately. Harvey's description of the circulation of blood was crucial, but not unopposed in his day. Similarly, Andreas Vesalius' anatomical work, De Humani Corporis Fabrica (1563) began the transformation of surgery – but not immediately.

The Enlightenment period engendered much intellectual debate. Discussion of this in detail is outwith the scope of this work,[5] but alongside the towering philosophical and theological intellects were medical men like William Cullen, who tried to produce new classification systems or nosologies of diseases (at a time when there was a desire for universal laws in nature). Cullen's system was erroneous but at least he attempted to do it. The first and second of the Alexander Monro triumvirate, who controlled anatomy teaching at Edinburgh University for much of the eighteenth century, contributed much to the description of lymphatic, muscular and nervous systems. In practical terms, the period produced microscopes and thermometers, but only gradually would these have an impact on the experience and treatment of pain, illness, disease or accident at any social level.

All of this, together with faster progress in elucidating the functions, or physiology, of the body by the mid-eighteenth century, would prove crucial for the future development of medical and surgical treatment, but for the moment medical practise lagged well behind medical knowledge, and consequently the everyday experience changed but slowly. What also changed slowly was the general acceptance that the will of God was paramount, both in the occurrence of disease and its cure. What most people sought from medical attendants was symptomatic relief – the cure required higher powers.

There is some merit in viewing the situation in terms of concentric circles of influence and consultation, with Edinburgh (and later Glasgow) at the epicentre. Within this central core, the experience of illness, disease and pain – in terms of how they were treated – was perhaps a little more complex than in the outer circles. Here were the qualified physicians, time-served surgeons and apothecaries; here would be the early medical schools and first hospitals; here would be the 'hotbed' of Enlightenment discussion; here would be many of the advances in anatomical knowledge. It was within this inner sphere that a medical orthodoxy emerged in the early modern period, centred on the urban medical institutions, which prescribed training and entry requirements. The identity of Scottish medicine was very much a hybrid of influences, but increasingly what was claimed to be the orthodoxy was Lowland, urban and 'professional', but in medical terms still very much centred on the humoral tradition.[6]

Further out from the centre, but within travelling or correspondence distance, the experience for some people was relatively similar to that in the towns, particularly for gentry estates and their households. In the farthest circles, the balance between qualified and unqualified medical practitioners was very different, so that as a spectrum of practice, the further from the epicentre, the less 'professional' was the practice, the less contact possible with qualified practitioners and the greater reliance on folk and domestic medicine. It was noted by one traveller that there was only one 'medical man' for 50 miles north of Aberdeen at the start of the eighteenth century. This was a Dr Beattie of Garioch, who apparently did his rounds 'on a shaggy pony'.[7] In all areas, epidemic or famine intensified the everyday experience of disease. The situation was a little paradoxical, though, as those who experienced the new clinical methods pioneered in the hospitals in the second half of the eighteenth century were generally from lower social levels. The elite did not consider it socially acceptable to enter a hospital, so in fact the bedrock of the new clinical medicine was the poor, or at least those who were able to gain sponsorship to enter a hospital. There was nothing clear-cut about the everyday experience of un-health in terms of social status or rank.

Professional medicine was exclusively male, but women played a significant role in the sphere of health and disease. By virtue of their role in household and family, they were involved in the care of the sick. Elite women circulated cures around their social circles, in the same way as they were passed around non-elite society. Veronica, countess of Kincardine, wrote to the earl of Tweeddale in 1686, requesting information on the 'dyet of steel', as some of her household were 'much affected w^t the scurvie' – this condition did not spare the elite, and many people consumed scurvy grass prophylactically.[8] A number of women, perhaps more so in rural and remoter areas, also acquired the status of wise women: that is, women who had somehow been given special knowledge, or who could effect cures for conditions affecting humans or animals. More dangerously, the role of women as healers and charmers became – in the minds of the politically powerful at least – subsumed under the general banner of witchcraft, with tragic consequences for some. This chapter will consider all of these aspects, focusing on the experience of the people by means of assessing diseases and their treatment at all social levels and in all areas of the country.

WHAT WERE THE EVERYDAY DISEASES AND INJURIES?

Throughout the whole period the population suffered from intermittent epidemics, including measles and typhus, many conditions being lumped together as fevers or agues. Endemic conditions included chincough (whooping cough), leprosy, consumption, scrofula or tuberculosis (King's evil) and scurvy. Designation of disease was a very inexact science, as was treatment.

In the early part of the period, plague was a constant fear and intermittent reality. The final attack of plague in Scotland took place in the 1640s, and thereafter the country was free of that devastating illness, though this would be replaced by others, particularly cholera and typhoid.[9] Regulations for containment rather than new ideas on cure were introduced at various times, though some awareness of causation is clear in orders given to poison mice and rats during the Brechin outbreak of 1647, which killed one-third of the town's inhabitants.[10]

Scotland was generally afflicted by the bubonic version of the disease, *pasteurella pestis*, rather than the pneumonic type. It attacked the lymphatic system, producing painful swellings, or bubos, accompanied by skin eruptions and characteristic, deeply-coloured spots. Most patients died within a week of contracting the disease, and severe outbreaks killed over 60 per cent of those afflicted. The attack in the 1640s affected over seventy parishes, including remote Highland areas as well as Lowland burghs. Burghs generally took action at the first sign of an attack. Isolation was the principal measure taken to contain outbreaks, and there are many instances of plague pits being dug, such as on the burgh muir in Edinburgh, while plague huts were built on Leith links in 1645 and similar structures erected at Kinnoul, in Perth.[11] The relatively cold Scottish climate may have at least in part explained the disappearance of plague, though awareness of the danger of further outbreaks continued. In 1665, for example, Peebles town council banned trade 'with inhabitants or merchants of Ingland', because of an outbreak in London.[12] The everyday experience of epidemic disease was shaped by corporate regulation and coercion, just as much as the individual symptoms or tragedies.

Smallpox was a consistent presence, not alleviated immediately by the innovations of inoculation from the early eighteenth century, and vaccination from the 1790s. In 1800 religion was still central to everyday life – perhaps not to the extent that it had been in 1600, but important none the less. Religion was cited as a counter-argument to prophylactic inoculation, for example, a view expressed in reports submitted to the *Statistical Account* (OSA) stating that opposition stemmed from a reluctance to interfere with the will of God. It was noted in the parish of Carmunnock that 'the small pox returns very often, and the distemper is never alleviated, as the people from a sort of blind fatality, will not hear of inoculation, though attempts have often been made to remove their scruples on this subject'.[13] New techniques collided with religious fatalism, even in an age of increasingly secular and supposedly enlightened philosophy.[14] In the barony parish of Glasgow, it was noted that inoculation was 'far from being generally practised', while in Hamilton, 'inoculation for the small-pox is practised, but the common people are not reconciled to it'.[15]

Medical professionals realised the benefits of the procedure, but many were wary about any sort of coercion to accept inoculation or vaccination. Administration of inoculation was not confined to professional medical practitioners though. Local ministers and amateur operators offered the service, and a few individuals, such as 'Camphor Johnnie' in Shetland, built up considerable reputations.[16] 'Johnnie' used a different method from some of his contemporaries, in that he did not use the smallpox matter he collected immediately, but buried it with camphor for a period, arguing that 'it always proves milder to the patient, when it has lost a considerable degree of its strength'.[17] Cabbage leaves were used to bind the patient's arm, rather than bandages or other dressings. The point could be made here that lay operators concentrating on one procedure might be more reliable than qualified practitioners doing it rarely (this was probably also the case with lithotomists who dealt with bladder stones, or cataract 'operators', who travelled the country removing cataracts, often on a public stage, claiming cures in all cases).

Venereal disease did not respect social status, and the highest in the land could be afflicted with gonorrhoea or syphilis. Burghs took measures to deal with outbreaks of 'grandgore' by isolating victims, and many treatments were offered, including the ubiquitous mercury. John Clerk of Penicuik, one of the key actors in the saga of the Union of 1707, wrote to his physicians indicating that he had 'ane gonorrhoea simplex', and outlining the self-treatment measures he had taken.[18] His physician concluded, perhaps benevolently, that the cause of Clerk's condition was 'riding much of latte in cold weather & under night [which] hes occasioned all the disorders of his bodie and that his coching [coughing] also latte at night hes occasioned a separation of sharp serous humours which has fallen on the testicle & seminal vessels whence is the tumor testis sinistri and the beginning of a gonorrhoea'. Dr Burnet considered that Clerk had 'ordered severall things for himself verie pertinentlie', and took the view that purging was the main line of treatment.[19] Clerk had treated himself with bloodletting, rhubarb, turpentine and senna, and was advised to take mercurius dulcis and Peruvian bark in addition, and to eat a 'cooling dyet' – all of this clearly focused on a humoral approach. Though an elite case, the treatments were widely available, and it is clear that the elite treated themselves before consulting medical opinion just as much as individuals lower down the social scale.

By the eighteenth century Scotland suffered fewer famines,[20] but there were still occasional subsistence crises. It appears also that there was general correlation between episodes of famine and reduced birth rate (measured in terms of numbers of baptisms), although there were individual variants from this general trend.[21] Famine produced severe malnutrition, which meant that diseases such as typhus had even more devastating effects on the population. Even in times of good harvests and economic stability, though, disease was still a feature at all levels of society and in all areas of the country. Fevers, whooping cough, typhoid and dysentery ('bloody flux') were all prevalent, and consumption was still the most frequent cause of death noted on bills of mortality, followed by 'fever' and smallpox.[22] Gradually the devastating effects of famine and disease in tandem were alleviated, although there were still outbreaks, particularly of smallpox, but also of 'putrid sore throat' and sibbens in Aberdeen in the 1790s, epidemic measles in Edinburgh in the 1720s and Kilmarnock in the 1740s.[23]

It is difficult to obtain rank-specific mortality or morbidity statistics for this period. Interestingly, though, evidence has been produced to show that in the eighteenth and nineteenth centuries the Scots were, on average, taller than the English, suggesting better nutritional or environmental conditions, and this is likely also to relate to social status.[24] This is confirmed by evidence showing that Writers to the Signet as a group had higher than average life expectancy.[25]

There was also, of course, the general background of un-health, in that diseases such as common colds, which are trivial nowadays, could well be lethal, while the debilitating effects of intestinal worms, or poor diet, meant that a state of health in modern terms could be achieved rarely. Constant manual labour produced early arthritis, while old age came prematurely, without the possibility of retirement for most. This, however, is one area where the effects of debility were more status-linked, as the elite could afford servants to care for them in their old age.

In terms of general endemic conditions, it was claimed that in Caithness, for example, ague (which may have been a form of malaria) and rheumatism were the most common everyday afflictions.[26] People here, as well as elsewhere in Scotland, suffered from sibbens (sivvens, civvans or Scottish yaws), a bacterial illness, characterised by raspberry-like spots on the skin. There were similarities with syphilis, but the disease was probably propagated by non-venereal means. Boyd notes that it has been referred to as 'Fromboisia Cromwelliana', allegedly brought to Scotland by Cromwell's troops after the battle of Dunbar in 1650.[27] Invading troops were a convenient focus of blame for the introduction of several afflictions, including plague and venereal diseases.

The OSA returns give good evidence of general levels of illness and disease. The report for the small east-coast fishing port of Eyemouth states:

> The air here is reckoned healthy. We are not afflicted with any infectious or epidemical diseases, except the small-pox, the bad effects of which have of late been prevented by inoculation. The only complaints that prove mortal in this place, are different kinds of fevers and consumptions; and these are mostly confined to the poorest class of people, and ascribed to their scanty diet.

In Orkney it was declared that the only 'epidemical distempers' to be found were smallpox, measles and chincough, while the endemic dampness of the weather produced stomach pains, the King's evil [tuberculosis], asthma, rheumatism and 'dropsy'.[28]

Another factor highlighted by some OSA contributors reflects the beginnings of industrialisation. The reporter for Corstorphine regretted the consequences of factory work on children, stating that 'the waste of the human species would not be easy to compute', while factory workers in the Glasgow Barony parish were subject to 'flatulency and diseases incident to sedentary people' – weavers were afflicted in particular by leg ulcers (which were often treated by the application of lime water).[29]

There were also common denominators in injuries: war; 'everyday' violence; and 'industrial' accident. Buildings were not subject to modern standards of control, which resulted in many injuries, including one where a child was hit by a piece of falling masonry, suffering a serious head injury. The records state colourfully that two children had been hit by a 'gryt stane lintell', which 'brak ane of their leggis all to pieces and dang in his harne pan [broke his skull]'.[30] The level of general background violence was high, and quarrels and domestic disputes also produced their fair share of injurious consequences. Fire and its devastating consequences were another factor. War was rather less of an everyday experience by the end of the period, but it was none the less a factor, and particularly in terms of the effects of gunshot wounds and consequent problems of ulceration and infection.

Maternal, infant and child mortality continued to affect all levels of society. Midwifery in the eighteenth century may have been more advanced in terms of anatomical knowledge and publications by professors of midwifery, such as Alexander Hamilton's *Treatise of Midwifery*,[31] but in reality, given factors of modesty, superstition, environment and ignorance of the causes of childbed fever or the consequences of mal-presentation of the infant in the womb, the dangers of childbirth were no less for those of higher rank. The emotional trauma of losing a child was no less severe at any level of society. Wilson claims that the gradual change from female to male midwifery resulted from advanced anatomical knowledge and the use of forceps to aid delivery,[32] though there were probably other factors, including the social symbolism of employing qualified physicians. The teaching of midwifery to medical students was also a significant factor, though, of course, in many areas a licensed midwife[33] or unqualified female birth attendant remained supreme. This is one area where the everyday was a little different, according to social level, but the elite consulted non-professionals too, an example being that of Beatrix Ruthven, the wife of an Edinburgh physician, who provided an acquaintance with 'some particulars to cause her to conceave with chyld', and then pursued her in the burgh court for payment of the fee, which had been agreed at £17 should the woman conceive, which she did.[34] The scourge of childbed fever did not spare the elite either, and it is also the case that professional treatment could not save mother or child, as seen in a case treated by Professor Hamilton:

> A poor woman . . . seized with the pains of childbirth in the sixth month of pregnancy, was delivered by Professor Hamilton, of three boys and a girl. The three boys were brought into the world alive, but . . . could not long exist. Instances of women conceiving as many children are extremely rare in this or any other country.[35]

Hamilton could do little in this case, though there was beginning to be some hope for surgical assistance in difficult circumstances. Caesarean section had hitherto been performed mainly to remove a dead child from a dead mother, but research on eight Caesarean sections carried out on live mothers in Edinburgh during the second half of the eighteenth century showed that all of the mothers died, but three of the infants survived. This is still tragic, but there was at least some hope.[36]

Attendance at childbirth had long been part of the female domestic and medical sphere, and, indeed, it was often the case that the same woman fulfilled the task of laying out the dead, thus influencing both the beginning and end of life. Tragically, she would often have to perform the task of laying out the mother of the infant she had helped to deliver. Quite naturally, the folk medicine sphere had its store of remedies and rituals to assist in childbirth and neonatal care, including girdles, bound ritually round the mother; or tying a red cloth at the foot of the bed to stem post-partum bleeding; or believing that a child born at full moon was lucky; or that birth was easier at high tide.[37] A recipe to 'stopp purging' in lying-in women contained pearl barley, rosebuds, sugar and 'syrrup of vitrioll' (sulphuric acid), combining chemical preparations with kitchen and garden ingredients (see Figure 4.1).[38]

THE INNER CIRCLE – URBAN HEALTH AND DISEASE

In 1600 most Scottish towns were small and dirty, with little or no sanitation or concept of hygiene. By 1800 there were more, larger towns, though most were still relatively small in comparison with other urbanised European countries. Edinburgh remained by far the largest town, but Glasgow was flourishing, while Aberdeen continued to be the most significant urban centre in the north. Despite the presence of five universities, no formal medical education was available in Scotland until the foundation of the Edinburgh Medical School in 1726 (there had been a mediciner in post in Aberdeen University since its foundation, but there is little evidence that any of them taught extensively, or even at all).[39] Medical students had to go abroad to receive training, and many did not return to Scotland to practice.

In 1600 the only medical institutions in Scotland were the Incorporation of Surgeons of Edinburgh, founded in 1505,[40] and the uniquely combined

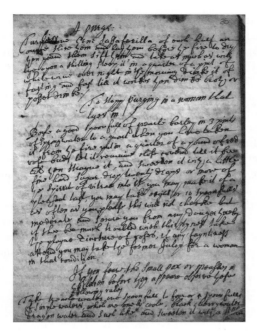

Figure 4.1   *Seventeenth-century recipe 'to stopp purging in a woman that lyin in', from a seventeenth-century manuscript recipe book. Source: © National Library of Scotland (www. scran.ac.uk).*

Faculty of Physicians and Surgeons of Glasgow, established in 1599.[41] These were concerned primarily with establishing occupational demarcation; what their members did in practice was another thing entirely. No amount of organisation could mask the fact that, with surgery in particular, very little could be achieved, though there is evidence that most practitioners sought to help their patients to the greatest extent possible. What urban patients may have experienced that was different from their rural counterparts concerned frequency of consultations rather than different kinds of cure. Apprentices were sent to change dressings, and potions could be acquired easily from an apothecary's shop. In remote areas this was much less possible.

Urban practitioners had the advantage of rudimentary collegialism; rural practitioners were isolated. Urban patients could consult a wide spectrum of opinion; rural patients were more restricted. Multiple consultation was not always profitable, though. This is demonstrated in the case of a minister who had symptoms of urinary stones, and consulted one physician, who used a solid catheter as a diagnostic tool and claimed to have identified a stone in the neck of the bladder. Treatment included diuretics and topical ointments. A second physician ordered bloodletting together with a poultice 'of cows dung or bread and milk'. A third physician repeated the bloodletting and concluded that the problem was inflammation, not a stone. Amid all this disagreement, the unfortunate patient 'fell wholly insensible with a comatous stupor and dy'd'; post-mortem examination confirmed a stone.[42] Triple consultation in this instance complicated the situation, with tragic consequences.

It was the patients' prerogative to consult widely, and they did so with enthusiasm, confirming the very broad medical marketplace in operation, and the close concern with health shared by most of the population.[43] Elites consulted qualified opinion, but they also consulted each other and a wide range of amateur practitioners, including the itinerant quacks who plied their trade around the countryside and towns. These amateur healers built up considerable reputations, and also underwent an image change over the period. In earlier times their wares were peddled as part of a show, with circus acts to warm up the audience,[44] but by the middle of the eighteenth century they were more likely to portray themselves as serious physicians, quoting numerous cures as advertisement for their skills – some had even undergone medical training. They included Francis Clerk, 'oculist', who advertised his expertise in the *Caledonian Mercury* in 1710, and James Black, who claimed in the same publication in 1726, that he could cure many diseases, including smallpox, measles, 'all other flying pains through the body', stating that he did not use vomits, purges or 'common dyet', which were all used by the qualified practitioners.[45] Newspaper advertisements were useful to all sorts of practitioners, who announced patent medicines, such as the 'ointment for curing of the King's Evil in any part of the body, in a very short time'.[46] The everyday experience was influenced by factors other than progress – or lack of it – in medicine. The expansion of the newspaper press was a significant factor here also.

The everyday experience of individuals who had access to qualified urban physicians did change somewhat over the period. Clinical medicine had been pioneered by the renowned Dutch physician, Hermann Boerhaave, who taught many Scottish medical students at the University of Leiden.[47] Boerhaave advocated physical examination, rather than relying on history, and this brought an individual aspect to the consultation experience. There is evidence that Boerhaave's advice was heeded in clinical practice, as shown in a recent analysis of the medical casebooks of a late-eighteenth-century Glasgow physician, Robert Cleghorn.[48] Cleghorn was ahead of his time, in that he was very much in favour of physical examination, including palpation, to assist diagnosis. He also took careful note of post-mortem findings as a test of his diagnostic powers. Cleghorn noted in his diary, concerning a patient with kidney disease, confirmed at post-mortem, that the case was 'another proof of the necessity of attending to local symptoms & to the feelings of the patient, no matter how bizarre these may appear & however contrary to nosology!'[49] It has been claimed that the 'clinical encounter' was at the heart of medical change from the early eighteenth century, and Cleghorn seems to be a good example to confirm this.[50] This meant that gradually there

Figure 4.2 *Edinburgh Royal Infirmary. Engraving of Royal Infirmary of Edinburgh, opened in 1741, by John Elphinstone. Source: © Lothian Health Services Archive (www. scran.ac.uk).*

was more focus on the individual and his or her specific symptoms, rather than relying on standard disease templates.

Individual bedside teaching also involved a further development: medical hospitals in which close observation of patients could be undertaken. Perhaps ironically, though, hospital medicine was experienced mostly by those at the lower end of the social scale. The elites could afford to summon a physician or surgeon and accommodate him for the duration of the treatment; hospitals were not for them. It is possible to claim, therefore, that the effects of hospital medicine on everyday life were in inverse proportion to the social status of the patient. Hospitals still, though, could only care rather than cure in many cases.

The first infirmary in Edinburgh opened 1726 and contained only six beds Surprisingly, the first listed patient came from Caithness – somewhat countering the argument that rural experience of treatment differed from urban. The conditions suffered by the initial inmates included thigh pain, cancer in the face, hysteric disorders, bloody flux, tertian ague, consumption, dropsy and 'inveterate scorbutick ulcer of the leg'.[51] The second infirmary, opened in 1741 (see Figure 4.2), had separate wards for soldiers and servants – it was in the interests of the elites to keep both groups as healthy as possible. The medicalisation of childbirth also resulted in a lying-in ward being established – somewhat ironically on the top floor – and later a separate lying-in hospital in 1791.

The Glasgow Royal Infirmary dates from 1794, the organising committee noting that 'an Infirmary for the Relief of Indigent Persons labouring under Poverty and Disease has long been wanted in the City of Glasgow and in the adjoining counties of Scotland'.[52] This is very much in line with the provision of hospitals as a method of caring for the sick poor, not because of new ideas on diagnosis or treatment. Conditions suffered by patients treated there included the common problems of ulcers, venereal disease, fevers and chest complaints. A key factor in the origins of the major urban hospitals was, of course, population increase, and this was particularly the case in Glasgow, which was expanding more rapidly than its ancient infrastructure could cope with.[53] As with all voluntary hospitals, admission depended on sponsorship, and accident cases were not admitted in the early years. Aberdeen's infirmary started life in the early 1740s, and was the only such institution in the north-east for some considerable time.[54]

Medicalisation of the hospitals would be crucial to the everyday experience of medicine in the nineteenth century, but the new, clinically-based methods did not change the basic approach to patient care. Research on the treatment of typhus at the Edinburgh Infirmary, for example, confirms that close observation, good diet, hygiene and ventilation were still considered to be as important as drugs which, if used, were mainly analgesics for symptomatic relief.[55]

Much general surgical work in the towns was concerned with dressing wounds and treating ulcers, often for lengthy periods. The account submitted by the surgeon appointed to treat Edinburgh's poorest in 1710 includes the case of a woman bitten by a dog, whose wound was 'drest 6 weeks w^t plasters, ointments & balsomes', and that of a man treated for several weeks for a large forehead wound and arm fracture, treatment including purges and emetics as well as plasters and spiced ointment.[56]

The range of surgical procedures which was practically possible was very limited. Amputation, excision of cataracts and closure of anal or lachrymal fistulas were the most common procedures carried out, although surgeons had the knowledge necessary to perform more complex operations. Amputations were performed in circumstances which nowadays would not require sacrifice of the limb, one example being an unfortunate minister, who broke his leg jumping over a ditch. The limb had to be amputated 'on account of the shocking manner in which the bone was fractured', but he died, 'leaving a wife and family unprovided for'.[57] Surgeons became expert in very rapid amputation techniques and there is evidence to show that it was possible, even in the most adverse of circumstances, to survive the procedure. One woman listed on the accounts for the Edinburgh surgeon to the poor survived amputation long enough to require the expenditure of £3 Scots on a 'timber leg' three months later.[58] An early surgical textbook written by Peter Lowe, one of the founders of the Faculty of Physicians and Surgeons of Glasgow and first published in 1597, contained clear advice as to the best and least distressing method of

Figure 4.3   *A set of blood-letting knives used by Hugh McFarquhar, who practised medicine in Tain, Ross-shire, from 1744 to 1794. Source: © Tain and District Museum (www.scran.ac.uk).*

carrying out the procedure.[59] Trepanning, one of the oldest known surgical procedures (believed to have been in use as early as 5000 BC), involving the drilling of a hole in the skull, was still carried out, but for different reasons than in past times, where the intention had been to release evil spirits.[60] By the early modern period it was realised that what had to be released was pressure from a blood clot under the bony skull – but the procedure was the same. Lowe, though, recommended caution, warning young surgeons against rushing to operate too hastily as 'it is not meet to trepan in all fractures as ye have heard, or to discover the brains without necessitous and good judgement, so that the young Chyrurgion may not so hastily, as in time past, trepan for every simple fracture'.[61] This may have resulted in patients experiencing a more conservative approach to their treatment in some areas.

A key facet of the surgeons' everyday work was, of course, bloodletting, both prophylactically and as part of an array of treatments prescribed for most conditions (Figure 4.3 shows a set of bloodletting knives from 1773). The humoral approach meant that treatment for most cases included purges and bloodletting to eliminate evil matters, before restoring the equilibrium of the body with Galenical drugs and tonics, together with advice on diet and lifestyle – and this was the case with surgical problems as well as medical.

In the inner circle, then, the everyday experience could be complex, but it was also firmly rooted in a common philosophy, which was not eclipsed, despite the growing numbers of qualified physicians and surgeons and the addition of medicalised hospitals to the sphere of illness and its experience. Everyday experience of illness in the towns could now involve hospital, professional treatment and patent medicines, but at the core of it all was still the everyday beliefs as to the causes of disease and illness.

BLURRED BOUNDARIES – BETWEEN TOWN AND COUNTRY

It is perhaps in the consultation circles between urban and peripheral that the situation was most complex. Urban medicine penetrated the countryside: that is, as far as it were possible for a physician to travel, and usually to the country house of a member of the gentry, who could afford the costs of consultation, accommodating the physician and stabling his horses. Urban medicine also reached remoter areas by correspondence, usually between gentry and their town physicians, one example being that of the physician, Sir John Wedderburn, who wrote to the countess of Queensberry in 1678, stating that he could not visit because of his 'valetudinary condition', but giving advice on treatment for scurvy, including scurvy grass, fumitary, sage, juniper lemons, rosemary and rue – depending on seasonal availability.[62]

A landed estate may be seen as a small town, given the numbers and occupations of servants and the ability of the landowner to consult urban medical practitioners. There is also clear evidence that servants received professional medical treatment, as they were attended by the family physicians, surgeons and apothecaries as part of their keep. It was, of course, in the interests of the estate that its servants should be kept fit for work, but it did mean that elite medicine was experienced as part of the everyday for estate workers. A useful example comes from the Dundas estate, where the first item on an account sent by apothecary, John Hamilton, in 1630 is 'a dose of pillules to a servant woman'. This account also demonstrates the use of mercury, as 9 shillings were expended on 'a quarter unce Mercury Sublimat'.[63] Other examples come from the papers of the Tweeddale estate. A lengthy bill for apothecary supplies to the earl of Tweeddale's household in 1670 contains 'a pott with cooling ointment to the porter', 'ane bagge of purging ingredients to the cooke', 'ane purging glister [enema] to one of the servants', 'ane pott w^t oyntment for the itch to the coachman' and 'a potione of manna to the postilione'.[64] The cost of the family's medications amounted to the considerable sum of £377 1s., and as well as showing that servants had access to the same medical care as the family, it confirms the close interest in health which was a prime feature of everyday life for all.

Some years later, an account sent to the Lord President of the Court of Session, Sir James Gilmour of Craigmillar, contained many items which appeared in domestic or folk cures, including lemon juice, rosewater, rosemary, marigolds, mugwort, sage water, oximel (vinegar and honey), violet water and hyssop water, some of which were used to treat servants and household members alike.[65] It also contains items which perhaps could not be so readily concocted by lay practitioners. These included 'gilded pills', 'a spiced cape', mastic patches and amber, while other items have a slightly amusing air as expressed in the language of the day, such as 'ane attractive plaister' (probably a poultice for drawing boils) and 'ane hysterick plaister'. Treatment was clearly given in many forms, including liquids, pills, ointments, plasters, emulsions, together with leeches, frequent purges and, of course, bloodletting.

Alongside this was the much more amateur face of rural and semi-rural medicine, where local idiosyncrasies and traditions persisted. In many communities the minister provided rudimentary medical care, being the natural focus of consultation in areas with few qualified physicians – it has been claimed that there were 2,300 physicians in Scotland by 1800, but this seems a generous estimate.[66] Administration of remedies by family members – 'medicine without doctors' – was a major facet of the experience of illness in all areas, but particularly in remoter parts.[67] Cures were handed down through the generations, often being written in commonplace books or inside the covers of printed books, every inch of spare paper being utilised. One example from the late sixteenth century gives a recipe 'to clenge ye heid, ye breast, ye stomache, and to make ane to haif gude appetyte':

> Take thre handfull of centery [centaury] & seith it in ane galloun of water, and then clenge it & put into any pynte of clarified hony & seith it to any quarter & drynke y[r] of two sponefull at once earlie in the morning, and lait in ye evening.

The same source contained a cure for 'scabbed legges that ake & burne', which would be in demand, given the endemic nature of skin conditions. This involved making a plaster with oil derived from a mixture of 'marigoldes, pety morel and plantayne' (plantain – astringent, cooling, used on wounds of all sorts),[68] while a remedy for 'impotence in ye body', contained 'centaury, rosemary and wormwoode' (relatively rare in Scotland, but used as nerve tonic), made into a syrup with white wine.[69]

As the period progressed, however, domestic medicine became almost a sub-division of official medicine, and professional practitioners published works aimed specifically at the domestic situation. Perhaps the most famous such publication was William Buchan's *Domestic Medicine*, first published in 1769 and still in use well into the nineteenth century.[70] Buchan was a Fellow of the Royal College of Physicians of Edinburgh, who moved to London in 1778, consulting at the Chapter Coffee House in the vicinity of St Paul's Cathedral. The full title of the book indicates the prevailing philosophies of self-help, simple remedies and good lifestyle. It must be remembered also that the book was published in the rising intellectual temperature of the Enlightenment, when common-sense philosophies were propounded and knowledge became more widely accessible.[71]

In many ways Buchan reflected the past. He stated that he was 'attentive to regimen' as people tended to 'lay too much stress on Medicine and too little on their own endeavours'.[72] Each disease or condition was discussed in terms of causes, symptoms, regimen and, lastly, medicine. Buchan covered all aspects of life, including appropriate children's clothes and food (Buchan disapproved of swaddling, and also of mixing wine with infants' milk),[73] and the role of religion in health, claiming that 'persons whose business it is to recommend religion to others should beware of dwelling too much on gloomy subjects'.[74] He was strongly in favour of inoculation – 'a salutary invention', lamenting that had the practice been advocated as a fashion rather than a medical treatment, 'it had long ago been universal'.[75]

In his drug treatments, Buchan relied on well-tested remedies, exhorting the use of Peruvian bark (cinchona, source of quinine) for many conditions, including mental afflictions, while mercury was also cited as treatment for madness consequent on animal bites – 1 drachm of mercury ointment to be rubbed around the wound (the recipe for mercury sublimate pills was included in the section of the book on drugs and their composition).[76] Peruvian bark was also suggested as part of the treatment complex for infertility, which also included astringent medicines, dragon's blood, steel, elixir of vitriol, and exercise – as 'affluence begets indolence'.[77] In summary, Buchan's work was very much in and of its time. It was detailed and presumed a reasonable level of both literacy and understanding. Those many households possessing a copy therefore owned a physical manifestation of long-held medical philosophy, and also had access to at least part of the consultation and prescribing sphere of the urban physician. Town dwellers may well have owned copies, but it was also an important method of propagating professional medicine in more distant parts.

OUTER CIRCLES – FOLK MEDICINE, SUPERSTITION AND TRADITION

The peripheral regions of Scotland had rather different everyday experiences in terms of lifestyle, domestic surroundings and work, and it would seem logical to conclude that this was true of health and disease also. However, underneath the cloak of region-specific cures, there were shared assumptions about illness and its relationship to the body and the environment. One account of healing traditions in the Highlands and Islands has the title *Healing Threads*, to highlight both the physical threads used as cures and also the threads of continuity from Celtic medicine.[78] This work also confirms that in the Highlands, as in the Lowlands, health and disease were viewed against the backcloth of balancing opposites – well and ill, light and dark, winter and summer, hot and cold. This binary cosmology was at the heart of many superstitions and beliefs. The struggles of those suffering from illness mirrored the conflict of good and evil forces within. This meant that explanations for many conditions were complex – most diseases having an 'eclectic pathology'.[79] The eclecticism of disease and illness was not just a Scottish or

British phenomenon, nor was it status-defined, and the evidence confirms that superstition, magic and ritual were 'in the mainstream of both elite and popular culture'.[80] It was also the case that some aspects of non-Christian magic were accepted as part of the wider Christian sphere, thus ascribing them some degree of legitimacy.[81] Most areas had distinctive folk remedies, such as a cure for jaundice from Galloway: 'Take half an ounce Saffron, 4 ounces sheep's droppings and 4 bottles beer: boil together for half an hour: put back in the bottles and take a dram three or four times per day';[82] or the Fifers' belief in tying red silk round the wrist to ward off rheumatism.[83]

Everyday experience of illness and medicine in the Highlands was not shaped by folk medicine and oral tradition alone. There was a significant core of learned medicine, based on Gaelic translations of the ancient medical classics. Knowledge was propagated dynastically; a detailed study of the Beaton family has demonstrated this effectively.[84] The structure of Gaelic society enabled this dynastic 'professionalisation' to take place and Gaelic translations of medical classics allowed Highland physicians to share the philosophy held by their Lowland counterparts. Few Gaelic works have been translated into English, but one which has is the *Regimen Sanitatis* of the Beaton family.[85] This regimen, dating from the early seventeenth century, is based squarely on the tenets of classical, humoral medicine, emphasising a good lifestyle in order to conserve and preserve health and reduce un-health or humoral imbalance. Precise advice is given about rising in the morning, stretching, putting on clean clothes and expelling 'the superfluities of first, second and third digestions by the mucous and superfluities of the nose and chest'.[86] One piece of advice which would be difficult to follow in the remote Highlands, though, was that teeth should be cleaned with a melon leaf. Following all this cleansing the next item on the regimen was to 'say Hail Mary or any other (similar) thing'.[87] Practitioners were cautioned against over-use of bloodletting, though still encouraged to use it prophylactically. It was not deemed advisable to 'let the cephalic vein beyond the end of forty years at the outside, for that will blind a person and it will pervert the memory'.[88] There were close similarities between the *Regimen* and Buchan's *Domestic Medicine*, despite the 150-year span between their publications.

There is also evidence of specialisation by Highland practitioners, particularly in areas such as lithotomy (cutting for bladder stones), a procedure approached with reluctance by qualified surgeons. One Highlander, Iomhar MacNeill, was appointed 'stone cutter' in Glasgow in 1661, while differences in phlebotomy techniques are suggested by the description of one individual as a 'Highland blooder'. Such tasks were often undertaken by individuals at a lower level in the Highland medical hierarchy than the learned family dynasties (in which there was no distinction between medicine and surgery).[89] Changes in the structure of Highland society in the later eighteenth century led to the breakdown of clan-based, dynastic medicine, with concomitant change in the everyday experiences of the Highland patient.

Parallel to this confirmation that classical, humoral medicine was practised by the learned Highland physicians, there was a very strong folk healing
strand, also based on humoral principles, but laced with superstition and
ritual. Everyday life was punctuated by superstitions of all sorts, and health
matters were no different. Alexander Carmichael's *Carmina Gadelica*, a
large collection of hymns and incantations, contains interesting entries on
medicine. The 'Gravel Charm', invoked Christian intervention for cases of
urinary stones:

> I have a charm for the gravel disease,
> For the disease that is perverse;
> I have a charm for the red disease,
> For the disease that is irritating.
> As runs a river cold, as grinds a rapid mill,
> Thou who didst ordain land and sea,
> Cease the blood and let flow the urine.
> In name of Father, and of Son,
> In name of Holy Spirit.[90]

A feature of these incantations is the apparent lack of pagan symbolism,
though there is a hint of the magical powers of the Christian trinity. A plea
for cure of seizures comprising several similar stanzas, stated:

> I trample on thee, though seizure
> As tramples whale on brine,
> Thou seizure of back, thou seizure of body
> Thou foul wasting of chest.
> May the strong Lord of life
> Destroy thy disease of body
> From the crown of thine head
> To the base of thy heel.[91]

Though incantations were to be found in all areas, they were potentially
more dangerous in Lowland parts, as it was easy to relate them to witchcraft.
Beith documents a case in Edinburgh in 1643, when Marion Fisher was sum-
moned to appear before the Kirk Session of St Cuthbert's, accused of charming and using spells. It proved difficult to obtain the testimony of witnesses,
though, and the accused was eventually ordered to don a sackcloth and sit in
a prominent place in the church in order to confess to her offences, which
allegedly included the following incantation:

> Our Lord to hunting red,
> His sooll soot sled;
> Doun he lighted,
> his sool sot righted
> Blod to blod

Shenew to shenew
To the other sent in God's name.
In the name of the father, Son, and Holy Ghost.[92]

The format and sentiment of these rituals shared much with the sort of charms and incantations related to white witchcraft, and it is easy to see – at least in part – why the majority of individuals prosecuted in the witch-hunts of the period were women. Of the 3,398 individuals involved in witchcraft cases between 1500 and 1740, some 140 involved folk healing.[93] This is a small number in comparison with accusations of malefice or demonic pact, but demonstrates, none the less, that the interface between healing and witchcraft was permeable and perilous. Examples of this include Janet McAlexander from Ayr (1618), who was cited as a witch, but accused of advising three women on how to heal their children, and Margaret Sandieson, accused of sprinkling water on someone's head as a cure (1635).[94]

Later in the period, similar evidence of the superstitious side of health comes from, for example, Morayshire in the 1770s, where woodbine wreaths were used in the cure of 'hectic fevers', the patient walking under the wreath 'in the increase of the March móon'.[95] This demonstrates several strands in the cosmology of healing – the plant, the ritual and the phases of the moon – all of which might be construed as witchcraft by those wishing to do so. Wise women have been identified in most periods of history. Hildegard of Bingen, for example, is well known as an eleventh-century nun who composed music, but she also wrote a treatise on the use of medicinal herbs.[96] However, the wise women (and occasionally men) and folk healers consulted by Scots remain largely anonymous, though their recommendations have passed down by means of the strong oral tradition of the time.

Toward the end of the seventeenth century the traveller, Martin Martin, made a journey of observation around the western islands of Scotland, taking detailed notes on many aspects of everyday lifestyle including superstitions and medical matters. He observed that in Shetland it was thought that long-distance charming could be effective, as there was:

> a charm for stopping excessive bleeding, either in man or beast, whether the cause be internal or external; which is performed by sending the name of the patient to the charmer, who adds some more words to it, and after repeating those words the cure is performed, though the charmer be several miles distance from the patient.[97]

Water was important in healing throughout the country, but it is easy to argue that remoteness perpetuated long-held superstitions. Martin notes one well where sick people would:

> make a turn sunways round it, and then leave an offering of some small token, such as a pin, needle, farthing, or the like, on the stone cover which is above the well. But if the patient is not likely to recover they send a proxy to the well, who

acts as above-mentioned, and carries home some of the water to be drank by the sick person. There is a little chapel beside this well, to which such as had found the benefit of the water, came back and returned thanks to God for their recovery.[98]

This demonstrates neatly the unproblematic juxtaposition of pagan and Christian ritual and elements of white witchcraft as part of the wider cosmology and healing process. Rain-water from hollows in gravestones was thought to be useful for dealing with warts, while people suffering from rickets in Wigtownshire were advised to wash in a burn at Dunskey.[99] In her work on charming, Joyce Miller has shown that water was by far the most important motif used.[100] What is also very interesting is that over the period the fascination with the curative powers of water was subsumed into elite culture, so that visits to healing spas such as Strathpeffer were a key part of the health tourism undertaken by wealthier Scots.[101] The combination of water with special objects was also central to folk healing. Enchanted stones, or stones dipped in healing water, were thought to be curative, and it was also believed in many areas that disease could be cured by transferring it to an object, such as a piece of cloth, which would be rinsed in healing water, or attached to a tree, so that the disease faded as the cloth degraded in the elements. These are illustrated in Figures 4.4 and 4.5, showing healing stones, and the 'clooty well at Munlochy'.

BREAKING THE MOULD – SEPARATION OF MENTAL AND PHYSICAL DISEASE

At the beginning of the period there was no real difference in the care of individuals suffering from mental or physical afflictions. The mentally-ill were accepted as 'different', or cursed in some way, but were still part of their everyday communities. By the mid-eighteenth century, some medical professionals began to take the view that mental illness had different causes from physical afflictions, and that those affected should be removed from society and cared for in institutions. There was also the question of changing perceptions on what was acceptable social behaviour. In most rural areas, an individual with learning problems or mental illness was viewed as eccentric or occasionally threatening, but still accepted as part of the community, whose members would normally protect the person from harm. By the end of the period, local cures and superstitions still held sway in rural areas, but in urban centres there was some attempt to provide medicalised explanations and treatment. This is all rather different from the treatment of mental illness in earlier times, which was referred to variously as melancholy, loss of sense, furiosity or possession. Then lunatics could be 'plunged into water wherein they were tossed about rather roughly'. They were then taken to the chapel of St Fillans, bound and left overnight. If the individual had managed to free himself by morning, 'hopes were entertained that he would recover

Figure 4.4 *Charming and healing stones used in Scotland, from various locations including Berwickshire, Ross and Cromarty and Kirkcudbrightshire. Source: © National Museums Scotland (www.scran.ac.uk).*

his reason'.[102] Joyce Miller describes similar treatments, which involved towing a sufferer behind a boat round an island in Loch Maree, before drinking water from a healing well – a process referred to as 'towing the loon'.[103] (Unexpected immersion was also tried in cases of tetanus, or lockjaw, and given the hydrophobia which was a major symptom in these cases, this was a drastic treatment.) The aim in all of these was clearly to shock the patient out of his or her state of un-sense and restore sense or 'right mind'.

The process of separating the mentally ill from their communities and the medicalisation of mental health care can be attributed to a number of possible causes. By the late eighteenth century more people were treated in hospitals for physical illnesses, thus instituting a key element of separation in the everyday treatment of disease in general. This separation reduced the role of the relatives and, indeed, of the patient, who had hitherto had a more active influence as 'agent' as well as patient.[104] The plans for the second Edinburgh Infirmary included restraining cells for the insane – this being the first part of the building to be completed. The situation was affected also by the growing numbers of medical men taking an interest in madness – perhaps the most famous being Andrew Duncan, whose proposal for a public lunatic

Figure 4.5 *The Clouty Well, Munlochy, dedicated to St Boniface. Pieces of cloth were hung around the well as a means of ensuring good health. It was believed that as the cloth disintegrated, so disease would disappear.* Source: © St Andrews University Library (www. scran.ac.uk).

asylum in Edinburgh came to fruition in 1807. Duncan had been particularly distressed at the conditions in which the poet, Robert Fergusson, had been kept in the Town Bedlam, and this stimulated his medical interest in mental illness.[105] This asylum was followed by similar institutions in Montrose, Aberdeen and Glasgow. These institutions were designated as asylums, not hospitals; but asylums for whom – the patients or the wider community, which would be rendered safe from embarrassment? Some of these institutions charged fees, and by 1820 the Dundee asylum had no fewer than six categories of patient, the fees ranging from 7 shillings to 3 guineas per week, indicating social stratification even within such a setting.[106]

The OSA respondent from Dumfries reported that insanity was an increasing problem in the town, and connected this to the opening of the Infirmary fifteen years previously, which had attracted 'a considerable number of persons unhappily labouring under both these disorders'. Some residents attributed this to the absence of warm summers which they remembered from half a century previously. The report also claims that the increasing numbers of 'lunatics' must be attributed to the presence of the hospital, which drew in patients from a wide area. There is an interesting question here as to whether the presence of a hospital altered the balance of attitudes toward individuals with mental illness, with the result that they were detached from family and community, and, importantly, labelled. A further possible reason for the upsurge in mental disorders is given as the 'excessive and increasing use of spirituous liquors amongst the lower ranks of people'.

This was one area of illness where it would seem that there was a distinctive urban/rural difference by the end of the period, a difference which was brought about by perhaps contradictory forces: advancing medical knowledge and Enlightenment freedom of thought, but also narrower parameters for what was considered to be acceptable behaviour. In this context, the upper ranks became more litigious in trying to have relatives declared insane and thus gain power of attorney over them and, of course, their assets – the social construction of madness was rather different at this level.[107] Specialisation in other areas of medicine took longer to develop, but the treatment of mental illness seems to have been one aspect which saw more rapid change. It goes without saying, though, that in remote, isolated areas, both the treatment of mental illness and the belief complex surrounding it changed much more slowly.

CONCLUSION

It seems clear that the everyday experience of physical illness, disease and pain was in many respects common throughout Scottish society, though there were regional and status variations. The prevalent philosophy meant that there was a strong common core to medical practice, both professional and lay, and the progress that was made during the second half of the eighteenth century in terms of elucidating the structure and function of the body did not lead to rapid change in treatments or offer more complex surgery, though more chemically-produced drugs were in use – these were rather slower to be adopted in Scotland than in England. Epidemic disease remained, but famine was generally less problematic. The circles of consultation were more demarcated by 1800, but it was still not the case that the everyday experience of illness or accident was fundamentally different for the elites of society from that of the so-called ordinary people. The knowledge and expertise claimed by 'legitimate' medical practitioners emerged, at least in major urban centres, as the medical orthodoxy, shedding some of the concentric layers of belief, superstition and folk medicine, but by no means all.[108] At the turn of the nineteenth century religion was still a key aspect of society, and fatalistic acceptance of illness, disease or pain remained part of the cosmology of un-health. Although Hamilton claims that the services

of qualified practitioners were available only to the elite, the evidence contra-
dicts this to a considerable extent.[109]

The everyday was thus a complex and changing combination of contrasts, continuities, convergences and commonalities. Health was a prime
concern for all, and there is considerable evidence to confirm the presence
of a common psychological attitude, or *mentalité*, in relation to matters
of everyday health and disease. The experience of health was modified by
factors, such as changing religious attitudes, the medicalisation of health (as
opposed to the philosophical, superstitions and religious sphere in which it
had resided for centuries), the changing nature of the consultation process,
the introduction of new drugs and the broader changes involved in demographic realignment and urbanisation, as well as the culture of print and
Enlightenment reason and empiricism. Nature was still at the heart of the
everyday, though, and the experience of illness and its treatment had many
common strands throughout Scottish society.

Notes

1. See, for example, L. Beier, *Sufferers and Healers. The Experience of Illness in
   Seventeenth-Century England* (London, 1987); R. Porter (ed.), *Patients and
   Practitioners. Lay Perceptions of Medicine in Pre-Industrial Society* (Cambridge,
   1985).
2. Full account in L. I. Conrad, M. Neve, V. Nutton, R. Porter and A. Wear,
   The Western Medical Tradition 800 BC–AD 1800 (Cambridge, 1995); see also R.
   Porter, *The Greatest Benefit to Mankind. A Medical History of Humanity from
   Antiquity to the Present* (London, 1997), pp. 6–8, 55–62, 73–7.
3. Edinburgh University Library (EUL), DC.8.130, *Ane Gude Boke of Medicines*,
   f6v–17r.
4. Full account of these and other plants in T. Darwin, *The Scots Herbal. The Plant
   Lore of Scotland* (Edinburgh, 1997).
5. For detailed account of the Enlightenment, see, for example, A. Broadie, *The
   Scottish Enlightenment. The Historical Age of the Historical Nation* (Edinburgh,
   2001).
6. H. M. Dingwall, *A History of Scottish Medicine. Themes and Influences* (Edinburgh,
   2003), pp. 102–3, 104–5.
7. J. D. Comrie, *History of Scottish Medicine* (London, 1932), i, p. 224.
8. H. M. Dingwall, *Physicians, Surgeons and Apothecaries. Medical Practice in
   Seventeenth-Century Edinburgh* (Edinburgh, 1995), p. 178.
9. Comrie, *History of Scottish Medicine*, pp. i, 202–22, D. Hamilton, *The Healers. A
   History of Medicine in Scotland* (Edinburgh, 1981), pp. 47–50.
10. Comrie, *History of Scottish Medicine*, pp. i, 218.
11. M. Flinn (ed.), *Scottish Population History* (Cambridge, 1977), p. 137; Hamilton,
    The Healers, pp. 47–8.
12. *Charters and Documents Relating to the Burgh of Peebles AD 1165–1710* (Scottish
    History Society, 1872), p. 398.

13. *The Statistical Account of Scotland* (OSA), Sir J. Sinclair (ed.), with new Introduction by M. Gray (Wakefield, 1981).
14. For assessment of the demographic impact of smallpox, see D. Brunton, 'Smallpox inoculation and demographic trends in eighteenth-century Scotland', *Medical History*, 32:4 (1996), 403–29.
15. OSA, vol. 7, p. 339.
16. B. Smith, 'Camphor, cabbage leaves and vaccination: the career of Johnnie "Notiones" Williamson, of Hamnavoe, Eshaness, Shetland', *Proceedings of the Royal College of Physicians of Edinburgh*, 28:3 (1998), 395–406.
17. Smith, 'Camphor, cabbage leaves and vaccination', p. 401.
18. Penicuik House, Clerk of Penicuik papers, GD18, 2129, 1696.
19. Penicuik House, Clerk of Penicuik papers, GD18, 2129, 1696.
20. Cullen and Smout note that episodes became much less frequent from mid-eighteenth century, but also that when they did occur, the effects were alleviated by better relief and improved agricultural techniques. L. M. Cullen and T. C. Smout (eds), *Comparative Aspects of Scottish and Irish Economic and Social History* (Edinburgh, 1977), p. 21.
21. Flinn (ed.), *Scottish Population History*, p. 148, table 3.4.1, demonstrating fewer baptisms in plague years.
22. Hamilton, *The Healers*, p. 95.
23. Hamilton, *The Healers*, pp. 239, 293, 296.
24. R. Floud, 'Medicine and the decline of mortality: indicators of nutritional status', in R. Schofield and D. Reher (eds), *The Decline of Mortality in Europe* (Oxford, 1991), pp. 146–57.
25. R. A. Houston, 'Writers to the Signet: estimates of adult mortality in Scotland from the sixteenth to the nineteenth centuries', *Social History of Medicine*, 8:1 (1995), 37–53.
26. D. H. A. Boyd, *Amulets to Isotopes. A History of Medicine in Caithness* (Edinburgh, 1998), pp. 14–15.
27. Boyd, *Amulets to Isotopes*, pp. 17–20.
28. OSA, vol. XIX, p. 126.
29. OSA, vol. II, p. 156; vol. VII, p. 340.
30. Edinburgh City Archive (ECA), Burgh Court Acts and Decreets, 13 November 1610.
31. A. Hamilton, *A Treatise of Midwifery Comprehending the Management of Female Complaints, and the Treatment of Children in Early Infancy* (London, 1781).
32. A. Wilson, *The Making of Man-Midwifery* (London, 1995), p. 66.
33. Midwives were licensed by Town Councils, though in Glasgow this function was performed by the Faculty of Physicians and Surgeons. J. Geyer-Kordesch and F. Macdonald, *Physicians and Surgeons in Glasgow. The History of the Royal College of Physicians and Surgeons of Glasgow 1599–1858* (Oxford, 1999), pp. 251–3. There is only a single instance of a midwife being examined by the Edinburgh Incorporation of Surgeons.
34. ECA, Burgh Court Acts and Decreets, 23 May 1672.
35. *Caledonian Mercury*, 16 April 1801.

36. M. H. Kaufman, 'Caesarean operations performed in Edinburgh during the eighteenth century', *British Journal of Obstetrics and Gynaecology*, 102 (1995), 186–91.

37. D. Buchan (ed.), *The Writings of David Rorie* (Edinburgh, 1994), pp. 79–80.

38. National Library of Scotland (NLS), Adv.MS.23.6.5, f35r.

39. The post of mediciner at King's College seems to have been a sinecure, though Gilbert Skene, appointed in 1556, wrote a treatise on the plague, deemed to be the first medical publication in Scots. M. Lynch and H. M. Dingwall, 'Elite society in town and country', in E. P. Dennison, D. Ditchburn and M. Lynch (eds), *Aberdeen before 1800. A New History* (East Linton, 2002), pp. 197–8.

40. Full account in H. M. Dingwall, *A Famous and Flourishing Society. The History of the Royal College of Surgeons of Edinburgh, 1505–2005* (Edinburgh, 2005).

41. Geyer-Kordesch and Macdonald, *Physicians and Surgeons in Glasgow.*

42. NLS, MS3774, p. 84.

43. This view is confirmed in relation to England by M. Pelling, *The Common Lot. Sickness, Medical Occupations and the Urban Poor in Early Modern England* (London, 1998).

44. R. Thin, 'Medical quacks in Edinburgh in the seventeenth and eighteenth centuries', *Book of the Old Edinburgh Club*, 22 (1939), 132–60.

45. *Caledonian Mercury*, 10–13 March 1710; 21 July 1726. Fuller coverage in H. M. Dingwall, '"To be insert in the *Mercury*": medical practitioners and the press in eighteenth-century Edinburgh', *Social History of Medicine*, 12:1 (2000), 40–2.

46. *Edinburgh Courant*, 6–8 August 1706.

47. E. A. Underwood, *Boerhaave's Men at Leyden and After* (Edinburgh, 1977).

48. F. A. Macdonald, 'Reading Cleghorn the clinician: the clinical case records of Dr Robert Cleghorn, 1785–1818', in C. W. J. Withers and P. Wood (eds), *Science and Medicine in the Scottish Enlightenment* (East Linton, 2002), pp. 255–79.

49. Withers and Wood (eds), *Science and Medicine*, pp. 260–1.

50. C. Lawrence, *Medicine in the Making of Modern Britain* (London, 1994), p. 3.

51. Comrie, *History of Scottish Medicine*, pp. ii, 450.

52. J. L. M, Jenkinson, M. S. Moss and I. F. Russell, *The Royal. The History of the Glasgow Royal Infirmary 1794–1994* (Glasgow, 1994), p. 11.

53. T. M. Devine and G. Jackson (eds), *Glasgow, Vol. I. Beginnings to 1830* (Manchester, 1995).

54. I. D. Levack and H. A. F. Dudley, *Aberdeen Infirmary. The People's Hospital of the North-East* (London, 1992).

55. G. Risse, '"Typhus" fever in eighteenth-century hospitals: new approaches to medical treatment', *Bulletin of the History of Medicine*, 59:2 (1985), 176–95.

56. ECA, Accounts for the Surgeon to the Poor, 1710.

57. *Edinburgh Advertiser*, 8–12 June 1787.

58. ECA, Accounts for Surgeon to the Poor, 1710.

59. P. Lowe, *The Whole Course of Chirurgerie: Wherein is Briefly Set Downe the Causes, Signes, Prognostications & Curations of All Sorts of Tumors, Wounds, Vlcers, Fractures, Dislocations & all Other Diseases, Vsually Practiced by Chirurgions, According to the Opinion of All Our Ancient Doctours in Chirurgerie* (London, 1597).

60. Porter, *Greatest Benefit*, p. 35.

61. Lowe, *Discourse*, p. 316.
62. NLS, MS 6502, Commonplace book of Sir John Wedderburn, f74. Advice was also given on diet and the most opportune time for bloodletting.
63. NLS, Adv.80.2.5, f175.
64. NLS, MS14636, ff23–6.
65. NLS, MS 5291, ff2r-6r.
66. M. Plant, *Domestic Life in Eighteenth-Century Scotland* (Edinburgh, 1952), pp. 24–5.
67. R. Porter 'The patient in England, *c.* 1660–1800', in A. Wear (ed.), *Medicine in Society: Historical Essays* (Cambridge, 1992), p. 97.
68. EUL, DC8.130, f54r.
69. EUL, DC8.130, f41r.
70. W. Buchan, *Domestic Medicine: or the Family Physician: Being an attempt to render the medical art more generally useful by shewing people what is in their own power both with respect to the prevention and cure of diseases. Chiefly calculated to recommend a proper attention to regimen and simple medicines* (Edinburgh, 1769). See also D. Lawrence, 'William Buchan', *Oxford Dictionary of National Biography* (Oxford, 2004–7).
71. Full coverage of this area in Withers and Wood (eds), *Science and Medicine*.
72. Buchan, *Domestic Medicine*, p. ix.
73. Buchan, *Domestic Medicine*, p. 38. He did, though, advocate cold baths as beneficial for children.
74. Buchan, *Domestic Medicine*, p. 124.
75. Buchan, *Domestic Medicine*, p. 212. Perhaps surprisingly, Buchan was in favour of amateur inoculators, believing that they would be under less restraint than qualified medical practitioners.
76. Buchan, *Domestic Medicine*, pp. 420–1. It was also noted that the patient should not eat meat or highly seasoned foods.
77. Buchan, *Domestic Medicine*, pp. 470–1.
78. M. Beith, *Healing Threads. Traditional Medicines of the Highlands and Islands* (Edinburgh, 1998).
79. S. Wilson, *The Magical Universe* (London, 2000), p. 316.
80. Wilson, *The Magical Universe*, p. 468.
81. A. Wear, 'Religious beliefs in early modern England', in H. Marland and M. Pelling (eds), *The Task of healing. Medicine, Religion and Gender in England and the Netherlands 1450–1800* (Rotterdam, 1996), p. 148.
82. NLS, SP2.90.201, *Old Galloway Recipes & Cures*, No. 2 (1730–40) (single card leaflet).
83. D. Buchan, *Writings of David Rorie* (Edinburgh, 1994), p. 45.
84. J. Bannerman, *The Beatons. A Medical Kindred in the Classic Gaelic Tradition* (Edinburgh, 1986).
85. H. C. Gillies (ed.), *Regimen Sanitatis. The rule of health. A Gaelic medical manuscript of the early sixteenth century or perhaps older: from the Vade mecum of the famous Macbeaths, physicians to the Lords of the Isles and the Kings of Scotland for several centuries* (Glasgow, 1911).

86. Gillies (ed.), *Regimen Sanitatis*, pp. 34–8.

87. Gillies (ed.), *Regimen Sanitatis*, p. 40.

88. Gillies (ed.), *Regimen Sanitatis*, p. 48. For fuller account of surviving Gaelic medical manuscripts, see Comrie, *History of Scottish Medicine*, pp. i, 92–104.

89. Bannerman, *The Beatons*, pp. 93, 95, 120.

90. A. Carmichael, *Carmina Gadelica. Hymns and Incantations Collected in the Highlands and Islands of Scotland in the Last Century* ([1910], Edinburgh, 1992), p. 160.

91. Carmichael, *Carmina Gadelica*, p. 413.

92. Beith, *Healing Threads*, pp. 84–5.

93. http://webdb.ucs.ed.ac.uk/witches/index.cfm?fuseaction=home.searchcase, Survey of Scottish Witchcraft database.

94. http://webdb.ucs.ed.ac.uk/witches/index.cfm?fuseaction=home.searchcase, 1618.

95. Wilson, *Magical Universe*, p. 340.

96. Porter, *Greatest Benefit*, p. 129.

97. M. Martin, *A Description of the Western Islands of Scotland circa 1695* (Edinburgh, 1999), p. 218.

98. Martin, *Description of the Western Isles*, p. 149.

99. L. Henderson, 'Charms, spells and Holy Wells. The repackaging of belief', *Review of Scottish Culture*, 19 (2007), 13–14.

100. J. Miller, 'Devices and directions. Folk healing aspects of witchcraft practice in seventeenth-century Scotland', in J. Goodare (ed.), *The Scottish Witch-Hunt in Context* (Manchester, 2002), p. 99. See also, J. Miller, 'Cantrips and carlins. Magic, medicine and society in the presbyteries of Haddington and Stirling, 1603–1638', unpublished Ph.D. thesis (University of Stirling, 1999).

101. A. Durie, 'Medicine, health and economic development: promoting spa and seaside resorts in Scotland c. 1750–1830', *Medical History*, 47:2 (2003), 195–216.

102. Comrie, *History of Scottish Medicine*, i, p. 88.

103. J. Miller, '"Towing the loon." Diagnosis and use of shock treatment for mental illness in early-modern Scotland', in H. de Waardt, J. M. Schmidt, H. C. E. Midelfort, S. Lorenz and D. R. Bouer (eds), *Dämonische Besessenheit: Zur Interpretation eines Kulturhistorischen Phänomens* (Bielefeld, 2005).

104. Porter, 'Patient in England', p. 91.

105. Fuller accounts in A. Duncan, *Short Account of the Rise, Progress and Present State of the Lunatic Asylum at Edinburgh* (Edinburgh, 1812); D. K. Henderson, *The Evolution of Psychiatry in Scotland* (Edinburgh, 1964).

106. R. A. Houston, 'Institutional care for the insane and idiots in Scotland before 1820: Part II', *History of Psychiatry*, 12 (2001), 12.

107. R. A. Houston, *Madness and Society in Eighteenth Century Scotland* (Oxford, 2000) – though most of the statistical detail is drawn from the early decades of the nineteenth century.

108. Dingwall, *History of Scottish Medicine*, pp. 102–3.

109. Hamilton, *The Healers*, p. 31.

Chapter 5

Necessities: Food and Clothing in the Long Eighteenth Century

Stana Nenadic

INTRODUCTION

The eighteenth century saw the everyday experience of ordinary Scots transformed from one of basic struggle for survival – marked by famines in the 1690s, when as many as a fifth of the population died in some northern areas[1] – to unprecedented plenty in food and clothing by the end of the century. There were short run crises, as in 1739–41 and again in 1782–3, but as demographers have shown, perhaps the greatest long-term indication of improvement in the basic necessities of life was reflected in falling death rates, particularly among infants, due to better feeding for mothers and their babies.[2] The greater height of ordinary Scots when compared with similar populations in England also suggests a generally well-fed population by the end of the century, though this advantage was to vanish in the nineteenth century.[3] The common experience was still one of uncertainty and poverty, but as observed by many commentators in the 1790s, 'there is a considerable alteration to the better, within these 20 years, in dress, manner of living, houses, etc.'.[4]

The necessities of life in the form of food and clothing are timeless human preoccupations. Most people in eighteenth-century Scotland spent most of their time working to provide the means of getting their basic food and clothing. In relative terms, the costs of housing and fuel were a lesser priority. Of course, the manner in which people acquired their food and clothing changed greatly over the century. In 1700, when subsistence conditions prevailed in many parts of the country, most foodstuffs were grown and consumed locally, often exchanged with neighbours for other commodities or as payment for work, with only limited commercial purchase through markets and fairs. Clothing was also locally produced from cloth made in great houses and cottages throughout the country. By 1800, although some local clothing manufacture survived and many rural folk still produced some elements of their own food, much of what was consumed or worn by Scots was commercially produced, increasingly imported from elsewhere in Britain or from abroad and purchased for cash from market stalls or shops.

There are several fine studies of food supply and diet in eighteenth-century Scotland.[5] The Industrial Revolution, which was first and foremost a revolution in textile manufacture, has also been the focus of much scholarly endeavour.[6] This chapter is concerned with food and clothing not as economic phenomena, but as social entities which were the product of changing cultures in Scotland, a focus for everyday social practices, a source of identity and part of a material world to which subtle social and even political meanings were attributed.[7] The political dimension of clothing was famously seen in Scotland at this time, for one of the only pieces of legislation in modern Britain to address the issue of clothing and identity was that concerning the wearing of tartan and plaid, passed after the Jacobite rebellion of 1745 in order to outlaw visible statements of loyalty to a dangerous political cause.[8] The politics of food was also contentious, particularly following the Act of Union when 'English' taxes on such basic commodities as salt and malt caused mass protests.[9]

The creation of a modern Scottish identity invested in its food and clothing was a product of eighteenth-century changes, which included growing numbers of English visitors who were struck by the distinct material cultures that prevailed north of the border and described them in print. The Scottish involvement in empire forged new habits of eating and dressing, some of them surviving to the present day. The century witnessed the flowering of a national celebration of Scottish food and clothing, seen, for instance, in the poetry of Allan Ramsay in the 1720s, whose 'Tartana: or, the Plaid' was a defence of traditional Scottish women's dress against French fashions.[10] And there was Robert Burns at the end of the century, whose 'Ode to the Haggis', compared the robust Scottish peasant, 'haggis-fed', with the 'spindle shank', fed on ragout and fricassee, who 'looks down wi' sneering, scornfu' view, on sic a dinner'.[11] The Enlightenment and new ideas of politeness shaped the clothing and foodways of elites, and late-eighteenth-century gentleman antiquarians debated long and hard over the 'true' character of Scottish dress and cuisine. Most ordinary people had little interest in such controversy. Their concerns tended to focus on keeping warm and getting enough food to support a life of mostly outdoor physical labour.

BASIC CONCERNS IN THE FIRST HALF OF THE EIGHTEENTH CENTURY

At the start of the eighteenth century, Scotland was similar to many northern European countries in being pre-modern in the character of much of its textile and food production. Home-spun and woven cloth made from sheep wool dominated clothing, and home-grown grain dominated food. Oats, which were easily produced in Scotland, provided, on average, three-quarters of the calories of ordinary Scots.[12] Oats were consumed as oatmeal and as oat bread. Meal was made into 'pottage' or porridge, by boiling in water, and was served in various forms and consistencies, hot or cold, with ale, or butter or milk. Sometimes it was served with fish and vegetables.[13] All classes of society had 'pottage' for their breakfast in the early eighteenth century, and the various ways of serving porridge survived among the working population into the nineteenth century. The same was true of oat bread and oatcakes, which were made to local recipes and graced even the most fashionable urban tables.

Early-eighteenth-century labouring people were often partly paid in oatmeal. According to Edmund Burt, an English soldier in Inverness in the 1720s, many households employed live-in teenage girls to do the housework and spinning 'at the wages of three half crowns a year each, a peck of oatmeal for a week's diet; and happy she that can get the skimming of a pot to mix with her oatmeal for better commons'.[14] Oatmeal was so ubiquitous that it was often not even mentioned in household accounts. In the Eglinton family house book, which details food purchases and daily menus for a wealthy Ayrshire family and their servants from 1733 to 1742, no mention is made of breakfast, though dinners and suppers were noted, and there is no record of oatmeal being consumed, though this would have appeared in some form at virtually every meal. On a typical day (8 October 1742) the family were served with 'hare broth, boiled beef and roast hens' for dinner, which was a midday meal, with 'roast pigeons, cold roast hens, turnip and eggs' for supper. It is likely that the lady of the household, the widowed Lady Eglinton, had some hand in the preparation of the food.[15] The only record of the servants' meals was the 'eggs' that they got for dinner, though on Sundays they also routinely ate both broth and beef. Other types of foods consumed in this household in October 1742 included cabbage broth, celery soup, herrings, collops (beef) and many different dishes of pigeons, including fricassee and ragout. Most was locally sourced and seasonal.[16]

Even the relatively privileged consumed vast and regular quantities of oatmeal. Students, mostly teenage boys of middling or genteel family, at St Andrews University in the 1730s were given a diet that was dominated by oatmeal, eggs and ale. For breakfast, they had a third of a ten-ounce oatmeal scone with a mutchkin of ale (about three-quarters of a pint) to wash it down. Dinner, the main meal of the day, comprised half an oatmeal scone, a mutchkin and a half of ale, and a dish of broth with a portion of beef, mutton, veal or chicken. If fish was served for dinner, it was accompanied by 'sapps', that is, wheat bread soaked in ale. Supper consisted of another half of scone, more ale and three eggs. As with servants in the Eglinton household, the Sabbath was marked with additional food for the students, who were given broth with meat for their supper on Sundays.[17] This regime provided almost 3,000 calories, mostly from the meal and ale, was high in protein and calcium, but like many Scottish diets was low in vitamins.[18]

Edmund Burt in Inverness in the 1720s provided a detailed account of the foods that were available in that northerly town for those with the money to buy it. The principal diet of the garrisoned English officers comprised salmon and trout from the river, hens and eggs, along with game birds and hares. But for much of the year they hankered after beef, mutton, veal and lamb, which was highly seasonal. They had plenty of 'roots and greens' from local market gardens and the manner of presenting food was very much in the French style, with heavy sauces, which Burt did not care for. Butter was the main fat used in cooking and lemons and sugar were always available in town, but when he travelled through the Highlands while undertaking his work as a military surveyor, the only foods that were available to buy from cottagers were oatmeal and eggs.[19]

In the first half of the eighteenth century ordinary Scots commonly enjoyed milk, butter and cheese. There was fish in some places, salt meat was available for many and a small amount of fresh meat was an occasional luxury.[20] The everyday experience of food was inevitably limited to the basics, but special occasions were celebrated with food and drink that was out of the ordinary in both quantity and range. An idea of the sorts of food that might be prepared and consumed by labouring people to mark a special event is given by Allan Ramsay in his poem *The Gentle Shepherd*, first published in 1725 and set among ordinary cottagers in the southern uplands. The feast organised by Glaud and his wife to mark the home-coming of the master, comprises two adult sheep from their own flock, one boiled and one roasted, ale, 'good cakes', that is oat cakes and haggis, made from the innards of the sheep, all prepared within the household.[21] A feast in a grander setting, this time in the Highlands, to celebrate the birth of a child, comprised:

> a great pyramid o' hens at the tap o' the table, an' anither pyramid o' ducks at the fit, an' a muckle stoup fu' o' posset [milk curdled with wine] i' the middle, an' aw kinds o' sweeties doon the sides.[22]

Highland funerals were similarly marked with elaborate foods, though those in the Lowlands were more modest affairs. As noted by Burt at one great funeral in the 1720s, there were 'several pyramids of plum cake, sweetmeats, and several dishes, with pipes and tobacco', along with wine and whisky in vast quantities.[23] Though women did not attend such funerals, they did make the food and organised the great displays, which was a conventional aspect of all elaborate hospitality. And they also got their share of the good things, for according to Burt, 'on the conclusion, some of the sweetmeats are put into your hat or thrust into your pocket, which enables you to make a great compliment to the women of your acquaintance'.[24]

If oatmeal dominated the diet in the first half of the eighteenth century, then the basic textile for clothing was home-spun, home-woven woollen cloth made from home-raised sheep. Like oatmeal, a piece of woollen cloth could be used in many different ways, and was worn by rich and poor alike. Most men in Scotland, like James Mork, candlemaker in Edinburgh, who died in 1720 (see Appendix) owned clothing that comprised a jacket or coat,

Figure 5.1 *John MacLeod and his wife, 1811. Poor and elderly highland peasant couple of c. 1800. Their simple and unstructured garments are home-made and inadequate for the climate. The man is shoeless. Source: © Gaidheil Alba/National Museums of Scotland (www.scran.ac.uk).*

breeches and a 'vest', or waistcoat – all woollen – with a flat round bonnet for the head.[25] The relatively well off had stockings, shirts, shoes, a hat and a wig, and, perhaps most important of all, a greatcoat. The latter had a high collar, fitted waist and full skirt reaching below the knees, with broad turned-up cuffs and big patch pockets with flaps on each side, sufficient to carry food and valuables. Men's clothing was mostly dull-coloured and practical, but, for those who could afford it, was embellished with buckles and buttons, sometimes made of silver, or with lace, including silver and gold lace for special occasions.

Women's basic clothing consisted of a close fitting bodice and loose skirt, an ensemble that was technically known as a mantua, but was called 'a gown' in Scotland, with a loose shift or petticoats underneath, the latter sometimes quilted for warmth.[26] As can be seen in the Appendix, some older women at the start of the century still wore stomachers, a flat, stiff panel at the front of a bodice. Women's clothing was more complex than that of men, and came in greater quantities and variety of names and fabrics, which included coloured silks for the well off. But they were less likely to wear shoes than their men folk and they did not wear wigs. Their over-garments were more flexible than those of men, with scarves and aprons and cloth head coverings rather than hats. The most important protective outer garment was often described as a 'plaid'.

The plaid was a striking aspect of clothing in Scotland, a survival from ancient times that continued to be worn throughout the eighteenth century and beyond. It was a garment made out of a single piece of cloth, draped about the body in various ways and held in place with pins, broaches, buckles or belts, some of these of high value or antiquity. The importance and value of this type of clothing was located in the fabric, which was often highly coloured, and in its interpretation and use by the wearer, for there was no cutting or design involved. In Highland areas it was known as the 'arisaid' when worn by women, or the belted plaid when worn by men, but it was not unique to the Highlands, for the plaid was a standard item of clothing for women throughout the country, and men in Lowland areas, particularly those involved in work with sheep, commonly wore a plaid over their jacket and breeches.[27]

Edmund Burt provides a contemporary description of the 'arisaid' in the 1720s:

> The plaid is the undress [informal dress] of the ladies; and to a genteel woman who adjusts it with a good air, is a becoming veil . . . It is made of silk or fine worsted, chequered with various lively colours, two breadths wide, and three yards in length; it is brought over the head, and may hide or discover the face according to the wearer's fancy or occasion; it reaches to the waist behind; one corner falls as low as the ankle on one side; and the other part, in folds, hangs down from the opposite arm.[28]

This type of dress was employed to give subtle social signals, much like a modern Indian sari today. It could indicate political allegiances according to which way it was draped, and in church it was pulled over the face by degrees to indicate the spiritual concentration of the wearer – though some ministers complained that this habit was merely to mask the fact that women were sleeping during their sermons.[29] Inventories for the early decades of the eighteenth century suggest that women of all social backgrounds routinely wore the 'arisaid', or plaid (see Appendix). Sophia Pettigrew, the widow of an Edinburgh vintner, who died in 1718, had two 'Glasgow plaids' in her extensive wardrobe, one described as 'the best'. And Agnes Wilson, a flesher's widow who died in 1740, also owned two plaids, one of silk and one of worsted wool. The garment went out of fashion among elites in the middle decades of the century, though London-produced political prints of the 1760s still show it being worn by Scots women to signal their national identity, suggesting that even though it was no longer current, it remained a part of a popular visual language in Britain.[30] Among labouring women, the piece of cloth worn as a shawl and as a protective working garment, continued to be worn into the nineteenth century.

Men in the Highlands also wore the plaid as their principal outer clothing,

A Lady in the Highlands of Scotland

The Plaid which is part of this Drefs, is a Piece of chequered Silk or Woollen Stuff of about three Yards long and two Breadths wide; the Lady generally difpose of it in such a manner as to reach the Waist behind, to let one Corner fall as low as the Ancle on one Side, and the other hang in Folds over the oppofite Arm.

Figure 5.2 *Arisaid worn by a gentlewoman, early eighteenth century. The shawl-like plaid was worn as an outer garment. They were valuable items, often of tartan design, though some were plain coloured. They were made of wool or wool and silk mixes and could be draped according to complex conventions to suggest political affiliation or flirtatious intent. Source: © Gaidheil Alba/National Museums of Scotland (www.scran.ac.uk).*

as was described in 1769 by Thomas Pennant, the antiquarian tourist, at an Inverness fair:

> A most singular group of Highlanders in all their motly dresses. Their *brechcan*, or plaid, consists of twelve or thirteen yards of narrow stuff, wrapt round the middle, and reaches to the knees: it is often fastened round the middle with a belt, and it is then called *brechcan-feill*; but in cold weather, is large enough to wrap round the whole body from head to feet . . . It is frequently fastened on the shoulders with a pin often of silver, and before with a brotche . . . which is sometimes of silver, and both large and extensive; the old ones have very frequently mottos. The stockings are short . . . the *cuaran* is a sort of laced shoe made of skin with the hairy side out, but now seldom worn. The *truis* were worn by the gentry, and were breeches and stocking made of one piece . . .[31]

Pennant also noted the wearing of the *feil-beg*, or little kilt, a constructed garment and 'modern substitute for the lower part of the plaid'. He went on to observe, 'almost all have a great pouch of badger and other skins, with tassels dangling before. In this they keep their tobacco and money.' Yet we

know from others that most men in the Highlands, even at the start of the
century, did not dress in this way. Here is Burt, again describing the population of Inverness in the 1720s:

> The gentlemen, magistrates, merchants, and shopkeepers are dressed after the
> English manner, and make a good appearance enough according to their several
> ranks, and the working tradesmen are not very ill clothed.[32]

The source and manufacture of clothing was complex. In the early eighteenth century, much of it was made at home from home-spun fabrics, either
by women in the household or by male tailors, some based in towns and
others who travelled a regular country circuit and made more complex clothing for men and women alike. Even among the aristocracy, some elements of
their clothing were made from woollen cloth woven on their estates.[33] But not
all clothing was new. Used clothing was given to servants and other workers
as payment or gifts from their masters and mistresses. Cut down or remade
clothing was seen in all sections of society. Indeed, most surviving clothing
artefacts from this period show evidence of frequent remaking or 'turning',
and this was also mentioned in descriptions of clothing in personal inventories, as in the case of Francis Wood, merchant and soap manufacturer, who
died in Edinburgh in 1759 and owned '4 suits of old body cloathes, all turned
but an upper coat' (see Appendix). There was also a robust and growing
market for second-hand clothes, particularly associated with country peddlers
and women clothing merchants operating in the bigger towns and cities.[34]

Clothing and food cultures could vary considerably across the different
regions of Scotland, partly determined by environment and work, but also
reflecting distinctive local fashion systems. The latter are hard to uncover
since they tended to be known only by the participants and were rarely
recorded. An English example probably reflected what also prevailed in
Scotland. A buckle-maker, James Gee, travelled from Dublin to Walsall
looking for work in the 1760s, wearing a smart cocked hat of which he was
proud, but was obliged to put this aside in favour of a more old-fashioned
round hat with brim, in order to be accepted into his new community.[35] In
this case the clothing was not associated in any particular way with the work
culture of Walsall, it was simply the 'custom of the place' to wear such hats.
In other instances the work was important, as seen among east coast merchants with regular contacts with Europe, who dressed in a more opulent
style than was usual among other Scots of similar status, and furnished their
houses likewise in a manner that was typical of merchants on the continent.[36]
Their communal identities were built on links that crossed oceans. This was
also true of some fishing communities of the north, as in Shetland, where
fisherman dressed in a distinctive waxed protective outer garment called a
'gansey', which was buttoned down the back to keep their under garments
dry and was of a style that had spread from Guernsey in the Channel Islands
through much of coastal Britain.[37]

Figure 5.3   *Shetland fishermen in traditional clothing, back-fastened protective working clothing made of oiled canvas, of a type that was found in all areas of coastal Britain by the early nineteenth century. The young woman, in common with women, and sometimes also men, in wool-producing areas, is busy knitting as she goes about her daily round. Source: © Shetland Museum (www.scran.ac.uk).*

Many parts of Scotland had distinctive food ways, little known to outsiders, and some communities concentrated on the commercial processing of certain foods. One that thrived in the early and middle decades of the eighteenth century was goat's whey production for the benefit of elite health and leisure tourists. The towns of Duns and Moffat in the Borders made a speciality of goat's whey to complement their mineral water springs. Certain inns in the Highlands were also famous for goat's whey. It was regarded as the best antidote to the effects of excessive alcohol consumption, but went out of fashion in the 1760s.[38]

CLOTHING AND FOOD AS CULTURAL SYMBOLS

The social systems that clothing and food comprised conveyed subtle symbolic messages, some specific to Scotland, others in evidence throughout Britain and Europe. As we have seen, gentlemen in the Highlands in the early century sometimes wore Highland clothing, but many dressed in Lowland styles, which did not go unnoticed. Burt in the 1720s noted the following:

Upon one of my peregrinations, accompanied by a Highland gentleman, who was one of the clans through which I was passing, I observed the women to be in great anger with him about something that I did not understand; at length, I asked wherein he had offended them? Upon this question he laughed, and told me his great-coat was the cause of their wrath; and that their reproach was, that he could not be contended with the garb of his ancestors, but was degenerated into a Lowlander, and condescended to follow their unmanly fashions.[39]

Perhaps with concern for local opinion in mind, some Highland gentlemen, including Colin Campbell of Glenure in the 1740s, wore different clothes in the Highlands to those they wore when visiting the Lowlands.[40] The Highland gentry were particularly associated with luxury in their clothing according to one late-eighteenth-century commentator, John Ramsay of Ochtertyre:

> The dress of our gentry resembled in some particulars their domestic economy. It was in general plain and frugal, but upon great occasions they scrupled no expense . . . It was the etiquette, not only when they married, but also upon paying their addresses, to get laced clothes and laced saddle furniture – an expense which neither suited their ordinary appearance nor their estates. No people formerly went deeper into that folly than the Highland gentry when they came to the low country.[41]

These observations were certainly reflected in the clothing purchases of Colin Campbell of Glenure, which included fine plaids and gold lace supplied by an Edinburgh merchant.[42]

Tartan and plaid assumed remarkable significance when they came to be associated with the aspirations of the Jacobites. The Proscription Act of 1746 was an attempt to outlaw a symbol of dangerous political challenge, though it seems many who were charged with its policing were anxious to accommodate the realities of life in a poor area where ordinary men and women could not afford to replace their clothing. This is how the legislation was interpreted by James Erskine, sheriff depute for Perthshire, writing to his sheriff substitute at Killin:

> You may take all the opportunities you can of letting it be known that tartan may still be worne in cloaks westcoats, breeches or trews, but that if they use loose plaids they may [be] of tartan but either all of one colour, or strip'ed with other colours than those formerly used, and if they have a mind to use their old plaids, I don't see but they may make them into the shape of a cloak and so wear them in that way, which tho' button'd or tied about the neck, if long enough, may be taken up at one side and thrown over the other shoulder by which it will answere most of the purposes of the loose plaid. And if they could come in to the way of wearing wide trowsers like the sailor's breeches it would answere all the conveniences of the kilt and philibeg for walking or climbing the hills.[43]

Those who commented on the passing of the Highland plaid and philibeg were not always that interested in the politics of the matter. A gentlewoman poet, Margaret Campbell, an Argyllshire minister's wife who wrote in Gaelic, was more concerned with the aesthetics of masculinity than the Stuart cause when she noted that Highland women were being denied the sight of their men folk's naked legs.[44]

One of the most important features of clothing in eighteenth-century Europe was the accumulation of large quantities of white garments in the form of shirts and shifts, handkerchiefs, petticoats and aprons. White clothing – either linen or cotton – was a mark of status and wealth because it required constant laundering, which was costly in servants.[45] It was also changed frequently, sometimes several times in a day, as a way of maintaining hygiene.[46] When young Roderick Random, in Tobias Smollet's eponymous novel of 1748, left Scotland for London to seek his fortune as a ship's surgeon, he described:

> my whole fortune consisting of one suit of cloaths, half a dozen ruffled shirts, as many plain, two pair worsted stockings, as many thread; a case of pocket instruments, a small edition of Horace, Wiseman's surgery, and ten guineas in cash.[47]

Working men and women could not afford to maintain white clothing and their labouring lifestyles rendered it impractical most of the time. Yet for special occasions there were white sleeves and neckpieces that could be worn by labouring men – and women could put a square of white cloth around their shoulders as a scarf. This is how the social subtleties of shirts in Scotland in the early eighteenth century were described in the 1790s:

> The poorer class of farmers, tradesmen and day labourers, some of whom did not aspire to the luxury of a shirt, commonly wore sarges [smocks] either grey, or tinged by a hasty blue. The richer class of farmers . . . contented themselves with a hardened [hemp] shirt; the collar and wrists of which were concealed at kirk and market by two pieces of linen, called *neck* and *sleeves*.[48]

And here is the cottager Glaud, in Allan Ramsay's *Gentle Shepherd*, who in celebration of the arrival of his master, calls to his wife; 'Gae get my Sunday's coat; wale out the whitest of my bobbit bands, my white-skin hose, and mittans for my hands.'[49]

As hinted by Ramsay, who was a wig-maker by training, most clothing cultures tend to focus on the extremities of head, hands and feet to symbolise broader concerns. Burt in the 1720s famously linked the primitive state of Highland society to the observation that most Highland women, including gentlewomen, carried their shoes and walked barefooted.[50] *The Gentle Shepherd* suggests another aspect of footwear, this time among men, which signalled wealth and a cosmopolitan identity. The young man Patie has come into good fortune and leaves his rural community for life in Edinburgh, London and Paris. When he returns, he intends to 'come hame strutting in my red-heeled shoon'.[51] Red high-heeled shoes signified that a young man had been on the Grand Tour of Europe, where, particularly in France, there was legislation to restrict their wearing to men of courtly status.[52] Shoes with high heels, which were worn by men and women alike, also indicated a lifestyle that required limited outdoor walking. Even in big towns, pavements were rare before the 1770s and to walk down the street required protective overshoes – either clogs or patterns – particularly for women, whose shoes were often made of fabric.[53]

Patie's red-heeled shoes also highlight the importance of colour and in particular red for special or high status clothing. Young women of fashion wore scarlet cloaks, as indicated in the inventory of Joan Robins, wife of a weaver in Glasgow, who died in 1760 (see Appendix). In Glasgow mid-century the wealthy tobacco lords, a business clique with a well-developed sense of their own importance, were said by contemporaries to have a regular promenade at the 'cross', 'which they trod in long scarlet cloaks and bushy wigs'.[54] In addition to their clothing, the wigs of these Atlantic merchants were also very distinct. Through much of the eighteenth century gentlemen and well-paid labouring men wore wigs to signal their propriety and respectability. Wigs were costly to buy and also required wig powder for dressing, to keep them white and free from infestations, which was expensive because it was taxed.[55] As a symbol of the elite, wigs were sometimes targeted by mobs, as in the 'levelling' disturbances of the early eighteenth century. For a man to loose his wig, or go wigless in public was to invite ridicule. This is indicated by John Galt in his comic novel of local political life in the eighteenth century, *The Provost*, when the whole town council, in a state of drunkenness following a celebratory dinner, are persuaded to burn their wigs as a statement of loyalty. Only Provost Pawkie, the narrator, saves face by sending home for his spare wig:

> It was observed by the commonality, when we sallied forth to go home, that I had on my wig, and it was thought I had a very meritorious command of myself, and was the only man in the town fit for a magistrate . . .[56]

Food and drink also carried powerful symbolic messages. Edward Topham's, *Letters from Edinburgh*, published in 1776, included many descriptions of food. He referred in disparaging terms to a special meal comprising haggis, 'a display of oatmeal, and sheep's liver and lights', with 'cocky-leaky', a broth comprising a chicken boiled with leeks. There was also a sheep's head and a 'Solan goose'. The latter had a 'strong, oily, unpalatable flavour', but there were other 'Scottish dishes' that he did enjoy, including 'cabbi-clow', 'barley-broth' and 'friars chicken':

> The first is cod-fish salted for a short time, and not dried in the manner of common salt-fish, and boiled with parsley and horse-radish. They eat it with egg sauce, and it is extremely luscious and palatable. Barley-broth is beef stewed with a quantity of pearl barley and greens of different sorts; and the other is chicken cut into small pieces, and boiled with parsley, cinnamon, and eggs in strong beef soup.[57]

He went on to remark, 'plenty of good claret and agreeable conversation made up other deficiencies'.[58] Many observed the heavy drinking culture that prevailed in Scotland, even among elite women:

Figure 5.4 *Gravestone of John Milne, master baker, and his five children, Arbroath churchyard, 1778. Gravestones provide an useful source of information on Scottish clothing and food. In this example, representations of bakery equipment and oatcakes are used for decorative effect. Source: © Royal Commission on the Ancient and Historical Monuments of Scotland; AN/6556 (www.scran.ac.uk).*

> During the supper, which continues for some time, the Scotch Ladies drink more wine than an English woman could well bear; but the climate requires it, and probably in some measure it may enliven their natural vivacity.[59]

The traditional basic foods of Scotland often figured symbolically in popular rituals. One that was described by several Highland ministers writing for the *Statistical Accounts* (OSA) was the Beltane festival of 1 May:

> It is chiefly celebrated by the cow-herds, who assemble by scores in the fields, to dress a dinner for themselves, of boiled milk and eggs. These dishes they eat with a sort of [oat] cakes baked for the occasion, and having small lumps in the form of nipples, raised all over the surface.[60]

At the other end of the social spectrum the prominence in Scottish cuisine of exotic fruits was also remarked. These were grown in hothouses, which were more common than elsewhere in Britain owing to the cheapness of coal in Scotland, and supplied most gentlemanly households with melons, grapes and particularly pineapples.[61] The pineapple was frequently represented in eighteenth-century Scottish design and architecture and was even celebrated in a remarkable building in Stirlingshire, the Dunmore Pineapple, a summer house in a great walled garden, built in 1761 by the earl of Dunmore, which still survives.

IMPACT OF NEW PROSPERITY AND FASHION

With rising prosperity in Scotland in the second half of the eighteenth century, clothing was increasingly likely to be purchased ready-made, particularly for men and boys, through shops in towns, where clothiers supplied coats and jackets, shirts and stockings, hats, boots and shoes to increasingly standardised sizes.[62] With regard to shoes, for which there is good contemporary data, this meant on average two pairs of shoes per year.[63] Change was evident even in the Highland districts, such as Dowally in Perthshre, for which the following observations, comparing the character of clothing in 1778 with 1798, were made:

> Then, there was not a hat worn by any of the tenants or their servants; now, there are many. Then, there was not one black cap; now, all the women wear them. Then, the gowns of the women were camblet [wool/silk] and their aprons woollen; now, the gowns are of printed linen, and the aprons of white muslin. Then, many of the men wore the philibeg; now, there are none who do so. Then, in short, the whole articles of the dress of the people were home-made, excepting their bonnets, and a few shoes; now, they are all bought from the merchants of Dunkeld.[64]

Not only was the clothing of ordinary people likely to be shop bought, it was increasingly made from non-Scottish materials that conveyed a fashionable image:

> The dress of all the country people in the district was, some years ago, both for men and women, of cloth made of their own sheep wool, Kilmarnock or Dundee bonnets, and shoes of leather tanned by themselves . . . Now every servant lad almost, must have his Sunday's coat of English broad cloth, a vest and breeches of Manchester cotton, a high crowned hat, and watch in his pocket.[65]

Clothing fashions in Scotland, as elsewhere, were increasingly influenced by new ideas of politeness. Adam Petrie, author of the first Scottish conduct book, published in 1720, which was mainly directed at young men, gave clear directions on what was proper for indoor use and for wearing out of doors.[66] Notions of working clothing among labouring people became increasingly differentiated from those of genteel status. As elite women retreated from the kitchen and dairy they abandoned the wearing of aprons. As elite young men increasingly flocked to join the army, military styles of dress, including the hessian or leather riding boots of cavalry officers, became fashionable. By the end of the eighteenth century the fact that so many of the ordinary people could afford to be dressed in styles of clothing that were once the preserve of elites, at least for their Sunday best, meant that 'the gentry can only be distinguished from plebeians by their superior manner, and by that elegant simplicity in dress which they now admire'.[67] In short, ostentation in quantity and range of clothing had been replaced by the principle of 'less is more', especially when the 'less' was signalled by exclusive design and expensive fabrics, such as the embroidered muslin favoured by women.

Conduct books also gave advice on polite ways of eating and changing fashions in meal times. A proliferation of tableware for serving food and drink was a new mark of status, which meant that communal drinking vessels or bowls, once common in all layers of society, were increasingly associated with poverty. The gradual shift in the genteel dinner hour from midday at the start of the century to early evening by the end also differentiated the polite classes from those whose hard physical labour required them to take a solid meal in the middle of the working day. That meal was increasingly likely to be based on market-bought foods. The commercialisation of food production and the evolution of a British market for grain gave rise to anxieties about the availability and price of basic foods in local markets that was often expressed through local rioting, particularly in port towns.[68] But most descriptions of late-eighteenth-century Scottish markets noted the growing regularity of supplies of all commodities and particularly of fresh meat. Of Wigton in the south-west, for instances, it was remarked in the 1790s:

> Though the practice of salting up meat is still continued, both in the town and country, yet beef and mutton are now almost constantly sold in the market, and all who can afford it, eat fresh meat though the whole course of the year.[69]

It was the same in Crieff, in the southern Highlands, where there was a 'weekly market on Thursday for all kinds of butchers meat, poultry, butter, cheese etc'.[70] The availability of a better range of foods impacted on children at local parish schools:

> In 1760, children at school had a piece of pease bread in their pockets for dinner. In 1790, children at school have wheaten bread, sweet milk, butter, cheese, eggs and sometimes roast meat.[71]

These Forfar children were now regular consumers of bakery-made wheaten bread made from grain transported from other parts of Britain or even abroad. The shift in the Scottish diet towards new grains and new types of shop-bought bakery took place among the rich in the big towns before it reached the ordinary people in country districts, as shown in a bill of 1744 that was presented to 'My Lord Justice Clark', an Edinburgh judge, by James Aitken a merchant in the city. The bill reveals that both oatmeal and wheaten flour were purchased by the household every three or four days, but the family also bought shortbread and French rolls from the same merchant, who operated a bakery business.[72] By the later eighteenth century a Wigton minister could observe the impact of this change in taste and supply of basic foodstuffs even in his own small town:

So little wheat bread was used in the town of Wigton, about 40 years ago, that one baker could not find sufficient employment; whereas the use of it is now become so general, that there are four or five bakers in town, by each of whom a consider-able quantity is sold.[73]

Yet the commercialisation of food supply also had negative conse-quences, for it meant that among the very poor there was pressure to sell the little luxuries that they might previously have consumed at home, to make much needed cash to purchase other commodities and pay their rents. In many areas, including Dunlop in Ayrshire, specialised high quality cheese production evolved among cottagers who never tasted their own produce, but sent it all to market. This was one of the reasons why for some there was an increase in the regularity of food consumption, but a decline in the range of foods and in the nutritional value.[74] Behind the following description by Pennant of an Inverness fair in 1769, there were many Highland families with increasingly dreary diets:

> The commodities [at the fair] were skins, various necessaries brought in by the Peddlers, coarse country cloths, cheese, butter and meal: the last in goat-skin bags; the butter lapped in cawls, or leaves of the broad *alga* or tan . . .[75]

One of principal sources of evidence about the impact of new prosperity and fashion on the food and clothing of the ordinary people was the OSA, penned in the 1790s on a parish-by-parish basis by Church of Scotland ministers in response to questions posed by the editor. Inevitably reflect-ing the preoccupations of clergymen, some of the changes were reported in moralising terms, while others were exaggerated to reflect well on the parish. Among the many trends that were widely reported were changes in the wages received by servants, which now routinely included one or two pairs of shoes per year rather than oatmeal. Another was seen in the gradual shift in the diet of the poor from grains to potatoes. The following budget for an ordinary labouring family with four small children in the parish of Gaitney, Dumfriesshire, offers an insight to modestly comfortable clothing, including the notion of Sunday clothes, and a growing range of foods. But oatmeal was still the largest single expenditure, comprising about a third of the annual budget.

	£ s d
House rent, including a small garden and potato-ground	1 9 0
1 ½ stones of oat meal a week, at 1s. 8d. the stone	6 10 0
Milk and butter a week, 1s.	2 12 0
Tea and sugar a year	0 15 0
Soap, candles and salt, etc.	0 15 0
Tear and wear of Sunday clothes	1 0 0
A working jacket, vest, breeches, shirts, stockings, clogs handkerchief, and hat, for the man	1 12 0

A bed gown, petticoats, shirt, stockings, clogs,		
handkerchief, and cap for his wife	1	0 0
A new vest, breeches, etc. for each of the four		
children at at 10s. each suit	2	0 0
School wages for two of the children	0	12 0

Total annual expenses £18 14s.

The minister who recorded this budget went on to remark:

> The annual expenses exceed the man's annual earning [by] £1 16s.; but the deficiency may be made up by the wife's industry, as she generally works in hay time and harvest, by which she may earn about £1, at an average, and by spinning the remainder of the year, may earn about 1s. a week, besides doing the business of her family. When potatoes are a good crop, there will be a saving in the article of oat-meal, which is generally expended in purchasing better clothes or a little butchers meat.[76]

Another budget for a labouring family with a similar income in Perthshire, made no reference to tea or sugar, but included 'cheese, bacon, or other meat' as a regular, if small, expenditure. It also noted that 'the garden, dressed by the man in the mornings and evenings, affords them cabbages, greens and potatoes'.[77] These budgets clearly represented the ordinary working population in the most favourable situations. For the sick, the elderly and widows – and most working people encountered such circumstances at some stage in their life – a capacity to furnish the basic necessities of life was diminished.

IMPACT OF THE EMPIRE

The integration of modern Scotland into a growing British empire, and the movement of people back and forth to far-flung places defined the identity of Scots and shaped their food and clothing cultures. The rise in the use of cotton for the clothing of ordinary men and women was as important as the impact of cotton manufacturing processes on their experience of work. In all parts of Scotland by the 1790s, ministers reported that women wore printed cotton gowns along with cotton thread stockings and muslin aprons and men wore cotton shirts and stockings. Even wealthy women, like Mrs Margaret Colville, widow of a merchant who died in Edinburgh's New Town in 1801, owned cotton clothing alongside their costly silks (see Appendix). Cotton was cheap, colourful, easy to wash and maintain and easily mixed with other fibres such as wool and silk. It represented a revolution in the dress and hygiene of ordinary Scots.[78]

Another impact of empire on the clothing of the Scots was seen in the formalisation of clan tartans, which evolved in conjunction with the militarisation of the Highlands post-1745 and the empire service of so many Highland regiments. Regimental tartans with their clan associations had become fashion fabrics by the later eighteenth century, worn by men and women alike and spawning a modern manufacturing industry. This was signalled by Donald McPherson, tailor in Inverness, when he wrote to Messrs William Wilson of Bannockburn, a notable firm of tartan weavers, 'send me good quality fine tartan as it is intended for the wear of Ladies who are desirous to dress in the uniform plaids of their husbands'.[79] Highland regimental garb was even said by one well informed contemporary, David Stewart of Garth, writing in the 1820s, to have influenced women to abandon the cloth pocket, a detachable pouch, worn among the petticoats for keeping money and other valuables, in favour of the leather purse, worn on the wrist or a belt, which was modelled on the sporran.[80]

The influence of empire on the 'nabobs', wealthy East India officials who returned to Scotland with exotic clothing and cuisine, was commonly satirised in Scottish novels of the early nineteenth century.[81] The colonial merchants of Glasgow, who imported the foods and textiles of empire, were famously brash and extravagant in their dress, as revealed in the following description of the scene in Glasgow's Exchange Coffee House in the early nineteenth century:

> Here was to be seen the counting-house blood, dressed in a box-coat, Belcher handkerchief, and top boots, or leather gaiters, discoursing . . . about brown sugar and genseng! Here was to be seen the counting house dandy, with whalebone stays, stiff neckcloth, surtout, Cossacks, a spur on his heel, a gold-headed cane on his wrist, and a Kent on his head, mincing primly to his brother dandy some question about pullicat handkerchiefs . . .[82]

One cannot help but feel that William Alexander, a young merchant's clerk, who died in Edinburgh in 1792, with his 'cassimir yellow breeches' and 'silk tartan waistcoat', as detailed in the Appendix, was another 'counting house dandy'.

Glasgow's colonial merchants were also famous for their vast dinners and elaborate hospitality. J. G. Lockhart described one such occasion: 'The dinner was excellent, although calculated, apparently, for forty people rather than for sixteen, which last number sat down.' The meal included 'fowls in curry; everything washed down by delicious old West India Madeira'. After the meal the serious masculine drinking was of rum punch, made in 'the china', a decorated porcelain bowl, out of sugar, lemons and limes, rum and hot water.[83] But this conspicuous influence of empire on the food ways of the rich was nothing new. As early as the 1720s, the agricultural reformer, William Macintosh of Borlum, reflected with regret on changing dining habits:

> Where I saw the table served in Scots clean fine linen, I see now Flemish and Dutch diaper and damask. And where with two or three substantial dishes of beef, mutton and fowl, garnished with their own wholesome gravy, I see now served

up several services of little expensive ashets, with English pickles, yea Indian mangoes, and catch-up [ketchup] or anchovy sauces . . .[84]

Even in the remote Highlands the store cupboard of a minor laird in 1752 included dried raisins, bottled fruit, anchovies, sugared almonds, spices, sugar and tea, along with great quantities of claret, port, rum and brandy, not to mention the locally produced whisky, cider and ale.[85] And James Boswell in 1773 was impressed by a meal he was served at Coirechatachan on Skye, the home of an elderly tacksman:

> We had for supper a large dish of minced beef collops, a large dish of fricassee of fowl, I believe a dish called fried chicken . . ., a dish of ham or tongue, some excellent haddocks, some herrings, a large bowl of rich milk, frothed, as good a bread-pudding as I ever tasted, full of raisins and lemon or orange peel, and sillabubs made with port wine and in sillabub glasses. There was a good table-cloth with napkins; china, silver spoons, porter if we chose it, and a large bowl of very good [rum] punch.[86]

Exotic imported foods were often used in elaborate household displays alongside fine glass and tableware.[87] Sugar with lemons or limes were ingredients in the distinct puddings and pastries that featured in contemporary cook books, and the sweet tooth of modern Scots can probably be traced to Glasgow where there was a relatively prosperous labouring population who adopted sugary foods because they were locally fashionable and available cheaply in the city. Fashionable drinking habits also impacted on ordinary men and women. The most important was tea, which was encouraged by government because it was easily taxed. Adopted in rich households from the later seventeenth century, it was a drink for all classes, and particularly for women, by the mid-nineteenth century. Even in remote parts of the Highlands in the first half of the eighteenth century, peddlers carried small packs of tea, along with imported tobacco and snuff, for sale to the locals.[88] The popularity of tea initially caused controversy in Scotland, not only because of the cost and the fashionable English associations, but also because of its feminine and leisured connections and the impact on more masculine, indigenous drinking habits. To quote William Macintosh of Borlum in 1729:

> When I came to my friend's house of a morning I used to be asked if I had my morning draught yet? I am now asked if I have had my tea? And in lieu of the big quaigh with strong ale and toast, and after a dram of good, wholesome Scots spirits, there is now the tea-kettle put to the fire, the tea-table and silver and china equipage brought in, and marmalade and cream.[89]

The tea party was the most important female-directed occasion for sociability and hospitality in eighteenth-century genteel and middle rank households.[90] Light food, particularly sweet pastry, was often offered with tea, valuable household objects such as tea china were put on display and poets, including Allan Ramsay in the 1720s, wrote poetry for reading and discussion over tea.[91] Tea drinking could take place at any time of the day and became the form of hospitality most likely to be offered to unexpected visitors. Gentlewomen also served tea to females of lesser status than themselves, such as their dressmaker, the wives of tenant farmers or trusted servants.

Tea has limited nutritional value, but it offered a little domestic luxury and it is not surprising that it was widely adopted as the beverage of choice by working-class housewives. Many ministers writing for the OSA in the 1790s highlighted the new role of tea in the changing budgets and social practices of ordinary Scots. But they were also critical of the 'debilitating' impact where it replaced 'pottage' for breakfast.[92] Even some ordinary men and women had their doubts about tea drinking. In Gargunnock near Stirling the following was noted: 'Tea is universally used. Even the poorest families have it occasionally, and the last cup is qualified with a little whisky, which is supposed to correct all the bad effects of the tea.'[93] In tea drinking, as in all aspects of food and clothing, the necessities of life were shaped by social practices of sometimes surprising complexity.

APPENDIX

Clothing inventories recorded at death

(1) James Mork, Candlemaker in Edinburgh, died in 1720 (National Archives of Scotland: Edinburgh Commissary Court Register of Testaments, 1 May 1718–22 February 1721: C8/8/87, p. 361):

> 2 coats
> 1 vest
> 1 pair of breeches
> a big coat and tartan geron
> a hatt and wigg
> 2 pairs of stockings
> 1 pair of shoes
> 1 pair of silver buckles.

(2) James Lawrie, Flesher in Edinburgh, died in 1740 (National Archives of Scotland: Edinburgh Commissary Court Register of Testaments, 24 December 1739–18 November 1840: CC8/8/103, p. 149):

> 3 suits of cloathes
> 5 shirts
> 5 stocks and 6 cravats
> 2 pairs of shoes and pair of silver buckles

3 pairs of stockings
hatt and wigg.

(3) James Baird, Painter in Edinburgh, died in 1780 (National Archives of Scotland: Edinburgh Commissary Court Register of Testaments, 5 January. 1780–27 December 1780: CC8/8/125/1, p. 1):

thread suit of body clothes
great coat much used
round hat
6 shirts and 6 stocks
6 pairs of stockings
2 pairs of shoes
1 pair of shoe and knee metal buckles
pinchbeck watch.

(4) William Alexander, sometime clerk to George Leslie, Merchant in Edinburgh, died in Nicholson Street, Edinburgh, 1792 (National Archives of Scotland: Edinburgh Commissary Court Register of Testaments, 3 January 1792–19 June 1793: CC8/8/129/1, p. 14):

great coat much wore
coat, green, in good order
coat, drab
stripped waistcoat
silk tartan waistcoat
white cotton waistcoat
light stripped waistcoat
pair of cassimir yellow breeches
pair of black breeches
2 pair of nankeen breeches with drawers to one
2 flannel under waistcoats
4 plain shirts
11 ruffled shirts
6 stocks
2 new neck cloths
4 flannel foot socks
red worsted night cap
4 pairs of white silk stockings
1 pair of coloured silk stockings
6 pairs of thread and cotton stockings
3 pairs of worsted stockings
1 pair of blue cotton stockings
old hat

pair of boots
silver watch and seal
pinchbeck oval ring.

(5) Sophia Petticrew, relict of Thomas Caddell, Vintner in Edinburgh, died
1718 (National Archives of Scotland: Edinburgh Commissary Court Register
of Testaments, 1 May 1718–22 February 1722: CC8/8/87, p. 52):

twilted black killimankie petticoat
light coloured silk and worsted gown with lemon coloured persian lining
stripped and flowered killimankie petticoat
Glasgow plaid, the best
black serge apron
blue and red serge petticoat
another Glasgow plaid, the worst
masquered gown lined with black serge
black masquered petticoat
black killimankie apron
fine black cloth petticoat
old dark coloured rocolar
blue and white apron
pair of stays and stammagor
pair of shoes
night cap
21 coarse clothes, laced and plain
black short ruffled silk apron
4 laced mutches
2 musline pinnons with lace
plain muslin hood
suite of damask head cloathes
½ muslin napkin with lace
cambrick napkin
stripped muslin hood
another plain muslin hood.

(6) Agnes Wilson, relict of Andrew Matheson, Flesher in Canongate,
Edinburgh, died 1740 (National Archives of Scotland: Edinburgh Commissary
Court Register of Testaments, 24 December 1739–18 November 1840:
CC8/8/103, p. 35):

old silk gown
2 silk and worsted gowns
3 washing gowns
1 druggat and 1 manky gown

a flaming gown and apron
4 twilted petticoats
2 smock petticoats
2 rocolas
1 silk and 1 worsted plaid
shirts, headcloths, handkerchiefs
3 pairs of stockings
2 pairs of shoes
3 pairs of clogs
6 plain rings, 2 stone rings, gold locket with beads.

(7) Joan Robins, wife of Robert Nivisson, weaver in Glasgow, died in 1760 (National Archives of Scotland: Glasgow Commissary Court Register of Testaments, 7 July 1757–19 February 1761: CC9/7/63, p. 220):

3 silk gowns
scarlet cloak
silk cloak
2 dozen shirts
2 pairs of stays
2 silk hats
fur typpet
2 twilted coats
12 mutches
1 pair of ruffles
10 aprons
10 napkins
2 pairs of shoes
2 rings
silver broach
silver breast and shoe buckles.

(8) Jean Scott, widow of John Cleghorn, Brewer in Edinburgh, died 1792 (National Archives of Scotland: Edinburgh Commissary Court Register of Testaments, 3 January 1792–19 June 1793: CC8/8/129/1, p. 17):

3 silk gowns
1 printed gown [cotton]
13 petticoats
12 small jackets
10 shirts
5 aprons
34 caps
6 pairs of stockings

6 handkerchiefs
13 napkins
4 pairs of pockets
4 cloaks
6 fans
2 ribbons.

(9) Mrs Margaret Colville, relict of Andrew Colville, Merchant, of 43 George Street, Edinburgh, died 1801 (National Archives of Scotland: Edinburgh Commissary Court Register of Testaments, 2 January 1801–30 December 1801: CC8/8/132, p. 83):

black bombazene gown and petticoat
2 black cotton gowns
1 black satin quilted petticoat
4 white dimity petticoats
2 pairs of pockets
12 shifts
10 pairs of stockings, some thread and some worsted
12 neck handkerchiefs
black silk handkerchief
black silk apron with crape
12 white pocket handkerchiefs
8 coloured pocket handkerchiefs
12 night caps
3 white bed gowns
black silk bonnet and cloak with crape
black satin cloak lined with fur
English shawl
clasped gold watch and jewel.

Notes

1. R. E. Tyson, 'Famine in Aberdeenshire, 1695–1699: anatomy of a crisis', in David Stevenson (ed.), *From Lairds to Louns: Country and Burgh Life in Aberdeen, 1600–1800* (Aberdeen, 1986), pp. 32–51.
2. M. Flinn (ed.), *Scottish Population History from the Seventeenth Century to the 1930s* (Cambridge, 1977).
3. R. Floud, K. Wachter and A. Gregory, *Height, Health and History; Nutritional Status in the United Kingdom, 1750–1890* (Cambridge, 1990), p. 73.
4. John Sinclair (ed.), *The Statistical Account of Scotland (OSA)*, 21 vols (Edinburgh, 1791–9), vol. 2, p. 494, Kinnell, County of Forfar.
5. A. J. S. Gibson and T. C. Smout, *Prices, Food and Wages in Scotland, 1550–1780* (Cambridge, 1995).

6. Alastair J. Durie, *The Scottish Linen Industry in the Eighteenth Century* (Edinburgh, 1979).

7. For background to this approach, see, Amy de la Haye and Elizabeth Wilson (eds), *Defining Dress: Dress as Object, Meaning and Identity* (Manchester, 1999).

8. John Telfer Dunbar, *A History of Highland Dress* (Edinburgh, 1962), ch. 4.

9. Christopher A. Whatley, *The Scots and the Union* (Edinburgh, 2006), ch. 9.

10. Dunbar, *Highland Dress*, pp. 98–9.

11. James Currie, *The Works of Robert Burns*, 4 vols (Montrose, 1816), vol. 3, p. 166.

12. Gibson and Smout, *Prices*, table 7.1.

13. Gibson and Smout *Prices*, p. 227.

14. Edmund Burt, *Letters from the North of Scotland* (Edinburgh, 1998), p. 49.

15. Stana Nenadic, *Lairds and Luxury: the Highland Gentry in Eighteenth Century Scotland* (Edinburgh, 2007), ch. 6.

16. National Library of Scotland (NLS), MS.15913.

17. William Croft Dickinson, *Two Students at St. Andrews, 1711–1716: Edited from the Delvine Papers* (Edinburgh, 1952), pp. lzvi–lxvii.

18. Gibson and Smout, *Prices*, table 7.2.

19. Burt, *Letters*, p. 65.

20. Gibson and Smout, *Prices*, ch. 7.

21. Allan Ramsay, *The Gentle Shepherd, a Pastoral Comedy*, 2 vols (Edinburgh, 1808), vol. 2. p. 539.

22. Susan Ferrier, *Marriage, a Novel* (Edinburgh, 1818), p. 287.

23. Burt, *Letters*, p. 119.

24. Burt, *Letters*, p. 119.

25. David Kuchta, *The Three Piece Suit and Modern Masculinity* (Berkeley, CA, 2002).

26. Avril Hart, 'The mantua: its evolution and fashionable significance in the seventeenth and eighteenth centuries', in Hay and Wilson (eds), *Defining Dress*.

27. Dunbar, *Highland Dress*, ch. 6.

28. Burt, *Letters*, p. 48.

29. Dunbar, *Highland Dress*, p. 95.

30. Lewis Walpole Library Digital Collection.

31. A. J. Youngson, *Beyond the Highland Line: Three Journals of Travel in Eighteenth Century Scotland. Burt, Pennant, Thornton* (London, 1974), p. 151.

32. Burt, *Letters*, p. 48.

33. Nenadic, *Lairds and Luxury*, ch. 7.

34. E. C. Sanderson, 'Nearly new: the second-hand clothing trade in eighteenth-century Edinburgh', *Costume*, 31 (1997), 38–48. John Styles, 'Clothing the North: the supply of non-elite clothing in the eighteenth-century North of England', *Textile History*, 25:2 (1994), 139–66.

35. John Styles, 'Custom or consumption? Plebian fashion in eighteenth century England', in Maxine Berg and Elizabeth Eger (eds), *Luxury in the Eighteenth Century: Debates, Desires and Delectable Goods* (Basingstoke, 2003), pp. 103–18.

36. William Mackay (ed.), *Letter Book of Bailie John Steuart of Inverness* (Edinburgh, 1915).

37. Engraving, Shetland Museum. SCRAN Image: 000-000-563-921-C.

38. Henry Grey Graham, *The Social Life of Scotland in the Eighteenth Century*, 2 vols (London, 1900), vol. 2, p. 217.

39. Burt, *Letters*, p. 235.

40. National Archives of Scotland. (NAS), GD170/314. Campbell Family of Barcaldine Papers, accounts for clothing and tailoring.

41. John Ramsay, *Scotland and Scotsmen in the Eighteenth Century*, 2 vols (Edinburgh, 1988) vol. 2, p. 83.

42. Nenadic, *Lairds and Luxury*, ch. 7.

43. NAS, GD170/1213. Campbell of Barcaldine family papers, letter from James Erskine to Duncan Campbell of Glenure, 22 November 1748.

44. Ronald Black, *An Lasair: Anthology of 18th Century Scottish Gaelic Verse* (Edinburgh, 2001), p. 189.

45. See, Daniel Roche, *The Culture of Clothing: Dress and Fashion in the Ancien Regime* (Cambridge, 1994).

46. See, G. Vigarello, *Concepts of Cleanliness. Changing Attitudes in France Since the Middle Ages* (Cambridge, 1988).

47. Tobias Smollet, *The Adventures of Roderick Random* (Oxford, 1969), p. 31.

48. OSA, vol. 21, p. 143.

49. Ramsay, *Gentle Shepherd*, p. 540.

50. Burt, *Letters*, p. 235.

51. Ramsay, *Gentle Shepherd*, p. 588.

52. Georgio Riello, *A Foot in the Past: Consumers, Producers and Footwear in the Long Eighteenth Century* (Oxford, 2006), p. 63.

53. Peter McNeill and Georgio Riello, 'The art and science of walking: gender, space and the fashionable body in the long eighteenth century', *Fashion Theory*, 9:2 (2005), 175–204.

54. James Cleland, *Statistical Facts Descriptive of the Former and Present State of Glasgow* (Glasgow, 1837), p. 39.

55. See, *Eighteenth-Century Studies*, (2004), 38:1 Special Edition, 'Hair'.

56. John Galt, *The Provost* (Oxford, 1982), p. 72.

57. Edward Topham, *Letters from Edinburgh* (London, 1776), p. 161.

58. Topham, *Letters*, pp. 157–61.

59. Topham, *Letters*, p. 67.

60. OSA, vol. 5, p. 84, Logierait, County of Perth.

61. Topham, *Letters*, p. 229.

62. Beverly Lemire, 'Developing consumerism and ready-made clothing in Britain, 1750–1800', *Textile History*, 15:1 (1984), 21–44.

63. Riello, *A Foot in the Past*, pp.18–22.

64. OSA, vol. 20, p. 480, Dowally, County of Perth.

65. OSA, vol. 10, p. 245, Cluny, County of Aberdeen.

66. Adam Petrie, *Rules of Good Deportment or of Good Breeding for the Use of Youth* (Edinburgh, 1720).

67. OSA, vol. 21, p. 144.

68. C. A. Whatley, 'The Union of 1707: integration of the Scottish burghs: the case of the 1720 food riots', *Scottish Historical Review*, 78 (1999), 192–218.

69. OSA, vol. 14, p. 482, Wigton, County of Wigton.
70. OSA, vol. 9, p. 595, Crieff, County of Perth.
71. OSA, vol. 5, p. 227, Mains of Fintry, County of Forfar.
72. NLS, MS16871, f.171.
73. OSA, vol. 14, p. 482, Wigton, County of Wigton.
74. Gibson and Smout, *Prices*, pp. 242–3.
75. Youngson, *Beyond the Highland Line*, p. 151.
76. OSA, vol. 9, p. 527, Graitney, County of Dumfries.
77. OSA, vol. 9, p. 502, Caputh, County of Perth.
78. Beverly Lemire, *Fashion's Favourite: the Cotton Trade and the Consumer in Britain, 1660–1800* (Oxford, 1991).
79. Dunbar, *Highland Dress*, p. 201.
80. David Stewart, *Sketches of the Character, Institutions and Customs of the Highlanders of Scotland* (Inverness, 1885), p. 94.
81. They were stock characters for both John Galt and Susan Ferrier.
82. J. G. Lockhart, *Peter's Letters to his Kinsfolk*, 3 vols (Edinburgh, 1819), vol. 3, pp. 169–70.
83. Lockhart, *Peter's Letters*, vol. 3, pp. 172–3.
84. William Macintosh, *Essay on Ways and Means for Inclosing, Fallowing, Planting etc.* (Edinburgh, 1729), p. 229.
85. NAS, GD170/329, Campbell Family of Barcaldine Papers, inventory of Glenure House, Argyll, 1752.
86. James Boswell, *Journal of a Tour to the Hebrides with Samuel Johnson* (New York, 1936), p. 120.
87. See, Stana Nenadic, 'Middle rank consumers and domestic culture in Edinburgh and Glasgow, 1720–1840', *Past and Present*, 145 (1994), 122–56.
88. Stana Nenadic, 'The Highlands of Scotland in the first half of the eighteenth century: consuming at a distance', *British Journal for Eighteenth Century Studies*, 28 (2005), 215–28.
89. Macintosh, *An Essay*, p. 231.
90. Elizabeth Kowaleski-Wallace, *Consuming Subjects: Women, Shopping and Business in the Eighteenth Century* (Columbia, NY, 1997), pp. 19–36.
91. Allan Ramsay, *The Tea-Table Miscellany: or, a Collection of Choice Songs, Scots and English* (Glasgow, 1753).
92. OSA, vol. 12, p. 55, Coldingham, County of Berwick.
93. OSA, vol. 18, p. 121, Gargunnock, County of Stirling.

Chapter 6

Communicating

Bob Harris

INTRODUCTION

Early modern Scotland, along with the rest of the British Isles and much of Europe, saw far-reaching changes to technologies and means of communicating, notably through the growing reach of print in its myriad and proliferating forms, but also through the increasing habit and practice of letter writing. Communication between individuals across Scotland (and indeed between Scotland and places well beyond its borders) quickened, as well as increased, owing to improvements in transport – new and better roads, and also sea traffic – the continuing and often growing mobility of large sections of the population and the growth of postal, carrier and coach services. Yet, for all these undoubted and often very important changes, much of the following chapter might equally well be written around the themes of slow evolution, the mutual dependencies of print and oral cultures, and the continuing centrality in many contexts of the spoken word. Scotland in 1800 remained a society in which many vital elements of communication were oral. This was the case, moreover, not just in the Highlands or rural areas, but also in the fast-growing towns of the later eighteenth century. The market place and the churchyard and church door, the doorway, close and street were still, as they had been in 1600, pre-eminent sites of public and much private communication, and towns continued, as they had done for centuries, to act as nodal points in circuits of communication which were formed in the main by personal interaction and mobility, by people moving to and from, within and through towns for different, although frequently overlapping, reasons. Print and other forms of written communication, such as letters, became infused into this set of realities and habits rather than transforming them.

LANGUAGE AND ACCENT

However, our starting point must be language, the basis of written and verbal communication. In contemporary European terms, early modern Scotland was linguistically relatively united.[1] The salient word is relatively, however; language played a central role in this period in dividing Scots, by area and region, by social rank and, increasingly, by age.

Gaelic had since at least the sixteenth century attracted the opprobrium of the Lowlander, and extirpating its use had become towards the end of that century an important element of state-sponsored efforts, albeit these were intermittent in effect, to impose civility and loyalty on the Highlander.[2] The decline of Gaelic was long-standing, being especially marked in areas which spanned the Highland–Lowland border. The main causes were two-fold: commercial pressures – the language of commerce was English; and population mobility – as a result both of temporary and permanent migration. In the eighteenth century, the pace of the decline accelerated. The main reason, apart from the continued operation of the causes already mentioned, was education.[3] In 1709 the Scottish Society for the Propagation of Christian Knowledge (SSPCK) was established in Edinburgh. Emerging out of the Reformation of Manners movement which had taken root in the capital from 1699, the SSPCK sought to establish schools in the Highlands which taught only in English, the language of civilisation and loyalty, as well as commerce.[4] Although their teachers did not always share the parent body's anti-Gaelic purism, this policy was reaffirmed in 1723, and even tightened in 1750, when it was ordered that children should speak English to the complete exclusion of Gaelic in school and also when playing around school premises. The mid-1750s, however, saw a sudden shift in attitudes, with the SSPCK commissioning its own Gaelic New Testament in 1754 – a work which eventually appeared in 1767 – and from 1766 Highland schoolmasters were allowed to 'teach their scholars to read both Erse and English'. The basic goal remained the same, however, to 'wear out' the use of Gaelic and ensure the supremacy of English. Over time, the effect of these policies was, in areas where such schools were established, to entrench and widen a generational divide along language lines. In 1794, the minister of Comrie, Perthshire recorded: 'The common language of the people is Gaelic. All the natives understand it; but many, especially the old, do not understand English well. All the young people can speak English.'[5] Within fast-expanding towns of the later eighteenth century, the linguistic division between the generations could prove starker still. In these places, a new generation of Highland descent were born who spoke and, it seems, commonly only understood English, while their parents spoke only Gaelic.[6]

Outside the Highlands, prior to the eighteenth century most people probably continued to speak in vernacular Scots or English spoken with a broad Scots accent.[7] Incorporating union with England, however, made speech, specifically speech in English, a much more urgent matter, creating strong pressures for cultural assimilation with an English metropolitan culture which threatened to achieve, even if it did not actually do so, hegemonic status in the eighteenth century. How one spoke became a vexed issue, which was all the more vexed because it was so singularly bound up with unwanted feelings of provincialism. As part of the same process, speech became freighted with new social, as well as national cultural, significance, in that it also became an important badge of civility among elite men and women. The elder Sheridan, who sent the Edinburgh Moderates into such a frenzy of hope and anxiety when he arrived in 1761 to deliver his lectures on elocution, argued that what he termed 'court pronunciation' was no less 'than a sort of proof that a person has kept good company'; 'rusticity of accent' was at any event definitely to be avoided.[8] Whether much beyond a narrow social stratum, people's speech began to change under the impact of becoming British (as well as Scottish) and aspiring to polite manners is difficult to say. Although it has been asserted that, 'English rather than Scots became the tongue of Scotland's landed, professional and aspirant mercantile classes',[9] pronounced Scots accents continued to be commonplace, even in the second half of the eighteenth century. In 1757, James Buchanan declared that Scottish English was that 'rough and uncouth brogue which is so harsh and unpleasant to an English ear'.[10] Even Scots who succeeded at the very heart of the British state and empire – Henry Dundas, to take the most obvious example – did not relinquish their native pronunciation.[11] In Scotland, coarseness of manners and a broad Scots accent presented no impediment to Robert McQueen, Lord Braxfield, rising to the top of the legal establishment. The Lord Chief Justice may have become a source of embarrassment in official circles for his conduct in political trials in 1793 involving radicals, but the accent in which he delivered his extreme anti-radical pronouncements in open court was not the problem.[12] In elite circles, talking with a pronounced Scots accent could become a defiant badge of age, as the Whig lawyer, Henry Cockburn, was to recall in the middle of the nineteenth century in relation to 'a singular race of excellent Scotch ladies'.[13]

How one spoke also no doubt depended significantly on context and to whom one was speaking. James Boswell continually swithered about whether he should pursue a career at the English bar, and immerse himself permanently in his beloved London, but felt peculiarly self-conscious about the Scottish tone of his pronunciation.[14] In 1794, he was disappointed at his son, Sandy's, 'loud familiarity of manner' and 'very broad pronunciation', habits picked up while studying law at the University of Edinburgh.[15] John Ramsay of Ochtertyre summed up the uneasy linguistic equilibrium which prevailed toward the end of the eighteenth century in the following terms:

> Besides the colloquial Scotch spoken in good company, there was likewise the oratorical, which was used by judges, lawyers and clergymen, in their several departments. In this, perhaps, there was greater variety than in the other; but it may be concluded, that such as wished to excel in their public appearances, strove to bring their speeches or sermons some degrees nearer pure English than their *ordinary talk* (emphasis added).[16]

As Ochtertyre's remarks imply, even among the elite the common result was a 'tempered medium', a form of spoken English distinctly inflected by Edinburgh or Scottish norms.[17] This presumably is what Boswell spoke.

Polishing away provincialism was a British and not merely a Scottish pre-occupation in the eighteenth century, while the drive for linguistic and grammatical standardisation was a feature of a number of European countries in the early modern period.[18] The broader effect was for language and accent to become ever more strongly a marker of social rank and social aspiration. Language, it has been remarked, was 'a vehicle of communication and excommunication'; and to a greater extent than hitherto this was becoming true during this period.[19] A hierarchy of forms of speech was one of the early modern era's strongest contributions to a more class-based society, something underlined by the fact that throughout the seventeenth and eighteenth centuries, and indeed some way beyond that, Scots continued to be the native tongue among the lower orders in the Lowlands, and Scottish dialects continued to be strongly regional. James Beattie, the Aberdeen professor, who had a keen interest in such things, claimed to be able to 'know by his speech, a native of Banffshire, Buchan, Aberdeen, Dee-side, Mearns, Angus, Lothian and Fife, as well as of Ross-shire and Inverness'.[20] Scotland was yet to become a unified nation at least at the popular level, but comprised a dense patchwork of communities divided by language and different ways of acting and perceiving.

LITERACY

If how one spoke served, increasingly, as a powerful badge of social identity, literacy created another set of divisions. The precise location of these is, none the less, elusive. As Brian Ward Perkins has written recently in a very different context, but in terms which can be applied equally well to early modern Scotland: 'it will never be possible to come up with reliable figures for the number of people comfortable with literacy, let alone provide a nuanced view of what level of literacy they had attained'.[21] In default of the existence of such figures, historians have focused on the ability to write one's name, partly because this has left obvious traces in the historical record. Defined in this way, literacy levels have been shown to correlate strongly with the rural–urban divide, social status and gender. By the end of the seventeenth century a majority of the male population were able to sign their names (one estimate puts this as high as 75 per cent in the 1710s), while female literacy was significantly lower (at 25–30 per cent).[22] Within individual communities, distinctions were even more fine-grained, depending on trade and occupation, as well as place of residence.[23]

Being able to write, however, was not the same thing as being able to read. There is plenty of evidence that reading was often taught before writing, through, for example, women teaching children to read in the home often using the Bible. This means that figures such as those cited above almost certainly misrepresent levels of literacy, especially so in relation to women.[24]

How, then, did most people learn to read? In the first place, this was at parish or burgh schools. The seventeenth century saw the development of a network of parish and burgh schools, partly funded by landowners and burghs and partly by fees.[25] By the early 1690s, in the eastern Lowlands and the southern and eastern Highlands, most parishes (perhaps around 90 per cent) had an official school and a schoolteacher. While this network was probably weakened by the effects and disruptions of the famines of the second half of the 1690s, renewed efforts were made to ensure provision in the aftermath of further legislation in 1696.[26] Beneath and around these official establishments there developed a large number of private schools in towns and rural areas, the rise of which also suggest the existence of a genuinely popular desire for literacy in this period. Parents frequently clubbed together to hire a schoolteacher, as occurred in the later eighteenth century in the Links, an area on the outskirts of Montrose.[27] By contrast, in the central and western Highlands provision of schooling remained very patchy, reflecting, on the one hand, the very slow and uneven penetration of that region by the kirk state and, on the other hand, cultural separation and distance.

Although information on what school was like for most people is scant, we do know that in rural areas schooling had to fit around the seasonal rhythms of agriculture and the periodic demands this created for child labour. Full-time schooling was of short duration and limited in summer. Older children returned to study in the evenings and in winter. Attendance could be of equally short duration in urban schools. In the burgh school in Cupar, Fife, half of attendees present between 1774 and 1778 were in school for a year or less, and 80 per cent three years or less. The attendance of girls was especially sporadic.[28] Kirk sessions in rural parishes and burghs regularly paid the fees of poor pupils, while the fees themselves were kept at a low level. This in itself is a measure of contemporary determination to ensure that schooling was available to as many people as possible, and was despite the adverse impact this had, especially in the second half of the eighteenth century, on the incomes of hard-pressed schoolmasters.

If schooling formed part of the lives of most of the Lowland population, at least for a brief period, a great deal of learning probably took place inside the home or in other, informal ways.[29] People's first experience of reading may well have been learning to read from the Bible at home under instruction from their mother, although nineteenth-century autobiographies of working men – one of the few sources which shed light on this – can be very vague on this point. 'At six', wrote the author of one, 'I was able to read the Bible pretty well, but the initiatory process has quite escaped my memory.'[30] The inference is that it was not as a result of formal schooling. Another records having been to school briefly from the age of five, but who was afterwards 'caused to improve what little [education] I had received by reading a portion of some easy book by my mother every day. It was not very long till I was able to read the Bible, and my task then was to sit down by her side and read three chapters daily.'[31]

Figure 6.1 *Self-portrait of artist and his mother and sister by Alexander Carse. Women
appear to have played an important role in teaching their offspring about the Bible
and aspects of Scottish history. Although literacy levels were lower among females than
males, women from the middling ranks were frequently avid readers and writers of letters.
Reproduced by permission of the Scottish National Portrait Gallery.*

The next stages of education – still the parish school in rural areas, the
grammar school and private schools in towns, and beyond that university
and during the later eighteenth century academies – furnished an ever nar-
rowing, although still socially quite mixed, section of society with more
advanced skills in literacy and numeracy.[32] From the later seventeenth
century, the range of subjects taught widened significantly in response
to new demands and cultural imperatives created by a commercialising
economy.[33] In smaller burghs, new subjects – book-keeping or geography,
for example – were added to the curricula of the grammar schools from at
least the 1720s, albeit in haphazard, piecemeal fashion. In Dundee, despite
the rapid mid-century expansion in its international and domestic trade and
manufacturing, the addition of geography came only in 1780, and followed
a petition 'by a number of inhabitants of Dundee having children at the
Grammar School'.[34] On the other hand it is likely that – given the significant
presence of merchants and ships' captains – there were private schools in
the town offering modern, more narrowly vocational subjects which remain
hidden from our view.[35] Using advertisements and notices placed in the
press, Charles Withers has counted sixty-four public lectures or classes in
geography across Scotland between 1708 and 1830.[36] Although the bulk of

these were in Edinburgh and Glasgow, this may be partially misleading in that it could simply reflect the relative lack of papers elsewhere before the early nineteenth century. Alongside geography, these private teachers usually taught navigation, astronomy, geometry, mathematics and arithmetic.

Across the country, the precise pattern of educational provision which emerged depended, to a significant extent, on a town's size and the density of the local population on which schools could draw for pupils. In Edinburgh and Glasgow, the grammar schools continued to confine themselves in the eighteenth century to a classical education since they had no difficulty attracting a sufficient number of pupils to make this approach viable; separate establishments existed to deliver other subjects. When Henry Cockburn went to the High School in Edinburgh in 1787, the only additional subject, apart from Latin, was Greek. The era, meanwhile, of the separate academy, designed to provide instruction to the sons of the mercantile and professional classes as a cheaper, hopefully (for the parents anyway) more moral, alternative to university, was relatively short-lived, lasting from 1760 with the formation of the Perth Academy to around 1800. One reason why the movement faltered was that the universities took growing steps, especially from mid-century, to revise and liberalise their curricula.[37]

Little is known about the actual experience of schooling at the level of the grammar school. After 1707 – but not generally before then[38] – the highest ranks of the landed classes tended to send their sons south to English public schools – notably Eton. Middling rank families continued to entrust their children to the burgh schools, which suggests the enduring appeal of such institutions. On the other hand, school could, it seems, be a rather brutal, uninspiring environment. Certainly, this was Cockburn's recollection of Edinburgh High School: 'kept about nine years at two dead languages, which we did not learn'.[39] Flogging seems to have been rife in some schools, although burgh councils sought to keep such tendencies in check.[40]

During the eighteenth century, there was also a strengthening and broadening demand for education for the daughters of the elites and prospering middling sorts. Largely confined in the later seventeenth and early eighteenth centuries to Edinburgh and one or two other places, in the later eighteenth century girls' boarding schools spread more widely, reflecting the diffusion of genteel culture and aspirations throughout propertied society. These schools taught an array of accomplishments, including foreign languages, music, *belles lettres*, needlework and drawing.[41] By the middle of the eighteenth century women might also gain access to private lectures in geography and other subjects, while some classes in the capital were specifically aimed at women.[42] By the early nineteenth century, most sizeable towns boasted a growing range of music teachers and drawing masters, again usually catering (although certainly not exclusively) for the instruction of young women.[43]

In broad terms, therefore, education, like language, underpinned, first, social hierarchy, although less so perhaps than in countries where there was no public provision of schools, and where access to university was impossible for members of the lower and lesser middling orders, and, secondly, gender differences. Instruction in the classical languages, Latin and Greek, was entirely a male preserve, as Mary Somerville, the astronomer, mathematician and writer, was to discover in the later eighteenth century.[44]

READING

What people read was obviously dependent on what was available, its cost and what they wanted and had time to read. Clearly, from the early seventeenth century, and even more so from the middle of the seventeenth century, a growing number of people read avidly and regularly, although such individuals were a sub-section of the elites, including professionals, ministers and members of the landed classes. The bulk of the population simply did not have the time to read except in stolen moments – in the workplace or the field – in childhood as part of their education, or on Sundays, although weavers might read or be read to in weaving shops as might women at the spinning wheel.[45] It is in contemporary diaries and journals that we occasionally glimpse individual readers. Boswell tended to read on Sundays, when ill in bed, or, when not dining or carousing, admittedly not that often, in the evening, unsurprisingly a common time for reading.[46] On the odd occasion, he is to be found reading aloud to his wife or her to him, or with a friend or acquaintance. In June 1782, he read Fielding's *Tom Jones* to his wife, a book she did not care for as much as her husband, disliking the novelist's 'turn for low life' and regarding Sophia, the heroine, as 'not quite refin'd'.[47] Sunday was more likely to involve reading from the Bible or other devotional works, often aloud. At different times in the seventeenth century (1622, 1625, 1642 and 1663), legislation sought to prescribe the possession of Bibles and psalm books in households above a certain rental value, while similar orders were issued periodically at the local level.[48] In January 1648, the minister and elders of Lasswade parish admonished a group of boys who guarded the cattle in Loanhead 'for comeing together and playing on the Sabbath day and not exercising themselves in reading or other godlie exercises'.[49] Female readers are less visible in the historical record. Some women clearly read very widely, although most of our information concerns elite women.[50] How far women's reading differed from men's, if at all, is unclear, although it has been argued recently that women's reading was more likely to be a social activity. The truth is that currently we do not know enough to say one or the other, although male reading was certainly not always solitary and 'associated with the study'.[51] Similarly, how far reading aloud was usual is hard to say, apart from reading from the Bible. Reading to children, however, seems to have been common at all social levels, albeit that what was being read almost certainly varied significantly according to social rank.[52]

Access to books and other forms of print increased very significantly during this period. Alistair Mann has suggested recently that bookselling activity doubled on average between the 1640s and early eighteenth century.[53] In Edinburgh, Perth, Glasgow, St Andrews and Aberdeen, separate booksellers appeared between the 1580s and 1610s. Thereafter, bookselling spread steadily to other burghs – Ayr, for example, had a bookseller from 1668 and Paisley from 1680 – connecting different parts of Scotland to a bookselling network which focused on Edinburgh and London, but also Ireland and the continent.[54] From the central decades of the eighteenth century, this network entered a further, new phase of growth, leaving few towns of any size without a separate bookseller by the end of the century. Prior to the mid-eighteenth century, public libraries – be they burgh, kirk, university and professional libraries – were relatively few in number, and access to them was restricted socially. From the 1750s circulating and subscription libraries started to be more widely established, although the main surge in their formation came at the very end of the eighteenth century. Robert Burns' father, William Burnes, was a founder member of the Ayr subscription library, established in 1761, frequently walking to and from his farm to collect books. Supported by the prospering middling ranks, tradesmen, the urban gentry, and neighbouring ministers and landed gentlemen, subscription libraries ensured that the major works of the Scottish, and often European, Enlightenment were disseminated much more widely in society.[55] Commercial circulating libraries, run by booksellers, were usually predominantly (although certainly not exclusively) stocked with novels and plays.[56]

Books could also be borrowed from the private libraries of individuals, which again became more common during this period, or handed around between friends and within social networks. Such forms of borrowing were probably much more frequent and important at all social levels than historians of reading have assumed. The farmworker and later radical, Alexander Somerville, testifies repeatedly to the importance of borrowing books among the labouring classes in rural areas in the early nineteenth century. A copy of Burns' *Poems* which he read as a boy was lent to him by an older farm labourer. 'It was', Somerville recalled, 'a volume that had been often read, well read and well worn. It had been in tatters, and was sewed again together, and I had special charges to take care of it, as it was not everyone that it would be lent to.'[57]

Large collections of books were commonplace among the nobility from the early seventeenth century, and several *virtuosi* – Robert Sibbald being the most eminent – and ministers were compiling libraries of considerable scale and diversity by the end of the century.[58] Private libraries, however, were much less ubiquitous at that date among the landed gentry. This was true even where individuals had ready access to Edinburgh and thus to books.[59] Trends after 1700 have yet to be documented, although inventories of moveable estates drawn up at the death of their owners provide one potentially very valuable source of information.[60]

A preliminary survey of surviving detailed inventories of household possessions for Angus in the eighteenth century suggests several tentative patterns.[61] The presence of books increased markedly in the second half of the century, as did the range of subject matter covered. Of those who are recorded as having possessed books, many, nevertheless, seem to have owned a fairly small number of volumes, typically fewer than ten. Substantial libraries do appear, but in the burghs seem to have commonly belonged to prospering professionals often with close links to landed society. One such individual was John Watt of Meathie, a provost of Forfar at the end of the eighteenth and early nineteenth centuries, whose library of 302 books was clearly a prized possession; Watt bequeathed this library to his son and his lawful descendants for a hundred years.[62] This was in addition, moreover, to a further 110 items which were not included in this bequest, and another thirty-one described as having been 'received' just before Watt's death and not included in the catalogue. Watt's interests were impressively wide-ranging and diverse, and reflected very directly the influence of the European and Scottish Enlightenments.

This was probably not typical, however, and many professionals seem to have limited themselves to books directly related to their work. The Montrose physician, Thomas Seaton, who died in 1743, owned forty volumes, almost all of them medical works.[63] Tom Devine has suggested that the reading material of merchants in the 1670s and 1680s was 'somewhat narrow and circumscribed', although by the 1720s there was a change towards more secular literature, in addition to the devotional material which remained commonplace. Among the collection of George Bogle, scion of the Glasgow merchant dynasty, were works by Pufendorf and Grotius;[64] whether Bogle was typical, however, is open to question. During the eighteenth century, merchants commonly seem to have collected only books which were work-related, apart from the obligatory Bible. By the later eighteenth century, however, there were merchant bibliophiles dotted around Scotland, important figures in a provincial Scottish enlightenment. Thomas Ross, a Montrose merchant who died in the early nineteenth century, had a very considerable library housed in a closet off the dining room. This included an almost complete collection – ninety-four volumes – of Voltaire's works in French; six volumes were missing.[65]

Why did people read? For entertainment and instruction certainly, for the sense of the wider community of learning that could be gained through print. The precise balance of motivations undoubtedly varied according to individual taste and circumstance. However, many regular readers throughout this period seem to have continued to read for primarily religious reasons. For families across a wide social spectrum reading the Bible was a weekly occurrence, a part of Sunday observance, as we saw earlier. This was a form of intensive reading, or re-reading of familiar texts in a semi-public setting, a type of reading which probably remained predominant among the bulk of the population throughout this period. Devotional literature was very widely circulated from the early seventeenth century; by the end of the same century it was being exported in large quantities to Ulster. Mann has emphasised a 'movement' in the later seventeenth century 'from a spiritual to a secular agenda' in publishing.[66] Nevertheless, the most popular and widely circulated works remained religious ones into the eighteenth century, that is apart from almanacs, which often contained religious material, and a few exceptional items, for example, William Buchan's *Domestic Medicine*, a self-help medical guide conceived of as a popular work, which was issued and re-issued in one-volume octavo format from 1769, and cheap, chapbook-style versions of Blind Harry's *Wallace*.[67] Many printed sermons and devotional works were repeatedly re-published, or issued in print runs which far exceeded those that were normal for secular works. George Penny, looking back from the 1830s, recalled of the later eighteenth century:

> At this period, the reading of the common people was limited to a few books of a religious character, such as the Bible, Confessions of Faith, Shorter Catechism;

Figure 6.2   Ballad and Penny History Stall, *by Walter Geikie. Although this Walter Geikie (1795–1837) drawing of a 'penny history' stall derives from the early nineteenth century, it captures an aspect of everyday life that dated back to the previous century and even earlier. Broadsheets, ballads and penny histories – also known as chapbooks – were a ubiquitous form of popular literature, which by the later eighteenth century were being sold by chapmen and read by ordinary people the length and breadth of the country.*
Source: H. Geikie, Etchings Illustrative of Scottish Character and Scenery *(1841).*

Boston's, Bunyan's and Willison's works and a few sermons. The lighter articles of literature were on a part with John Cheap and Leper the Tailor, with a miscellaneous collection of ballads.[68]

Christopher Smout has called the eighteenth century the 'age of ballad and chapbooks';[69] it was also, like the preceding century, an age of devotional reading.

Another strong motivation for regular reading was to keep abreast of news and current events. For the merchant classes, this, along with reading for instruction, was probably the most common type of reading they did, although their sources of news were by no means confined to printed ones. The rise in the later eighteenth century of the subscription newsroom, with its ever expanding range of newspapers available – Scottish, English, Irish and international – was a symptom of this need and habit, as was the growth of the commercial reading room, usually run by booksellers.[70] These newsrooms supplemented other sources of information about events abroad and in the world of trade: letters; ship news; and personal contacts. From the later seventeenth century, coffee rooms may also have provided a similar service to that offered later by the subscription newsrooms. These first appeared in Edinburgh and Glasgow in 1673 and, as south of the border, were viewed with suspicion if not downright hostility in official circles for disseminating 'false' and seditious news and views.[71] How fast they spread beyond the two main cities is currently unknown, although certainly Aberdeen boasted one by the 1710s and Dundee by 1721 at the latest; Inverness may have had more than one. In the later seventeenth century, it was likely to be newsletters as much as, or rather than, newspapers which were the main sources of news. Burgh authorities subscribed to newsletters and increasingly newspapers, usually from Edinburgh but also on occasion from London, from the later 1650s and 1660s.[72] Typically, these were housed in the townhouse, where they were accessible to the council members, but may well also have been passed around locally. In 1696, a complaint was made to the authorities in Dumfries that the weekly newsletter from Edinburgh was being frequently borrowed by neighbouring gentlemen 'so that those who purchased it lost the use of it'. The council duly ordered that 'it should not be sent abroad out of town in all tyme coming', but should be kept in the town clerk's office 'for the use and benefit of this burgh'.[73] Although the coffee rooms and newsrooms were not frequented by women unless as servants, household account books indicate that elite women subscribed regularly to often a variety of newspapers.[74]

How fast or how widely newspaper reading spread is currently unknown and may well be unknowable due to gaps in the evidence. In the mid-seventeenth century and during the Exclusion crisis, when England witnessed an explosion of newsprint of various kinds, nothing remotely similar was seen in Scotland.[75] Those few news-books which did circulate intermittently were, moreover, usually of English origin. The growth of a Scottish press – which began in 1699 with the foundation of the *Edinburgh Gazette* – was slow, and the circulations of individual papers were modest when compared with their London and English provincial counterparts.[76] In the early nineteenth century, circulations of most papers remained in the low hundreds, while in rural areas among the lower orders they remained a relative rarity into the 1830s.[77] The appetite for news was, nevertheless, strong and widespread at a much earlier date, and ironically was fed by the growing habit in the second half of the seventeenth century of agencies of government – the privy council, ministers, and parliament – of printing proclamations and acts and seeking to defend their actions in print, although this was, in turn, a response to the circulation of Covenanting propaganda, much of which was produced in the United Provinces. In the 1680s, as much as 36 per cent of printed output in Scotland was accounted for by such information publishing.[78] That a new fabric of communication networks was taking shape in this period, and at the same time serving to re-shape political culture, is suggested by the range of publications – some of which were explicitly aimed at a popular readership – generated by the Darien adventure in 1696 and 1699 and even more strikingly the Union in 1705–6.[79] Edinburgh, with its literate artisan population, its stationers and booksellers, its 'paper cryers', and with handbills posted up on walls, was by the later seventeenth a relatively print-rich environment.[80]

The dependency on English news and newspapers, evident from the mid-seventeenth century, continued after 1707, with the circulation of English newspapers increasing markedly in the final third of the century. There was also a steady increase in the number of newspapers published in Scotland from the middle of the century.[81] Their growing availability may be why the practice of burgh councils purchasing newspapers for the use of their members seems to have died out or become much less important from the same period.[82] By the end of the century, under the impact of the French Revolution, and with their presence in tap rooms, taverns, barbers' shops, coffee rooms and reading rooms, and the growing practice of collective purchase, skilled artisans and lesser tradesmen had become regular readers of newspapers. A visitor to Perth in the early 1790s declared: 'PERTH, like all other great towns in North Britain, has its public subscription coffee house, for the perusal of the periodical public prints; and the study of politics may be reckoned one of the favourite amusements of *every order of persons in the town*' (added emphasis).[83] This new lower-class readership also extended through the Lowland manufacturing villages and hamlets.[84]

The practice of collective purchase of newspapers on the part of the labouring classes was in many ways a natural extension of a habit of buying reading matter evident from much earlier in the eighteenth century, especially among weaving and mining communities in the west and west-central regions.[85] It was from within these communities, with their deep traditions of reading and debate, that the weaver poets of the later eighteenth century emerged.[86] In the 1790s, in what looks very like a manifestation of a genuinely popular Enlightenment, groups of artisans, especially in these same areas, established reading societies.[87] Members of these societies pooled money to purchase books, which were lent out, before being auctioned off to the members after a set period of time, typically a year or two. As far as we can tell, the works being bought were major Enlightenment texts, and certainly not novels. Similar reading groups were a feature of Presbyterian Ulster at this time.[88]

WRITING

The circulation of print, in all its forms, depended, to a greater extent than most other places in the British Isles, on the existence of postal services. Newspapers and the post had been interlinked very closely from the outset in Scotland, as throughout early modern Europe, and this relationship persisted with newspapers depending on the arrival through the post of London papers for the bulk of their information and comment and being distributed to readers through the post.[89] Newspapers as a form developed from newsletters, and letters, in addition to newsletters *per se*, which remained an extremely important source of news for producers of newspapers and private individuals during the eighteenth century. This was partly because, depending on their authorship, they could contain privileged information. Many correspondents used (and expected to use) letters in this period to convey news. During the Highland war of 1689–91, the stopping of the posts from England appears to have allowed the Jacobites to manufacture 'false news', partly using the device of forged letters.[90]

The postal service expanded significantly in this period, in the process moving far beyond its origins as a government relay for messages.[91] In the seventeenth century, expansion tended to have a military or political logic, although official services were supplemented by private ones or services directed by burgh authorities. From the later seventeenth century, these private services were incorporated within or overtaken by official ones, a circumstance reinforced by the Union – which brought Scotland within a British postal system. Official services were supplemented on occasion after 1707 by private initiative, an example being the Edinburgh penny post established by the colourful Peter Williamson in the 1770s.[92] During the eighteenth century, the number of post towns steadily grew – from thirty-four in 1708, around sixty in 1715, to 140 in 1781 – while postal services also became faster and more frequent.[93] Growth was driven by demand, a great deal of which was commercial in origin, a symptom of the crucial role of information in creating and elaborating marketing and business networks. From the sixteenth century, merchants – overseas and domestic – had come to rely heavily on correspondence to conduct their business.[94] Politics and public business involved letter writing from the end of the fifteenth century; although no doubt this became much more common in the seventeenth century, partly because politics came to depend on connections which crossed national boundaries. Letters from MPs describing parliamentary business after 1707 were on occasion copied to increase their circulation.[95] Religious networks were formed or reinforced by letter writing, as were scholarly ones. At the beginning of the eighteenth century, Robert Wodrow sat in the middle of a vast, far-flung epistolary network which was international in scope and which, in his eyes, was some compensation for his isolation in Glasgow.[96] By the second half of the seventeenth century estate business was frequently conducted, or at least monitored in part, through letter writing between factor and absentee landowner.

What we know less about is letter writing as a feature of building and cementing social networks, and as a 'site', as one writer has recently put it, 'for the construction of self'.[97] During this period, letter writing, like speech, became much more closely regulated by notions of propriety and appropriate style.[98] Letters were seen, in such cases, as self-conscious acts of revelation or concealment. Burns paid particular attention to such things, training himself carefully in the art of epistolary communication.[99]

Members of landed families had by the eighteenth century produced a great deal of correspondence. What is clear is the role of letters in sustaining deeply affectionate and companionate relations between, say, husband and wife. Lord George Murray's wife wrote her husband, who had remained in Scotland, lengthy epistles – often of six pages or more – from London on a near daily basis in the mid-1770s.[100] Given the mobility of the landed classes in this period, their peripatetic habits and the tendency particularly of younger sons to seek their fortunes overseas or in the armed services in the eighteenth century, letters took on added importance in maintaining relationships. They also had a vital role in oiling the patronage networks which were so crucial to Scottish success in infiltrating and profiting from the British state and empire in the eighteenth century.[101] Correspondence may have been especially important to women of the landed classes, especially married women, helping to maintain their networks of friends and companions. Below the level of the landed classes, the picture is more obscure, although on occasion we are afforded glimpses of the potential importance of letters. An Aberdeen merchant snatched the hand of a daughter of a minister on Shetland from under the latter's disapproving nose using a secret correspondence.[102] Kate Telscher has recently remarked on the 'playful intimacy' which characterised the young servant of the East India Company, George Bogle, in his letters to his sisters back in Scotland in the 1770s.[103] Below this level, a tantalising hint about the significance and pervasiveness of letter writing comes in the form of official concern during the Napoleonic Wars, with a postal surveyor remarking, in relation to the area around Tain, where a post office had recently been established, of 'the lower classes now receiving and sending their letters under privilege as soldiers and which there is much reason to believe is not confined to those only who are strictly entitled to it'.[104] The desire to write letters in order to defeat the tyrannies of distance, to re-knit fragmented families, may well have had a peculiar importance given the unusual mobility of the Scottish population in this period; it may also have been a further factor behind a striving for literacy skills among the lower orders.[105]

TALKING AND SINGING

The spoken word remained central to everyday life throughout this period. One of the strongest indicators of this is the barely diminished importance of the pulpit. Before the age of mass literacy and a genuinely popular newspaper press, this constituted the sole means of communicating with the bulk of the population. In 1643, the Commission of the General Assembly approached the Convention of Estates with a proposal that parish ministers should be used to convey the news, the stated rationale for which says much about both the potential power of the pulpit and the dominance of talk and rumour in the creation of news at this stage. 'Because', the proposal urged, 'thruch want of sure and tymous intelligence a greate pairte of the people are aither left to uncertane rumoures or flicked by the negligence of common bearers, or abuseith with malignant informationes that thei nather know thair awin danger nor the danger of religion in the countrey.'[106] Almost a century later, Mackintosh of Borlum, seeking to drive forward agricultural improvement, could write to Lord Loudon as Lord High Commissioner, urging: 'The greatest Difficulty I apprehend, is, the unaccountable aversion our Commons have to Inclosing, indeed any thing new: There Parish Ministers are the only sett of men they believe: They do all with them . . .'[107] During the passage of the Union, and at subsequent moments of crisis for the eighteenth-century British state the support, or certainly quiescence, of ministers and churchmen was seen as vital to securing the Union and to shoring up the political status quo. In 1708, 1715–6, 1745–6, 1792–3, 1794–5 and 1797–1805, ministers were expected to lead their flocks to a position of exemplary, and ideally, very visible loyalty.[108]

The pulpit and the church therefore, played a central role in communications networks in this period. Proclamations was read out from the pulpit and often pinned up on the door of the kirk. Sermons had an importance and weight in society and culture which is easily underestimated, and the sermon was central to church services.[109] On fast days and Sundays, so far as we can tell, churches tended to be well attended and ministers' sermons closely attended to, even written down later.[110]

The culture of the Highlands remained an overwhelmingly oral one. It was a culture in which story and song played a large role. This did not mean that the Highland population was cut off from the outside world, as in rural societies in more modern periods – for example, China in the early part

of the twentieth century.[111] News may well, in fact, have circulated quite
quickly, carried by bards, travellers of different kinds, and, on occasion and
between 1689 and the later 1750s, spread by agents of the exiled Stuart court
and Catholic missionary priests.[112] In the seventeenth-century context, Allan
Macinnes has emphasised that: 'Topical information was disseminated and
public opinion shaped through the *ceilidh*', a spontaneous folk gathering.[113]
Vernacular poets, such as Iain Lom from Keppoch, used song to disseminate
a traditionalist critique of commercialising clan elites throughout the second
half of the seventeenth century, a critique which in the subsequent century
fed into a popular Highland ideology of Jacobitism. Among the bulk of
the Lowland rural population, story telling and song were central elements
of an intensely local, communal culture which revolved around fairs and
harvest and winter suppers provided by landowners and farmers. Alexander
Somerville, referred to earlier, recalled that his father was always ready on
such occasions with 'droll stories, jokes, and songs with a meaning in them'.[114]
A strict anti-burgher, who took his family home at 10 pm on such occasions
in order to prepare for the Sabbath, Somerville senior was able, nevertheless,
to contribute fully to the entertainment. Village inns resounded to the singing
of 'glees and other songs'. The elderly played an important role in transmit-
ting familial and communal memories and stories to younger generations;
while women have been depicted as key perpetuators of an oral ballad tradition which was deeply rooted in, but not confined to, rural culture.[115]

Ballads and song were also an important part of urban life, although our
knowledge of the circulation of printed ballads in this period is limited.[116]
Penny, the Perth historian, recalled: 'A great many of our old Scotch songs
were sung, chiefly picked up by the ear from the maids at the wheel.'[117]
Penny implies that these were part of an oral tradition, although their original source may equally have been a printed ballad or chapbook.[118] Psalm
singing was a central feature of religious devotion and worship, in town and
country, and song was frequently used in the context of popular protest and
demonstration.[119] Much of the growing urban and semi-urban population
in this period comprised incomers from rural areas and villages, and they
brought rural cultural traditions and habits with them.

If the role of song, therefore, transcended a simple division between town
and country, in various ways, this was equally true of the spoken word.
The reputations of most townsfolk in this period were constructed, circulated and challenged through speech, although they might, in the case of
merchants, for example, also depend on written and printed forms: letters;
bills of exchange; and bonds. Edinburgh, and perhaps Glasgow and one or
two other places, may have been somewhat different in this respect in that
print was on occasion turned to in pursuit of personal and political rivalries.
Yet, what differences there were do seem to have been matters of degree. In
contrast to London and, indeed, other places south of the border, contests
over public reputations do not generally seem to have been conducted by

means of print, or through written libels. It may be that there are such cases waiting to be discovered in national and local archives; currently, however, it is their relative rarity which stands out.[120] Scottish newspapers tended by and large to avoid personal disputes; or at least many Scots sought to keep their disputes out of the newspapers.

Most towns, moreover, remained compact settlements during this period, while most urban dwellers were part of, by later, nineteenth- and twentieth-century standards, modest populations. Towns were places where visual communication still played an influential role, as emphasised, for example, by the theatrical elements of the punishment of crime and misdemeanours or the rich symbolism of much civic and associational life. They were known to their inhabitants through sight and memory and talk; not through print. In face-to-face societies, status was also personal, not primarily a function of office, and reputations were jealously guarded and easily injured by hostile gossip. Legal records contain large numbers of cases of magistrates defending their reputations against public challenge – usually in the form of words rather than print. In Perth, loud contempt for a magistrate by a recruiting sergeant uttered in the town's main street led the injured magistrate to pursue retribution in the local burgh court.[121] Reputations were of moment, of course, for more than simply those in positions of public authority. Merchants, tradesmen and retailers depended on their good name for success in business and, indeed, survival, while domestic servants could see their livelihoods irreparably damaged by malicious talk.[122] In 1758, a case of slander before the Argyll sheriff court involved both the public authority of a magistrate and the private reputation of a merchant. The complainant had found himself called a liar in court in relation to a claim about settlement of a deal involving the sale of timber in Ireland. What seems to have swayed the court against the defendant was, that despite his producing witnesses in his defence, his offence had been against 'a magistrate and a Trading Merchant' as well as having been in open court. The sentence comprised a substantial fine and the requirement that he 'make a public Acknowledgement' of his fault 'at the Cross in Campbelltown [sic]' and 'beg pardon' from the complainant.[123] Words mattered, but in the eyes of the law they mattered more for certain people than for others; so did where they were spoken.

Privacy was rare in early modern urban life, or rather it was the privilege of the very wealthy. For the majority, the division between private and public, the visible and the unregarded, could be extremely narrow. Words spilled out from doors or were spoken at doors in full hearing of the rest of the close or street. In such circumstances, key qualities of good neighbourliness were being 'discreet and quiet'.[124] Nor was a 'venomous tongue' necessarily less potentially destructive of reputations, livelihoods and, on occasion, social and domestic harmony in rural areas, although this was obviously not so much a consequence of social propinquity or relative audibility in confined areas.[125]

The spoken word was interwoven with the nature of urban life in other ways. Public notices were delivered by word of mouth. Print barely changed this, although handbills were on occasion issued by larger burgh authorities in the face of popular protests, such as food riots as part of efforts to defuse popular anger.[126] The market cross or market place was often where news was announced or spread from, although the original source of the news might be a written or printed report. In 1769, when Ilay Campbell rode back to Edinburgh with news of the House of Lords decision in the famous Douglas case, on arrival he went straight to the cross in the High Street, threw his hat in the air, and cried 'Douglas for ever!'.[127] From the later seventeenth century, coffee houses were places where print was regularly alchemised into 'common report', which then travelled through towns and into villages and rural areas in their environs. Food riots had their origins not just in high food prices, but in the circulation of information and rumour about specific malpractices or actions by individual dealers, or millers or landowners; this emanated from a thickly populated realm of talk which is only partially and occasionally visible in the historical record. In the market place, it was very often women who gathered and circulated information and rumour about prices and the behaviour of retailers, bakers and farmers or landowners.[128] As Bernard Capp has shown in an English context, women in this period tended to form what he has called 'gossip networks', reflecting their population of distinct spaces within towns, including doorways and the home, networks which could be mobilised, as in food protests, to defend communal interests and values, but which, on a day-to-day basis, served as a crucial form of support in the struggle against the vagaries and instabilities of life.[129] These networks might also offer some protection, in the context of a society which was deeply patriarchal in its customs and beliefs, against attacks on their reputation and person, from neighbours and, indeed, husbands. In rural communities, the kirk and the kirk door could play a similar role to the market place in the town. Even in the urban political sphere, where print had by the end of the eighteenth century assumed considerable importance, what is striking is just how much political talk remained just that. Local affairs – the politics of the parish and the burgh council – rarely intruded into newspapers or print; newspapers were read in this period for news of what was happening in London or Europe or further afield. In sum, for the bulk of the population, despite the growth of print and the increasing speed with which information, news and people travelled between communities, the world of communications in 1800 continued to have much in common with that of 1600.

Notes

1. See R. A. Houston, *Literacy in Early Modern Europe: Culture and Education 1500–1800*, 2nd edn (London, 2002), ch. 9; Peter Burke, *Languages and Communities in Early Modern Europe* (Cambridge, 2004).

2. Julian Goodare, *The Government of Scotland 1560–1625* (Oxford, 2004), ch. 10; Charles W. J. Withers, *Gaelic Scotland: The Transformation of a Culture Region* (London, 1988), especially ch. 3.

3. Charles W. J. Withers, *Gaelic in Scotland, 1698–1981: The Geographical History of a Language* (Edinburgh, 1984); V. E. Durcacz, *The Decline of the Celtic Languages* (Edinburgh, 1983).

4. D. J. Withrington, 'The SSPCK and Highland schools in the mid-eighteenth century', *Scottish Historical Review*, XLI (1962), 88–99; Withers, *Gaelic Scotland*, pp. 120–37.

5. Quoted in Charles W. J. Withers, *Urban Highlanders: Highland–Lowland Migration and Urban Gaelic Culture, 1700–1900* (East Linton, 1998), p. 201.

6. Withers, *Urban Highlanders*, ch. 6.

7. J. Derrick McClure, 'English in Scotland', in R. Burchfield (ed.), *The Cambridge History of the English Language, Vol. V: English in Britain and Overseas: Origins and Development* (Cambridge, 1994), pp. 29–93.

8. Quoted in Burke, *Languages and Communities*, p. 41. For Sheridan's visit to Edinburgh and its impact, see Janet Adam Smith, 'Some eighteenth-century ideas of Scotland', in N. T. Phillipson and R. Mitchison (eds), *Scotland in the Age of Improvement: Essays in Scottish History in the Eighteenth Century* (Edinburgh, 1970), pp. 110–11.

9. Houston, *Literacy in Early Modern Europe*, p. 229.

10. Quoted in Charles Jones and Wilson McLeod, 'Standards and differences: languages in Scotland, 1707–1918', in I. Brown, T. O. Clancy, S. Manning and M. Pittock (eds), *The Edinburgh History of Scottish Literature Vol. Two: Enlightenment, Britain and Empire* (Edinburgh, 2007), p. 28.

11. As noted in Paul Langford, 'South Britons' reception of North Britons, 1707–1820', in T. C. Smout (ed.), *Anglo-Scottish Relations from 1603 to 1900* (Oxford, 2005), pp. 164–5.

12. Henry W. Meikle, *Scotland and the French Revolution* (Glasgow, 1912), pp. 150–1; Michael Fry, *The Dundas Despotism* (Edinburgh, 1992), p. 171.

13. Henry Grey Graham, *Social Life of Scotland in the Eighteenth Century* (London, 1906), p. 76.

14. See R. Crawford, *Devolving English Literature*, 2nd edn (Edinburgh, 2000), p. 75.

15. *Boswell's Edinburgh Journals*, pp. 469, 548.

16. Quoted in David Hewitt, 'James Beattie and the languages of Scotland', in Jennifer J. Carter and Joan M. Pittock (eds), *Aberdeen and the Enlightenment* (Aberdeen, 1987), p. 252.

17. See relevant comment in Jones and McLeod, 'Standards and differences', p. 28.

18. For this, see Burke, *Languages and Communities*, chs 4, 6.

19. P. J. Waller, 'Democracy and dialect, speech and class', quoted in A. Fox, *Oral and Literate Culture in England, 1500–1700* (Oxford 2000), p. 53.

20. Quoted in Hewitt, 'James Beattie', p. 257.

21. Brian Ward Perkins, *The Fall of Rome and the End of Civilization* (Oxford, 2005), pp. 151–2.

22. R. A. Houston, 'The literacy myth?: illiteracy in Scotland 1660–1760', *Past and Present*, 96 (1982), 90.

23. R. A. Houston, 'Literacy, education and the culture of print in Enlightenment Edinburgh', *History*, 78 (1993), 373–92.

24. See T. C. Smout, 'Born again at Cambuslang: new evidence on popular religion and literacy in eighteenth-century Scotland', *Past and Present*, 97 (1982), 114–27.

25. R. D. Anderson, *Scottish Education since the Reformation* (Dundee, 1997), ch. 1.

26. D. J. Withrington, 'Education and society in the eighteenth century', in N. T. Phillipson and R. Mitchison (eds), *Scotland in the Age of Improvement* (Edinburgh, 1970), pp. 169–99.

27. Angus Archives, Restenneth, Montrose Burgh Records, EK/6, Petitions etc. 1800–1808, Petition by several inhabitants in the Links requesting ground to build a new school, 1800.

28. Paula Martin, *Cupar: the History of a Small Scottish Town* (Edinburgh, 2006), p. 128.

29. This is also stressed by Smout, 'Born again at Cambuslang', pp. 125–6.

30. Anon., 'Life of a letterpress printer, written by himself', *The Commonwealth*, 7 February 1857, p. 3. I am grateful to Vivienne Dunstan for this reference.

31. Anon., 'Life of a handloom weaver, written by himself', *The Commonwealth*, 25 April 1857, p. 1.

32. See the summary of findings on the social composition of university students in Anderson, *Scottish Education*, pp. 18–19. See also Houston, *Scottish Literacy*, pp. 244–7. Houston has emphasised how few individuals went to university in this period, around 1.5–2 per cent of the relevant age group in the population.

33. Withrington, 'Education and society in the eighteenth century', pp. 169–83.

34. Dundee Archives and Records Centre (DARC), Dundee Town Council Minute Book, entry for 31 January 1780.

35. The first Dundee trade directory, published in 1782, lists nine private teachers in the town, but gives no indication of what they taught: *The Dundee Register of Merchants and Trades, with the Public Officers, &c for MDCCLXXXIII* (Dundee, 1782), pp. 38–9.

36. Charles W. J. Withers, *Geography, Science and National Identity: Scotland since 1520* (Cambridge, 2001), p. 119.

37. As summarised in Withrington, 'Education and society', pp. 184–91; Anderson, *Scottish Education*, ch. 2.

38. As emphasised in Keith M. Brown, 'The origins of a British aristocracy: integration and its limitations before the treaty of Union', in Steven G. Ellis and Sarah Barber (eds), *Conquest and Union: Fashioning a British State, 1485–1725* (London, 1995), pp. 233–4.

39. *Oxford Dictionary of National Biography*, entry for Cockburn.

40. For one example, see Martin, *Cupar*, p. 129.

41. See the advertisement for Miss Thomson's boarding school in Dundee in the *Edinburgh Advertiser*, 21 October 1777.

42. Withers, *Geography, Science, and National Identity*, p. 124.

43. See Bob Harris, 'Towns, improvement and cultural change in Georgian Scotland: the evidence of the Angus burghs, c. 1760–1820', *Urban History*, 33 (2006), 203.

44. D. McMillan (ed.), *Queen of Science: Personal Recollections of Mary Somerville* (Edinburgh, 2001), p. 24.

45. For evidence on this in Scotland there is nothing to compare to Raymond Gillespie's *Reading Ireland: Print, Reading and Social Change in Early Modern Ireland* (Manchester, 2005) or the considerable body of relevant work on England. For a useful, if rather schematic, summary of existing knowledge, however, see J. Crawford, 'Reading and book use in eighteenth-century Scotland', *Bibliotheck*, 19 (1994), 23–43; and R. A. Houston, *Scottish Literacy and the Scottish Identity*, (Cambridge, 1983), pp. 163–78.

46. *Boswell's Edinburgh Journals*, p. 457.

47. *Boswell's Edinburgh Journals*, p. 462.

48. Alistair J. Mann, *The Scottish Book Trade 1500–1720: Print, Commerce and Print Control in Early Modern Scotland* (East Linton, 2000), pp. 52, 161.

49. Quoted in Houston, *Scottish Literacy and the Scottish Identity*, p. 188.

50. See Elizabeth Rose of Kilravock (1747–1815), whose reading list covering the years 1775–80 is reproduced in H. W. Drescher (ed.), *Henry Mackenzie Letters to Elizabeth Rose of Kilravock: On Literature, Events and People 1768–1815* (Munster, 1967), pp. 229–40; or the commonplace books of Mary Eleanor Bowes (1749–1800), 9th countess of Strathmore and Kinghorne, which survive in the Strathmore muniments, Glamis Castle, Angus. For a recent valuable discussion of one small group of such readers, see Katherine Glover, 'The female mind: Scottish Enlightenment femininity and the world of letters. A case study of the women of the Fletcher of Saltoun family in the mid-eighteenth century', *Journal of Scottish Historical Studies*, 25 (2005), 1–20.

51. See comment in Glover, 'The female mind', p. 7.

52. See George Penny, *Traditions of Perth* (reprinted, Coupar Angus, 1986), pp. 120–2, where Penny notes that *Satan's Invisible World Discovered* was commonly read in the presence of children.

53. Mann, *Scottish Book Trade*, p. 222.

54. Jonquil Bevan, 'Scotland', in John Barnard and D. F. McKenzie (eds), *The Cambridge History of the Book in Britain. Volume IV, 1557–1695* (Cambridge, 2002), pp. 698–9.

55. See David Allan, 'The Scottish Enlightenment and the readers of late Georgian Lancaster: light in the North', *Northern History*, 36 (2000), 267–81; Martin, *Cupar*, p. 134; Crawford, 'Reading and book use', pp. 34–5.

56. E. Jacobs, 'Eighteenth-century British circulating libraries and cultural book history', *Book History*, 6 (2003), 19; Crawford, 'Reading and book use', p. 33.

57. *The Autobiography of a Working Man: Alexander Somerville* (London, 1967), pp. 25, 55–6.

58. Keith M. Brown, *Noble Society in Scotland: Wealth, Family and Culture from Reformation to Revolution* (Edinburgh, 2000), pp. 219–20; Roger L. Emerson, 'Scottish cultural change 1660–1710 and the Union of 1707', in John Robertson

(ed.), *A Union for Empire: Political Thought and the Union of 1707* (Cambridge, 1995), pp. 130–41.

59. *Foulis of Ravelston's Account Book 1671–1707* (Edinburgh, 1894); *The Diary and General Expenditure Book of William Cunningham of Craigends . . . Kept Chiefly From 1673 to 1680* (Edinburgh, 1887).

60. This source will be much more extensively discussed in forthcoming work by Vivienne Dunstan, currently a Ph.D. student at the University of Dundee.

61. Research conducted by David Barrie and Vivienne Dunstan as part of separate research projects on the early modern history of Dundee and other burghs in Angus. The results of Barrie's examination have been deposited with the Dundee University Archives and Museum Services.

62. National Archives of Scotland (NAS), CC20/7/7, inventory of the personal estate of John Watt Esq, 1815.

63. NAS, CC3/4/20, 1868–76, articles of roup of Thomas Seaton, physician in Montrose, 1743.

64. T. M. Devine, 'The Scottish merchant community, 1680–1740', in R. H. Campbell and A. S. Skinner (eds), *The Origins and Nature of the Scottish Enlightenment* (Edinburgh, 1982), p. 34.

65. NAS, Court of Session Productions, CS96/819, inventory of household furniture and other moveable property, belonging to Thomas Ross, merchant in Montrose, 27 July 1819.

66. Mann, *Scottish Book Trade*, p. 217.

67. For Buchan's *Domestic Medicine*, see Richard B. Sher, 'William Buchan's domestic medicine: laying book history open', in Peter Isaac and Barry McKay (eds), *The Human Face of the Book Trade: Print Culture and its Creators* (Winchester, 1999), pp. 45–64.

68. Penny, *Traditions*, p. 38.

69. T. C. Smout, 'Scotland and north Britain: the historical background, 1707–1918', in Brown *et al.*, *The Edinburgh History of Scottish Literature*, p. 6.

70. One of the earliest, and certainly the most famous and most remarked on, of the newsrooms was the Glasgow tontine subscription newsroom, which opened in 1781. Commercial reading rooms could subscribe to an equally wide range of newspapers and periodicals as, for example, in the case of the Trongate Literary Museum run by John Murdoch, a Glasgow bookseller, stationer and perfumer. This held eleven newspapers and ten periodicals (advertisement in *Glasgow Courier*, 18 January 1800).

71. See Clare Jackson, *Restoration Scotland 1660–1690: Royalist Politics, Religion and Ideas* (Woodbridge, 2003), p. 41.

72. 'News lettres' were supplied to Montrose Town Council as early as 1654 from an Edinburgh agent (James G. Low and W. Low, 'Bibliography of Montrose periodical literature', *Scottish Notes and Queries*, 3, 1889–90). Aberdeen town council minutes record a payment in 1657 to an individual to supply 'ane weekly diurnal' (W. J. Couper, *The Edinburgh Periodical Press*, 2 vols (Stirling, 1908), I, p. 48), while Glasgow had a correspondent in Edinburgh from 1652 and was receiving a weekly journal from London from 1657 (George Eyre Todd, *History*

of Glasgow, ii, From the Reformation to the Revolution (Glasgow, 1931), p. 258). In some cases, such arrangements seem to have lapsed, partly owing to their cost and partly because of a feeling that they were not required in peacetime.

73. William McDowall, *History of the Burgh of Dumfries, with Notices of Nithsdale, Annandale and the Western Border*, 4th edn (revised, 1896), p. 514. Montrose burgh council members were allowed to keep papers for a week in 1694.

74. University of St Andrews Special Collections, MS CS479.A8, Elizabeth Maitland Household account book, 1767–1803. See also Glover, 'The female mind', pp. 9–10.

75. See Joad Raymond, *The Invention of the Newspaper: English Newsbooks 1641–1649* (Oxford, 1996); Joad Redmond, *Pamphlets and Pamphleteering in Early Modern Britain* (Cambridge, 2003); Carolyn Nelson and Matthew Seccombe, 'The creation of the periodical press 1620–1695', in Barnard and McKenzie, *The Cambridge History of the Book in Britain*, pp. 533–50.

76. There is no adequate modern study of the eighteenth-century Scottish press or the nature of news networks in Scotland prior to 1700. See, however, W. J. Couper, *The Edinburgh Periodical Press: Being a Bibliographical Account of the Newspapers, Journals, and Magazines issued in Edinburgh from the Earliest Times to 1800*, 2 vols (Stirling, 1908); M. E. Craig, *The Scottish Periodical Press 1750–1789* (Edinburgh, 1931).

77. Details of one early-nineteenth-century newspaper can be found in National Library of Scotland, Acc. 10262/2, View of the present state of the *Dumfries & Galloway Courier*, 10 October 1811. The paper had 620 subscribers, a number which had grown by ninety since 1 January.

78. Mann, *Scottish Book Trade*, p. 148.

79. Karin Bowie, *Scottish Public Opinion and the Anglo-Scottish Union, 1699–1707* (Woodbridge, 2007); see also, Karin Bowie, 'Public opinion, popular politics and the Union of 1707', *Scottish Historical Review*, LXXXII (2003), 226–60; and Christopher A. Whatley, *The Scots and the Union* (Edinburgh, 2006).

80. For a general discussion, see Houston, 'Literacy, education and the culture of print'.

81. Bob Harris, 'Scotland's newspapers, the French Revolution and domestic radicalism (c. 1789–1794)', *Scottish Historical Review*, LXXXIV (2005), 38–62

82. Some councils continued to purchase papers – Dundee, for example, subscribed throughout the second half of the eighteenth century to the *Edinburgh Evening Courant* and the *Edinburgh Advertiser* – but whether arrangements for reading them continued in the same way from this period is not always clear.

83. John Lettice, *Letters on a Tour Through Various Parts of SCOTLAND in the Year 1792* (London, 1794), p. 454.

84. Harris, 'Scotland's newspapers', p. 60.

85. See Ned C. Landsman, 'Presbyterians and provincial society: the Evangelical Enlightenment in the west of Scotland, 1740–1775', in John Dwyer and Richard B. Sher (eds), *Sociability and Society in Eighteenth-Century Scotland* (Edinburgh, 1993), pp. 194–209; Ned C. Landsman, 'Evangelists and their hearers: popular

interpretation of Revivalist preaching in eighteenth-century Scotland', *Journal of British Studies*, 28 (1989), 131, 146.

86. See Andrew Noble, 'Displaced persons: Burns and the Renfrew Radicals', in Bob Harris (ed.), *Scotland in the Age of the French Revolution* (Edinburgh, 2005), pp. 196–225.

87. These reading societies, which numbered around fifty, are described in a remarkable and little remarked on series of articles in the *Scots Chronicle*, 20 October, 30 December 1796; 20 January, 10 February, 24 February, 4 April, 19, 30 May, 7 July, 10 November, 5 December 1797; 16 February, 16 March 1798. See also Crawford, 'Reading and book use', p. 37, where the author refers to the Encyclopaedia Club of Paisley, a debating society, which was in existence as early as 1770, membership of which included a blacksmith, barber and hand-loom weaver.

88. J. R. R. Adams, *The Printed Word and the Common Man: Popular Culture in Ulster 1700–1900* (Belfast, 1987), pp. 39–40.

89. For a European perspective, see Paul Arblaster, 'Posts, newsletters, newspapers: England in a European system of communications', in Joad Raymond (ed.), *News Networks in Seventeenth-Century Britain and Europe* (Basingstoke, 2006), pp. 19–34.

90. *Culloden Papers, Correspondence from 1625 to 1748* (London, 1815), pp. 14–15, memoir of a plan for preserving the peace of the Highlands.

91. A. R. B. Haldane, *Three Centuries of Scottish Posts* (Edinburgh, 1971).

92. Haldane, *Three Centuries*, pp. 108–9.

93. Horse posts, for example, were introduced from the 1710s and mail coaches from the 1780s.

94. Arblaster, 'Posts, newsletters, newspapers', p. 20.

95. Bob Harris, 'The Scots, the Westminster Parliament, and the British state in the eighteenth century', in Julian Hoppit (ed.), *Parliaments, Nations and Identities in Britain and Ireland, 1660–1850* (Manchester, 2003), p. 130.

96. L. W. Sharp (ed.), *Early Letters of Robert Wodrow,1698–1709* (Edinburgh, 1937).

97. Rebecca Earle (ed.), *Epistolary Selves: Letters and Letter Writers 1600–1945* (Aldershot, 1999), p. 2.

98. On this, see relevant comment in Susan Whyman, 'Paper visits": The post-Restoration letter as seen through the Verney family archive', in Earle, *Epistolary Selves*, pp. 15–36.

99. Katrina Williamson, 'The emergence of privacy: letters, journals and domestic writing', in Brown *et al.*, *The Edinburgh History of Scottish Literature*, p. 60.

100. Blair Castle, Atholl Papers, 65 (6), 24, 115, 121.

101. For a recent study of such networks, see Douglas J. Hamilton, *Scotland, the Caribbean and the Atlantic World, 1750–1820* (Manchester, 2005).

102. *Diary of the Reverend John Mill, Minister in Shetland* (Edinburgh, 1889), p. 52.

103. Kate Teltscher, 'The sentimental ambassador: the letters of George Bogle from Bengal, Bhutan, and Tibet, 1770–1781', in Earle, *Epistolary Selves*, pp. 81, 84–5.

104. Haldane, *Three Centuries of Scottish Posts*, p. 59.

105. I owe this insight to discussion with Susan Whyman. I am grateful to her for

allowing me to read some unpublished work on letter writing and literacy in northern England in this period.

106. Quoted in Couper, *Edinburgh Periodical Press*, p. 79.

107. National Register of Archives Scotland, Loudoun Papers, Mountstuart House, Box 90, bundle 14, 'A Lover of his Country' [i.e. Mackintosh of Borlum] to Lord Loudoun, 18 May 1730.

108. Emma Vincent, 'The responses of Scottish churchmen to the French Revolution, 1789–1802', *Scottish Historical Review*, LXXIII (1994), 191–215. See also Bob Harris, *The Scottish People and the French Revolution* (London, 2008).

109. See the discussion of this in Margo Todd, *The Culture of Protestantism in Early Modern Scotland* (New Haven, CT, 2002), ch. 1.

110. Edinburgh Central Library, DA 1861.789, Journal of Andrew Armstrong, 1789–93.

111. See the discussion in Henrietta Harrison, 'Newspapers and nationalism in rural China 1890–1929', *Past and Present*, 166 (2000), 181–204.

112. See relevant comment in Bob Harris, *Politics and the Nation: Britain in the Mid Eighteenth Century* (Oxford, 2002), p. 167; Houston, *Scottish Literacy*, pp. 197–8.

113. Allan Macinnes, 'Gaelic culture in the seventeenth century: polarization and assimilation', in Ellis and Barber, *Conquest and Union*, p. 164.

114. *Autobiography of a Working Man*, p. 19.

115. *Autobiography of a Working Man*, pp. 24–5. For the role of women as conduits of oral tradition, see Deborah Symonds, *Weep Not For Me: Women, Ballads, and Infanticide in Early Modern Scotland* (University Park, PA, 1997).

116. Mann suggests that, along with other forms of cheap print, 'bawdy ballads' became much more common in the early eighteenth century (Mann, *Scottish Book Trade*, p. 208). In England, printed ballads and broadsheets were very widely circulated from the sixteenth century.

117. Penny, *Traditions*, p. 117.

118. For comment on the 'impurity' of the Scottish ballad tradition, see Edward J. Cowan, 'Hunting the ballad', in E. J. Cowan (ed.), *The Ballad in Scottish History* (East Linton, 2000), p. 9; Thomas Crawford, *Society and the Lyric: A Study of the Song Culture of Eighteenth Century* (Edinburgh, 1979), p. 7.

119. For psalm singing, see Todd, *Culture of Protestantism*, pp. 72–3; Landsman, 'Evangelists and their hearers', pp. 144–5. For an example of the use of song in protests and demonstrations, see Douglas Watt, *The Price of Scotland: Darien, Union and the Wealth of Nations* (Edinburgh, 2007), p. 198; and more generally the singing of Jacobite songs in Murray G. H. Pittock, *Poetry and Jacobite Politics in Eighteenth-Century Britain and Ireland* (Cambridge, 1994).

120. Leah Leneman noted just two cases of defamation involving print in her 'Defamation in Scotland, 1750–1800', *Continuity and Change*, 15 (2000), 209–34.

121. Perth and Kinross Council Archives, Perth, B59/26/11/1/2/23, copy of process Baillie Scot Ag.t Preston soldier, 29 June 1726.

122. See Leneman, 'Defamation in Scotland'.

123. NAS, CC2/2/53/4, Alexander McMillan, merchant & Baillie in Campbeltown agt William Watson jun there, 5 August 1758.

124. As suggested by NAS, CC8/6/42, Anna Colvill, spouse of Benjamin Bate, soldier in the 31st regiment of foot, & him for himself agt Ann Dickson & her spouse, James Dickson, residenter at West Kirk Braehead near Edinburgh, 13 February 1783.

125. The term 'venomous tongue' is taken from a case of scandal involving a mother-in-law alleging an adulterous affair between her son-in-law, who was a portioner of Drimllilie, and a married woman which was heard before the Argyll sheriff court in 1769 (NAS, CC2/2/70/5).

126. For one example of this, see Christopher A. Whatley, *Scottish Society: Beyond Jacobitism towards Industrialisation* (Manchester, 2000), p. 207.

127. *Boswell's Edinburgh Journals*, p. 76.

128. See Whatley, *Scottish Society*, ch. 5.

129. Bernard Capp, *When Gossips Meet: Women, Family, and Neighbourhood in Early Modern England* (Oxford, 2003)

Chapter 7

Order and Disorder

Christopher A. Whatley

INTRODUCTION

Early modern Scotland has been portrayed as relatively well-ordered, rather authoritarian society. Such an image, however, applies better to the Lowlands than the Highlands (where feuding lasted longer – well into the seventeenth century, while cattle raiding carried on until the mid-1700s), and towards the end of the period under review rather than earlier.[1] But the unruliness of Highland society can be exaggerated – the last clan battle was fought in 1688 – as can the contrast with the Lowlands. There were fewer armed men in the north at the turn of the eighteenth century than has often been assumed; even in the previous century most clansmen had little more than a sword.[2] Yet in the early seventeenth century the country had been wracked by civil war, and later James VII (and II) and his ministers were forced to flee from Scotland. Armed conflict followed the Glorious Revolution in 1688–9. There was a further eruption of civil conflict again in the first four decades after the Union of 1707. Scotland was not settled until the 1750s, and then only through the imposition of 'systematic state terrorism' was Highland Jacobitism finally defeated.[3] At the century's end there appeared the challenge of political radicalism and the French Revolution, although historians are divided about the degree of support these twin causes attracted, and what threat to the state they posed in Scotland.[4]

However, behind these ideological, dynastic and confessional conflicts, key structures of Scottish society were in place even by 1600, and firmly so by the end of the seventeenth century, certainly in most of the Lowlands. These ordering mechanisms were sufficiently robust to create a somewhat different pattern of disorder in Scotland than was commonplace in other parts of early modern Europe. Levels of serious crime appear to have been lower in Scotland than in England – although an exception may have been child murder, often by the use of particularly gruesome methods.[5] Even in Edinburgh, the country's teeming capital, there appear to have been fewer violent deaths than might be anticipated – whether by accident, suicide, execution or homicide.[6] Fewer Scots – again proportionately – were transported to Australia at the turn of the nineteenth century.[7] But the indications are that once brought to trial, there was a greater likelihood in Scotland compared with other parts of the British Isles that the accused, or 'panel', would be found guilty.[8] Acquittals too were rare.[9] There were good reasons, therefore, to abide by the law. But when the noose was called for, it was more likely to have been round the neck of a female murderer in Scotland than a male's – and almost as many women in this category were subject to aggravated execution, that is, public dissection following death.[10] Courts in Enlightenment Scotland were not known for their mercy, particularly when dealing with violent women – the antithesis of civil society then in the making.

Central government was one of the least effective of the ordering structures. Governance from the centre was rather ineffectual until steps began to be taken in the later seventeenth century to enforce stronger legal control through the reconstituted High Court of Justiciary (1672). Unlike England's, Scotland's justices of the peace – introduced in 1609 – had carried little force, although ultimately they managed to make something of a mark in dealing with the poor, and at least one local study suggests they may have played a more significant role in regulating moral and social behaviour than has usually been allowed.[11] With the creation of circuit courts in 1708, however, the net of the criminal justice system was cast over the whole country. It was not until 1747, however, that the landowners' feudal heritable jurisdictions were abolished; thereafter the business of the circuit courts mushroomed.

This is not to suggest that Scotland was exempt from the everyday tensions and disorders that were found elsewhere, either in England or further afield. Mobbing and rioting were much more part and parcel of Scottish social life than was thought previously, even if they were not, by any stretch of the imagination, everyday occurrences.[12] Even so, each of the main waves of food rioting in England and Wales during the eighteenth century had its Scottish counterpart, and in this respect can be interpreted as integral features of Scottish life in the Lowlands.[13] Combinations of workers, and strikes too, were much in evidence from the 1720s, but can be dated from the later seventeenth century; skilled workers in Scotland were no less averse than their counterparts elsewhere in Europe to the changes brought about by capitalist modernisation.[14] That such instances of collective behaviour occurred at all hints at the existence of a set of evolving but distinctively plebeian beliefs, norms and responses, reproduced down the generations. How ordinary people understood and justified their actions, what they thought and believed, is often hard to fathom, and requires empathy and imaginative inference.[15] Within communities, there were particular individuals – probably literate and moderately subversive – who were prepared to adopt the role of defenders of what has been termed the moral economy of the poor, of natural justice and as spokespersons for and leaders of the common people.[16]

In Scotland there were variants of most kinds of disturbance found in other parts of early modern Europe. For example, if relatively few Scots lost their lives as a result of premeditated murder between 1600 and 1800, the incidence of assault involving customs and excise officers, and soldiers, in the first half of the eighteenth century was as great as the worst-afflicted regions anywhere.[17] Elements of disorderliness, which Scotland also shared with other parts of Europe, included that associated with vagrants, usually on the move, sometimes in bands – much to the concern of the inhabitants of towns and rural settlements they passed through, often demanding food and succour. In dealing with vagrancy the measures implemented by the authorities in Scotland were little different from those adopted in England and elsewhere. Steps taken included the rounding up and arrest of vagrants and directing them back to their home parishes and banishment; less successful were attempts to force them into employment, although Edinburgh had a correction house in which the inmates were put to work making various sorts of cloth from 1643.[18]

Yet, there was a lower level of disorders that are more properly understood as everyday, such as drunkenness, neighbourhood disputes, sexual misdemeanours, assaults and other comparatively minor crimes. What may at first sight appear to be disorderly events, however, may actually be nothing of the sort, but rather controlled excesses – permitted by the authorities as part of the business of maintaining order in the longer run. In the sixteenth century there are even instances where abbots of unrule and Robin Hoods of the May Games were appointed by the town authorities; hardly a world turned upside down.[19]

To be considered too, are shifts in the concerns of the authorities over specific types of disorder and criminality. Priorities and fears changed, as is most clearly seen in the irregular surges in witchcraft persecutions. Lack of information is not be equated with an absence of disorderly behaviour. For example, it was only in 1699 that the twice-weekly *Edinburgh Gazette* appeared, and what this and subsequent newspapers reported was patchy.[20] It is only from a proclamation in 1781 issued by Glasgow's magistrates about improvements to the city's policing arrangements and banning various street games, including stone throwing (probably the widespread sport of 'bulleting'[21]) and making bonfires in public places, that we discover that these had evidently been sufficiently extensive and long-standing to have caused middle and upper rank anxiety.[22]

ORDERING STRUCTURES

Notwithstanding the limitations of central government during much of the seventeenth century, and the periodic difficulties in ensuring regular sittings of the lower courts, by the start of the eighteenth century there had emerged in Scotland a multi-layered, interlocking justice system. This involved the higher secular courts and beneath them county sheriffs, justices of the peace and commissioners of supply, and in the towns, burgh courts. In the countryside, until 1748, were the franchised barony and regality courts, the preserve of the landed class. Landowners also convened parish boards of heritors, responsible for the construction and upkeep of the church and its graveyard and the support of the minister. Often bridging the formal distinctions between the various bodies was their membership, which was mainly drawn from the ranks of the gentry, that is, owners of moderate sized estates.[23] The other link was the kirk: a 'vital arm of the state in early modern Scotland'.[24]

Of the factors that kept ordinary Scots in check during their daily lives, there is little doubt that the church was by far the most significant. By 1600 the Protestant Reformation was well-entrenched, even if the supporters of episcopacy and presbyterianism continued their contest for national ascendancy until the latter was finally secured following the Glorious Revolution of 1688–9. Presbyterians in Scotland created a Church governed by a series of courts, ranging from a national general assembly, through synods and presbyteries, down to local kirk sessions, established in every parish. And it was at the local level, in the most densely populated parts of the nation – largely the Lowlands – that what has been described as a cultural revolution in the lives of ordinary Scots was achieved with remarkable speed, and with an unrivalled intensity.[25]

Adherence to Roman Catholicism, the religion of the majority until 1560, had shrivelled to as little as 2 per cent of the population, confined mainly to the Gaelic-speaking Highlands and Islands, and the north-eastern county of Banff. More numerous were their oft-times allies the Episcopalians, whose liturgy, prayer book and celebrations of saints' days were almost equally despised by Presbyterian reformers. On manners and morals, however, there was little difference between presbyterianism and episcopalianism.[26] With protestantism on the march under the leadership of its firebrand Calvinist preachers, and the demise of the Catholic Church, under attack were a series of religious festivals, pageants and what have been described as the 'sensuous' aspects of the old worship, such as statues and other imagery including stained-glass windows (the 'books of the humble'), incense and harmonised music. Some holy days simply disappeared, formally at least. In their place were imposed days of fasting and prayer. Formerly integral elements of the everyday life of ordinary people were the focus of Presbyterian disapproval: belief in the supernatural, including fairies; charming; pilgrimages to holy wells. Greater emphasis was placed upon Old Testament biblical teaching, sobriety and catechism, along with regular attendance at church (for two lengthy sermons each Sunday, frequently led by hectoring ministers), where an unharmonised vernacular psalter, with simple tunes, was introduced.[27]

Calvinist dogma, with its belief in man's innate sinfulness, was the order of the day, at least until the mid-eighteenth century, when presbyterianism in Scotland became increasingly Arminian – and salvationist – in tone. In the lives of ordinary Scots godly discipline was exercised by their parish ministers, aided by a posse of elders and deacons, who had no compunction about intruding into the most intimate aspects of the lives of their parishioners. Their rule was absolute, and held sway over their ministers too. Parish populations typically ranged in number between 600 and 3,000 – readily manageable numbers for an active kirk session. In many burghs the sessions included at least one town baillie, and were often assisted in their work by the town councils and the burgh courts. In Aberdeen during the second half of the seventeenth century most offenders appeared in both secular and church courts.[28] In the countryside an elder was appointed from each barony.[29] Few, therefore, escaped the elders' gimlet-eyed gaze. This was directed toward the streets, wynds and public places in the towns, and country lanes and fields. Elders peered – literally – into the everyday activities of parishioners in their homes, workshops and barns. They used their ears too, to detect illicit love-making, or to grasp at whispers of scandal and reports of suspected pregnancies among spinsters, or of adulterous liaisons and wife-beating. It was by the kirk, too, that information was gleaned about charming and suspected cases of witchcraft, even if further enquiry and punishment required the intervention of civil magistrates and lairds.[30] At various points during their lifetimes, most people came face-to-face with their fastidious parish governors: to ask for marriage banns to be proclaimed; and to request that their bairns be baptised. Even in death, to be buried in the parish mortcloth – deemed essential by believers – required the sanction of the session. Others would appear to complain about their neighbours' behaviour, or as witnesses for and against in cases before the kirk court. But the sacrament of communion – the poet Robert Burns' 'holy fair' – was the contact point each year which mattered most to individuals, and was a precondition of social acceptability. Conscientious ministers tried to visit their flocks in person at least as often as once a year, in part to examine their worthiness to receive the sacrament.[31]

Those suspected of breaches of godly discipline were summonsed to appear before the elders, quizzed relentlessly, pressed to acknowledge their sin and demonstrate a willingness to repent. Failure to appear could instigate action by the justices of the peace.[32] Breaches included failing to attend church – or worse, working or drinking during the time of sermon (even 'standing idle' could bring a reprimand). Also likely to bring down the wrath of the kirk were activities like dancing 'promiscuously', or engaging in a range of sexual misbehaviours, including what the Englishman, Edmund Burt, thought the 'extraordinary' offence of 'antenuptial fornication'. This was detected months after the event by checking a new-born child's date of birth against the parents' wedding date. In sexual matters and even ostensibly innocent relations between the sexes, like touching, let alone kissing in public (both activities coming under the heading of scandalous carriage), the regime was unremittingly severe.[33] Women were demonised, their bodies judged to be the locus of sin, a misogynous belief that restricted women, especially unmarried domestic servants, in their mobility, employment,

Figure 7.1 The Mauchline Holy Fair, *by Alexander Carse. Holy fair – or communion – was an annual (and sometimes twice-yearly) event that attracted large numbers, even hundreds of parishioners. Preaching and prayers preceded communion itself, but despite its religious purpose, by the end of the eighteenth century the occasion was also associated with drunkenness and other forms of licentiousness. This is captured in Robert Burns' 'The Holy Fair', the energy of which is strangely absent from this painting – which was inspired by Burns' poem. © Courtesy of the Trustees of Burns Monument and Burns Cottage (www. scran.ac.uk).*

wages, residence and credit.[34] It was women who were most often suspected as witches – as many as 90 per cent of the total named in some counties. The breasts of women denying pregnancy were forcibly pressed in search of the tell-tale eruptions of 'green milk'. Concealing pregnancy was judged in the relevant statute – the Act Anent Child Murder (1690) – to be as heinous a crime as child murder. In insisting on ritual public humiliation of offenders Scottish presbyterianism stood at the more extreme end of the scale of punishment practices in Protestant Europe.[35] Typically, the guilty parties were barefoot and dressed in sackcloth and forced to sit on the high, backless, 'stool of repentance' in full view of the church congregation (that is, their neighbours, acquaintances, employers, friends and family, sometimes for a succession of Sundays).

Additionally, punitive fines were imposed by sessions on adulterers, while other penalties included periods in the stocks or jougs (a device similar to the stocks) and imprisonment. Finding it harder to pay their fines, it was women who were more likely to be subject to punishments like ducking, having their heads shaven, whipping and ritual banishment by the hangman.[36]

Few parishioners were immune, although more often than not substantial landowners managed to escape public penance, often by payment of a fine (a means increasingly used by others able to afford to pay in the eighteenth century); their servants too generally avoided kirk discipline. Neither were soldiers subject to the dictates of the ruling elders. Like sailors, most had left by the time it had become evident that they had fathered an illegitimate child.

The impact of such a thick blanket of moral policing was profound. It led in part to an 'obsessive' introspection, a concern with salvation and anxiety to know and carry out God's will.[37] The kirk provided much of the nation's elementary schooling (though boys were more often participants than girls), played a major role in the universities and, from 1592, had been responsible for setting the terms of poor relief. The distinction was quickly made between the deserving poor: the 'cruiket folk, seik folk and waik folk'; and the undeserving, that is, 'sturdy beggars', the semi-criminalised vagrants.[38] Those belonging to the last group included 'actors of unlawful plays', 'Egyptians' and 'others who pretend[ed] to power of charming'. In 1700, in response to the swollen numbers of the poor on the move resulting from the famine conditions of the second half of the 1690s, one alarmed writer distinguished between the 'truly poor' and those of both sexes who lived 'as Beasts . . . Promiscuously', with no regard for the law, civil or God-given.[39]

It was from church pulpits that efforts were made to shape local opinion and from which were intimated important items of public news, although peripatetic tradesmen, chapmen, and tinkers performed this role as well.[40] As in the immediate aftermath of the Reformation not all parishes were either keen or able to follow John Knox's injunctions to impose rigid church discipline; it was not until the mid-seventeenth century that most sessions really got into gear. Another wave of intense endeavour to stamp out vice swept the country from the 1690s through to the 1710s, aided and abetted in Edinburgh by the Society for the Reformation of Manners, and even royal exhortations against prophanity and immorality.[41] Although its origins lay in England, the 1690 Act against infanticide was passed on the urging of the ruling patriarchy of the General Assembly in Scotland, and ushered in a period of half a century or so when hanging was the favoured punishment for women found guilty of child murder; few suffered this fate after 1750.[42] If in Edinburgh by the 1720s there were signs of a waning of the intense religious fervour of earlier times,[43] it was not until the last quarter of the eighteenth century that the kirk's grip on social behaviour really loosened, prised free by the moderatism of the Scottish Enlightenment, the growth of humanitarianism and an emergent belief in individualism. Increased population mobility and rapid urbanisation made it more difficult for elders to track their prey by the device of the 'testificat', a certificate of good behaviour from a person's last parish, without which movement up to this point had been difficult.[44] But until relatively late in the century, visitors to Scotland continued to be struck by what might be considered the kirk's residual effects, notably the air of relative calm on the sabbath. Attendance levels at church were high. Perhaps as many as one-third of Scots sat in the pews in 1780; more would have attended if there had been room for them, or seats that they could afford.[45]

It is where kirk controls were less prevalent that it can be seen, by comparison, how effective they were when in place. Thus, in the Highlands, the northern isles and the north-east, where presbyterianism was weakly established prior to the mid-eighteenth century, customary support for saints' days remained buoyant under the aegis of the Catholic and Episcopalian ministries. In the central Lowlands and south-east by contrast, popular culture has been described as 'ritually impoverished'.[46] If this is a judgement that requires qualification, what is certainly the case is that there was little in these parts of Scotland that resembled the religious feasts, carnivals and festivals of Misrule that occurred in English towns in the medieval period and beyond (and more spectacularly on mainland Europe) and, indeed, in Scotland prior to the Reformation.[47] Under the influence of the church and state, celebratory events in the capital, Edinburgh, tended to be for royal birthdays and to mark naval or military victories. Most public spectacles were carefully planned and orchestrated. With bell-ringing, bonfires and cannon and small-arms fire heightening passions, prudent management was essential.[48] In the parishes, strict enforcement of kirk discipline appears to have impacted on sexual behaviour, by holding down illegitimacy rates (which fell, nationally, from the 1660s to the 1720s) at 5 per cent or less; regionally, they were lowest where the Church's authority was strongest, and began to rise only as the kirk's hold slackened from the 1760s.[49] Most children in central Lowland Scotland were born to married couples.[50] Indeed in St Andrews, under the ministry of James Melville, fornication and adultery were stamped out almost completely for a short time during the mid-1590s.[51] By contrast, in the booming but small Shetland fishing town of Lerwick (the population of which was under 1,200 in 1755), where a minister and kirk session were appointed only after 1701, fornication and offences against kirk morality were rife. Cases of the former reached levels twice as high as in Lowland Scotland in the first decades of the eighteenth century, and were three times higher than in the nearby parish of Sandwick, where session control was longer established and clearly tighter.[52]

As noted, other agencies also contributed to the sought-for orderliness of early modern Scottish society. In the countryside, the landed classes monitored the farmtowns not only through the kirk sessions but also via the birlaw courts and the aforementioned courts of barony and regality, which often worked hand-in-hand with the church. Like the kirk's 'parish states', baron courts were numerous; at least sixteen administered the Glenorchy estates of the Campbells – earls of Breadalbane from 1681 – for instance.[53] In the early part of the period at least, and perhaps until the second half of the eighteenth century in the north-east, where peasant farming survived for longer, there appears to have been a marked sense of community, a commitment to the principles of good neighbourhood and less of the antipathy between lairds and their tenantry than would emerge later.[54] Landlord absenteeism was rare, the gulf in the material conditions between laird and tenants and sub-tenants was narrower and linguistically the two were bound by the use of vernacular Scots; there was recognition, in a world where the forces of nature could so easily upset the balance and create crisis conditions, of mutual dependency. There was mutual respect too, with little of the obsequiousness on the part of the lower orders, the absence of which was afterwards regretted by those above them as rural society became increasingly commercialised and conflict-ridden.[55]

Where disputes between neighbours did occur, it was the main function of the birlaw-men to adjudicate on these – over matters such as boundaries and animal trespassing and rights to peat and other fuel. Where squabbles could not be resolved amicably, good behaviour was insisted upon by the baron courts, in effect the lairds' private courts of jurisdiction through which they could exert control over their estates.[56] In theory baron courts could hang offenders for some crimes – murder and certain kinds of theft – but few did after 1600. Instead, they were kept fully occupied by dealing with a host of lesser offences: rent arrears; poaching; and theft of, or damage to, wood were among the most numerous. Miscreants could be fined, or in the most serious cases, imprisoned in the barony 'pit', or 'hole', a rudimentary gaol, although this was rarely used in the eighteenth century. Other concerns for the courts included setting the prices that country tradesmen could charge or, often overlapping with the less formal birlaw court, establishing and maintaining the rules of good neighbourly husbandry. Order was better maintained when the landowner himself participated in the court's proceedings, as well as when the courts met regularly – at least once a year; the same was true when an absent laird's wife stepped into the breach.[57] After 1747, landlord influence in the countryside was ensured through the strengthened sheriff courts and sheriff-deputes, who were invariably recruited from the landed classes. But not to be overlooked as promoters of order in rural Scotland for virtually the entire period are the justices of the peace who, when working effectively, offered another option to landowners anxious to suppress the cutting of green wood and trespassing, for example. They were also an arbiter to which ordinary people could complain about minor thefts, encroachments and assaults.[58] The labouring poor, too, had an interest in maintaining good neighbourly relations and containing petty crime.

It was not solely the application of strict estate justice allied to the inculcation of a strong sense of communal interest that explains the apparent quiescence of rural Lowland Scotland, even after c. 1760, when Scottish landowners embarked on a programme of radical estate reorganisation.[59] Arguably, the longevity of many landed families' dominance bolstered the

effectiveness of the courts of regality and barony.[60] Patronage and paternalism played their parts in ensuring the loyalty and obedience of the people
below.[61] By these means landlords were able to call on their tenants and
dependants to defend their common interests. Feuding was a feature in the
Lowlands as well as the Highlands. Inter-family feuds were commonplace
in south-west Scotland at the turn of the seventeenth century, while a late,
and rarer, instance comes from 1708 when Robert Cunninghame, laird of
Auchenharvie in Ayrshire, persuaded a broad social mix of the inhabitants
of his barony to pour sand down the coal-pit of a rival coal-mine owner.[62]

The close partnership of burgh magistrates and parish sessions in dealing
with immoral behaviour has been noted; the closer the association, it would
seem, the more respectable the behaviour of the citizenry. Dundee is a case
in point. There, the authority of the kirk appears to have been internalised
more deeply than its more northerly east coast neighbour, Aberdeen. For
example, in Dundee the illegitimacy ratio was consistently lower, the detection rate was higher and, from the second half of the seventeenth century
through to the end of the eighteenth century, men were considerably more
likely to admit paternity.[63] In Edinburgh, on the other hand, the magistrates
and town council were not always as firm in their backing for moral reform
as the more zealous of their citizens might have wished. They recognised the
downsides of adhering too tightly to kirk strictures, as in 1730 when, contrary to the demands of sabbatarians, the council ordered that street lamps
should be lit on Sundays, as every other evening.[64]

Burgh courts also stamped down on offences such as prostitution and
vagrancy, drunkenness and brawling. Breaches of public order of this sort
took most of the burgh courts' time.[65] Reputation mattered in small communities. Women (and in the sixteenth century a few men) found guilty of
false accusations, making threats, or mouthing insults – often very wittily
and in the quasi-theatrical form of 'flyting'[66] – could find themselves ordered
to be constrained by the branks, the 'scold's bridle'. This was a metal cage-
like device which enclosed the offenders head and pierced or held in check
the offender's tongue. Branks were used fairly commonly in the seventeenth
century, although thereafter they fell out of favour. The humiliation was
more effective if the offender's plaid was removed: there was nowhere to
hide. Doubling the shame was that most victims were of modest burgess
rank, not the poor or vagrants. For women who broke with other norms of
acceptable neighbourly behaviour in the Scottish towns there were even cru-
eller fates. For those charged with witchcraft – often resulting from everyday
quarrels that had apparently taken a demonic turn – there was strangling,
burning and drowning.[67] But there were clearly also women whose commitment to the kirk's moral values were as strong as those of any kirk session.
Having failed perhaps to persuade a pregnant girl to throw herself at the
mercy of the church, it was older women who came forward with the testimonies that were used to prosecute those suspected of infanticide. A 'close

cousin' of witchcraft, this was 'a woman's crime . . . suspected by women, and usually brought to light by women'.[68]

To enforce the law in the towns, many councils employed constables or officers, who were often clothed at the expense of the burgh, and sometimes uniformed. In the larger burghs they could be full-time, and part-time elsewhere. Sometimes they were old or retired soldiers, although in Edinburgh there was a distinction between the permanent town guard and the trained bands – which comprised craftsmen and tradesmen at times when they were not working. The town officers' role was an onerous one, requiring them to deal with a range of offences and offenders, at any time of night or day.[69] Trades incorporations could also play an important part in maintaining urban order. Formed in many cases in the sixteenth century and in some instances even earlier, and functioning primarily as employers' organisations designed to restrict entry to their crafts, maintain high standards of workmanship and support their members in sickness and old age, the incorporations also supplemented the activities of the kirk sessions and the town councils. Members of the trades were expected to attend church – where they often had their own clearly identifiable pews – and to ensure the good behaviour of their workpeople and families (daughters, for instance, were expected to remain virgins as long as they were unmarried). Masters applied strict rules to their apprentices, in whose houses they were usually accommodated and fed. Card and dice playing were frequently banned, while there were rules in some places that apprentices should be in their masters' houses by ten at night. Often indentures required regular attendance at church, forbade fornication and adultery and other types of loose living. Those breaching the crafts' rules could be fined, and for serious offences, such as theft, insubordination, assisting in mobs or forming associations, expelled.[70]

Private initiatives were also taken by burgh inhabitants. Thus, in 1754, concerned about a rise in property theft, possibly carried out by a posse of 'Gypsies' and beggars, fifty or so 'gentlemen of Glasgow' formed the Glasgow Friendly Society, a vigilante body the aim of which was to bring private prosecutions against suspected culprits.[71] At the very end of the eighteenth century, several such associations were formed, like that of Dundee in October 1794, 'for the purpose of aiding the civil magistrates for the preventing of riots, tumults or disorder within the burgh'.[72] Hitherto, and much more frequently than has usually been assumed, the lords provosts, magistrates and town councils had been able to request the aid of the military in quelling serious disorder. All of the major outbreaks of crowd violence in Scotland from the Union of 1707 through to the 1770s had required the use of the army to restore order, as did many smaller, less well-documented disturbances. Within their communities, aggrieved Scots could strike fear into the hearts of those in authority who had caused them offence; without military intervention, there may have been considerably more blood-letting, beating and wounding than actually happened.[73] But from 1793 the army's priority was the war with France, and calls for military assistance at home were less likely to be answered.

Towns, too, were where the circuit courts were held, twice-yearly; the most serious cases were heard at the High Court in Edinburgh. Where the courts convened, the inhabitants were left in little doubt as to the importance of the proceedings. The theatrical props of rank and authority were designed to impress and cow. These included powdered wigs, fine clothing and 'hauteur of bearing and expression' which accompanied the slow procession of the judges to each sitting. It was where the courts sat too that most death sentences were carried out; those after the Murder Act of 1752 were deliberately made more shocking – and intimidating. But although huge numbers assembled to watch, it was only at the start of the nineteenth century that hangings began to be carried out more frequently where the crime had been committed.[74] Even in the smaller places, however, corporal punishment was something virtually everyone would have witnessed. Few people would not have seen a public whipping, an offender's ear pinned to the townhouse door or someone chained by the neck in the aforementioned jougs to the townhouse wall for a period of hours, so presenting an inviting target for those drawn to mock, or further humiliate the guilty party by pelting them with eggs or mud. Banishment might follow, as it did when two women in Hawick in 1697 were found guilty of theft, taken out of the irons in which they were held, publicly whipped and scourged – on the busy market day. The ritual culminated at the east end of the town, when the culprits were 'brunt on the chiek with the letter H' (for Hawick) and then expelled, to the sound of a single drum beating. Normally with a label attached to the breast of the offender stating in large characters what he or she had been guilty of, those watching were made acutely aware of what would follow if they were to step out of line.[75]

DISORDER: ITS EXTENT AND CAUSES

Despite the array of instruments in place which could be applied to discourage disorderly behaviour, and the structures of Scottish society which appear to have militated against it, what is striking is the extent to which unruliness prevailed. It is difficult to construct a simple chronology of disorder. There were surges in the intensity of certain forms of collective violence for example, which can be linked to particular circumstances. War often produced hardship – and disorder – as, of course, did harvest failures. Not surprisingly, it was during periods of economic difficulty that concerns about vagrancy intensified: thus, coinciding with the downturn of the early 1770s, a plan was drawn up by the justices of peace for Perthshire designed to stop 'vagrant beggars' from thieving fish, wood, fruit, grass, peas, potatoes, cabbage, kail and turnips from 'Pounds, Gardens or Fields'.[76] The problem was chronic rather than acute in the Highlands, however, although it was in large part the cumulative consequence of episodic dislocation. Roaming bands of caterans – principally landless men who sought subsistence through banditry – were responsible for most of the serious disorder there was in the Highlands and the contiguous parts of Lowland Scotland in the seventeenth century. Their crimes ranged from theft of livestock, through fire-raising to murder.[77]

Customs officials in Scotland had been the target of angry mobs before 1707. Union, however, heralded an increase in the levels of taxation on a wider range of commodities, and was accompanied by much more determined efforts on the part of the newly-created British state to make sure that taxes were actually collected. Within weeks of the treaty being inaugurated there were reports of collective violence directed against customs and excise officers, followed in many cases by furious assaults on the parties of soldiers sent to assist the officers in their duty. In virtually all the seaward parts of Lowland Scotland, customs officers, and the town magistrates and soldiers found themselves harangued, bloodied, beaten and sometimes taken prisoner by ferocious crowds rarely comprising less than thirty or forty people, and frequently many more. Most participants carried weapons of some sort, usually stones, clubs, staves and pitchforks, and occasionally firearms. In the worst affected districts – Dumfriesshire and the south-west coastline to Greenock, and low-lying Angus with its ports of Arbroath, Dundee and Montrose, further inland, too, in and around Stirling and Perth, for instance – officials were overwhelmed, as indeed sometimes was the military sent in to protect them.[78] In this regard Scotland was, simply, ungovernable; in England guerrilla war of this kind – resisting and routing customs officers – was far more localised. In Scotland the disorder was national and stretched as far north as Shetland – where popularly connived-at smuggling took much longer to suppress than elsewhere.[79] What is remarkable is not the number of major disturbances where fatalities resulted, or which reached the ears of the Lord Advocate and went to a High Court trial. Such cases were the proverbial tips of the iceberg, which mask the compelling evidence there is of the daily disorder surrounding smuggling and the authorities' attempts to deal with it. Most smuggling was small-scale, with contraband goods being sold at lower than market price. This was a major boon for the bulk of ordinary Scots who struggled to make ends meet, and in part accounts for the prominence of women among the riotous crowds, acting in defence of the aforementioned 'moral economy' of the poor. Some of the largest and most threatening in Dumfries and Galloway, in fact, were virtually all-female; even in mixed crowds women were often in the vanguard, exploiting perhaps the belief that in confrontations with authority they would be less likely to be arrested.[80] However, that between 1750 and 1815 in the Lowlands, slightly more women – usually married – than males were indicted for assaults against revenue officers, demonstrates that this popular notion bore little relation to reality, perhaps as the authorities became less forgiving in their attitudes.[81]

Also welcome among a penurious people was the casual employment created by smuggling gangs who often relied on 'country people' to do much of their 'running' for them, assisting in unloading contraband on quiet shore-lines and in creeks and then concealing in caves, on moorland and inside barns, barrels of brandy or wine and tobacco, tea, gin and other dutiable goods.[82] Adding other dimensions to the disturbances were the widespread unpopularity of the Union, and the association of smuggling with Jacobitism. There was an unwillingness, too, on the part of Jacobite justices of the peace to prosecute offenders. There was also a deep-seated resentment on the part of ordinary people at the encroachment of the tentacles of the centralising state which customs and excise officers represented – especially as early on they were acting in the interests of the less than popular Hanoverian regime; in this respect, modest merchants, artisans and labouring men and women – and even children – found common cause. Incidents involving large crowds had reduced by the mid-eighteenth century, although small groups could cause equal discomfort for the victims they 'deforced'. However, the will to defy the exciseman remained strong up to and even beyond 1800, inten-sifying in parts of the Highlands from the 1760s with the rising demand for whisky, illicitly distilled by thousands of necessitous poor peasants each autumn, and was the subject of much of the business of the lesser courts.[83]

Only exceptionally did disorder in the countryside reach the ears of gov-ernment in London. There were instances of large-scale riot, mainly against enclosing and during which offending walls and dykes were pulled down, but these were sporadic – decades could go by without another occurrence – and localised. Similar were instances of resistance on the part of town dwellers to the encroachment by neighbouring landowners over common land which had been used to graze livestock, or as a supply of kindling and peat, or stones or turf divots for house-building purposes.[84] But behind many of these eruptions of collective anger was deep-seated resentment and rumbling unrest about the effects of growing commercialisation on rural society, although the intensity of this varied across the country and over time. Few landlords, however, were spared some discomfort of this kind. Even James Boswell of Auchinleck estate in Ayrshire, who revelled in his role as paternalist proprietor, fretted about the 'cunning' of his tenants and their apparent disregard for his prop-erty, although in this Boswell in the later eighteenth century was simply dis-covering what other lairds had known for a long time; adherence to customary rights – and a belief in the right of the individual to make a living – was tena-cious. With the inequalities of power and authority that characterised rural Scotland, prudence decreed that this would manifest itself in other ways, anonymously, and often under cover of darkness. [85] Even large-scale actions sometimes took place at night, where discovery and arrest were less likely.

Less dramatic, but widely utilised 'weapons of the weak', were small-scale, even personal acts of defiance which included theft of peat and green wood, and breaking through recently built enclosure walls and newly planted hedges, perhaps to maintain customary rights of way and to secure access to graze and shelter cattle, sheep, horses – and the goats that were a particular menace to growing wood.[86] Given the reluctance among the lower orders 'to change old customs and relinquish habits which have acquired the sanction of time', threats, prosecutions and the exercise of formal power, judged one early-nineteenth-century observer of the Scottish countryside, would achieve little.[87] Indeed, it became apparent during periods of intense social stress, as during the 1790s, that threats from below, some of which were delivered anonymously, could induce terror even among those who wielded the instruments of formal power: of Annandale, following the introduction of the Militia Act in 1797, the duke of Buccleuch reported, 'The Constables dare not appear, and the gentlemen of the county dare not show their faces in the towns and villages. God knows where this will end.'[88] Fatal assaults on men of rank were rare, however: by and large it was their agents – factors, ministers, town officers and the like – who bore the brunt of any physical force. What was a constant presence though was the lurking, watchful, usually conservative, sometimes rebellious, but collectively fearless mob.

There were clearly limits to the influence of the kirk on everyday behaviour. The Clerks of Penicuik on their Loanhead estate near Edinburgh tried over a period of several decades to reform the morals of their coal workers and agricultural tenants. Yet swearing, drunkenness, disobedience, Sabbath breach and irregular working by being absent from work on time-honoured days such as Mondays, Fridays when a marriage was announced, were as much complained of in 1750 as they had been a century earlier.[89] Clashes of value systems as landowners, employers and others sought to achieve social hegemony were neither unique to pre-industrialised Scotland, nor to Loanhead. Fife's salt workers, for example, openly defied the kirk sessions in the seventeenth century by keeping their pans fired on Sundays. Much to the irritation of their employers, salters too were known to take extraordinarily long breaks at new year.[90]

Kirk session minute books teem with cases of moral delinquency. Their focus was on sexual offences, primarily fornication and adultery (which accounted for around 60 per cent of cases), although those suspected of bigamy were also investigated.[91] The frequency with which the same individuals appeared before the session, however, is suggestive of a high level of individual promiscuity. Few though were as bare-faced in their contempt for the kirk in Scotland as the members of Fife's Beggars Benison, formed around 1732, a club of otherwise 'respectable' males devoted to convivial celebration of free sex and penis worship, including masturbation, although the men were linked also by their interest in smuggling.[92] The Benison spawned Edinburgh's Wig Club.

Yet the extent to which males in Scotland denied paternity suggests such clubs simply formalised urges and behaviours that would have had John Knox birling in his grave. Figures that have been calculated for those parishioners eligible for communion also point to rather a low level of religiosity, other perhaps than during the c. 1690–1720s period of more intense kirk fervour.[93] On the other hand, not least because of the considerable quantities of wine that were disbursed, as well as unusually generous handouts for the poor, the yearly communion had its attractions – as a boisterous holiday – and, therefore, its moralising detractors.[94] That there were in most communities sizeable minorities, perhaps as much as a third of the population of a town like Glasgow, who seemed oblivious to or were prepared to ignore the efforts of parish elders to coral them, is indicated by the frequency with which complaints were made of idling, drinking, playing games and working on the sabbath. Even servant girls drawing water from wells on a Sunday was disapproved of in Dundee as late as 1796.[95]

It was this kind of low level disorder that permeated Scottish society. In Edinburgh, most malicious but relatively minor damage to property and small-scale vandalism, robberies, and muggings were random events, carried out in the main by young males who had had too much to drink.[96] Drunken brawling was for men, largely. Women perpetrating violent assaults, including robberies, were much more likely to have been sober and to have planned their crimes.[97] Much of what happened to disrupt daily life can be classified as unneighbourly conduct, such as name-calling or fighting, as in Hawick in 1645 when James Scott was accused by Gilbert Watt of calling him a 'twa facet thief, and ane runnigat beggar', or in the same place in 1642 when Thomas Oliver, described as a traveller, drew 'ane sword to James Burne, baillie'.[98] Provosts, town councillors, magistrates and baillies often found themselves on the receiving end of abuse, both verbal and physical, more often than might be anticipated and despite the insistence of the magistrates in Perth, for example, that those passing them doff their hats.[99] Ritualistic torment for the town's dignitaries had become more or less the norm by the 1770s on the annual occasion of the king's birthday celebrations, an event – in all of its rumbustiousness – captured in Robert Fergusson's 'The King's Birthday in Edinburgh' (1772). Glasgow's *Mercury* newspaper in 1792 treated the 'daring' outrages of the day more seriously, and condemned the actions of the 'loose disorderly rabble throwing brick bats, dead dogs and cats, by which several of the military were severely cut'.[100] It was the state that had led moves to mark the monarch's birthday after the Restoration. Celebrations had been orchestrated by a number of burghs, but as early as the 1730s the town authorities in Lanark and Stirling had had to take stern action to deal with the day's disturbances.[101] Although in the early eighteenth century there were contests between Jacobite celebrants of the birthday of the Old Pretender and Hanoverians, by the time Fergusson was writing it is clear that the occasion had been hijacked by the towns' youths and other ordinary inhabitants. The king's birthday had been become a much-anticipated and energetically planned-for occasion upon which they could prick the pomposity of their social superiors and remind them, in the manner of the carnivalesque – a Europe-wide phenomenon – that the lower orders had their place in urban society together with the means of enforcing their will.[102]

This they did also, on their own terms, by forcing those who ignored standards of acceptable behaviour to 'ride the stang', a long pole which involved the victim struggling to remain upright while being paraded in public. They rarely managed, however, and spent much time upside down, their head and upper body scraping along the rough road surface or through mud. Victims included merchants who demanded what were deemed to be over-high prices for meal during a period of dearth, adulterers, wife-beaters and nagging and over-domineering wives.[103] Uncomfortable and unseemly though such displays of lower class behaviour may have been in the eyes of the middling sort and upper classes, such charivari-esque rituals of social inversion were a price worth paying, as the letting off of steam on a short-term basis which ensured longer-term social stability.[104]

But there were other catalysts for urban unruliness, although most were rooted in an unwritten but commonly understood sense of what was right – and wrong. Perth's early-nineteenth-century chronicler of the preceding decades, George Penny, for example, wrote of 'dreadful riots' at public whippings, partly inspired by the sight of and sense of injustice about the lashing of bare-headed and bare-backed women. Perceived harshness in the application of military discipline – such as the flogging of ordinary soldiers for stealing in order to compensate for the inadequacies of army pay – could lead to violent intervention on the part of the town's washerwomen, who worked in the vicinity of the punishment ground. This was despite the general antipathy in the burgh to billeting. Meal rioters subjected to public whipping also induced the sympathy of the assembled multitudes. Hangings periodically ended with a mob chasing and stoning the hangman.[105]

There was an uglier side to periodic disorders of this sort, however: antipathy to outsiders. These could include not only soldiers (and customs and excise men), but also non-burgesses, the English, Roman Catholics and Quakers. The trickle of anti-Englishness rarely dried up during the seventeenth and eighteenth centuries, but its usual manifestation was surliness, cold-shouldering and mildly abusive treatment, as experienced by Daniel Defoe on his tour of Scotland during the 1720s – in the aftermath of the still unpopular incorporating Union when he had feared for his safety.[106] Only occasionally did it erupt into a flash flood of barely containable disorder, as in 1705 when deteriorating Anglo-Scottish relations led to the hanging on Leith sands of the English captain and some crew of the *Worcester*, to the accompaniment of the braying of a vast xenophobic mob. The boil lanced, tempers cooled. Catholics fared rather less well overall, and were subject to rampaging mobs inspired by their sense of Protestant duty, to terrorise, beat, maim and even kill their victims. Even so, such eruptions were rare, as in Edinburgh in 1686, and again in 1688 when the chapel in the abbey at Holyrood was desecrated and the houses of the chancellor the Catholic earl of Perth and his co-religionists pillaged.[107]

Yet a sign of the less than comprehensive impact of the Reformed Church on everyday life is the degree to which the old pre-Reformation calendar days were adhered to, albeit in altered forms.[108] In Shetland a series of 'Popish' festivals was still being honoured in 1774.[109] If the great carnivals had disappeared, ordinary people themselves made good much of the deficit. Football, for example, 'the most plebeian sport in early modern England',[110] was played with equal energy and almost certainly as ubiquitously in Scotland. The favourite occasion for this was Fastern's E'en (in effect, Shrove Tuesday), although the game was also played at New Year or Yuletide in some places.[111] Fastern's E'en, too, was when cock-fighting took place, although again there were the usual regional exceptions: in the Highlands and Islands the cock-fight was associated with Candlemas. Inherent in activities of this sort was a marked level of violence – the football games involved large numbers of people, whose aim might not only to be to transport the ball from one end of a street or burgh to the other, or across a burn, but also to inflict maximum physical damage on the other side. In such a way old grudges could be settled in the general melee.[112] Ordinarily, the several days of sport and festivity which punctuated the working lives of the labouring poor in Scotland went off trouble-free. Nevertheless, while such revels were licensed or at least tolerated by the authorities for much of the period under review – with many employers even supplying the ale and bonfires for special days, what became disconcerting was how frequently the boundaries of acceptable behaviour were breached. Too often serious disorder ensued, and this at a time when greater orderliness was wanted.

Intention and outcome could also diverge during the common ridings, the annual perambulations on horseback of the burghs' boundaries that were organised in many places from the sixteenth century. Instigated not only to assert ownership of town lands but also as a highly theatrical means of forging civic harmony, they often became associated with drunkenness and sexual excess.[113] It was behaviour of this kind that led, at different times throughout Scotland, to attempts to contain particular kinds of popular cultural activity. Thus, in 1716, the council in Hawick felt obliged to fine a number of people for their part in misdemeanours, riots and bloodshed at the 'annual boon-fyr', traditionally held on the town's common to celebrate Beltane (a day marked by similar festivities in most Scottish parishes), but which had become the occasion for violent inter-communal rivalry.[114] However, any kind of gathering together of ordinary people was potentially dangerous, especially when copious quantities of liquor were consumed. Thus, fairs, of which there were many hundreds through Scotland, were a frequent flash point. By the end of the eighteenth century Glasgow's main July fair had become a 'scene of riot and dissipation', not least when youths from town and country clashed (as they did at other town fairs). Boisterous, too, were ubiquitous 'penny weddings', the scale and excessive abandon of which country ministers in particular railed at futilely throughout the period. Even funerals brought disorder

Figure 7.2   The Village Ba' Game, *by Alexander Carse. In many Lowland towns the daily routine was punctuated by sports and games that involved large numbers of their inhabitants. Ball games of the sort depicted here, where one neighbourhood was set against another, were fairly common – from the Borders in the south and to the northern isles. Such occasions were keenly anticipated and involved much physical violence, with attempts by the authorities to stamp them out meeting strong popular resistance. Source: © McManus Galleries and Museum, Dundee.*

in their wake. By the later decades of the eighteenth century the ubiquity of drunkenness was much more complained about than sabbath breach. Heavy drinking and the new work discipline that required regular attendance in the factory or workshop were incompatible.[115]

If the kirk in Lowland Scotland was far from hegemonic in its influence, we should be clear that it acted as an important bulwark for the Hanoverian regime nationally as well as in the localities. Nevertheless, neither its ministers nor its communicants were always reliable allies. Presbyterians' propensity to use force in the face of state oppression – during the unpopular re-imposition of episcopacy after the Restoration – had been demonstrated in a series of armed rebellions and disturbances, commencing in 1666 with the Pentland rising.[116] Enclosing landlords in the south-west during the levellers' revolt in 1724–5 – who were suspected of being Jacobite sympathisers – had to defend their dykes against displaced peasant farmers steeped in the blood-tinged traditions and ideology of the Covenanters, who also found support among evangelical Church of Scotland ministers. There was a Presbyterian edge to the malt tax disturbances in Glasgow and elsewhere in 1725. In 1736 there were reports that ministers had demanded revenge – in blood – not for the hanging by the state of a smuggler but for the subsequent firing on the crowd by a Captain Porteous and his men that resulted in the riots of the same name in Edinburgh. It was in the wake of anti-papist preaching by ministers, and at the instigation of the Protestant Association that brutal sectarian riots broke out in Glasgow against the Catholic Relief Bill in 1778.[117] That the common people had at least in part internalised church teaching is further suggested by an assault directed against customs and excise officers and soldiers at Fraserburgh in 1735: that houses had been searched on the sabbath had angered women there and was the immediate cause of the dispute, which only turned into a 'most atrocious Ryot' on the Monday.[118] Conscience over-rode the requirement to obey the law.

Nowhere is this seen more starkly than in the many patronage disputes that were 'the most persistent and geographically widespread cause of popular unrest in Scotland' after 1730.[119] Patronage had been re-introduced by Westminster in 1712, although parishioners retained the right to dissent at the choice of minister made. Men and women (single rather than married) more likely to be drawn from the ranks of the evangelical, salvationist Presbyterians and artisans rather than the lowest classes, forcibly blocked the introduction of new ministers – invariably the heritors' candidates. Not unusually, the military was required to enforce the new incumbent's entry. There were numerous instances, however, where the protestors' will prevailed, at least in the short term, as at Alloa in 1750 when they rang the church bell 'from morning till night, and in the afternoon, displayed a flag from the steeple', to declare that they had the upper hand.[120]

CONCLUSION

By and large, and with a judicious mix of authority and licence, those responsible for maintaining law and order in early modern Scotland were moderately successful. It was in most people's interests that this should be so; there was majority consent to the systems of control that were in place. Equally importantly, there were shared values: about the undesirability of adultery, for example, or theft. It is clear that there were circumstances where ordinary people felt justified in taking the law into their own hands within their communities. Sometimes this reinforced community norms: by punishing merchant profiteers during a period of high food prices, for example. But the consensus was far from universal. There was widespread rule breaking, and low-level disorderliness was rife. Agents of the state, whether national or local, had a hard time, and were often the targets of verbal and physical abuse. Resistance to unpopular taxes predated the Union of 1707 and carried on until the end of the eighteenth century, but the extent and longevity of the violent confrontations between the authorities and the sizeable numbers of ordinary people that followed the Union were extraordinary. Parts of the country were out of control, and in some districts – the Highlands for instance – excise collection continued to be difficult until the following century. What is also striking is the extent to which women were prepared to act in defiance of the forces of law and order.

It is difficult to say whether the level of everyday disorder was any greater in 1800 than it had been two centuries earlier. There seems to have been more crime, but definitions of criminality had changed. Contemporaries from the middling ranks were sure they could detect a changing in attitude among the lower orders in the later decades of the eighteenth century. William Fullarton, in his *General View of the Agriculture of the County of Ayr*, published in 1793, observed that the 'manufacturing part of the community' was causing 'dread' among the 'established orders', who now feared any kind of disturbance. Notwithstanding improvements in the standard of living in the countryside, 'the manners and morals of the different ranks', he was sure, had 'by no means ameliorated'. On the contrary, 'the civil cordial manners of the former generation' were 'wearing fast away', and being replaced by a 'regardless, brutal, and democratic harshness of demeanour'. Religion and a deep sense of morality, which had kept crime at a low level, were less in evidence; by contrast, the drinking of spirits was on the increase, as were 'levelling manners' and attendance at fairs and markets and other encouragements to dissolution and vice.[121] Industrial and agrarian capitalism were clearly effecting fundamental changes in social relations. So, too, did cultural differentiation. Larger towns, where a growing proportion of Scots were living, made it more difficult for the authorities to comprehend the motives and intentions of those of their inhabitants who engaged in collective action; what had before been familiar and predictable was no longer the case. But even smaller, apparently more socially harmonious places could turn disorderly, almost at the drop of a hat. Felt to be under challenge was the state itself, with the agencies responsible for keeping the peace unsure that they could keep the lid on.

Notes

1. R. A. Houston and I. D. Whyte, 'Introduction', in R. A. Houston and I. D. Whyte (eds), *Scottish Society, 1500–1800* (Cambridge, 1989), pp. 21–9; T. C. Smout, *A History of the Scottish People, 1560–1830* (London, 1969), pp. 222–9; R. A. Dodgshon, *From Chiefs to Landlords: Social and Economic Change in the Western Highlands and Islands, c. 1493–1820* (Edinburgh, 1998), pp. 87–8.

2. A. Mackillop, *'More Fruitful than the Soil': Army, Empire and the Scottish Highlands, 1715–1815* (East Linton, 2000), p. 7; A. I. Macinnes, *Clanship, Commerce and the House of Stuart, 1603–1788* (East Linton, 1996), p. 31.

3. Bob Harris, *Politics and the Nation: Britain in the Mid-Eighteenth Century* (Oxford, 2002), pp. 165–86.

4. For a recent study of the period, see Bob Harris (ed.), *Scotland in the Age of the French Revolution* (Edinburgh, 2005).

5. S. J. Connolly, 'Unnatural death in four nations: contrasts and comparisons', in S. J. Connolly (ed.), *Kingdoms United? Great Britain and Ireland Since 1500* (Dublin, 1998), pp. 210–12; A.-M. Kilday, 'Maternal monsters: murdering mothers in south-west Scotland, 1750–1815', in Y. G. Brown and R. Ferguson (eds), *Twisted Sisters: Women, Crime and Deviance in Scotland since 1400* (East Linton, 2002), pp. 156–77.

6. R. A. Houston, *Social Change in the Age of the Enlightenment: Edinburgh, 1660–1760* (Oxford, 1994), p. 169.

7. I. Donnachie, 'Scottish criminals and transportation to Australia, 1786–1852', *Scottish Economic & Social History*, 4 (1984), pp. 21–4.

8. S. J. Connolly, 'Albion's fatal twigs: justice and law in the eighteenth century', in R. Mitchison and P. Roebuck (eds), *Economy and Society in Scotland and Ireland, 1500–1939* (Edinburgh, 1988), p. 121.

9. See S. J. Davies, 'The courts and the Scottish legal system, 1600–1747: the case of Stirlingshire', in V. A. C. Gattrell, B. Lenman and G. Parker (eds), *Crime and the Law: The Social History of Crime in Western Europe since 1500* (London, 1980), pp. 120–54.

10. A.-M. Kilday, *Women and Violent Crime in Enlightenment Scotland* (Woodbridge, 2007), pp. 54–6, 155.

11. A. Whetstone, *Scottish County Government in the Eighteenth and Nineteenth Centuries* (Edinburgh, 1981), pp. 27–9; J. G. Harrison, 'The justices of the peace for Stirlingshire 1660 to 1706', *Scottish Archives*, 12 (2006), 46–7.

12. K. J. Logue, *Popular Disturbances in Scotland, 1780–1815* (Edinburgh, 1979).

13. C. A. Whatley, 'An uninflammable people?', in I. Donnachie and C. A Whatley (eds), *The Manufacture of Scottish History* (Edinburgh, 1992), pp. 51–71.

14. W. H. Fraser, *Conflict and Class: Scottish Workers, 1700–1838* (Edinburgh, 1988), ch. 3.

15. For a useful introduction to these issues, see A. J. Fletcher and J. Stevenson, 'Introduction', in A. Fletcher and J. Stevenson (eds), *Order & Disorder in Early Modern England* (Cambridge, 1987 edn.), pp. 1–40, and also the seminal work of E. P. Thompson, in, for example, *Customs in Common* (London, 1991).

16. C. A. Whatley, *Scottish Society 1707–1830: Beyond Jacobitism, Towards Industrialisation* (Manchester, 2000), pp. 199–200.

17. See, J. R. Ruff, *Violence in Early Modern Europe, 1500–1800* (Cambridge, 2001), pp. 118, 239–47.

18. R. Mitchison, *The Old Poor Law in Scotland: The Experience of Poverty, 1574–1845* (Edinburgh, 2000), pp. 45–55; see also, I. D. Whyte, 'Scottish population and social structures in the seventeenth and eighteenth centuries: new sources and perspectives', *Archives*, XX: 84 (April 1997), 30–41; H. M. Dingwall, *Late 17th-Century Edinburgh: A Demographic Study* (Aldershot, 1994), p. 262,

19. E. P. Dennison, 'Urban society and economy', in Bob Harris and A. Macdonald (eds), *Scotland: The Making and Unmaking of the Nation, c. 1100–1707* (Dundee, 2007), p. 161.

20. K. Bowie, *Scottish Public Opinion and the Anglo-Scottish Union, 1699–1707* (Woodbridge, 2007), pp. 21–2.

21. J. Burnett, *Riot, Revelry and Rout: Sport in Lowland Scotland Before 1860* (East Linton, 2000), pp. 32–5.

22. C. A. Whatley, 'Labour in the industrialising city *c.* 1660–1830', in T. M. Devine and G. Jackson (eds), *Glasgow, Volume 1: Beginnings to 1830* (Manchester, 1995), p. 383.

23. R. Mitchison and L. Leneman, *Girls in Trouble: Sexuality and Social Control in Rural Scotland, 1660–1780* (Edinburgh, 1998), p. 13; for a study of the system as it worked in Argyll, see F. Bigwood, 'The courts of Argyll, 1664–1825', *Scottish Archives*, 10 (2004), 26–38.

24. C. G. Brown, *Up-Helly-AA: Custom, Culture and Community in Shetland* (Manchester, 1998), pp. 65–6.

25. See M. Todd, *The Culture of Protestantism in Early Modern Scotland* (New Haven, CT, 2002); and, for the eighteenth century and later, C. G. Brown, *Religion and Society in Scotland since 1707* (Edinburgh, 1997 edn).

26. M. Lynch, G. DesBrisay and M. G. H. Pittock, 'The faith of the people', in E. P. Dennison, D. Ditchburn and M. Lynch (eds), *Aberdeen Before 1800: A New History* (East Linton, 2002), p. 301.

27. Todd, 'Church and religion', pp. 116–18.

28. R. Mitchison and L. Leneman, *Sin in the City: Sexuality and Social Control in Urban Scotland, 1660–1780* (Edinburgh, 1998), pp. 19–39.

29. G. Parker, 'The "kirk by law established" and the origins of "the taming of Scotland": St Andrews, 1559–1600', in L. Leneman (ed.), *Perspectives in Scottish Social History* (Aberdeen, 1988), p. 5.

30. J. Goodare, 'Introduction', in J. Goodare (ed.), *The Scottish Witch-hunt in Context* (Manchester, 2002), p. 4; S. Macdonald, *The Witches of Fife: Witch-hunting in a Scottish Shire, 1560–1710* (East Linton, 2002), pp. 172–3.

31. Houston, *Social Change*, pp. 186–7; P. Cadell, 'The Reverend John Brand and the Bo'ness of the 1690s', in G. Cruickshank (ed.), *A Sense of Place: Studies in Scottish Local History* (Edinburgh, 1988), p. 7.

32. Harrison, 'Justices', p. 48.

33. Mitchison and Leneman, *Girls*, p. 92.

34. C. G. Brown, 'Religion', in L. Abrams, E. Gordon, D. Simonton and E. J. Yeo (eds), *Gender in Scottish History since 1700* (Edinburgh, 2006), p. 88; Macdonald, *Witches*, pp. 155–7; G. DesBrisay, 'Twisted by definition: women under godly discipline in seventeenth-century Scottish towns', in Brown and Ferguson, *Twisted Sisters*, p. 138.

35. Todd, 'Church and religion', p. 117.

36. DesBrisay, 'Twisted', pp. 141–2.

37. C. A. Whatley, *The Scots and the Union* (Edinburgh, 2006), pp. 239, 269.

38. Dingwall, *Late 17th-Century Edinburgh*, p. 247.

39. K. J. Cullen, 'Famine in Scotland in the 1690s: causes and consequence', unpublished Ph.D. (University of Dundee, 2004), p. 168.

40. See, for example, Revd W. M. Inglis, *Annals of an Angus Parish* (Dundee, 1888); D. Buchan, *The Ballad and the Folk* (East Linton, [1972] 1997 edn), p. 25.

41. Houston, *Social Change*, pp. 195–6.

42. D. A. Symonds, *Weep Not for Me: Women, Ballads, and Infanticide in Early Modern Scotland* (University Park, PA, 1997), pp. 92–4, 127–38.
43. Houston, *Social Change*, p. 194.
44. Mitchison and Leneman, *Girls in Trouble*, pp. 15–17, 33–7.
45. C. G. Brown, *The People in the Pews: Religion and Society in Scotland since 1780* (Edinburgh, 1993), p. 7.
46. Houston and Whyte, 'Introduction', pp. 34–5.
47. See C. Humphrey, *The Politics of Carnival: Festive misrule in medieval England* (Manchester, 2001); P. Burke, *Popular Culture in Early Modern Europe* (Aldershot, 1978), pp. 178–204.
48. Houston, *Social Change*, pp. 48–54.
49. Mitchison and Leneman, *Girls in Trouble*, pp. 73–8.
50. R. Mitchison and L. Leneman, *Sexuality and Social Control: Scotland, 1660–1760* (Oxford, 1989), p. 142.
51. Parker, '"Kirk By Law Established"', pp. 14–19.
52. Brown, *Up Helly-AA*, pp. 65–71.
53. F. Watson, 'Rights and responsibilities: wood-management as seen through baron court records', in T. C. Smout (ed.), *Scottish Woodland History* (Edinburgh, 1997), p. 102.
54. Buchan, *Ballad*, pp. 21–7; see also A. B. Barty, *The History of Dunblane* (Stirling, 1994), pp. 142–6.
55. M. H. B. Sanderson, *Scottish Rural Society in the 16th Century* (Edinburgh, 1982), pp. 169–71; Buchan, *Ballad*, pp. 39–40.
56. Smout, *History*, pp. 123–6.
57. Whatley, *Scottish Society*, pp. 145–7.
58. Bigwood, 'Courts of Argyll', pp. 34–5.
59. See, for example, S. Clark and J. S. Donnelly (eds), *Irish Peasants: Violence & Political Unrest, 1780–1914* (Dublin, 1983).
60. K. M. Brown, *Kingdom or Province? Scotland and the Regal Union, 1603–1715* (Houndmills, 1992), p. 34.
61. See T. M. Devine, 'Unrest and stability in rural Ireland and Scotland, 1760–1840', in Mitchison and Roebuck, *Economy and Society*, pp. 126–31.
62. M. Stewart, '"A sober and peaceable deportment": the court and council books of Dumfries, 1561–1661', in A. Gardener-Medwin and J. H. Williams (eds), *A Day Festival: Essays on the Music, Poetry and History of Scotland and England Previously Unpublished* (Aberdeen, 1990), pp. 146–7; Whatley, *Scottish Society*, p. 151.
63. Mitchison and Leneman, *Sin in the City*, pp. 52–3, 72–4.
64. Houston, *Social Change*, pp. 198–9.
65. Bigwood, 'Courts of Argyll', pp. 32–3.
66. K. G. Simpson, 'The legacy of flyting', *Studies in Scottish Literature*, XXVI (1991), 503–14.
67. J. Harrison, 'Women and the branks in Stirling, c. 1600–c. 1730', *Scottish Economic & Social History*, 18:2 (1998), 114–31; M. F. Graham, 'Women and the church courts in Reformation-era Scotland', in E. Ewan and M. M. Meikle

(eds), *Women in Scotland, c. 1100–c. 1750* (East Linton, 1999), pp. 189–92; L. Martin, 'The devil and the domestic: witchcraft, quarrels and women's work in Scotland', in Goodare, *Scottish Witch-hunt*, p. 85.

68. Kilday, *Women*, p. 63; Symonds, *Weep Not for Me*, p. 83.
69. I am indebted to David Barrie for this information, drawn from his forthcoming book on the development of policing in Scotland.
70. A. M. Smith, *The Nine Trades of Dundee* (Dundee, 1995); PKCA, PE 67/22, Index, Glovers Incorporation of Perth
71. Whatley, 'Labour', p. 382.
72. Dundee Archive and Record Centre, Dundee Town Council Minute Books, XIII, 1793–1805, 23 October 1794.
73. Whatley, *Scottish Society*, pp. 162–4.
74. *Scots Magazine*, June 1801.
75. G. Penny, *Traditions of Perth* (Perth, 1836, Coupar Angus, 1986 edn), pp. 96–8.
76. L. Leneman, *Living in Atholl, 1685–1785* (Edinburgh, 1986), p. 162; Whatley, *Scottish Society*, p. 159.
77. Macinnes, *Clanship*, pp. 32–7.
78. See, for example, F. Wilkins, *The Smuggling Story of Two Firths* (Kidderminster, 1993).
79. P. W. J. Riley, *The English Ministers and Scotland, 1707–1727* (London, 1964), p. 135; on Sussex, see C. Winslow, 'Sussex smugglers', in D. Hay, P. Linebaugh, J. G. Rule, E. P. Thompson and C. Winslow (eds), *Albion's Fatal Tree: Crime and Society in Eighteenth-Century England* (London, 1975), pp. 119–66; Brown, *Up Hell-AA*, pp. 71–5.
80. C. A. Whatley, 'How tame were the Scottish Lowlanders during the eighteenth century?', in T. M. Devine (ed.), *Conflict and Stability in Scottish Society, 1700–1850* (Edinburgh, 1990), p. 13.
81. Kilday, *Women*, p. 98.
82. Whatley, *Scottish Society*, pp. 195–6; Stevenson, *Beggars Benison*, pp. 122–4.
83. B. Lenman, *The Jacobite Risings in Britain, 1689–1746* (London, 1980), p. 232; Whatley, 'Labour', p. 379; Bigwood, 'Courts of Argyll', p. 36; T. M. Devine, *Clanship to Crofters' War* (Manchester, 1994), pp. 119–34.
84. Whatley, *Scottish Society*, pp. 154–6.
85. See Thompson, *Customs*, chs II and III.
86. See Watson, 'Rights', p. 109.
87. Whatley, *Scottish Society*, p. 158; Buchan, *Ballad*, pp. 180–4.
88. C. A. Whatley, 'Roots of 1790s radicalism: reviewing the economic and social background', in Harris, *Scotland*, pp. 36–43.
89. R. A. Houston, 'Coal, class and culture: labour relations in a Scottish mining community, 1650–1750', *Social History*, 8:1 (January 1983), 1–18.
90. Macdonald, *Witches*, p. 185; C. A. Whatley, *The Scottish Salt Industry, 1570–1850* (Aberdeen, 1987), pp. 112–13.
91. Brown, 'Religion', pp. 88–9; Houston, *Social Change*, p. 180.
92. D. Stevenson, *The Beggar's Benison: Sex Clubs of Enlightenment Scotland and their Rituals* (East Linton, 2001).

93. Brown, *Social History*, p. 73; Houston, *Social Change*, pp. 183–5.

94. Houston, *Social Change*, p. 184; Inglis, *Annals*, pp. 142–3; Barty, *History*, p. 148.

95. Dundee Archive and Record Centre, Church of Scotland Records, Dundee Kirk Session, CH2/12/1218/7, 10 August 1796.

96. Houston, *Social Change*, pp. 168–9.

97. Kilday, *Women*, pp. 134–46.

98. Wilson, *Annals*, pp. 56, 65.

99. Penny, *Traditions*, p. 15.

100. Whatley, 'Labour', p. 383.

101. C. A. Whatley, 'Royal day, people's day: the monarch's birthday in Scotland, *c.* 1660–1860', in R. Mason and N. Macdougall (eds), *People and Power in Scotland* (Edinburgh, 1992), p. 178

102. See B. Bushaway, *By Rite: Custom, Ceremony and Community in England, 1700– 1880* (London, 1982), p. 168.

103. Whatley, *Scottish Society*, p. 161; Penny, *Traditions*, p. 111; Kilday, *Women*, pp. 88–90.

104. For a discussion about how such events might be interpreted, see C. Humphrey, *The Politics of Carnival: Festive Misrule in Medieval England* (Manchester, 2001), pp. 1–37.

105. Penny, *Traditions*, pp. 61–3, 97–8; 102–3.

106. Whatley, *Scottish Society*, p. 194.

107. Whatley, *Scots*, pp. 200–1; Houston, *Social Change*, pp. 305–9.

108. Cadell, 'Reverend John Brand', p. 14.

109. Brown, *Up Helly-AA*, p. 78.

110. D. Underdown, 'Regional cultures? local variations in popular culture during the early modern period', in T. Harris (ed.), *Popular Culture in England, c. 1500–1850* (Basingstoke, 1995), p. 37.

111. Burnett, *Riot*, pp. 87–93; R. S. Fittis, *Sports and Pastimes of Scotland* (Paisley, 1891), pp. 163–70.

112. Penny, *Traditions*, p. 115.

113. K. R. Bogle, *Scotland's Common Ridings* (Stroud, 2002), chs 2 and 4; R. S. Craig and A. Laing, *The Hawick Tradition of 1514* (Hawick, 1898), pp. 163–4.

114. Wilson, *Annals*, pp. 129–30.

115. Whatley, 'Labour', pp. 364–5.

116. C. Jackson, *Restoration Scotland, 1660–1690: Royalist Politics, Religion and Ideas* (Woodbridge, 2003), pp. 145–55, 157.

117. R. K. Donovan, 'Voices of distrust: the expression of anti-Catholic feeling in Scotland, 1778–1781', *Innes Review*, XXX (1979), 62–76; *Scots Magazine*, December 1778, pp. 684–5.

118. Whatley, *Scottish Society*, pp. 167–8; Houston, *Social Change*, p. 213.

119. C. G. Brown, 'Protest in the pews. Interpreting Presbyterianism and society in fracture during the Scottish economic revolution', in Devine, *Conflict*, p. 99.

120. Whatley, *Scottish Society*, p. 169; Kilday, *Women*, pp. 119–24

121. D. McClure (ed.), *Ayrshire in the Age of Improvement* (Ayr, 2002), pp. 121, 136–7.

Chapter 8

Sensory Experiences: Smells, Sounds and Touch*

Elizabeth Foyster

INTRODUCTION

'Ours is a nearly sense-less profession', George H. Roeder wrote over a decade ago, describing how historians have neglected to study the five senses of smell, hearing, touch, sight and taste.[1] When we survey research conducted into the senses by historians of Scotland, the same observation could certainly be made today. Yet, we neglect the senses to our peril, since the senses were a crucial part of the everyday. The senses shaped everyday experiences, could act as triggers to memory and provoked powerful emotions. Being alert to the senses gives the historian a key to understanding the worlds of our predecessors, and in particular, to their culture. To take just one example for our period, the senses were central to Scottish witchcraft beliefs and practice. The 'evil eye' of the witch was thought to cause harm to those she gazed upon (sight); witches kissed the devil before he left his mark on their private parts, while witch-finders pricked suspected witches to see whether they were insensible to pain (touch); and the presence of the Devil could be detected by the foul smell of sulphur he was believed to exude.[2] Ideas about the senses could be both nationally and regionally distinctive. To continue our examination of the magical world, the Scots, and Highlanders in particular, were legendary for their possession of 'second sight': the ability to be able to see into the future.[3]

So why, if they were important, have historians failed to examine the senses for so long? Part of the reason may lie with the nature of our sources: there is a limit to the extent to which we can recapture the sensory experiences of the past. As one writer has put it, succinctly, 'written down, shit does not smell'.[4] There will always remain an important difference between the lived experience and the written record. Furthermore, as with many aspects of everyday life, it could take 'outsiders', or visitors to Scotland to note the sensory experiences that Scots themselves took so much for granted that they never bothered to record. Writing about smell in the past, one archaeologist has made the useful distinction between 'acute and dynamic smells (that carry new information and influence human decisions) and chronic or static smells (a constant and unavoidable part of the cultural landscape)'.[5] We have far more evidence of the former than the latter. But as this chapter will show, this does not mean we should agree with the assumption made by Patrick Süskind in his novel, *Perfume*, that smell was part of a sensory domain that 'leaves no traces in history'.[6] Instead, it is from the traces that we can begin to piece together the meanings that our early modern predecessors gave to the senses. The changing sights of early modern Scotland were commented upon and are examined in many parts of this volume, while new tastes are discussed in Stana Nenadic's chapter on 'Necessities' during her consideration of changing diet. This chapter will focus upon sound, smell and touch. Whereas historians of our period have paid attention to music, it is the many other sounds that Scots heard that will be analysed here. In this chapter the sensory landscape of everyday life will be examined initially, followed by a discussion of how the interpretation of the senses could provoke debate and ending with a consideration of how the senses played a part in everyday relationships.

SENSORY WORLDS

Smells and sounds were an inescapable feature of life in early modern Scotland. For the inhabitants of Scottish towns, they marked out both space and time. So distinctive were the smells and sounds of many early modern trades, such as those produced by tanners, dyers, butchers, bakers and brewers, and as town authorities became increasingly strict about where these trades could be located, so concentrated, that if an early modern Scot had been led round a town blind-folded, he would know where he was by what he smelt and heard.

Within towns the sound of bells signalled the passing of time.[7] The authorities in Aberdeen ruled that church bells should be rung in the town at five in the morning and nine in the evening, and that notice of the start and end of the day should be given by the town's drummers who were directed to go through the streets an hour beforehand.[8] The sound of bells structured the everyday experiences of people from an early age, as bells would be rung as lessons began and finished within schools.[9] Since regulations for street cleaning always stipulated the times of day when this was to be carried out, smells and their removal also signalled the transitions between day and night, work and leisure.[10] Additional attempts to clear the streets of waste could be announced by the town drummer, who in April 1637 was ordered to march through the streets of Aberdeen, charging its citizens to remove the middens outside their homes. Such was the special nature of Sunday, that Edinburgh's regulations stated that 'nuisances' (the collective term given to all waste) were 'on no pretence' to be laid out or collected on the Sabbath.[11] The passing seasons had a place on this olfactory calendar. In the summer months, Scottish burghs tended to multiply the numbers of orders for the removal of waste, as rising temperatures increased the fear of disease from rotting matter, while cities such as Edinburgh faced extra problems when streams and nearby lochs dried up, preventing the removal of sewage.[12]

Figure 8.1 *Detail of the tomb of William Baxter, Old Parish Church, Duffus, Moray, 1762. This recessed panel on the top of a table tomb shows many of the symbols associated with death. As well as an hourglass (demonstrating life's brevity), a skull and crossed bones and the tools of a gravedigger, there are two 'deid' (dead) bells, which would be rung at funerals. Sounds had strong associations with stages in the life-cycle, and played an important part in the rituals that accompanied them. Source: © Royal Commission on the Ancient and Historical Monuments of Scotland; C/23405/12 (www.scran.ac.uk).*

Sounds and smells also marked the passage of individual time, and seem to have played a particularly important role at the end of the life cycle. There were many sounds that were believed to be the omens of death, including: humming in the ear; the crowing of a cock; the howling of a dog; and in the Shetlands the song of the common quail, which was known locally as the 'dead-shak'.[13] The odour of death and decay was a key consideration in the location of burial grounds, and hence played a part within the topography of the Scottish town. A seventeenth-century clergyman noted that Greyfriars graveyard was positioned outside Edinburgh's city walls so that its citizens would 'thereby lose the scents which must needs attend such places'.[14] In the Highlands the dead were carried to burial accompanied by the wails of women, whose cries and praises for the deceased were called the coronach.[15] In Lowland towns, such as Dunbar and Bo'ness, the town's bell-man would go through the streets announcing the death, inviting citizens to the funeral, and then walk alongside the funeral procession ringing his bell.[16] Touch, the most intimate of the senses, and the one closely associated by contemporaries with the body and sexuality, could also bear significance for life-cycle rituals. The poet Robert Burns and Mary Campbell were one famous couple who practised handfasting, in which they kissed the thumbs of their right hands and then held them together, or held their hands across a stream to signify betrothal and marriage.[17] Like sounds and smells, touch could also serve as a useful information provider. In October 1666 when four widows in South Ronaldsay, Orkney, became suspicious that their husbands had not died of natural causes, but had been murdered, all those who were known to the men were ordered to touch their exhumed bodies. If they had been killed, it was believed that the murderer's touch would cause the corpses to bleed. In this case nothing happened, but the ordeal was repeated in other Scottish criminal trials.[18]

Sounds and smells varied between Scottish towns and contributed to civic identity as each town offered a distinctive mix of everyday sensory experiences. The sound of every church bell was unique, and burgh authorities deployed sounds for different purposes. Edinburgh's special place as the seat of government and royalty, for example, was emphasised through the burgh's directions to its drummers. When parliament sat the city's drummers were paid extra for their additional duties, and when the king entered the city, new drummers had to be found to mark the occasion.[19] The diverse sounds of Scottish accents, as Bob Harris shows in this volume, could be an indicator of place. 'The tone of voice, the cadence and manner of speaking in this town', an Inveresk minister visiting Aberdeen in 1765 noted, 'is so different from that in the south country.' The explanation for this difference in vocal sound was temperament, he thought;

> The sharp notes they use, and the high key in which they speak, may possible [sic] be owing to the vivacity of the people in this northern region. They are certainly brisk, lively and acute far above the people in other parts of Scotland.[20]

Thus, sound was thought to have the potential to reflect mood and emotion, as well as shape it. By varying across space, sound could also bind people together by creating speech and acoustic communities. As David Garrioch has put it, 'the familiar soundscape helped create a sense of belonging: it was part of the "feel" of a particular city, town or neighbourhood, a key component of people's sense of place'.[21] Contrasts were frequently drawn between Edinburgh and Glasgow by visitors, which suggest that they smelt quite different. It was the smell of the inhabitants of Edinburgh that was thought particularly repugnant. One Cheshire gentleman, travelling to the capital in 1636, found the smells so powerful that they also affected his sense of taste; 'the sluttishness and nastiness of this people is such . . . their houses, and halls, and kitchens, have such a noisome taste, a savour, and that so strong, as it doth offend you so soon as you come within their wall'.[22] In the eighteenth century the smells of Edinburgh continued to provoke comment. Joseph Taylor, travelling to the city in 1705, wrote that 'in a morning the scent was so offensive, that we were forc't to hold our Noses as we past the streets'; Wesley visiting in May 1761 wondered 'how long shall the capital city of Scotland, yea, the chief street of it, stink worse than a common sewer?'; and in 1773 James Boswell repeated the observation that 'walking the streets of Edinburgh at night was pretty perilous, and a good deal odiferous'[23]. The condemnation of Edinburgh on olfactory grounds differs from the praise afforded to Glasgow: 'For pleasantness of sight, sweetness of air, and delightfulness of its gardens and orchards', Glasgow 'surpasseth all other places' noted one visitor to Scotland in 1669.[24] A century later, there was appreciation of how Glasgow's markets for fish and meat were 'constantly kept sweet and neat' by the channels of water that ran from them.[25]

Rural society had its own smells. These could be pleasant. Martin Martin, travelling to the Isle of Harris at the end of the seventeenth century, noted the 'most fragrant smell' of the fields of clover and daisies.[26] But the rural economy meant that it was more often unwelcome smells that met the visitor. The fertility of the soil was enhanced using a variety of human and animal manure, lime from shells and seaweed, each producing a distinctive aroma.[27] Rural trades were well known for their smell. Kelp was burnt to manufacture potash, and the curing of fish, especially the strong smelling herring and salmon was essential to their preservation. The maxim 'you are what you eat' was certainly current at this time: an eighteenth-century reporter to the *Statistical Account* noted that those who lived around Lochcarron, Wester Ross, ate so much herring that 'their breath smelled strongly of fish'.[28] Spices were added to meat, especially in the winter months to disguise its rotting smell and aromatic herbs, such as fennel, thyme, mint, anise, juniper and cranberries were routinely used to flavour whisky.[29] The English satirised the Scots by suggesting that the poor often stank of garlic.[30] Such a strongly smelling diet was certainly not to everyone's taste, and was too much for both Boswell and Samuel Johnson, who loathed a Highland habit of eating cheese, 'which mingles its less grateful odours with the fragrance of the tea' at breakfast.[31] Cooking smells mixed with those of the fuels that were used in stoves and on the hearths of Scottish homes. In Lowland areas this could be coal, but in the Highlands and Islands peat predominated. 'In some places', Johnson noted of peat, 'it has an offensive smell', which because chimneys of cottages could not be placed directly above fires lest rainwater extinguished them, tended to linger.[32] A more widely appreciated smell was that of Scots pine, the roots of which Highlanders lit to serve as candles in their homes.[33] Of course, many aspects of Scottish domestic life were shared in common, and in the early modern period we should not exaggerate the distinction between the smells and sounds of urban and rural life. The citizens of Aberdeen were troubled in August 1654, for example, by a great number of pigs who were roaming through the streets, uncovering corpses in the graveyard, mixing in dunghills and gutters, and were said to have raised an 'infectious and intolerable smell'.[34] Similarly, the sounds of rural life were not confined to the countryside. The noise of horses' hooves, sheep, cows and pigs being transported to slaughter, as well as cats, dogs and birds, were all heard within Scottish towns.[35]

The sounds of Scottish wildlife could be staggering to the visitor. In 1636 one Englishman on route to Edinburgh, noted that the seabirds on Bass Rock made such a noise 'that you may hear them and nothing else a mile before you come to them'.[36] Thomas Pennant, travelling in the eighteenth century, remarked upon a similarly 'deafening chorus' of seabirds on Ailsa Craig, but enjoyed the sounds of the songbirds on the isle of Bute.[37] Johnson and Boswell believed that they had never heard the wind howl so loudly as on the island of Coll, and thought that it was the absence of trees which increased its sound.[38] It was an onslaught of different sensory phenomena, meanwhile, that gave Boswell a sleepless night at Slains Castle in August 1773:

> I had a most elegant room; but there was a fire in it which blazed; and the sea, to which my windows looked, roared; and the pillows were made of the feathers of some sea-fowl, which had to me a disagreeable smell: so that by all these causes, I was kept awake a good while.

No doubt Boswell was a fussy traveller, but his writings, and those of other visitors suggest that at this time Scotland offered a very different everyday sensory experience from her nearest neighbour. The early modern period provides ample evidence of how within Scottish history smells have changed over time. New smells were introduced to Scottish society as habits of personal consumption altered. Coffee, tea and drinking chocolate were all aromatic drinks that were consumed in increasing quantities as the period progressed. Another foreign import, which as we will see provoked considerably more controversy, was tobacco. Hawkers, peddlers, stall-holders at markets and ballad singers all used the sounds of their voices to market and sell these new goods. The manufacture of smells that most agreed were pleasant, within perfumes for use on the body, clothes or in homes, was also subject to change. Whereas recipes for making perfumes continued to be passed on by women through generations of elite families, the commercial manufacture of perfume became big business by the end of our period.[39] According to William Creech, perfumers had 'splendid shops in every principal street' of Edinburgh by 1783.[40] Here we see certain smells commercialised as commodities. Garden design was also affected by changing ideas about scent. In the sixteenth and seventeenth centuries, the fashion for building walled gardens adjoining castles such as Kellie and Edzell, can at least partly be explained by the desire to contain and intensify the smell of the herbs and flowering plants that were cultivated there.[41]

The changing nature and pace of Scottish industry brought its own new olfactory experiences. Those who reported the conditions of the early Paisley cotton mills foresaw the health problems that would be suffered by children who daily breathed 'an air . . . contaminated with the effluvia of rancid oil, arising from the machinery'.[42] Yet, to other commentators, such as Thomas

Pennant who visited the same area in 1774, the changing everyday sounds of such communities offered much hope:

> It must be extremely agreeable to every man who wishes well to his country . . . to hear, at all seasons, as he passes along the streets, the industrious and agreeable noise of weavers' looms and twist-mills.[43]

Such opposing interpretations of Scotland's changing sensory world were by no means confined to the end of our period, or to industrial change, as we shall now see.

CONTESTED MEANINGS

There was deeply divided opinion within Scottish society about the meanings of smells, sounds and touch, and what distinguished a 'bad' smell, an unwelcome 'noise', illicit or dangerous touch from a 'good one'. Exploring these differences allows us an insight into early modern beliefs, fears and prejudices. In particular, that many disputed meanings about smells or touch focused upon whether they offered explanations for illness and disease, or could provide much needed salves or cures, demonstrates the centrality of concerns about health to the everyday lives of our early modern predecessors. Contemporary ideas about how disease was spread, and how illness was treated, are central to understanding how smells were interpreted at this time. Before the discovery of germs, miasmatic theories held that it was the smell of rotting matter which was the cause of disease. Hence, when plague struck, it was thought crucial that the sick were separated from the healthy, and the dead and their clothing were removed from the living if the spread of plague was to be controlled. Less serious illnesses were also thought to stem from smells. When Isabel McKay was examined by her doctor in 1781–2, she told him that it was the 'disagreeable smell' of Edinburgh that had made her suffer from a cough and fever. In the eighteenth century the miners and smelters of Lanarkshire's lead industry were subject to what could be a fatal illness known as the 'mill-reek' from inhaling its fumes. Meanwhile, lead-workers, silver refiners and painters admitted to Edinburgh Royal Infirmary all blamed their exposure to lead or mercury fumes for their abdominal cramps.[44] At the same time, smells were thought to be the key to curing people from disease. Medicines were inhaled, not swallowed, because the nose was thought to be the channel that provided a direct link to the central organ of the body, the brain. So aromatherapy played a key part in therapeutic medicine in the early modern period.[45] In this context, the relatively 'fresh', untainted air of Scotland's Highlands and Islands gained a reputation for its healthy and curative qualities. Many invalids were said to flock to the isle of Arran, for example, because the air was known to be 'remarkably salubrious'.[46] The rarity of Scots suffering from agues compared with the English, was explained by reference to air quality. One enterprising Scottish physician, ignoring the adverse publicity about the stench of Edinburgh, claimed that such were the advantages of the city's high position, that its wholesome air gave English patients a 5:1 chance of recovery from agues if they visited him there.[47]

Strong smells were not necessarily understood to be 'bad' smells, but could instead be seen as powerful tools for repelling disease. When people travelled through the streets of early modern towns, many carried pomanders, which were originally oranges stuck with cloves, to try and counteract the less pleasant odours they met along their way.[48] In Orkney and Shetland the strong smells of excreta were used as cures for a wide range of common ailments until at least the nineteenth century. According to one researcher, 'a bleeding nose was plugged with fresh pig dung, a bruise was poulticed with cow dung, sweetened urine was considered an excellent remedy for jaundice, and milk in which sheep droppings had been boiled was drunk by people suffering from smallpox'.[49] Smells thus had many and complex meanings. Smells could act as warnings of danger, as represented by the contemporary expression 'to smell a rat'.[50] But the ambivalent nature of smell is perhaps best summarised by the soap industry. Soap was manufactured in towns such as Leith from the early seventeenth century, and produced to different qualities, the best being castle soap. This was a product that was intended to remove or mask what were regarded as the undesirable smells of the body. Yet ironically, because soap was made using whale oil and fish offal, soapworks themselves were notoriously noxious places.[51]

There could be disagreement about the impact of a particular smell, as demonstrated by attitudes towards tobacco. From its introduction to Scotland, tobacco could be viewed negatively. Smoking was portrayed as an assault upon the senses by James VI/I: it was 'a custom loathsome to the eye' and 'hateful to the nose', producing a 'black stinking fume'.[52] Yet James had to admit that its smell could serve medicinal purposes.[53] The supposed health benefits of tobacco were widely known. William Barclay, a sixteenth-century Aberdeen physician, wrote of the 'virtues of tobacco', and argued that tobacco had a positive effect on the senses. 'It maketh a clear voice', he wrote, 'it maketh a sweet breath, it cleareth the sight, it openeth the ears . . . and openeth the passage of the nose.'[54] Martin related the story of an elderly woman on the isle of Harris who cured herself of the loss of one sense through a heavy dosage of another; she poured tobacco in her ear to relieve her deafness.[55] By the end of the eighteenth century, tobacco was even being advocated as a cure for yellow fever.[56]

Touch could also be regarded as both the cause of disease and the key to its relief. Concern about contagious touch was magnified in our period through the experience of bubonic plague and venereal disease. The last visitation of bubonic plague in Leith was in 1645, when infected families were isolated in purpose-built shacks on the East Links, and fear of handling the dead was so widespread that the authorities found it increasingly difficult to

Figure 8.2 *Tobacco box engraved with symbols of the malt-making trade, c. 1737. From the outset, the consumption of tobacco, and the smells that it generated, attracted controversy. Like other aromatic consumer goods that were introduced in early modern Scotland, notably coffee, tea and drinking chocolate, tobacco consumption contributed to the production of a variety of associated utensils. These could enhance the pleasure of consumption, and as with this tobacco box, serve as symbols of social status. Source: © National Museums Scotland (www.scran.ac.uk).*

find workers to supervise burials.[57] Venereal disease was seen by many as evidence of the danger and sin of illicit sexual touch, and its sufferers were socially ostracised. Those who were infected could be banished to the island of Inchkeith in the middle of the Forth.[58]

While touch could be fatal, it could also prove to be the solution. Stories circulated of Scots who had been cured from a range of diseases, especially those relating to the skin, when they had come into contact with the water found in holy wells found across the country. The importance of water in healing traditions is further discussed in Helen Dingwall's chapter (Chapter 4) in this volume.[59] The royal touch for scrofula was not practised by the time the Hanoverians ascended to the throne, but popular belief proved more resilient. In 1838 coins bearing the effigy of Charles I were still being used in Shetland as remedies for the King's evil.[60] Touch was to play a part in medical science as well as folk cures. By the eighteenth century the measurement of a patient's pulse, achieved by touching and holding their wrist, had become standard practice in Edinburgh's Royal Infirmary. In 1744 the Scottish physician, William Tossach, published the first account of mouth-to-mouth resuscitation, or what we call the 'kiss of life', which he had performed successfully on a miner who had been overcome by toxic fumes while working in a mineshaft. Touch thus had the potential to save lives. Such recourse to the senses anticipated the use of percussion and stethoscopy at the end of the century, when Scottish doctors who trained their ears to the sounds of the body would be at the forefront of these developments in medical diagnosis.[61]

POWER SYMBOLS

> Mrs Hunter declared that she frequently heard noise in said house, at unseasonable hours – with which she was much disturbed as she lives directly above it – And that particularly last Thursday night she heard loud noises much horrid swearing and cries of murder.[62]

Everyday the senses played a crucial part in negotiating relationships between individuals in early modern Scotland. Sound could be used to both further and alleviate social conflict; within towns the voices of quarrelling neighbours were commonly heard and often recorded in legal cases for defamation.[63] For Mrs Hunter, the sound of her neighbours had become an intolerable noise, and she hoped in June 1765 that by approaching the Dundee General Sessions she might solve the problem. In similar ways, across the country those in positions of authority came to determine who could make certain sounds, and what and when sound was acceptable. The same power to decide the limits of the tolerable was exercised over smell and touch. Hence, the senses could play a political role in the management and experience of everyday life. As we shall see, although control of the senses could reinforce existing ideas of social, gender and national hierarchy, there could also be popular resistance to such control. Silence, as one historian has remarked, was the 'sound of authority'.[64] To many early modern Scots, silence was associated with good order. Night was intended to contrast with day because of its silence. Sounds at night were linked with lawlessness and suspicious activity. So when John Horsbruik, his wife and servant were fined in Peebles for riot, it was emphasised that this had been 'under silence and cloud of night'.[65] It could be one particular sound that signalled the start of the soundlessness of night. For example, in 1584 the authorities in Edinburgh ruled that the 'great bell' should be rung nightly at ten o'clock 'for keeping good order within this burgh and eschewing trouble and night walking'.[66] It was considered respectful to be silent when in the presence of those in positions of authority. Hence, talk during church services was frowned upon, while the sound of the minister's voice was amplified by the soundboard that was suspended over the pulpit. When young gentlemen were tutored in good manners, they were told to gain the attention of their superiors 'with as little noise as ye can'.[67] It is clear that smell could serve to reinforce distinctions between the powerful and the powerless in Scottish society. It was the wealthy who could afford to suppress bodily smells through the use of soap and perfumes, and it was the poor who sweated as they worked in foul smelling industries and agriculture. The Scottish philosopher, David Hume, advocated cleanliness because 'it naturally renders us agreeable' to company, but as politeness insisted upon being sweet smelling, it also highlighted the differences between Scots.[68] Visiting Dumfries in 1656, Richard Franck described seeing the 'rabble . . . that nauseate the very air with their tainted breath, so perfumed with onions'.[69] One result of what Norbert Elias has labelled as the 'civilising process' was that the elite could find bodily smells, sounds or touch socially embarrassing. Adam Petrie's *Rules of Good Deportment* (1720), for example, advised young men that it was rude to smell their food, 'break wind', 'laugh too loud', 'bite your lip or nail, pick your teeth or nose' or 'touch' any food with their fingers.[70] Here we see the upwardly mobile attempting to adapt their sensory behaviour in order to distance themselves from those they viewed as socially inferior.

The senses were also understood to reflect ideas of gender difference. Of course, much of women's domestic work was concerned with managing the smells of the home and family, whether through cooking, cleaning or laundry. But smells could be regarded as the first indicators of degeneracy: 'we may say of cities in a moral sense, what they do in a natural sense, they have an ill air', preached one Edinburgh minister.[71] This idea was applied especially to women. Desirable women smelt sweet: it was as much for the fragrance as for the appearance that Burns compared his love to *A Red, Red Rose* (1796). In contrast, women who were fornicators, adulteresses or prostitutes were described in numerous kirk sessions as unclean, corrupted and carrying the foul smell of venereal disease.[72] Thus, anxieties about women's reproductive and sexual bodies were expressed through popular beliefs about smell. It was because women were thought closer to the animal state than men that they were held to have a more sensitive sense of smell, and this sense was further heightened during pregnancy.[73]

It was the smell of the Scots, and Scottish women in particular, that was most frequently taken by the English as a marker of the less civilised and inferior state of the Scottish nation. The Scots gained an unfortunate reputation in this period for smelling bad. According to Samuel Pepys, 'so universal a rooted nastiness hangs about the person of every Scot (man and woman), that renders the finest show that they can make nauseous, even among those of the first quality'.[74] As for Scottish women, according to one Englishman writing in 1617:

> the ladies are of opinion, that Susanna could not be chaste, because she bathed so often . . . [Scottish women's] flesh naturally abhors cleanliness; their body smells

of sweat, and their splay feet never offend in socks. To be chained in marriage with one of them, were to be tied to a dead carcass, and cast into a stinking ditch.[75]

National prejudice also abounded when the English described the voices of Scottish women, who were described by one commentator as 'barren of manners . . . lavish of their tongues . . . noisy and vile . . . to be silent, is to be a fool'.[76] Within Scotland attempts to police the senses were not always successful. How to control the 'stink' that arose from tanning processes, for example, was a question that taxed burgh authorities, but their decisions were sometimes challenged by those whose livelihoods depended on these industries.[77] Following the Reformation, the Presbyterians tried to discourage grieving relatives from ringing the death knell, believing that such rituals were superstitious remnants of Catholicism. But evidence suggests that bell ringing at funerals continued to be popular. Aberdeen burgh council, for example, was exasperated in 1643 that 'notwithstanding . . . sundry acts', such practices were still common.[78] Similarly, clergy disapproved of the coronach, but there is little indication that the attempt to prohibit it by the 1642 Synod of Argyll had much effect.[79] Efforts to censure popular customs in which the senses played a role may even have reinvigorated them. When Aberdeen kirk session fined a woman in 1630 for sending her sick child to be washed in a well, for example, their actions could have served to advertise its reputed healing qualities.[80] Beliefs about the senses were entrenched within Scottish popular custom, and because they could serve to reassure and comfort ordinary people confronting the harsh realities of everyday life, they were not easily eroded.

CONCLUSION

The senses provided structure and meaning to the patterns of everyday life in early modern Scotland. Contemporaries who described their world made frequent reference to the senses, and it was the senses that could play a crucial role in cementing community and individual identities, as well as highlighting and explaining difference. The centrality of the senses to everyday life was evident in the treatment of those who could not experience the full range of senses because of disability. Generous provision for those who were blind or deaf often assumed that these individuals would find compensation for their misfortune by developing their remaining senses. Hence, a blind man in Edinburgh was given a musical instrument to play by the burgh authorities in 1582, and some two hundred years later a father received money from the kirk session for his blind son to have board and lessons with a musician living in Dundee.[81] In 1760 the second school in Europe for deaf children opened in Edinburgh (the first was in Paris), much to the praise of visitors; Johnson thought that the progress of students there was 'wonderful'.[82]

Through its study of early modern sources, this chapter suggests that Scotland presents an alternative chronology of sensory change to the one put forward by other historians of smell and sound. The pioneers in the history of smell, most notably Alain Corbin and Constance Classen, have each argued that there was a European 'olfactory revolution' in the late eighteenth and nineteenth centuries, when urban authorities took unprecedented measures to sanitise and deodorise their communities, and individuals became less tolerant of the bodily odours of others.[83] Similarly, Peter Bailey has pointed to the Victorian period as a time when people became particularly concerned about the noises of the city, and especially its working-class inhabitants.[84] But there is so much evidence before the end of the eighteenth century of the sensitivity of Scots to smell and sound, and through burgh records of attempts to control both smells and noise, that at least for the Scottish case, their claims of revolutionary change are exaggerated. As Clare Brant has put it, 'sensitivity to smell is not the monopoly of moderns'.[85] Furthermore, although conduct books that taught Scots good manners may present a view that people were becoming more aware and even embarrassed by personal or bodily smells and sounds, the records we have of touch indicate that there had long been recognition of the body's potential to communicate meaning and significance in everyday social interaction. To study early modern Scotland without an appreciation of the role of the senses, this chapter has argued, is to miss out on a crucial part of everyday life.

Notes

* I am grateful to Mark Hall, Stana Nenadic and Chris Whatley for their suggestions of references and helpful comments on this chapter. For ease of comprehension, all spellings and punctuation have been modernised.

1. G. H. Roeder, 'Coming to our senses', *Journal of American History*, 81:3 (1994), 1112.

2. W. G. Black, *Folk-Medicine: A Chapter in the History of Culture* (New York, 1970), pp. 22, 24; R. Pitcairn (ed.), *Criminal Trials in Scotland from 1488 to 1624* (Edinburgh, 1833), vol. 3, p. 599; J. Durrant, 'The *osculum infame*: heresy, secular culture and the image of the witches' sabbath', in K. Harvey (ed.), *The Kiss in History* (Manchester, 2005), pp. 40–1; and H. McLachlan and K. Swales, 'The betwitchment of Christian Shaw: A reassessment of the famous Paisley witchcraft case of 1697', in Y. G. Brown and R. Ferguson (eds), *Twisted Sisters: Women, Crime and Deviance in Scotland since 1400* (East Linton, 2002), p. 59.

3. T. Pennant, *A Tour in Scotland and Voyage to the Hebrides* (Chester, 1774), pp. 282, 310; S. Johnson, *A Journey to the Western Islands of Scotland* (1775) J. D. Fleeman (ed.) (Oxford, 1985), pp. 89–91; and M. Hunter (ed.), *The Occult Laboratory: Magic, Science and Second Sight in Late Seventeenth-Century Scotland* (Woodbridge, 2001).

4. R. Barthes, *Sade, Fourier, Loyola* (Paris, 1971), p. 140, as translated and cited in, M. S. R. Jenner, 'Civilization and deodorization? Smell in early modern

English culture', in P. Burke, B. Harrison and P. Slack (eds), *Civil Histories: Essays Presented to Sir Keith Thomas* (Oxford, 2000), p. 128.

5. L. Bartosiewicz, '"There's something rotten in the state . . .": Bad smells in antiquity', *European Journal of Archaeology*, 6:2 (2003), 188.

6. P. Süskind, *Perfume: The Story of a Murderer*, trans. J. E. Woods (Harmondsworth, 1986), p. 3.

7. For comparative discussion of the significance of bells, see, D. Garrioch, 'Sounds of the city: the soundscape of early modern European towns', *Urban History*, 30:1 (2003), 5–25.

8. *Extracts from the Council Register of the Burgh of Aberdeen 1625–1642* (Scottish Burgh Records Society, Edinburgh, 1871), p. 40.

9. *Extracts Burgh of Aberdeen*, p. 190.

10. See, for example, J. S. Marshall, *The Life and Times of Leith* (Edinburgh, 1986), p. 74; M. S. R. Jenner, 'Early modern English conceptions of "cleanliness" and "dirt" as reflected in the environmental regulation of London c. 1530–c. 1700', unpublished D.Phil (Oxford, 1991), p. 133.

11. T. Brown, *A New Guide to the City of Edinburgh* (Edinburgh, 1792), p. 118.

11. W. Makey, 'Edinburgh in mid-seventeenth', in M. Lynch (ed.), *The Early Modern Town in Scotland* (London, 1987), p. 201; Jenner, 'Early modern English conceptions', pp. 151–2.

13. E. W. Marwick, *The Folklore of Orkney and Shetland* (London, 1975), p. 92; 'Death and burial customs and superstitions', in W. Andrews (ed.), *Bygone Church Life in Scotland* (London, 1899), p. 237.

14. P. Hume Brown (ed.), *Early Travellers in Scotland* (Edinburgh, 1891), p. 283.

15. J. Ramsay, *Scotland and Scotsmen in the Eighteenth Century*, 2 vols (Edinburgh, 1888), pp. ii, 430–1.

16. Hume Brown (ed.), *Early Travellers*, p. 239; M. Steven, *Parish Life in Eighteenth-Century Scotland: A Review of the Old Statistical Account* (OSA) (Aberdeen, 1995), p. 32.

17. 'Marriage laws and customs', in Andrews (ed.), *Bygone Life*, pp. 212–13.

18. Marwick, *Folklore*, p. 97; Pitcairn (ed.), *Criminal Trials*, pp. 182–99.

19. *Extracts from the Records of the Burgh of Edinburgh 1528–1557* (Scottish Burgh Records Society, Edinburgh, 1871), vol. 2, p. 219; vol. 4, p. 122.

20. R. B. Sher (ed.), *Journal of a Tour to the North of Scotland, 1765* (Aberdeen, 1981), p. 17.

21. Garrioch, 'Sounds of the city', p. 14; see also B. R. Smith, *The Acoustic World of Early Modern England: Attending to the O-Factor* (London, 1999), pp. 37, 46.

22. Hume Brown (ed.), *Early Travellers*, p. 142.

23. J. Taylor, *A Journey to Edenborough in Scotland* (Edinburgh, 1903), p. 134; G. Birkbeck Hill (ed.), *Boswell's Life of Johnson* (Oxford, 1964), vol. 5: *Journal of a Tour to the Hebrides with Samuel Johnson* (1785), pp. 22–3; for further contemporary remarks on the unpleasant smells of Edinburgh, see Charles McKean, Chapter 2, above.

24. Hume Brown (ed.), *Early Travellers*, p. 248.

25. Pennant, *Tour in Scotland*, pp. 127–8; A. Gibb, *Glasgow: The Making of a City* (London, 1983), p. 75.

26. M. Martin, *A Description of the Western Islands of Scotland*, 2nd ed (London, 1716), p. 31.

27. Makey, 'Edinburgh', p. 201; Steven, *Parish Life*, pp. 125–6.

28. Steven, *Parish Life*, p. 70.

29. E. P. Dennison, G. Des Brisay and H. Lesley Diack, 'Health in the two towns', in E. P. Dennison, D. Ditchburn and M. Lynch (eds), *Aberdeen Before 1800: A New History* (East Linton, 2002), p. 71; M. Beith, *Healing Threads: Traditional Medicines of the Highlands and Islands* (Edinburgh, 1995), p. 60.

30. Jenner, 'Civilization and deodorization?', p. 139.

31. Johnson, *A Journey*, p. 45; Boswell, *Journal of a Tour*, p. 167.

32. Johnson, *A Journey*, pp. 24, 84; see also, Hume Brown (ed.), *Early Travellers*, p. 276.

33. R. Genders, *A History of Scent* (London, 1972), p. 144.

34. *Extracts from the Council Register of the Burgh of Aberdeen 1643–1747* (Scottish Burgh Records Society Edinburgh, 1872), p. 143; pigs were frequently a nuisance in English towns as well, see E. Cockayne, *Hubbub: Filth, Noise and Stench in England 1600–1770* (New Haven, CT, 2007), pp. 18–19, 107, 193.

35. Garrioch, 'Sounds of the city', p. 7.

36. Hume Brown (ed.), *Early Travellers*, p. 135.

37. Pennant, *Tour in Scotland*, pp. 158, 190.

38. Johnson, *Journey to the Western Islands*, p. 103.

39. For books containing recipes for perfume see, for example, one owned by the eighteenth-century countesses of Strathmore in Dundee University Archive, Glamis, vol. 245.

40. W. Creech, *Letters Addressed to Sir John Sinclair* (Edinburgh, 1793), p. 17.

41. C. Classen, *Worlds of Sense: Exploring the Senses in History and Across Cultures* (London, 1993), p. 22.

42. Steven, *Parish Life*, p. 97.

43. Pennant, *Tour in Scotland*, p. 145.

44. Pennant, *Tour in Scotland*, p. 114; G. B. Risse, *Hospital Life in Enlightenment Scotland: Care and Teaching at the Royal Infirmary of Edinburgh* (Cambridge, 1986), pp. 8, 10.

45. R. Palmer, 'In bad odour: smell and its significance in medicine from antiquity to the seventeenth century', in W. F. Bynum and R. Porter (eds), *Medicine and the Five Senses* (Cambridge, 1993), pp. 61–8.

46. Pennant, *Tour in Scotland*, p. 175; see also, Martin, *A Description*, pp. 202, 232.

47. R. Boyle, *The General History of the Air* (London, 1692), p. 239; see also, Hume Brown (ed.), *Early Travellers*, pp. 82–3.

48. Classen, *Worlds of Sense*, p. 21.

49. Marwick, *The Folklore of Orkney and Shetland*, p. 130.

50. See, for example, National Archives of Scotland (NAS), CH12/23/1094, Records of the Episcopal Church of Scotland (25 August 1759).

51. Marshall, *The Life and Times of Leith*, p. 45; H. Kelsall and K. Kelsall, *Scottish Lifestyle 300 Years Ago* (Aberdeen, 1993), pp. 195–6.

52. *A Counterblaste to Tobacco* (London, 1604), in J. Craigie (ed.), *Minor Prose Works by King James VI and I* (Edinburgh, 1982), p. 99.

53. *A Counterblaste to Tobacco*, p. 95.

54. L. B. Taylor (ed.), *Aberdeen Council Letters*, vol. 1: 1552–1633 (London, 1942), pp. xxxiv–xxxv.

55. Martin, *A Description*, pp. 39–40.

56. NAS, GD51/2/72, Papers of the Dundas Family of Melville (17 March 1797).

57. Marshall, *Life and Times*, pp. 66–8.

58. Brown, *A New Guide*, p. 10; M. Healy, 'Anxious and fatal contacts: taming the contagious touch', in Harvey (ed.), *Sensible Flesh*, pp. 22, 32–3.

59. T. Frost, 'Saints and holy wells', in Andrews (ed.), *Bygone Church Life*, pp. 46–63.

60. M. Bloch, *The Royal Touch: Sacred Monarchy and Scrofula in England and France*, trans. J. E. Anderson (London, 1973); W. G. Black, *Folk-medicine: A Chapter in the History of Culture* (New York, 1970), pp. 140–3.

61. Risse, *Hospital Life*, p. 112; L. Davidson, 'The kiss of life in the eighteenth century: the fate of the ambiguous kiss', in Harvey (ed.), *The Kiss in History*, pp. 98–100; M. Nicolson, 'The introduction of percussion and stethoscopy to early nineteenth-century Edinburgh', in Bynum and Porter (eds), *Medicine and the Five Senses*, pp. 134–53.

62. Dundee Archive and Record Centre, CH2/1218/4, 12 June 1765.

63. See, for example, L. Leneman, 'Defamation in Scotland, 1750–1800', *Continuity and Change*, 15:2 (2000), 209–34.

64. P. Bailey, 'Breaking the sound barrier: a historian listens to noise', *Body and Society*, 2:2 (1996), 53.

65. *Extracts from the Records of the Burgh of Peebles, 1652–1714* (Scottish Burgh Records Society, Glasgow, 1910), p. 63.

66. *Extracts from the Records of the Burgh of Edinburgh 1573–1589* (Scottish Burgh Records Society, Edinburgh, 1882) vol. 4, p. 346.

67. A. Petrie, *Rules of Good Deportment, or Of Good Breeding. For the Use of Youth* (Edinburgh, 1720), pp. 129, 18.

68. D. Hume, *A Treatise of Human Nature* (1739–40), as cited in K. Thomas, 'Cleanliness and godliness in early modern England', in A. Fletcher and P. Roberts (eds), *Religion, Culture and Society in Early Modern Britain: Essays in Honour of Patrick Collinson* (Cambridge, 1994), p. 69.

69. Hume Brown (ed.), *Early Travellers*, p. 185.

70. Petrie, *Rules of Good Deportment*, pp. 19–20, 58, 82–4.

71. As cited in R. A. Houston, *Social Change in the Age of Enlightenment: Edinburgh, 1660–1760* (Oxford, 1994), p. 149.

72. See, for example, L. Leneman and R. Mitchison, *Sin in the City: Sexuality and Social Control in Urban Scotland 1660–1780* (Edinburgh, 1998), p. 31.

73. Palmer, 'In bad odour', pp. 65, 68; Jenner, 'Civilization and deoderization?', pp. 132–3.

74. R. G. Howarth (ed.), *The Letters and Second Diary of Samuel Pepys* (1933), p. 139, as cited in Thomas, 'Cleanliness and godliness', p. 67.

75. Hume Brown (ed.), *Early Travellers*, pp. 102–3.

76. *A Trip Lately to Scotland with the True Character of the Country and People* (London, 1705), p. 11.

77. See, for example, NAS, GD124/10/134, Papers concerning the tanning of leather in Edinburgh (28 June 1617), and *Extracts from the Records of the Burgh of Peebles*, pp. 174, 175.

78. E. Howlett, 'Bell lore', in W. Andrews (ed.), *Bygone Church Life*, pp. 44–5; *Extracts from the Council Register of the Burgh of Aberdeen 1643–1747*, pp. 5–6.

79. J. L. Campbell (ed.), *A Collection of Highland Rites and Customes* (Cambridge, 1975), p. 86.

80. Frost, 'Saints and holy wells', p. 61.

81. *Extracts from the Records of the Burgh of Edinburgh 1573–1589*, pp. 563–4; Dundee Archive and Record Centre, Auchterhouse Session Minutes, CH2/23/2, 21 April 1793.

82. A. F. Dimmock, *Cruel Legacy: An Introduction to the Record of Deaf People in History* (Edinburgh, 1993), pp. 17, 20–1; Johnson, *Journey to the Western Islands*, p. 136.

83. A. Corbin, *The Foul and the Fragrant: Odor and the French Social Imagination* (Leamington Spa, 1986); and C. Classen, D. Howes and A. Synnott, *Aroma: The Cultural History of Smell* (London, 1994). See also, G. Vigarello, *Concepts of Cleanliness: Changing Attitudes in France Since the Middle Ages*, trans. J. Birrell (Cambridge, 1988).

84. Bailey, 'Breaking the sound barrier', pp. 57–60.

85. C. Brant, 'Fume and perfume: some eighteenth-century uses of smell', *Journal of British Studies*, 43:4 (2004), 446.

Chapter 9

Beliefs, Religions, Fears and Neuroses

Joyce Miller

INTRODUCTION

The life of ordinary Scottish men and women during the early modern period was dominated by a Judaeo-Christian world view. The church had been, and continued to be, the most powerful social and cultural force on society, despite its own organisational struggles with royal supremacy during the 1600s and beyond.[1] From the time of the first missionaries, the Christian Church was an organisation of social control which influenced individual and community behaviour and beliefs. Yet 'beliefs' had existed before the arrival of Christianity. One of the most fundamental beliefs, which underpinned much of how early modern society perceived their world, was fear, related to survival – or the lack of it.[2] Illness, injury, lack of food, loss of livestock, inability to pay rent, warfare and death; all of these fears affected people of all levels on a day-to-day basis. Compared with our modern twenty-first century standards, life was very insecure and a variety of beliefs and practices, of whatever kind or nature, provided the means to offer some comfort and an impression, perhaps illusory but nevertheless valuable, of control over a somewhat arduous and precarious existence.

This chapter will examine the phenomena of fears and neuroses experienced during the seventeenth and eighteenth centuries, particularly those in relation to demonising certain sections of society, and consider their relationship with beliefs and religions. These centuries saw much change on a major national scale and also on a more subtle, personal level. From the highest in the land to the lowest, Scottish society experienced a huge range of political, economic, religious and social changes.[3] Nevertheless, the journey to the rational and improved eighteenth century of Whiggish propaganda, was not easy and Scottish society experienced a variety of stressful cultural and social disturbances along the way.

When discussing fears and neuroses it is important to consider what these terms have been taken to mean for the purposes of this chapter. Fear can be regarded as a quite rational emotion, a reaction to frightening circumstances. On the other hand, neurosis is more of an irrational mental condition, characterised by hysteria, anxiety, depression or obsessive behaviours which are not necessarily always caused by frightening circumstances. There is no doubt that in the early modern period, illnesses were recorded as demonstrating a variety of physical and mental symptoms, but did people suffer from anxiety, depression and neurosis as we recognise these conditions today? Emotional symptoms, such as melancholia, mania, possession, distraction and loss of wits, as well as physical symptoms such as sweating, nausea, paralysis and debilitation, were all described in the seventeenth and eighteenth centuries, but their causes were debated and so, by extension, were their cures. This chapter, therefore, is an examination of fears, rational or irrational, that were experienced at that time, the factors that contributed to them and the means by which they were controlled. Although the personal fears and anxieties experienced by individuals are undoubtedly important, what is also relevant are the fears and anxieties expressed by the country as a whole. The fear and insecurity of some sections of Scottish society, particularly the church and state, resulted in the creation of a climate of fear by the manipulation of ordinary people's emotions. Thus, fears were experienced at both a personal and national level.

In the pre-scientific age of the seventeenth and eighteenth centuries, people experienced a variety of emotional and physical symptoms.[4] Diseases were not defined or identified by a number of symptoms as they are today. Instead each symptom was treated individually. Society believed emotional symptoms, like physical ones, could be caused by natural or unnatural forces. In other words, some symptoms did not appear to have a rational cause which could be treated or explained. Sir George McKenzie, a noted lawyer and prosecutor of witches and Covenanters, observed that: 'there are many diseases whereof the cures, as well as the causes, are unknown to us. Nature is very subtle in its operations, and we are very ignorant in our inquiries.'[5] If an educated lawyer could acknowledge that there were more things on this earth than could be explained by nature, then the ordinary population would be unlikely to have exhibited different beliefs. The vocabulary of disease used in popular discourse indicates very clearly what, for many, was the most likely cause of ill health or disease: some form of supernatural force. Terms such as 'bewitched', 'blasted by an ill wind', 'forespoken', 'brash of seikness through an ill ee', 'the skaith of an evil mind', were all used in descriptions of both physical and mental symptoms and demonstrate a fundamental belief in the supernatural as a cause of illness.

Since the perceived causes of illness were very different from our current approaches, their cures were also somewhat dissimilar. Emotional problems, described as 'the loss of one's wits', or senses, may be taken to equate to a degree of depression or anxiety and were recognised as needing treatment. A fairly typical popular cure for people who had lost their wits or were distracted in some way involved the use of water and a holy site. A typical case is illustrated by Agnes Simpson, who was left for two nights at the chapel at Struthill, near Muthill in Stirlingshire, in 1668.[6] She was tied up and left alone overnight for two nights. After the second night, when her tethers had been miraculously loosened without any assistance from anyone, she was reported to have come to her 'healthe and witts againe and continued so to this day'.[7] Emotional distress may have been a problem, but society had a means to try to cure, or at least to improve, the condition, which they found acceptable. Agnes may have been distressed by her treatment but to all intents and purposes it appeared to work for her – and presumably for many others in a similar condition.

At the national level, although some of the social changes experienced in the seventeenth century might, with hindsight, be seen as general improvements, there is no doubt that at the time they brought with them a certain amount of tension and anxiety, fear and panic. The eighteenth century might be regarded as a century of enlightened, rational thought exemplified by Hume, Smith, Ferguson and Robertson, but it followed more than a century of struggle and violence, much of it caused by the Reformed Church's attempt to create a perfect godly society. While the Presbyterian form of Christianity struggled to find a firm foothold in Scotland, what was not in doubt was the position of Christianity itself. Scottish society was unquestionably Christian during the seventeenth and eighteenth centuries but, as in earlier centuries, people modified their Christianity with other more informal beliefs, something which was absolutely unacceptable to the Protestant Church. Society may well have accepted and believed in the Judaeo-Christian world view as taught through church sermons and catechisms, but at the same time most people also paid more than just lip service to acknowledging that the world and nature were not things they could always control through officially sanctioned ritual. God may well have been the official, universal and predominant, spiritual power, but most people hedged their bets by attempting to propitiate various unofficial 'other' spiritual powers. For many, inexplicable and unseen forces and powers affected daily life – the sun, the moon, the stars, the planets, the fairies, ghosts or spirits – all of which could be harmful or beneficial depending on the circumstances. Most people incorporated belief in these various forces, which they regarded as relatively harmless, into their daily lives.

Magic was a means of allowing people to understand, and even manage, supernatural powers for their own purposes and survival. Running through the justification of belief in supernatural forces was the concept of limited good: this meant that there was only so much good luck, in the way of food, love, health, wealth and so forth to go round. To compensate, as a means of survival, people tried to maximise their share of good luck.[8] At the same time, the Reformed Church's decades long campaign to become the dominant social and political force in Scottish society manifested itself by provoking a climate of fear and anxiety and by attacking these beliefs and practices.

Seventeenth-century Scottish society was riven by fear and anxiety. Everyday personal fears about illness and the struggle to survive were

Newes from Scotland.

Figure 9.1 *Image of the Devil, 1591. The Devil, in the shape of a winged and cloven-hooved beast, emerging from a tree stump to preach to an assembled group of witches. During the early modern period, the Devil was perceived to be a real threat to the authority of the Protestant Church in Scotland, because of the reluctance of some to abandon pre-Reformation Church ritual and other popular religious practices. Taken from* Newes from Scotland *(1591, reprinted 1816). Reproduced by permission of the British Library.*

matched by more generalised, intellectual concerns which resulted from the church's desire to establish an ideal Christian society. The key issue that this chapter will address is how far the anxieties about the difficulties of life, which contributed to fears about witches, plagues and famines, were heightened by the kirk campaign to inculcate Protestant belief and control society.

MAGIC

The Protestant organisation and doctrine of the church in Scotland meant it had officially rejected many of the tenets and rituals which were part of pre-Reformation or Roman Catholic worship. These included rituals such as visiting holy wells, belief in the power of relics and praying for saintly intercession. Nevertheless, for ordinary people, many aspects of belief continued to be practised, unofficially, through the use of rituals. The church may have controlled official public worship, but unofficial private rituals continued to provide more personal consolation. In 1581 the Scottish parliament passed an act against pilgrimages and other superstitious observations:

> and pairtlie throw the peruers inclinatioun of manis ingyne to superstitious, the dregges of Idolatrie yit remanis in divers pairtes of the realme be using of pilgramage to sum chappellis, wellis, croces and sic uther monumentis of Idolatrie. As also be observing of the festuall dayis of the santes, sumtyme namit their patronis, in setting furth of bain fyres, singing of caroles within and about kirkis at certane seasones of the yeir and observing of sic utheris superstitious and papisticall rytes.[9]

Some of these 'superstitious' observances were undoubtedly pre-Reformation in tone or emphasis, but many were less specific than this and reflected a widespread popular belief in the power of magic. For the most part, the popular magical beliefs and rituals that were practised by the majority were not the high or elite magic of alchemists or *magi* who performed obscure and complex rituals to invoke powers or to reveal secret knowledge. They tended to be the quite ordinary or mundane and, most certainly, pragmatic magic of everyday life. Popular magic was used to solve everyday problems, to counter any perceived bad luck or alternatively to ensure as much good luck as possible. Nevertheless, as illustrated by the 1581 Act, the tension between the official church and some of its less compliant members over the continued observance of 'ignorant superstition' would contribute to a great deal of conflict in the 1600s.

The dividing line between religion and magic, and even science, was, for the majority, quite blurred. Most people, at all levels of society, had no problem in reconciling attending Protestant church service on Sunday morning and carrying out protective rituals over their goods and animals in the afternoon. The early seventeenth century was pre-scientific: rationalism and the mechanical world view were still, for most people, some decades off in the future. A Copernican heliocentric interpretation about the universe was hardly widely accepted, neither were Cartesian philosophical ideas about the distinction between the mind and the body, although by the end of the century these theories had found some support among the educated elite. These early defenders of Copernican and Cartesian philosophy found themselves in an awkward position, often accused by traditional theologians of endorsing atheism.[10] Intellectual and philosophical debates held little interest for the majority of the population, for whom survival was paramount. They did, however, pose another threat to the authority of the church. The church was beset on all sides: the pressure from an elite minority of intellectuals and philosophers was, for some theologians, as serious as that caused by the rituals and beliefs practised by the popular majority.

POPULAR RELIGIOUS PRACTICES

In what ways did popular religion manifest itself in post-Reformation Scotland? Undoubtedly the most obvious way was by the carrying out a variety of protective or restorative rituals, often observing rules and restrictions that had obscure origins, many of which had been acceptable to the pre-Reformation Church. These rituals related to general agricultural matters, including work on the land, work in the house, calendar customs, weather and animals. On a more personal level they were associated with the human condition and the cycle of life, including: significant rites of passage such as marriage, for example, visiting shrines or other sites believed to have an effect on the fertility; pregnancy and childbirth, including the placing of iron under a bed during labour; infancy and childhood – offerings of silver to protect newborns from being stolen by the fairies; and death and dying – placing iron or salt on the chest of a corpse. General illness and disease were also important themes, as were the observation and interpretation of divinatory signs and omens. Rituals were carried out at certain times or on particular days. The location was also often significant, as was the manner in which the rituals were carried out. Certain motifs, such as the use of words, water, objects and numbers, have also been identified as being associated with popular religious practices in general, and particularly with those associated with healing and protection.[11]

Many of the motifs identified in popular religious rituals were similar to those seen in Christian religious ritual, or may have been associated with older belief systems. The use of the number three as a representation of the Trinity was widespread. Individuals often walked three times around a holy well, a tree, a house or some other site which was believed to possess special powers, with the afflicted or with the suspected cause of the problem, possibly someone suspected of using witchcraft. Clearly the number three has recognisable Christian overtones, but it also has older origins as tripartite divisions were a fundamental aspect of Indo-European culture and society, and three-fold patterns or shapes were recorded in pre-Christian Pictish symbols and stones.[12] Other numbers were also used in specific rituals: four, five, seven, nine and even eleven, but three was the most commonly used.

Esoteric words, spoken or written, were a powerful characteristic of both magic and religion and were believed to have intrinsic power. Certain passages of the Bible were also believed, by a mostly non-literate society, to have special virtue, as did spoken words in the form of an invocation or petitionary prayer. During the seventeenth and eighteenth centuries, the use of parts of, or whole, verses of pre-Reformation prayers in Latin, particularly 'Ave Maria' and the 'Paternoster', or prefacing or completing a spoken charm with, 'In the name of the Father, the Son and the Holy Ghost', was still common. The use of a few words of Latin, albeit without full comprehension, may have had the effect of making the verse or spell seem more special and secret, and almost certainly implied that at least a part of the origin of the charm was the pre-Reformation Church liturgy, something which was certainly not acceptable to the Protestant Church.

On the other hand, many prayers used vernacular Scots, which would have been fully understood by most people: 'Three bitter thingis hes yow bitten, ill heart, ill ee, ill toung all meast. Uther thingis may thee beit, the Father, the Sone and the Holy Ghost,' was a blessing that continued to be used often throughout Scotland, and other parts of the British Isles in a similar version well after the Reformation. The use of prayer itself was not against Reformed practice, but the use of overtly pre-Reformation prayer was, particularly if it involved any plea for saintly intercession as in the verse: 'Oaken post stand hail; bairn's maw turns hail; god and St Birnibane [Barnabas] the bright, turn my my bairn's maw [nausea] right. In god's name.' Nevertheless, despite opposition from the Reformed Church, many people continued to use petitionary prayers that were a combination of pre-Reformation and local practice as a means to provide some relief from suffering.

Another feature of popular religious practice, which demonstrated a degree of overlap with Christian doctrine, was the use of water, particularly from a holy well or spring, which was used to cleanse an afflicted person. Many of these wells were associated with local or international Christian saints, for example, St Maelrubha, St Triduana, St Columba, St Mary and St John. Some of the local wells were often associated with a particular ailment or complaint experienced by either animals or humans; they were not known by a saint's name but were instead often named after the condition they reportedly helped. A number were given the name kinkhost, as they were believed to be efficacious in the treatment of whooping cough – in Scots, kinkhost or chincough. Water was used to treat a variety of other complaints including: eye diseases (St Triduana); toothache, fertility (the Virgin Mary); mental illness (St Fillan); or rheumatism (St Fillan again).[13] It is possible that a number of these wells may have had an unusual mineral content and the water may, therefore, have had some medicinal effect, but the belief in the power of the water was what mattered most. They did not need scientific explanations about why water from a particular site helped them. The belief that certain wells had special powers was more likely the result of local stories of miracle cures or from hagiographical legends about particular saints. Whatever the reason, the belief in the power of the water was quite logical and accepted by local communities.

Fear of illness and death, with limited access to trained physicians and surgeons, meant that the belief in the power of special water and other rituals was an important source of comfort for many people. Special or holy water and other objects were also used to bless animals, crops, households and other physical objects and, until the time of the Reformation, these ceremonies had the support of the church. The ritual carried out at all these wells or shrines was more or less universal: the person or their representative would go to the well, usually at sunrise, walk around the well sunwise – or *deasil*

– three times, collect some of the water and then use it to wash the sufferer or offer it as a drink; the sufferer would be cleansed externally and/or internally. Some small token would usually be left as a votive offering, which could take the form of a coin, a pebble, a pin, or a ribbon or thread. These healing, or purifying, rituals were essentially those of pilgrimage to sites that may have had pre-Christian origins but which had been assimilated into the Christian, pre-Reformation Church calendar and had been given official sanction. Unfortunately for seventeenth- and eighteenth-century Scottish men and women, these rites and sites were no longer acceptable to the new church.

REFORMED RELIGIOUS PRACTICE

The new church abandoned older practices and beliefs and, in order to enable congregations to become part of a perfect godly society, the key features of the new, Reformed worship were intended to prepare and instruct congregations to recognise their sins, cleanse their souls and improve their behaviour: Sabbath service; fasting; repentance; and communion. The Sunday service involved extensive and intensive preaching of God's word; the minister's sermon was indisputably the most important part of the service. As most people were unable to read the Bible for themselves (although by the eighteenth century the percentage of people who were able to do so had increased), congregations required instruction in order to understand the meaning of the scripture. Readings, catechisms, lessons and sermons – usually more than one – were all included in Sunday services and congregations were expected to attend and listen attentively. Preaching instructed and exhorted congregations to examine their lives and behaviour and eliminate sin. Individual moral misdemeanours were to be eradicated and the dangers and risks posed by threats to the integrity of the Godly society, by sinful practices and observances, were stressed. The Reformed Church of the seventeenth century was far from secure, and by pointing out the dangers of sinful behaviour to individuals and society as a whole, the church was, in many ways, addressing its fear for its own survival.

While the Reformed Church stressed the danger of sins of omission, as much as commission, that were present in everyday life, it no longer offered a range of rituals as a means of comfort to compensate or commiserate. The rituals and ceremonies sanctioned by the kirk were much more restricted. As part of the Protestant Church reforms, pilgrimages to wells had been made illegal in 1581. Despite such legislation, however, it would appear that the population were reluctant to change their habits as the Privy Council issued a further declaration in 1629 stating that pilgrimage: 'is so frequent and common in this kingdom'.[14] Seasonal celebrations for saints and other calendar festivals, including yule or midsummer were also outlawed. Public ceremonies, which combined civic and religious observances, such as Corpus Christi, and even Easter, were abolished; May plays and other folk plays had been declared illegal prior to the Reformation parliament of 1560.[15] Other forms of festivity and ceremony associated with marriage and burials were restricted. Helen Bull was questioned by the presbytery of Haddington in 1647 about putting pieces of bread on children's chests when they were baptised,[16] and in 1651 the kirk session in Pencaitland questioned Agnes Bennet about why she put a nail on top of a corpse before the winding sheet was put in place. Her reply was that the nail 'was to keep her [the dead woman's] spirit from coming again . . .'.[17] These women were typical of those who were interrogated as part of the clampdown on a range of customs that the new church condemned as 'ignorant superstition' and profane past times.[18]

The rituals the reformers offered in their place took the form of sacrament and repentance, particularly the latter. The main sacrament was communion (baptism was the only other sacrament allowed by the Protestant Church) and participating in, and the taking of, communion was an extremely serious matter and not one to be undertaken or accepted lightly. In many places communion was offered only once a year (as had been the case prior to 1560); although one of the main objectives of the new church was to offer communion quarterly, this was not achieved in most areas of the country. To reflect the serious nature of the ceremony, communicants were expected to undergo mental and physical preparation. As well as attending a number of preparatory sermons, examinations and tests were conducted – often taking many hours – to assess the communicants' suitability to be allowed to participate. If they passed, they would be issued with a token which would allow them admission to the communion ceremony.[19] The communion service was also preceded by a fast, sometimes of several days, often accompanied by fasting sermons when ministers would preach sermons encouraging congregations to examine their souls and repent their sinful behaviours.

Fasting was carried out in order to cleanse society of its sins and request God's forgiveness. Liturgical fasting was ordained and regulated by the church as a means of obviating the punishments inflicted by God because of society's sins. Although the Protestant Church in Scotland introduced liturgical fasting in the sixteenth century, its counterpoint, thanksgiving celebrations to mark God's blessing, featured less frequently.[20] The message was: less self-congratulation and more self-mortification. According to the church, Godly reproofs manifested themselves in a variety of disasters and crises, including famines and plagues, which society feared greatly. According to the new church, these disasters were beyond human control but with repentance and God's forgiveness, their effect could be reduced. Protestant fasts were not calendar events associated with regular, annual festivals, as formerly, but were ordered in reaction to individual local or national events: outbreaks of disease or harvest failure; threats to the security of the realm or the king; threats to the security of the authority of the church – all were interpreted as demonstrations of God's anger and signs that Scottish society was not as 'Good and Godly' as it could be.

It was the responsibility of the church to root out unacceptable behaviours and punish them in order to eradicate them. Repentance for one's sins and a request for God's forgiveness was an important liturgical ritual permitted by the new church as it was associated with being given permission to take communion, as well as the manner in which it was taken. In many ways repentance became the means through which the church made most impact on society. Instead of being ordered to carry out a penance, often done privately, on the instructions of a priest, after the Reformation individuals were encouraged to make a public personal repentance.

For the Protestant Church, although sexual misdemeanours were by far the most common, blasphemy and carrying out superstitious rituals – such as visiting a well – were far more serious, as these practices indicated a continuance of pre-Reformation observance. In cases of blasphemy or the carrying out of unacceptable rituals, the sin could be defined as that of apostasy, either through a misguided lapse or a deliberate continuation of practice. These serious misdemeanours involved careful investigation by the kirk sessions, and even the presbytery, in order to ascertain whether or not there had been any deliberate rejection of the authority of the church. In most cases, despite the concerns of the general assembly, kirk sessions tended to regard these transgressions as the result of ignorance, rather than the much more serious sin of deliberate apostasy. Nevertheless, as will be discussed later, the church would not always be so lenient but would view such practices as the most unacceptable kind of apostasy, that of demonic worship.

For those who were sick, however, there was little in the way of comforting ritual offered by the new church. For the Protestant Church the cause of illness or misfortune was the result of an individual's own behaviour: in other words fitting punishment for sins. The only recourses were prayer and asking God's forgiveness. In 1670 the presbytery of Haddington recorded that the minister should:

> visit the sick . . . [and] endeavours to awaken in them a sense of their sins that they may confess, repent and be humbled for them, and that recourse to god through Jesus Christ, for pardons, and stirr them up to resolv if god shall lengthen their days. To live more Christianlie; exhorting them to pactions under the hand of god and cheerful submission to his will.[21]

Possibly because of such hard-line policies and despite fear of punishment, people were generally reluctant to abandon their traditional practices, even if they were condemned by the new church, its ministers and elders.

UNGODLY BEHAVIOUR AND FEAR

Ungodly behaviour included anything that did not conform to the Protestant ideal, from deliberate Roman Catholic recusancy to accidental transgressions of non-observance of Protestant practice. As the many socio-economic and political crises of the seventeenth century contributed to a general climate of fear, this fear and anxiety was used by the church to stimulate further disquiet by attributing the causes of harvest failures, illness and plague, civil and military disruption, poverty and hunger to society itself. These crises or disasters were God's punishments for sinful behaviour. Fear was used to generate conformity in order to shape Scottish society into an idealised Godly population. However, by trying to create a perfectly obedient society, the church only added to the general atmosphere of fear and contributed to the disruption of the seventeenth century.

Nevertheless, in spite of legislation and the theoretical authority of the church, people continued to carry out what they regarded as traditional rituals because they provided them with comfort and reassurance – even if they did not always work. During the 1600s the church continued to be concerned about incidents of non-conformity – a century later non-conformity and disagreement over polity culminated in further schism and the formation of the original secession church in 1740. One of the 'superstitious' rituals or non-conforming practices that survived among the ordinary population, despite numerous pieces of legislation against, was pilgrimage. Typically, the synod of Dunblane recorded in 1649 that:

> ane general ordinance was passed that the several Presbyteries within the bounds be careful that all superstitious wells and chapels whereunto people resort may be carefullie abandoned, and diligence used for craving the assistance of the heritors and others within their bounds for restraining the said superstitions resorting, apprehending and punishing of such persons as do resort to such superstitious places.[22]

The church clearly had a continuing problem convincing its congregations that these popular religious rituals were unacceptable, and this was a serious threat to the church's authority. While a lack of correct observance of Protestant practice was troublesome, for the church a serious and dangerous reason for transgression was the evil influence of the devil. Ignorance of the Scripture, non-observance of Protestant regulations and continued use of pre-Reformation ritual were all interpreted as not simply a reluctance to conform, but as evidence of the threat from the devil to the security of the Protestant Church. As if there were not enough problems for people to face, the church started to preach messages of imminent disaster: repent or suffer. The message was quite straightforward: the church's fight to maintain its position as the dominant religious organisation and social and cultural force in the country, was a metaphor for a much larger contest as the devil and God struggled for control over society itself. The devil, Scottish congregations were told, was a real and present danger. Praying for, or believing in, any supernatural power other than God in order to relieve suffering was absolutely unacceptable. Invocations of, or petitions to, other spiritual agents – angels, saints, fairies or elves, ghosts, nature spirits, whether pre-Christian or pre-Reformation Christian – were not permitted. The only acceptable supernatural power was God; anything else was ultimately demonic. During the 1600s, many spirit figures of popular culture, particularly fairies and ghosts, were removed from popular culture by the church and replaced by the much more ominous figure of the devil.[23]

Fear of the power of the devil was a crucial aspect of Christian theology. The devil was antithetical to God and Christ, for both Roman Catholic and Protestant Churches and, as such, was an opponent against whom society had to be defended. Any rival to the authority of the church was demonised and recast as an enemy of God or the antichrist.[24] For the Protestant Church in sixteenth- and seventeenth-century Scotland, this enemy was the pre-Reformation Church and, principally, the figure of the pope, who was identified as the antichrist in early Scottish Protestant propaganda, such as the bond of the lords of congregation of 1557. Thus, the continuation of pre-Reformation religious rituals was regarded as not only being in direct opposition to the orders of the Protestant Church, but was an indication of support for papal authority, in other words, the antichrist. However, although the pope and the pre-Reformation Church may have been rejected, at least in theory, in 1560, the struggle to win over the hearts and minds of congregations took much longer. Many ordinary people were clearly reluctant to abandon a, possibly innocent, belief in the power of special places, things or people, based on local or personal tradition and which had been permitted by the old church before 1560. Unfortunately, people could be, and often were, regarded as having indulged in demonic practices, the most common of which was witchcraft and, as a result, would suffer serious consequences.

Most people denied that they had anything to do with the devil when they carried out popular religious customs. The image and power of the devil was something with which all levels of society in the seventeenth century, from the elite to the ordinary people, were familiar. James VI identified himself as God's Protestant magistrate after the demonic threat to the security and safety of the king, and by extension that of the country as a whole, had been identified and defeated with the North Berwick witchcraft trials of 1590.[25] Non-literate sections of the population were just as aware of the concept of the devil. Although Protestant Church buildings no longer contained painted or carved images of the devil – most having been destroyed during the early years of the Reformation – sermons using biblical chapter and verse, particularly from the Book of Revelation, instructed non-literate congregations about the very real threat from the devil. The devil, people were told, could take any form or appearance and would tempt people with offers of reward in the way of food, wealth, promises of good health or power. In a country which was relatively impoverished and where survival for many was often very difficult, the prospect of obtaining food, drink or clothing must have been quite tempting.

While the church struggled to mould a Godly population, many ordinary people were implicated and accused of demonic worship and witchcraft because of their reluctance to give up traditional beliefs and practices. For a church that was endeavouring to create a perfect Godly state, popular belief and practice appeared to have more in common with the devil than God.[26] Clearly many of those who practised what were regarded as non-conforming rituals had no desire to invoke the devil or to participate in demonic worship, but the church needed to suppress all forms of unorthodox practice in order to demonstrate its authority. Popular rituals were dangerous, profane and heretical and amounted to apostasy which needed to be stamped out.

FEAR OF THE DEVIL AND CRIMINALISATION OF BELIEFS AND PRACTICES

As all aspects of unorthodox observance were deemed demonic, so beliefs and practices long regarded as traditional were questioned, criminalised and eventually denounced as being demonic witchcraft. The Protestant Church's fear of the devil, coupled with people's fear of witches, resulted in around 4,000 people being accused of witchcraft in Scotland between 1563 and 1736.[27] This apparent increased incidence of demonic witchcraft was not the result of unusually large numbers of women and men renouncing their baptisms and becoming servants of the devil. Instead, it was a result of the demonising of popular culture and belief by the state and the church and recasting it as something dangerous and frightening.[28]

There is no doubt that ordinary people understood the concept of witch-craft before it was officially criminalised in Scotland in 1563. As a method of manipulating supernatural powers, witchcraft was an aspect of the spectrum of popular beliefs that included religion and magic. For the most part, witch-craft was regarded as a harmful power which was used to spoil ale, ruin crops, stop milk from churning and cause illness, injury and even death. However, if people believed their bad luck was the result of witchcraft, they were able to redress the negative effects of malefice, or harm, by using counter-witchcraft. A range of popular rituals were carried out to provide protection or good luck against what was perceived by many as being malicious witch-craft. In other words, ironically, the popular religio-magical rituals, which the Reformed Church had categorised as being witchcraft, were usually used to protect against perceived acts of witchcraft. In 1636, Andrew Aitken was called before the presbytery of Stirling to answer charges about his skill of taking-off witchcraft and curing people and animals. Aitken used a variety of rituals including a spoken verse, fire and south-running water and, when asked why he had been at Bothkennar at Beltane the previous year, stated that he had collected some south-running water which he had sprinkled on the ground over which he had passed his 'guids' (livestock) in order to protect them during the following year.[29] He did not give any indication that he invoked demonic powers but showed a typical belief in the apotropaic power of ritual. Yet his actions, and those of many others, caused the church much concern.

By the mid-seventeenth century, the Reformed Church regarded almost every use of witchcraft, whether malicious or beneficial, as demonic. The explanation was quite straightforward: in order to acquire particular skills either to heal or to cause harm (the understanding was that the ability to do one, gave the ability to do the other), an individual must have entered into a relationship with the devil and participated in a demonic pact. In theory the demonic pact featured a number of key elements, the most crucial being the renunciation of Christian baptism. Other features included: being given a new name; receiving the devil's mark; acknowledging the devil as their master; and participating in worshipping the devil in a sacrilegious manner. The question about whether or not the power of witchcraft was real or not was not in doubt for early modern society: since the devil was regarded as a real threat to the security of the church and state, the reality of witchcraft was unquestionable.

The problem for someone like Andrew Aitken was that, although he did not mention anything about demonic pact or demonic involvement, according to the authorities the devil's involvement was implicit in his actions and explanations. Some of those who participated in rituals were deemed to have committed simple superstition, like the group of eleven people who were called to explain why they had gone to Christ's Well in 1607 and who were ordered to 'mak public repentance at thair next sabbath . . .'.[30] Others, often those who did not appear before kirk session or presbyterial committees to answer for their superstitious practices, were excommunicated. But those whose practices were regarded as clearly demonic were treated far more harshly: the penalty for practising demonic witchcraft and participating in demonic pact was strangulation followed by burning.

People's genuine fear of malicious witchcraft was manipulated by the church into a widespread fear of witches, which culminated in thousands of people being accused of practising demonic witchcraft. Although this fear had existed prior to the Protestant Reformation, society had its own way of countering it. Harmful witchcraft could be neutralised either by using healing rituals or requesting the person suspected of having caused the problem to remove the spell. Like others, Andrew Aitken advised sick people to go to the person they suspected had laid the illness on them and ask for the return of their health 'for god's sake'.[31] Once healing rituals or personal requests had been forbidden by the church and state, society had no personal means by which to control the threat from, or their fear of, witchcraft. Official means of sanction – the church and secular authorities – took over the dispensing of justice. The fight for the souls of Scottish society was played out not only in the theatre of religious instruction and reprimand, but in the prosecution and execution of men and women whose deaths were used to persuade society to change their practices and beliefs.

CHANGING FEARS: FROM THE DEMONIC TO THE JACOBITE

By the end of the seventeenth century, attitudes began to change and fears about the threat from witches and the devil appear to have declined, or at least not to have dominated so much, partly as a result of changing attitudes and increased scepticism. The church was not necessarily in a more confident or successful position; indeed, it continued to attack heresy and atheism, but ultimately discontented elements within the church ended up attacking the church organisation itself and fragmenting into a number of sects in the eighteenth century. By this time, the fears of the state had been replaced by others, notably Roman Catholicism and Jacobitism. James, Duke of York's (later James VII and II) open support for Catholics, the attacking of conventicles and the passing of the 1681 Test Act all contributed to yet another period of religious tension. Although the number of Catholics in Scotland at this time was small, James VII's policies did little to ease perceived distrust or fear. By the mid-eighteenth century, there was an increase in antagonism by the state toward the Gailhealtachd, who were regarded as supporters of both Roman Catholicism and Jacobitism; the anti-Highland policies of earlier Stewart kings were rekindled as the government in London tried to assess the strength of the threat to national security and royal authority.

The areas where Jacobitism was rooted out and punished during the late seventeenth and eighteenth centuries were located in the Gailhealtachd – the area where Gaelic was the main language during the early modern period – which was mostly north of the Highland line.[32] A more mountainous landscape made many Highland areas unsuitable for arable farming and contributed to the longer survival of small, isolated, joint tenancy farm touns. Catholicism continued to be practised for longer in some areas of the Gailhealtachd, despite the presence of powerful Protestant clans such as the Campbells of Argyll; and finding Gaelic-speaking Protestant ministers was not an easy task in the early years of the seventeenth century. The customs and traditions associated with Gaelic-speaking areas are often cited as being quite different from those of Lowland Scotland, and yet on closer examination it can be seen that there were also similarities. The customs recorded in these areas were the same customs recorded in most agricultural communities in the Lowlands or Highlands, and revolved around rituals and observances that were intended to provide protection and good fortune.

Yet, for all there were similarities and differences, the Highlanders were persecuted and demonised in the eighteenth century. Just like the ordinary people who were classified as witches in the seventeenth century, Highlanders were regarded as a threat to the security and authority of the Protestant Church and state, and so fear and distrust of another section of society was manipulated and increased. Ironically, in areas where the population was demonised because of certain social and cultural differences, there had been relatively little prosecution of witchcraft, and in these areas popular religious beliefs and rituals would continue to be practised the longest; in some communities well into the twentieth century and up to the present day.

CONCLUSION

Popular religious rituals survived and continued to be observed, even in Lowland areas, despite the decades-long attack by the Protestant Church and long after the church had moved on to other internal organisational crises. By the end of the eighteenth century the Protestant Church was no longer as anxious about the problem of superstitious observance: for them the battle had been fought and won, ignorant superstition had been defeated. In fact, ordinary people persisted with their traditional practices; they were just more subtle about what they did. Despite the anxieties of theologians like Sir George Sinclair, Christianity had also survived, but a single, united Protestant Church had not.[33] The fear of the devil in the seventeenth century had been replaced by a genteel rationalism and a feeling of regret and guilt about the policies of demonisation and punishment that had been meted out against certain sections of society. By the end of the eighteenth century, antiquarians and historians began to recast popular religious rituals, and Highland society, as quaint, relics of a primitive past; they were no longer a threat but a memento of a bygone age.

Notes

1. There are many titles which cover the history of the political struggles of the church in the seventeenth century including: M. Lee, *The Road to Revolution: Scotland under Charles I, 1625–37* (Urbana, IL, 1985); D. Mullan, *Scottish Puritanism, 1590–1638* (Oxford, 1998); D. Stevenson, *The Scottish Revolution, 1637–44* (Edinburgh, 2003); D. Stevenson, *Revolution and Counter-Revolution, 1644–51* (Edinburgh, 2003). For an examination of the wider social and cultural impact of the church, see M. Graham, *The Uses of Reform: 'Godly Discipline' and Popular Behavior in Scotland and Beyond, 1560–1610* (Leiden, 1996); L. Leneman and R. Mitchison, *Sin in the City: Sexuality and Social Control in Urban Scotland, 1660–1780* (Edinburgh, 1998); R. Mitchison and L. Leneman, *Girls in Trouble: Sexuality and Social Control in Rural Scotland, 1660–1780* (Edinburgh, 1998); M. Todd, *The Culture of Protestantism in Early Modern Scotland* (New Haven, CT, 2002).
2. For a selection of chapters on the broad theme of fear see W. Naphy and P. Roberts (eds), *Fear in Early Modern Society* (Manchester, 1997).
3. I. D. Whyte, *Scotland Before the Industrial Revolution: An Economic and Social History, c. 1050–c. 1750* (Harlow, 1995) is a very good examination of social and economic aspects of both urban and rural society. There are also a number of publications by E. P. Dennison and R. Coleman looking at individual burghs, for example, *Historic Linlithgow, The Archaeological Implications of Development* (Edinburgh, 2000). H. Dingwall, *Late Seventeenth Century Edinburgh: a Demographic*

Study (Aldershot, 1994) is a useful examination of Edinburgh and there are a number of useful chapters in M. Lynch (ed.), *The Early Modern Town in Scotland* (London, 1987). For the rural experience see T. M. Devine, *The Transformation of Rural Scotland: Social Change and Agrarian Economy* (Edinburgh, 1994).

4. For a discussion of everyday attitudes to illness and disease in Scotland, see Helen Dingwall, Chapter 4, above, and her *Physicians, Surgeons and Apothecaries: Medical Practice in Seventeenth-Century Edinburgh* (East Linton, 1995).

5. G. McKenzie, *Pleadings in Some Remarkable Cases* (Edinburgh, 1672), p. 186.

6. Stirling Council Archives, Stirling Presbytery records, CH2/722/7.

7. For a discussion of this case and others see J. Miller, '"Towing the loon": diagnosis and use of shock treatment for mental illness in early-modern Scotland', in H. de Waardt, J. M. Schmidt, H. C. E. Midelfort, S. Lorenz and D. R. Bauer (eds), *Dämonische Besessenheit: Zur Interpretation eines kulturhistorischen Phänomens (Demonic Possession: Interpretations of a Historico-Cultural Phenomenon)* (Bielefeld, 2005), especially pp. 131–2.

8. S. Clark, *Thinking with Demons: The Idea of Witchcraft in Early Modern Europe* (Oxford, 1997), p. 472; K. Thomas, *Religion and the Decline of Magic* (London, 1971), p. 5; S. Wilson, *The Magical Universe: Everyday Ritual and Magic in Pre-Modern Europe* (London, 2000), pp. xviii, 467.

9. *Acts of Parliament of Scotland* (APS), vol. III, p. 212.

10. Clark, *Thinking with Demons*, pp. 300–4 points out that those who supported the new theories of mechanism were accused of supporting an atheistic philosophy. M. Wasser, '"What dangerous principles they are": the mechanical world-view and the decline of witch beliefs in Scotland', in J. Goodare, L. Martin and J. Miller (eds), *Witchcraft and Belief in Early Modern Scotland* (Basingstoke, 2008).

11. J. Miller, 'Devices and directions: folk healing aspects of witchcraft practice in seventeenth-century Scotland', in J. Goodare (ed.), *The Scottish Witch-Hunt in Context* (Manchester, 2002), especially pp. 97–104.

12. E. Lyle, *Archaic Chaos* (Edinburgh, 1990), pp. 142–55; J. Miller, 'Cantrips and carlins: magic, medicine and society in the presbyteries of Haddington and Stirling, 1603–1688', unpublished Ph.D. thesis (University of Stirling, 1999), pp. 284–6; Wilson, *Magical Universe*, pp. 446–9.

13. R. Morris and F. Morris, *Scottish Healing Wells* (Sandy, 1982).

14. *Records of the Privy Council*, 2nd series, vol. III, p. 241.

15. May plays and other folk plays had been made illegal by the parliament before the Reformation in 1555, *APS*, vol. II. The general assembly also tried to forbid 'clerk plays, comedies or tragedies' in 1574, Todd, *Culture of Protestantism*, p. 224.

16. National Archives of Scotland (NAS), Haddington Presbytery records, CH2/185/5.

17. NAS, Pencaitland Kirk Session records, CH2/296/1.

18. Todd, *Culture of Protestantism*, ch, 4.

19. Todd, *Culture of Protestantism*, ch. 2, especially pp. 85–98.

20. Todd, *Culture of Protestantism*, ch. 7, especially pp. 344–52.

21. NAS, Haddington Presbytery Records, CH2/185/7. Although Reformed Church

ministers were expected to care for the suffering of the spirit, at the same time many also offered more practical advice. Many had attended some basic lectures in medicine while they were at university and so were able to recommend treatments and prescriptions for a variety of illnesses. See, for example, National Library of Scotland (NLS), MS 548, Journal of Reverend Robert Landess, 1660–1705. Landess was minister at Robroyston.

22. J. Wilson (ed.), *Register of the Diocesan Synod of Dunblane, 1662–1688* (Edinburgh, 1877), p. 263.

23. L. Henderson, and E. J. Cowan, *Scottish Fairy Belief* (East Linton, 2001), ch. 4, especially pp. 116–18.

24. Clark, *Thinking With Demons*, ch. 6, especially p. 81.

25. Much has been written about the North Berwick witch trials and James VI's involvement. Some of the more useful works include: S. Clark, 'King James's *Daemonologie*: witchcraft and kingship', in S. Anglo (ed.), *The Damned Art: Essays in the Language of Witchcraft* (London, 1977); P. Maxwell-Stuart, 'The fear of the king is death: James VI and the witches of East Lothian', in W. Naphy and P. Roberts (eds), *Fear in Early Modern Society* (Manchester, 1997); L. Normand and G. Roberts, *Witchcraft in Early Modern Scotland: James VI's* Demonology *and the North Berwick Witches* (Exeter, 2000); J. Wormald, 'The witches, the devil and the king', in T. Brotherstone and D. Ditchburn, *Freedom and Authority: Scotland c. 1050–c. 1650: Historical and Historiographical Essays Presented to Grant E. Simpson* (East Linton, 2000).

26. For a discussion of the devil and popular culture in seventeenth century, see J. Miller, 'Men in black: appearances of the devil in early modern Scottish witchcraft discourse', in J. Goodare, L. Martin and J. Miller (eds), *Witchcraft and Belief in Early Modern Scotland* (Basingstoke, 2008).

27. See www.shc.ed.ac.uk/Research/witches for information about witchcraft belief and the prosecution of those accused of witchcraft between 1563 and 1736 in Scotland.

28. For a discussion about the attack on, and demonising of, folk culture in the late sixteenth century, see E. J. Cowan, 'Witch persecution and folk belief in Lowland Scotland: the devil's decade', in Goodare *et al.*, *Witchcraft and Belief in Early Modern Scotland*.

29. SCA, Stirling Presbytery records, CH2/722/5. The location of the well was not specified in the records.

30. SCA, Stirling Presbytery records, CH2/722/4.

31. SCA, Stirling Presbytery records, CH2/722/5.

32. For a definition and location of the Gaidhealtachd I have used Whyte's definition in his *Scotland Before the Industrial Revolution*, p. 252.

33. G. Sinclair, *Satan's Invisible World Discovered* (Edinburgh, 1685). Sinclair was professor of natural philosophy at the University of Glasgow, but was profoundly concerned about what he saw as the atheistic threat from Cartesian theories and wrote *Satan's Invisible World Discovered* in order to prove the reality of the threat from the devil and other supernatural powers.

Chapter 10

Movement, Transport and Travel

Alastair Durie

> Good roads, canals and navigable rivers . . . are the greatest of all improvements.[1]
>
> Adam Smith, *The Wealth of Nations* (1776)

INTRODUCTION

Writers on economic matters such as Smith were in no doubt as to the significance of better transport to the development of any economy, including that of Scotland. His contemporary as a political economist, Sir James Steuart, converted analysis into argument. Author of a pamphlet in 1769 which advocated better roads in Lanarkshire, he was one of many voices who called for the further improvement of the roads, although welcoming the change that had taken place within recent times. 'A hundred years ago, there was not one cart with iron shod wheels in any country parish. All carriages were on the back of horses.'[2] A strong supporter of the Forth and Clyde canal, he was concerned about what he called the dismal situation of the county roads, which meant that during the winter, when the roads were 'terrible until they join the turnpike road', every access to Glasgow was quite cut off.[3] Better surfaces meant that all-year-round carting could be introduced, which would cut costs and enable grain to be moved to markets much more cheaply, and would benefit all. That would be one clear gain – there would be others – for everyday life.

The relationship, of course, between better transport and economic growth is a complex one; sometimes change in transport leads to development, sometimes it follows it, or the two run in tandem. And there was always the vexed question, that Steuart addresses, of who was to finance change, given that the state had little in the way of resources, which thrust the onus on to local landowning and mercantile interests. For whatever cause, whether poor administration, limited techniques or lack of finance, it is generally agreed that pre-Improvement transport was poor: as Hamilton says, the state of the roads was 'deplorable'.[4] Traffic was light in the countryside, except perhaps nearer the larger burghs, with little moving in the winter or at night, though crop failure could result in a flow of beggars and the destitute in search of subsistence. The run of bad harvests in the 1690s, and resulting large-scale starvation forced tens of thousands – perhaps even more – of the poor on the move to find relief.[5] And some on this desperate trek perished on the way: the parish of Montrose, to name but one of many, between November 1697 and May 1698 had to organise four burials for 'people who had died on the hills'.

But these times when the roads were choked with misery were abnormal, and thankfully becoming more and more infrequent. In better seasons there would be some of the gentry, their families and servants, other riders on business, occasional peddlers and tinkers, even a funeral party, complete with ale, spirits and shortbread on the road, but mostly life was slow and undisturbed by movement to or through the parishes.[6] Poor transport was a symptom of and confirmed the backwardness of the economy. Many communities were trapped at subsistence level, and while people would move, or even emigrate – which has given Scotland the reputation of a mobile society – these were mostly one-off movements forced by famine or war, or drawn by opportunity rather than the lower level, less remarkable daily or weekly trips of the maturing economy to fair, or market or dealer. It has been suggested that emigration implies high levels of internal mobility, but whether that correlates with movement on a daily or regular basis remains open.[7] Also, what movement there was, often tended to be, as far as the lower orders were concerned, dictated by others: carting or other duties; a servant or nurse following their master or mistress in their travels. Many men in the countryside may have spent more time working on the roads – every man aged between fifteen and sixty was supposed by law to do three days work in the summer and another three in the autumn – than they ever did travelling on them. That such (unpaid) work was grudgingly given, and inefficiently performed, can have come as no surprise.[8] They could choose to pay a fee ('commutation') for the parish to hire a substitute, but 3d. a day was a heavy drain on slight pockets, and inadequate help as far as the road authorities were concerned as they had to pay three times that for a day labourer. And the care of the roads, filling in potholes, surfacing and other work was labour intensive. Dr James Anderson may well have voiced the common mood well when he observed in 1794 that 'the roads are all made by the labour of the poor . . . many of whom have neither horses nor carriages ever to travel on those roads . . . [b]ut the rich in consequence of their labour are enabled to loll in their carriages at their ease' – while these same vehicles cut up the roads which the poor were forced to work to maintain.[9] Repairing the roads took a lot of labour, and building new roads even more: the army had powers of direction and control over its working parties which the civilian administrations must have envied. To muster 500 to 1,000 men for months of work, as Wade and Cauldfield did on the military roads was an undertaking mostly beyond parish or county competence.[10]

SOME PRELIMINARY OBSERVATIONS

There is, however, an assumption to challenge, that everyday life was penalised by bad transport. There is no question but that all island and many coastal communities had to face the reality of periods of isolation, sometimes protracted, because of sea and storm, a situation not really addressed until the coming of the steamships in the nineteenth century. But a bold question is to ask what difference did it make to the mainland communities of the cot-, kirk- or fermtoun? The miller was, perhaps, in a rather different position; he needed to be able to move grain in and meal out. But people could, and did walk, and everywhere. Age and physical condition, and if there was anything to be carried, clearly were limiting factors, but those who wanted to could cover a lot of ground. The thirty-year-old Coleridge, by no means a person in peak physical condition, on his walking tour in Highland Scotland averaged thirty to thirty-five miles a day for eight days.[11] Religion would be as powerful a motivation, perhaps more so for some, than pleasure or work to travel. Daniel Defoe in the early 1720s remarked on a field meeting or conventicle being held in Dumfriesshire. An old Cameronian preacher, John Hepburn, preached for seven hours (with a short break in the middle) to a huge gathering of 7,000 people. To Defoe, the commitment of these people was remarkable, as many of them had to come fifteen or sixteen miles to hear Hepburn, and 'had all the way to go home again on foot'.[12] There would, it can be agreed, have been severe disadvantages to a community of isolation: among other things there could be local shortages of food which converted into famine, or of imported raw materials which could bring rural outwork to a stop. But there were also advantages of isolation for some, which were to appear in a modernising economy when the inefficient rural producer or worker was no longer protected by the cost of transport. Improvement was a two-edged sword: factory-made products, for example, mill-spun yarn or cloth, were to undercut rural production and hand spinning once the protection of high transport costs was removed.

Scotland was not a society without movement, but most movements were only short in distance, collecting water and fuel, to the fields, infield or 'out', pasture or commons or to the shielings. In some areas there was the slog of cutting and collecting peats, perhaps from a moss at some distance.[13] Peddlers, packsmen, chapmen, letter carriers, collectors of rags, vagrants, disabled seamen and sailors made their way through the countryside, as did the cattle dealers, drovers (and their dogs).[14] In the early summer there might be a few Highland girls on their way to seek work on the Lowland harvest, a trickle that was to become a stream in the later eighteenth century as Scottish agriculture modernised.[15] Migrants from the countryside, usually young and single, did find their way to the towns for domestic service or apprenticeship. There would on occasion be emigrants on the road to the ports, pushed out by privation or improvement, or drawn on by promise of better things abroad. At times, there could be a substantial group on their way to an occasional or annual visit to a healing well or spring, a practice long rooted in country culture.[16] Despite Presbyterian disapproval, the folk still went to the familiar places, perhaps not at a long distance but a day's walk. 'Every parish has still its sainted well, which is regarded by the vulgar with a degree of veneration, not very distant from that which in Papist and Hindoos we pity as degrading,' harrumphed the famous medical writer of the late eighteenth century, Dr William Buchan.[17]

Whether everyday life was really constricted is, therefore, one question. There would have been potential gains if there had been better transport, and indirect losses because there was not, but the system was in equilibrium at a low level. There was a catch 22 situation: poverty kept transport poor, but equally poor communications confirmed the poverty. It is arguable that the poorness of the system in part reflected lack of demand for anything better as well as a lack of means. And when improvement came, who benefited? Longer distance trade in weighty commodities was a clear gainer, and cheaper fuel and grain helped the urban communities, but here and even more so in the countryside, did this not really benefit only the elite of the landowning and the merchant class? Did the rural poor find their lives much altered? In the later eighteenth century we shall see the arrival of travellers and tourists in increasing numbers, travelling for leisure and pleasure, and their increasing presence around Scotland. To what extent, however, did the population of Scotland share in this other than those who were in the landed and moneyed elite: did the other sections of society share in these new forms of travel? These are issues to be addressed below.

A key problem which dogs discussion of this topic is that we have little, if any, hard evidence as to the scale, distances and frequency of internal movement. There are receipts from takings at the toll bridges and the turnpikes, and some customs evidence as to the number of cattle crossing the border. Upper class and business travellers have left some record of their travels, and there are some odd statistics. Creech, for example, states that the number of four-wheeled chaises in Edinburgh rose from 396 in 1763 to 1,427 in 1790, a three-fold increase. He adds that in the latter year there were more than 6,450 wains (that is, heavy wagons) and carts, with 'stage coaches, flies and diligences available to every considerable town in Scotland'.[18] But these wheeled conveyances were for the better-off, and the carts for goods. Much, in fact, virtually all, of the movement of the ordinary people has left no trace, especially humdrum and mundane, the daily round, the weekly trip to market or fair, to church on Sunday (virtually the only traffic on the Sabbath) and even the occasional outing to a well or spring. We know something about once-in-a-life time movement, emigration or, as Houston and Whyte have shown from study of apprenticeship and marriage records, migration pre-1800: there was appreciable movement to the Scottish cities of young men and women.[19] In the nineteenth century and perhaps earlier this was to generate a reverse flow: the holiday visit to friends and relations in the countryside. It can be asked whether this was a new development. Perhaps it was, aided by better transport, more leisure time and disposable income. Or equally it may have been a traditional pattern. But it, like so many forms of movement, cannot be tracked. It easier to talk about how and why people may have travelled, what the problems were and the issues for those who moved and those whom they moved among, than to assess the scale or understand the experience. Also largely hidden from history is the experience of those who travelled as wives or servants or children. In short, much of the mundane and the everyday is off the screen.

THE OLD ORDER IN TRANSPORT

If there is one issue on which late eighteenth century writers agreed, (whether in the *First* or *Old Statistical Accounts* (OSA) or the General Surveys of Agriculture, and current academic assessment has followed) it is as to how difficult it was to make your way round Scotland before things were improved. Sea travel faced the difficulties of wind, wave and tide, and naviga-tion without charts or lighthouses, with privateering an additional problem during periods of war. Ferry crossings were a lottery with the humour and condition of the ferrymen always uncertain. A petition in 1739 about the fer-ryman at Cambusbarron complained that he was 'rude, unnatural and always drunk and out of the way'.[20] Fords were dangerous especially when rivers were in spate, and bridges were few and far between. To cross some bridges required the payment of a much grudged toll. The roads were ill kept, not signposted, with goods moved either by packhorse or on a sledge. There were some carts, but any kind of wheeled vehicle was quite unknown in many parishes.[21] 'A hundred years ago there was not one cart with iron-shod wheels in any country parish. All carriages were on the back of horses' was the view of Sir James Steuart.[22] Chris Smout quotes Grant of Monymusk's retrospective view of the dismal state of transport about 1716: 'no repair of roads, all bad, and very few wheel carriages; no coach, carriage or chaise and few carts benorth Tay'.[23] Traffic was confined to the day and to the better weather: 'few travelled in winter if they could help it'.[24] Retreat forced the Jacobite army to leave Aberdeen in ferocious winter weather, but few if any ordinary people could have managed thirty-nine miles in two days under such conditions on what were merely tracks.[25] Travellers' accounts stressed with feeling how big the contrast was between the old and the new. In the summer of 1758, Sir John Burrell followed the new road that the military were making between Inveraray and Tyndrum, but when it came to an end after four miles, he and his party found themselves on 'the most horrid paths than can be conceived'.[26] Adam Bald, a young Glasgow merchant, was returning home to Glasgow from Stirling in November 1792 on the new road being made by way of Cumbernauld. About a mile or so south of the village he came on a part of the road which in his words was 'not cut', and had to scramble through field and heather for about three miles. Six months later it was still not completed and was little more than a 'quagmire'.[27]

Yet the picture of the deficiencies of the old system and its administration by local justices of the peace may have been overdrawn. Things certainly got better in the later eighteenth century, but they were not necessarily quite as bad before then as is assumed. There is a story made popular by Henry Graham (picked up by Christopher Smout) which has coloured our view of how bad things were. This is an anecdote of the locals turning out to gape at a wheeled cart in Cambuslang in 1723, a cart carrying a small load of coals from East Kilbride: 'crowds of people went out to see the wonderful machine: they looked with surprise and returned with astonishment'. The original source for this, is David Ure's history of Rutherglen and East Kilbride.[28] It seems to imply, and so it has been read, that it was the sight of wheels that was the source of wonder. But an alternative reading which the text will equally support is that the emphasis should be put on the fact that it was the first 'to be made in the parish'. In any case this was a recollection which was not first hand, but of something said to have happened some '70 years ago' when there was not a cart in the parish and very few sledges. Ure's account of the parish in the 1790s for Sir John Sinclair, used this anecdote from the past to point to the remarkable improvement in affairs. Two-wheeled horse-drawn wagons were in common use, with a carry of some one-and-a-half tons of coal each, capable of taking several loads a day to Glasgow. This story, of the amazed crowd, is wheeled out to confirm how great the recent advance had been and to corroborate the widely held view that before the Industrial Revolution, the roads system was primitive, and as a result wheeled transport a rarity. But perhaps it should be taken with a pinch of salt.

John Harrison's important work on the roads in and around Stirling, which needs testing for other areas, serves as an important corrective. He shows that from the early 1660s to the mid-1690s, the system had built several new bridges and repaired others, and that 'the main roads, and perhaps some of the lesser ones now had better surfaces'.[29] The use of statute labour could be made to work, not that common folk necessarily enjoyed their days' labour, nor was it always put to good use. To the maintenance of the roads was added the making of bridges, often by public subscription, over rivers such as the Clyde and the Tay. There was the Bow Bridge over the Lossie at Elgin, which bears the inscription '*foundit 1630, finishit 1635*',[30] that at Montrose over the Esk, prompted by the dangers of the ford,[31] and the one over the Don at Inverurie. There were gaps, as at Fochabers, and drovers did lose beasts trying to swim them across firths and rivers.[32] The crossings of the estuarial Forth or the Tay were a continuing hazard: there the ferries remained to the dismay of many travellers. But people could and did travel. The recently published diary for 1689–90 of John Allan gives pause for reflection. Allan was a thirty-year-old itinerant preacher, and authentic voice, who was making his way round the north-east of Scotland and up to the Black Isle. There were, indeed, difficulties for him. In October 1689 he got lost among the mosses on the moor of Balnagowan, near Tain. The locals spoke only Gaelic (the language barrier in the north may have been echoed for the

Figure 10.1   *Leckie Bridge, 1673. One of a number of small, but sturdy and serviceable bridges built in Stirlingshire during the 1670s, this at Leckie near Gargunnock from 1673 carries the inscription in Latin 'built out of benevolence for safety's sake'. Source: John G. Harrison.*

visitor elsewhere by the challenge of dialect) and he could not follow their instructions. This caused him to wander to and fro at length until he found a boy coming up the hill who had 'Scots and knew the way – I was much comforted'. But the surprising thing is how often he seems to have travelled even in quite remote areas without too much fuss here and there. Although in May 1690 he was held up in Aberdeen by a shortage of horses to hire, mostly he could find a supply, even if there was an element of accident (or what he would have called providence) involved. His entry for 5 December when he was on the Black Isle records that he 'met with some who had empty horses, from whom I got one betwixt the ferries and sent back that which I had. I had two miles to go on foot to Newmore after crossing the ferry of Inverbrackie, for I could not get a horse for hire. But got a boy who carried my boots & clock [*cloak?*] the most of the way.'[33]

A CHANGED WORLD OF TRANSPORT

The supply of horses for hire was in part related to the growth of the postal system, which meant that postmasters had a stock of horses available for hire. There was also the rise of carting as a separate occupation, rather than just a fill-in activity for farm workers: the incorporation of carters at Leith could afford their own convening house by 1726.[34] Haldane's study of the postal system in Scotland shows that during the seventeenth century there was an evolving network of posting offices.[35] The mail was carried from the south by horse to Edinburgh with a distribution network onwards, by horse on the main routes and on foot to the rural areas thereafter. As a rule, poor people neither sent nor received letters; the lowest stratum was perhaps a master manufacturer or a tenant farmer. But the arrival of the post carrier on his weekly trudge must have been a source of interest and of news, something to lighten the day, and break up the routine. At Inveraray during the period from 27 April to 31 December 1734 over 2,450 letters – incoming and outgoing – passed through the hands of the postmaster there, brought by a weekly runner from Dumbarton.[36] Having been sorted, they were sent onwards by a further network of runners. The letter carrier was sometimes paid only when the letter was delivered, remunerated by the addressee not the sender, a mechanism that ensured delivery.

Prior to 1715, except for the horse post to and from England, mail was carried everywhere on foot. But this began to change; a new horse post was inaugurated to Stirling from November 1715, to Glasgow in 1717 and a faster network spread out. The three dispatches a week conveyed by relays of horses from Edinburgh to Aberdeen had become five from 1763. The heaviest traffic was on the road to and from Berwick: mail to London in the early 1750s took eighty-five hours while the return ('inexplicably') took 131 hours! As the weight of traffic increased, thanks to newspapers, packets and letters, the introduction of mail coaches was forced, first on the Edinburgh to London route in 1785 and then elsewhere. The improvement in the postal service was but one facet of a developing economy, and one element in the increase in traffic on the roads which fed off better roads and into the need for better surfaces. The foot traveller, and the drover, with his self-propelled freight, was probably affected least (except insofar as harder road surfaces hurt the hooves of his cattle). If there were goods to be taken to market – cloth, shoes, peats – the local worker benefited, with the wheelbarrow an increasingly common sight. The longer-distance traveller with money benefited most from better roads and more regular services, as did the merchant with bulky commodities to move and, indeed, from coastal shipping services. Foodstuffs and fuel were moved with increasing ease and at lower cost, and suppliers and buyers, but not the less efficient producer, alike reaped the benefit.

There was, therefore, a substantial rise in traffic, which the roads saw, and the rural community (depending on location) would have seen both many more people passing through their parishes and a more varied cast of travellers. There would still have been the tinkers, vagrants and the poor on the road in search of relief or work. Recruiting parties, 'decked in all the glory of war paint, preceded by fife and drum' were a sight some sought and others avoided.[37] There could have even be the occasional soul on their way to seek treatment at a spa as was Margaret Stirling of Stirling, her passage to Moffat in 1755 eased by five shillings from Cowane's hospital.[38] In the summer, migrant harvest labour would have been on the move, their ranks swollen by artisan workers from the villages and towns taking a change of work as a break.[39] Boys, and some girls, from some of the rural burghs were hired out for herding during the summer.[40] A quickening economy meant more goods were sent to market by packhorse and by cart, with more raw materials in transit. Development required supervision; there were agents, factors, surveyors, yarn and cloth inspectors on the road not just for an occasional trip. Patrick MacGillvrie, the Board of Trustees' surveyor of bleaching, undertook a fifteen-week tour of finishing greens in eastern Scotland in 1763.[41] Significantly, the Board's top man in the field was called the *Riding* Inspector of Manufactures. There were more of the great and the good en route: more law and administration meant that there were the retinues of the judges on circuit; the landowners, their families and servants; delegates en route to the Convention of Royal Burghs; and presbyters to the General Assembly. There were also the members of parliament. The Union of 1707 created forty-six members from Scottish constituencies elected to serve in parliament at London, which usually met for five or six months beginning in November or December. It is interesting to ask how often did they attend, and if so how did they (and the increasing numbers of lobbyists for the Convention of Royal Burghs, for example) travel from Scotland? By what means did someone like Sir Alexander Cumming of Culter, MP for Aberdeenshire get to London where he voted in the debate over the Repeal of the Conformity and Schism Acts in January 1719?[42] Or Henry Cunningham of Bolquhan, MP for Stirling Burghs, when he voted in June 1717? Or, indeed, whether some who might have travelled south, and perhaps should have done so, did not because of the inconvenience. We do know that after the terms of the Union had been settled, the queen's commissioner in Scotland, the duke of Queensberry, and his entourage travelled in April 1707 to London in two coaches, accompanied by servants on horseback.[43] But his was a required trip, and others either less fit or less motivated, might not have gone. It is perhaps no accident that the road south from Edinburgh was improved after the Union, to the benefit of the dedicated and energetic politician. The first coach service to London began in 1734 with eighty stout horses stationed at proper distances to allow the journey to be performed in nine days. Glasgow to Edinburgh followed in 1749. Travel by coach became an accepted part of life among the better off, uncomfortable as it must often have been: heavy expense, jolting and long delays was one verdict. Things were rather more relaxed in the north. It was not unknown for the Inverness coach to take a scenic diversion of a few miles to oblige a lady or a tourist, or to take a stop for an afternoon tumbler of whisky or glass of port.[44] Those who had their own carriages had more flexibility as to when and at what pace they travelled. Sir John Sinclair, for example, in the 1780s, using his own carriage rather than the public stage coach service, was able to come back from London during the short Christmas recess. During the summer in Scotland he was equally able to go up and down between Caithness where his estates were, and Edinburgh where he had a range of official interests.[45]

CHANGE AND IMPROVEMENT: HOW WAS THIS ACHIEVED?

While the old order may have been less awful than has been painted, it was nevertheless poor. One can accept as a broad-brush assessment Ann Gordon's view that transport improvement 'really began in the eighteenth century' and that from the 1750s the scale and nature of change was remarkable.[46] Most attention has been paid to road making; but it is worth noting that coastal shipping services also improved. Voyages were not necessarily any faster, but they were now scheduled on the main sea routes: Leith–London, for example. Ferry crossings remained problematic; neither travellers nor their horses took kindly to the service on even quiet water. And there were all too frequent accidents. Eighteen people were drowned when the over-crowded Moulin ferry across the Tay capsized on the evening of a Fair day in February 1767; the local response was to build a bridge to do away with the ferry crossing entirely.[47] The pace of change to the mainland roads varied from area to area, but a sure sign of improvement was the arrival of wheeled transport; the cart for goods and the carriage for people. Much attention has been paid to the 'new form' of road, or innovation of the turnpike: the first Act, and each scheme required parliamentary sanction, was for Midlothian in 1713. Progress was slow thereafter: by 1788 there were only eighteen turnpike trusts in Scotland, none north of Perth. But the pace quickened: according to Sinclair over 3,000 miles of turnpike road had been created by 1810, three-quarters of them in the previous twenty years. Contemporaries were enthusiastic. The minister at Sanquhar, the Revd William Ranken, described in 1793 how tolls bars had been erected on the road from Dumfries to Ayr, an important route. Gradients had been smoothed out and a more direct line taken in places, with the result that the road was much easier for wheeled traffic.[48] There was no doubt, he concluded, as to 'the expediency and utility of turnpike roads'. Yet they had their critics. Not all were as well made, nor did income always match expectation, thanks to the country folk evading the toll houses where they could, which had an effect on the level of maintenance. Moreover not every new road was a toll road. Ranken also drew attention, perhaps with his stipend in mind, to the twenty-two miles of work on the great road between Dumfries and Ayr which the late duke of Queensberry had had 'cut' at his own expense, at the cost of some £1,500. And the construction or improvement of various cross roads was also credited to the duke. The drive to improve not just the longer distance routes, but what were called the county roads, and the local estate and byroads, was a very important part of the process. The *Sketch of a Plan for Executing a Set of Roads all over the County of Lanark*, which was drawn up following a meeting of the freeholders at Hamilton on 28 March 1769, addressed the key question of how to finance better roads. A problem was that some essential roads simply did not have enough traffic for a toll road.[49] Unpopular though it might be, parish funding was going to have to answer for these.

The roads were improved, in some areas faster than in others. Better surfaces and alignments, bridges and embankments allowed more year-round traffic at a smarter pace, and the movement of goods more cheaply. The use of the sledge, once common, died away, except in the very remotest areas. In 1786, Alexander de La Rochefoucauld found a few still in use in and around Fort William, where he thought that part of the problem was that the locals 'didn't much like the hard work of road building'.[50] Signposts, which were required on turnpike roads, gave a much better sense of distance and of direction.[51] The movement of grain, coal and other bulk goods had been a particular problem and the advantages of carting – or canals, or even wagon-way – over packhorse carriage was considerable. Coal masters, landowners and farmers benefited, as did the towns. Merchants and others found their travels eased: the new Edinburgh and Glasgow diligence, *The Mercury*, a neat post chaise, offered in 1790 a straight through trip for a select few – just three – passengers at 10s. 6d., which it thought would be convenient for 'people in business'.[52] But what did these changes mean for everyday life and ordinary people? It is clear to see that the upper and professional classes, those with money and time to travel, did prosper. Movement from townhouse or business office to a country retreat was eased. Their interest grew in a season at a spa, either within Scotland – Moffat, Peterhead or Strathpeffer – or down south to the more fashionable resorts of Harrogate, Bath and Cheltenham. Smoother conveyance, though the comforts of carriage travel should not be exaggerated, was particularly appreciated by the delicate and invalid. It meant the better off could travel south, and equally tourists start to come north. By the last quarter of the eighteenth century, tourism, fed by Ossian, a changed perspective on the natural beauties of Scotland and the romance of the Highlands was a discernible presence. The English gaze, once fixed only on the Continent, turned north: Mrs Diggle from Northamptonshire wrote to her sister in 1788 that 'All the world is travelling to Scotland or Ireland. People are coming north at a great rate, it seems.' There were even Continental visitors, some drawn by the intellectual reputation of Edinburgh.

TRAVEL FOR LEISURE AND PLEASURE

What assisted and, indeed, fanned this movement was better transport, and more information: guidebooks, milestones and maps which kept the travel-ler on track.[53] Defoe's tour was one of the first to be widely read. William

Burrell had with him the fourth edition, published in 1742 and also the more recent (1745) Andrew Rutherford's *Exact Plan of His Majesty's Great Roads Through the Highlands of Scotland*.[54] Strip road maps for significant routes and local county maps were also in the making.[55] There were still acute problems of navigation in the more remote areas, especially in the Highlands where language was a complication, but getting less so. There is some evidence to suggest that the decline of Gaelic was linked to the flow of English-speaking visitors into the north. During an excursion into the Highlands in June 1807 a Methodist lady from Hull was rowed across Loch Lomond by a local girl. This intelligent lass, as the excursionist in question, Mrs Thompson called her, said that while her mother spoke good Gaelic, it was little in use among them now, 'especially amongst younger people'.[56] Military roads had markers, but they – like the one put up in 1754 at the Lecht – tended to say only which regiment had built that stretch of road.[57] Everywhere the local sense of distance might be a difficulty – not helped by the difference between English and Scottish miles (the Scottish mile being more than a step longer at 1,984 yards) – or even of what ground was passable on horse as opposed to on foot. Sir William Burrell was 'misguided by the stupidity of the country people' into taking a bad route between Biel and Yester, with the result that his horse got stuck in a bog, from which it had to be rescued by ropes.[58] That East Lothian experience in 1758 was to be repeated by many another traveller who strayed off the beaten track over the next fifty years.

More travel meant a need for accommodation en route or at the destination, unless, of course, the traveller was possessed of sufficient social standing to be able to request accommodation from the local gentry, using perhaps a letter of introduction. They were accustomed to visit and be visited, sometimes without much notice. During her stay at Murthly Castle (near Dunkeld) as part of a tour in Scotland in the early summer of 1788, Mrs Diggle noted that there was a steady turnover among those resident. She commented that 'people come here to visit their neighbours & stay a day or two at a time without any previous notice: a very agreeable circumstance in a remote place with a large house, & quite in the style of ancient hospitality before inns were invented'.[59] The demands of hospitality and courtesy could become rather wearing, as the numbers of visitors from a distance increased, inclined as they might be to outstay their welcome. In a letter to his daughter in 1773, Lord Breadalbane at Taymouth Castle showed how his tolerance was being stretched. It was after a summer when there had been a stream of people undertaking a tour in the Highlands, which had become a fashionable pursuit: 'We have had a good deal of company here this summer, sixteen often at table for several days together, many of them from England, some of whom I knew before, and others recommended to me . . . being always in a crowd is not agreeable.'[60] There was a long tradition among the upper classes of offering hospitality in the form of free board and accommodation to their own, but the numbers coming from the south put a strain on this.

The duke of Argyll built an inn at Inveraray essentially to act as an overflow facility should the castle be full. In the moving around the country or county and the moving between house and house of the landowning classes, the servants were also involved, and provision of a much more modest kind had to be made for them. At Castle Moy in 1762 there were six different outside latrines, access to which was governed by position in the household – one wonders which did visiting servants get to use? And on what basis: their own job description or their master's or mistress' standing?

If the great house was a first choice option for the well connected, there was a spectrum of possibilities for the less well off, ranging down from a hotel or inn through an outhouse or for the unlucky a stable or byre. And in rural areas the inns were not always distinguishable as signs, especially in the Highlands, were not generally put up. Indeed, it is said that one gentleman at the end of day's walk, believing the building in front of him to be the inn, marched boldly to order dinner into what was, in fact, a gentleman's house, and was as quickly thrown out. Thereafter he was very careful to check for fear of 'affronting a Highland chief'.[61] There is little dispute as to how poor accommodation could be for the general traveller, or at least those who did not want to sleep rough.

A contemporary view, that of Hugh Sommerville, about Scottish inns in the mid-eighteenth century was that 'few could be met with in which the traveller could either eat or sleep with comfort'.[62] The experience of an overnight stay would vary from place to place. It depended on the individual's background, and what they were used to: it could be affected by who else was in the place. Neither sharing with drovers, nor finding oneself, if a lady travelling, alone in a parlour full of shooting men, were enjoyed.[63] Factors such as how bad or good the trip had been would colour the view taken of the quality of food and the service.[64] Burns, for one, has left his resentment of the treatment given to him at Inveraray where the servants were preoccupied with the duke's guests, rather than lesser lights like himself: 'There's naething here but Highland pride, and Highland scab and hunger.' In the back of her journal (1788) Mrs Diggle noted her assessment of the inns at which she had either stopped or stayed or just heard about during her time in Scotland. Thirty-two are ranked on the journey from Gretna to Dalmally, and then back to England by way of Edinburgh and Berwick. Six were good or very good, most satisfactory and only five 'bad' or 'very bad', those at Cairndow, Dalmally, Luss, Falkirk and Linlithgow, a list which includes Lowland premises, not just those which were remote or Highland. And some travellers were pleasantly surprised. It did depend what the yardstick was. A French traveller travelling north in a small party in 1785 said of the inn at Inverbervie that compared with the English inns it was pitiful, but that it was very much better than the great majority of those on the Continent away from the main roads.[65] The same writer commented of Highland inns that they were not very sophisticated, but that it was impossible to find them wretched or inadequate:

'You always seem to be able to find tea, sugar, rum and wine, and to eat as we did here [Portnacroish], fresh eggs, calf's head ragout, boiled chicken and an excellent bullock's tongue, with a potato cake'. They were to have much less satisfactory experiences, notably in the inn on Loch Ness, well named the General's Hut, where the innkeeper, his wife and children had scabies. As the Highland kitchen doubled as the family's parlour and bedroom, the French would not eat the food that was prepared by hand and tackled fresh eggs only after putting on gloves even to peel the eggshells!

The later eighteenth century saw a marked increase in the number of places offering purpose-built accommodation for the traveller, either for the night or even for a longer stay, should one wish to fish or take the waters. There were improvements, renovations and extensions in some of the older country inns, the conversion of farmhouses which had doubled as stopping points, and the building of hotels, with extensive stabling, particularly in the cities or burghs, at the new spa resorts or at ferry points such as at South Queensferry, Alloa and Kinghorn.[66] The separate bedroom, rather than a communal dormitory, was a feature of these new establishments, reflecting what the market now wanted and could afford to pay for. Opened in 1754, the Saracen's Head in Glasgow's Gallowgate boasted of some thirty-six fine rooms, with, it was advertised, the bedchambers all separate, 'none of them entering through another, so there is no need of going out of doors to get to them'. The proprietor promised that the beds were all 'very good, clean and free from Bugs'. By the 1790s, if the ministers of Inverness are to be believed, the inns there, which had been indifferent, were able to match any in Lowland Scotland for 'attendance, entertainment and beds'; and were able to offer for hire several four-wheeled chaises.[67] William Gordon, late of the Edinburgh Coffee house, at the New Inn in Aberdeen, advertised in the summer of 1792 that he could promise excellent stabling and elegant post chaises available on the shortest notice for 'Nobility Gentry and Travellers'.[68] It would be a mistake to exaggerate this improvement into a national network of good accommodation; the weary and benighted traveller on the Back Pentland road to Edinburgh could expect shelter only in one of the Old Spittal out-houses, with some straw allocated for that purpose.[69]

How far down the social ladder did the increasing taste for travel pen-etrate? The more prosperous had already established a pattern of movement: at Montrose during the summer, the ministers reported, many went to the wells or retired to the countryside to enjoy 'rural felicity'.[70] It would cer-tainly seem more than likely that with rising incomes amongst the middle and lower classes, some part of their surplus might be spent on travel for leisure, pleasure health, or, indeed, on sport. By the 1790s the Leith races were drawing crowds of some 20,000, not all of whom were local or from the landed or professional classes.[71] Burnett quotes an anonymous later-eighteenth-century poet's description of those present: 'Vulcans and cart-wrights, drouthy pairs, come frae the country clachans.'[72]

Better transport and a variety of conveyances took the weight off the feet. The wealthy had their chaises and carriages, although Coleridge saw none in Glasgow.[73] Why he did not is a mystery: advertisements in the local press confirm the existence of an active market in wheeled vehicles of all kinds.[74] But in rural areas, carts, of which there were very large numbers, were not in continuous use, and there were times in the year when, suitably cleaned, they could be pressed into service for an outing. There is a nice description from Gray about the popularity of the chaise cart among farmers: 'they go with their wives and daughters to church on Sunday in it, and on other days to the markets and fair in the neighbourhood. They jaunt about with it, pay visits in it to dine or drink tea, and they often in the fine weather in the summer, make long excursions to see their distant friends or relatives.'[75]

The taste for travel spread, and the means, admittedly modest, for a foray or trip which was more than a walk, with display as much as destination the motive, were available. What is not easy to establish is how far down the social ladder this practice had spread by 1800. It does appear from what evidence we do have that there was increasing participation in travel among a wider range of classes than had once been true. While many of the visitors were from the immediate vicinity, the Visitors' Books for the period 1795 to 1799 at New Lanark Cotton mills and the nearby Falls of Clyde show a considerable number of visitors from Edinburgh and Glasgow, as well as English travellers breaking their journey north. And whereas the signatories all say where they are from, when they do add their occupation, there can be found among them lawyers, ministers and army men, an accountant, surgeons, a landscape painter (Alexander Nasmyth, 12 August 1798), a cabinetmaker, a surveyor and a currier.[76] Travel for pleasure, if this source is representative, was no longer the preserve of the leisured elite. An interesting, perhaps even unique, window into travel which provides confirmation is provided by the commonplace book of a Glasgow shopkeeper cum merchant, Adam Bald. This records his travels, trips, jaunts and visits over nearly half a century, starting as a twenty-year-old in April 1790 with a five-day trip to what he called the 'North Country', to some of his relatives in and around Stirling. Bald took several trips each year, and not just in the summer months. Sometimes he travelled on foot (a pedestrian trip to Gartness over a weekend in early October 1790), or by horse or coach, close by Glasgow or further afield, across to Edinburgh, up to Inveraray, down to Ayr and even beyond to Liverpool, the Lakes, London and the north of Ireland. Sometimes a specific event drew him, the Doune horse fair, or the Leith races, but on occasion he and his friends set off without a fixed itinerary in mind. He climbed Ben Lomond at least twice, on the second occasion in August 1793, without one of the guides from the inn who were making their living from this form of tourism.[77] This was movement for pleasure, for scrapes with serving girls and escapes in which ferry crossings loom large. But what emerges incidentally is that his taste for travel was representative of a wider trend among the business and commercial class. He was an enthusiast of sea bathing, but so were many others: in July 1791 he visited relatives staying at Gourock who had been 'seized with the Saltwater mania'. The seaside had once been colonised in the summer, he observed, only by those who were ill or convalescent, but 'now the plump and the jolly are to be found everywhere. Nought now will satisfy either the married or unmarried, aged or young, but a trip for the summer to the Sea Coast.' Bald certainly came across visitors from the south; at the crowded Rowardennan Inn in August 1799 he met with three young ladies from Cornwall, coming in 'drookit' after an ascent of Ben Lomond.[78] A less happy meeting during the same trip was with an aged tinker; his cart overloaded and his wife walking alongside with a child on her back. He and his two friends assisted the ill-used horse over the summit, and as recompense, the tinker (or so Bald reports) offered them his wife to be their companion. Much of his travelling within Scotland, however, is with friends and to relations, and in this he would have been far from alone.

CONCLUSION

Isolation was still very much part of rural, and particularly remote or island life, a situation only really to be challenged by the arrival of the steamship. But on the mainland by the late eighteenth century, travel was easier, faster and better, depending, of course, on one's income and means. The new transport had shrunk the country. The advances of the nineteenth century have tended to greatly overshadow the improvements that had gone on before. But from the perspective of ordinary folk, if they had been able to look forward from the 1690s, the world of the 1790s would have been as different to them as it would have been to their great-grandchildren of the 1890s looking back.

Movement became more and more part of life. Travel for and to work was no new element but an increasingly significant one. Farm servants shifted around; especially on flitting day, in March at Whitsun or less commonly on 28 November.[79] Seasonal movement grew, whether to the bleachfield or on the harvest. According to Knox in 1783, at least half of the young females in the southern fringes of the Highlands were going south for the harvest.[80] Skilled workers and unskilled labourers alike sought employment, which might be at a distance. An illustration of this is to be found in the most complete parish statistical account written in the 1790s. It is that of the Revd Robert Rennie for the parish of Kilsyth, where he describes a scheme in 1794 for the cutting of a new channel for the Kelvin so as to drain what had been a meandering morass. The project, under the direction of Robert Whitworth engineer, was finished within a few months, thanks to labourers from England, Ireland and Scotland arriving as soon as they had heard of it.[81] One result was more work for the locals in haymaking during the summer on the once soggy meadows, 'in the summer during the haymaking it presents one of the gayest and grandest scenes of the kind to be seen any where'. Rennie also complained of the way in which 'amazing crowds of sturdy beggars infest us at all times, especially during harvest'. Failure could, and did, produce forced movement, but economic advance made for a more opportunistically footloose workforce. The novel development was travel for leisure and pleasure, of which the upper classes took greatest use and reaped the greater benefit. But it was a taste that was spreading down in society. For whatever motive, and by whatever means, there was with a developing economy, more movement.

Notes

1. R.H. Campbell and A.S. Skinner (eds), *Adam Smith, An Enquiry into the Nature and Causes of the Wealth of Nations* (Oxford, 1976), vol. 1, p. 163.
2. Sir James Steuart [Robert Frame], *Considerations on the Interest of the County of Lanark* (Glasgow, 1769), p. 6: author also of a *Sketch of a Plan for Executing a Set of Roads all over the County of Lanark* (Glasgow, 1770); *Enquiry into the Principles of Political Economy* (London, 1767).
3. Steuart, *Considerations*, p. 50.
4. Henry Hamilton, *An Economic History of Modern Scotland* (Oxford, 1963), p. 223.
5. Karen J. Cullen, Christopher Whatley and Mary Young, 'King William's ill years: new evidence on the impact of scarcity and harvest failure during the crisis of the 1690s on Tayside', *Scottish Historical Review*, XXXV (October 2006), 270.
6. David Ure, *The History of Rutherglen and East Kilbride* (Glasgow, 1793), p. 205. Ure was not an enthusiast for the way that funerals were conducted in his locality, which he described as tedious, expensive and laborious. He was critical of the way that the corpse was usually carried on spokes, 'which circumstance, from the badness of the roads, makes the service exceedingly unpleasant'.
7. I. D. Whyte, 'Population mobility in early modern Scotland', in R. A. Houston and I. D. Whyte (eds), *Scottish Society 1500–1800* (Cambridge, 1989), p. 43.
8. John Patrick, *The Coming of Turnpikes to Aberdeenshire* (Aberdeen, 1985), p. 4 cites the minister at New Machar describing such statute work as done 'with reluctance'.
9. Dr James Anderson, *General Survey of the Agriculture of Aberdeenshire* (Edinburgh, 1794), cited in Patrick, *The Coming of Turnpikes*, p. 8.
10. William Taylor, *The Military Roads in Scotland* (Newton Abbot, 1976), p. 35: the number of men used by Wade on any one road was usually 500.
11. Carol Kyros Walker, *Breaking Away. Coleridge in Scotland* (New Haven, CT, 2002), p. 21.
12. Pat Rogers (ed.), *Daniel Defoe, A Tour Through the Whole Island of Great Britain* (London, 1989), Letter 12, p. 208.
13. Sir John Sinclair, *The Statistical Account of Scotland (OSA)* (Edinburgh, 1791–9), Vol. IX (1793) *Parish of Birnie*, Morayshire, p. 162: 'Two hundred loads of peats are requisite to keep a good fire in a room, and another in the kitchen, for a year.'

They cannot be cast, dried and carried home, at the distance of four miles, for less than 1s the load.'

14. R. M. Mitchison, *The Old Poor Law in Scotland. The Experience of Poverty* (Edinburgh, 2000), p. 41.

15. John Beech, 'On the move. An overview of Scottish migration and emigration', in John Beech (ed.), *Scottish Life and Society. A Compendium of Scottish Ethnography. Vol. 9, The Individual and Community Life* (Edinburgh, 2005), p. 439.

16. Joyce Miller, *Magic and Witchcraft in Scotland* (Musselburgh, 2004), pp. 46–7.

17. Dr William Buchan, *Domestic Medicine, or The Family Physician* (Glasgow, 1819 edn), p. 681.

18. OSA, vol. VI (1793), *City of Edinburgh*, p. 592.

19. Christopher A. Whatley, *Scottish Society 1707–1830. Beyond Jacobitism, towards Industrialisation* (Manchester, 2000), p. 29.

20. Linda Chapman, 'Cambuskenneth Ferry between 1709 and 1935', *Scottish Local History* (Spring 2007), p. 24: 'Complaint and Petition of the Inhabitants of the Abbey, 11 August 1739'.

21. T.C. Smout, *Scottish Trade on the Eve of Union* (Edinburgh, 1963), p. 9.

22. Glasgow University Library, Special Collections, 'Sketch of a Plan for Executing a set of roads all over the County of Lanark' (ND c 1769).

23. Smout, *Scottish Trade*, p. 11.

24. Bruce Lenman, *An Economic History of Modern Scotland* (London, 1977), p. 27: 'Scotland was not in fact a very convenient country to travel in if you were a stranger. The easiest way was often to move by water. Water barriers were crossed by ferry or ford rather than by bridge. People did not travel in winter if they could help it.'

25. Frank McLynn, *Charles Edward Stewart* (New York, 1988), pp. 244–5, citing John Daniel's account: 'When we marched out of Aberdeen, it blew, snowed, hailed and froze to such an degree that few pictures ever presented winter better than many of us did that day. And very easy it was too to lose our companions, the road being bad, and the leading over large commons, and the paths immediately filled up with drifted snow.'

26. John G. Dunbar (ed.), *Sir William Burrell's Northern Tour, 1758* (East Linton, 1995), p. 85: 'the instant we left the new road we found ourselves in the most horrid paths that can be conceived, up and down steep hills, through bogs in some place, in others filled with large loose stones where our horses had no firm footing.'

27. Glasgow City Archives, TD 19/6: Adam Bald Commonplace Book.

28. David Ure, *The History of Rutherglen and East Kilbride, with plates* (Glasgow, 1793), p. 187. OSA, vol. IX (1793), *Parish of Rutherglen*, p. 8. In similar vein about the miserable state of the roads, see James Anderson, *General View of the Agriculture of the County of Aberdeenshire* (Edinburgh, 1794), p. 64: 'for the greatest part of the year it is more difficult to drag an empty cart along these roads than it would be to drawn one fully loaded were they in a proper state of repair'.

29. John G. Harrison, 'Improving the roads and bridges of the Stirling area c. 1660–1706', *Proceedings of the Scottish Society of Antiquaries*, 135 (2005), 287–307.

30. Gillian Nelson, *Highland Bridges* (Aberdeen, 1990), p. 55.

31. OSA, vol. V (1793), *Parish of Montrose*, p. 25: 'the ford, often varying, it frequently proved fatal to travellers'.

32. According to A. R. B. Haldane, *Drove Roads in Scotland* (Edinburgh, 1968), p. 40; the father of Alexander McCombie, the notable nineteenth-century Aberdeenshire cattle dealer, lost eighteen cattle on one occasion when trying to cross the Spey.

33. John R. Barrett, *Mr. James Allan. The Journey of a Lifetime* (Kinloss, 2004), p. 274.

34. Information from a headstone in South Leith Parish graveyard, which shows a horse and a two-wheeled cart. The inscription reads 'Great God whose potent arm drives the sun, the carters bless while wheels of time shall turn, guide thou their hands and steps in every road.'

35. A. R. B. Haldane, *Three Centuries of Scottish Posts, A Historical Survey to 1830* (Edinburgh, 1971), chs 2 and 3, pp. 32–73.

36. Haldane, *Scottish Posts*, p. 44.

37. George Gray, 'Recollections of Huntly seventy years ago (1892),' in D. S. Robb (ed.), *Huntly in Former Days; Two Studies* (Knaphill, 1998), p. 16: 'the several recruiting parties were allocated to the householders for a week's lodging'.

38. Stirling Archives, B66/21/10. Stirling Town Council Book, 21 March 1755. 'Account for a crown to Margaret Stirling, 'for helping to carry her to Moffat Wells for recovering her health'.

39. See A. J. Durie, 'Rural industries', in Kenneth Veitch (ed.), *Scottish Life and Society: Compendium of Scottish Ethnography*, vol. 2 (forthcoming).

40. Gray, *Huntly*, p. 46.

41. A. J. Durie, *The Scottish Linen Industry in the Eighteenth Century* (East Linton, 1978), p. 83.

42. Romney Sedgwick, *The House of Commons. The History of Parliament* (London 1970), p. 597.

43. Personal communication from Professor C. A. Whatley, 13 May 2007.

44. *The Inverness Courier*, 'Improved travelling in the Highlands', cited in the *Glasgow Herald*, Friday, 22 July 1836.

45. R. M. Mitchison, *Agricultural Sir John. The Life of Sir John Sinclair of Ulbster* (London, 1962), p. 63. In this vein, see also OSA, vol. VI (1793) *City of Edinburgh*, *Appendix* by William Creech, p. 587. 'A person may now set out on Sunday afternoon after divine service from Edinburgh to London; may stay a whole day in London; and be again in Edinburgh on Saturday at six in the morning.' He added that forty years ago it was common for people to make their will before setting out on a London journey.

46. Anne Gordon, *To Move with the Times. The Story of Transport and Travel in Scotland* (Aberdeen, 1988), p. 7.

47. OSA, vol. V (1793), *Parish of Moulin*, p. 71.

48. OSA vol. VI (1793), *Parish of Sanquhar*, p. 458.

49. [G. Frame?], *Sketch of a Plan for Executing a Set of Roads all over the County of Lanark* (Glasgow, 1769), p. 6. See also p. 10 with respect to the value of parish

statute labour: 'Were this faithfully performed under better regulations, what wonderful effects in a few years would proceed from it!'

50. Norman Scarfe, *To the Highlands in 1786, The Inquisitive Journey of a Young French Aristocrat* (Suffolk, 2001), p. 172.

51. Jim Thomson, *The Balfron Heritage* (Loanhead, 1991) carries a nice photograph of a signpost with hand pointing, '*Glasgow Royal Exchange, 19 [miles]*'.

52. *The Glasgow Advertiser*, July 1790. The advertisement is headed by a delightful block of a coach and horses.

53. J. Gold and M. Gold, *Imagining Scotland. Tradition, Representation and Promotion in Scottish Tourism since 1750* (Aldershot, 1995), pp. 50–1.

54. Burrell, *Northern Tour*, p. 133.

55. Gold, *Imagining Scotland*, pp. 49–53.

56. Arthur B. Robinson, *Seeking the Scots. An English Woman's Journey in Scotland* (York, 2006), p. 62.

57. Taylor, *Military Roads*, plate 15. The inscription reads 'AD 1754. Five companies of 33rd Regiment Right Honorable Lord Charles Hay Colonel made the Road from here to the Spey.'

58. *Burrell*, p. 120.

59. Glasgow University Library, Special Collections, Gen 738, *Elizabeth Diggle, Journal of a Tour from London to the Highlands 1788*, Letter 14 [from Murthy Castle], 1 June 1788.

60. James Holloway and Lindsay Errington, *The Discovery of Scotland* (Edinburgh, 1978), p. 63.

61. Diggle, *Journal*, p. 10.

62. Haldane, *Drove Roads*, p. 41.

63. The English traveller, Topham, was rather taken aback in 1770, having been recommended to the Black Bull as the best Inn in Edinburgh to find himself sharing room with twenty drovers, finishing off a meal of potatoes and whisky. See also Mrs Murray's experience at Tyndrum in September 1796. A. J. Durie, *Scotland for the Holidays* (East Linton, 2003), pp. 29–30

64. See Durie, *Scotland for the Holidays*, pp. 27–31.

65. Scarfe, *To The Highlands*, p. xvi.

66. This draws on David Walker, 'Inns, hotels and related building types', in *Scotland Buildings, Compendium of Scottish Ethnology*, Vol. 3 (Edinburgh, 2003), pp. 127–40. See also Durie, *Scotland for the Holidays*, pp. 28–31.

67. OSA, vol. IX (1793), *Parish of Inverness*, p. 630: 'the present time is distinguished by the number of carriages in the town and parish'.

68. *The Edinburgh Evening Courant*, advertisement repeated throughout July 1792 that his new inn was 'now open for the reception of Company'.

69. OSA, vol. XV (1795), *Appendix to the Account of the Parish of Penecuik*, p. 604.

70. OSA, vol. V (1793), *Parish of Montrose*, p. 48.

71. John Burnett, *Scotland's Past in Action. Sporting Scotland* (Edinburgh, 1995), p. 17.

72. John Burnett, *Riot, Revelry and Rout: Sport in Lowland Scotland Before 1860* (East Linton, 2000), p. 107.

73. Kyros Walker, *Coleridge in Scotland*, p. 144: 'At Glasgow the hurry and Crowd of People & also of carts, marking a populous trading city, but no coaches or carriages.'

74. For example, *The Glasgow Advertiser*, 11 June 1790 carried a notice of a sale by auction at the Gallowgate of a four-wheeled chaise.

75. Cited by Patrick, *Coming of the Turnpikes*, p. 20.

76. Glasgow University Archives, UGD 42/7/1/1 Visitor Books, New Lanark Cotton Mills, 1795–9. Also listed is a party of students from St Andrews, 10 May 1798.

77. Bald comments 'such a solitary undertaking I would not advise any person to attempt for many casualties may happen which only an experienced guide can extricate you from'.

78. Bald describes it as 'often in summer [a scene] of bustle, confusion and disappointment from the crowds of visitors from different parts of the world of different ranks and degrees huddled together in a small and but indifferently plenished inn'.

79. Burnett, *Riot, Revelry and Sport*, p. 84

80. T. M. Devine, *Clanship to Crofters' War*, *The Migrant Tradition* (Manchester, 1994), p. 136.

81. OSA, vol. XVIII (1796), *Parish of Kilsyth*, p. 224: 'It may be noted worthy of observation that as soon as the work was contracted for, numbers from England and Ireland as well as Scotland flocked to it.'

Chapter 11

Work, Time and Pastimes

Christopher A. Whatley

INTRODUCTION

For all but a privileged few – as well as the very old, the infirm and those otherwise incapacitated, and in theory supported under the tight strictures of the Scottish Poor Law of 1574 – making a living in early modern Scotland meant working. Work was the means by which most men and women and their dependants were able to eat, clothe themselves and find shelter from the elements. Local, regional and sometimes international market conditions were one set of factors that determined what work was available.[1]

Establishing the importance of employment – and work – in early modern Scotland is relatively easy. Capturing and articulating the everyday features of work are more problematic. The broad outlines of the contexts of everyday working lives can be identified, but drilling beneath the surface exposes a kaleidoscopic array of experience which frequently defies generalisation. Changing circumstances over time add another layer of complexity.

What work was done and when it was carried out were in large part determined by the seasons and the weather, although by the end of the eighteenth century the sharp rise in the application of power sources, such as water and steam used to drive continuous processes like cotton spinning, had the effect of flattening seasonal variations for workers in such employments, although by no means did these disappear. Otherwise, most people were drawn in some way into the remorseless cycle of agricultural production. The seasons, weather and the state of the harvest in Scotland (but also overseas) combined even to govern the operations of merchants involved in the grain trade, both coastwise and across the North Sea to Scandinavia and the Baltic. During the winter months few if any ships were freighted for deep-sea voyages, but even coastal shipping eased off between November and March, with the result that sailors and many ancillary workers at the harboursides, such as carters and coopers, were laid off.[2]

Residence in the countryside though was not essential for direct involvement in agriculture. In the seventeenth century in towns like Aberdeen and Edinburgh, farmers (and gardeners and cottars) appear in census records, albeit in numbers that diminished over time. Early modern burghs (towns) in Scotland frequently owned or claimed rights over commons or moors, upon which the burgesses' livestock were grazed and from where turf and peats were taken for roofs and as fuel for fires, respectively. Burgh lands needed to be harvested, and a number of burghs held hiring markets within their bounds. The commons served too as urban sports-fields, the locus of short periods of respite from everyday working life, and until well into the eighteenth century were jealously protected by the burghs' inhabitants.[3]

The calendar of activity generated by the agricultural cycle was as important to the great and the good as it was to the labouring poor; for the former though it was rarely a matter of life and, in the case of harvest failure, privation and even starvation. Prior to the Union of 1707, estate owning members of the Scottish parliament tended to stay away from Edinburgh, the nation's political capital, to oversee farming operations early in the spring and at the harvest; attendance at sittings at these times was lower, while those present were anxious to be gone.[4] Most of the main landowners took a close interest in their estate accounts and liaised with factors, agents and chamberlains over matters such as seed procurement, planting, harvesting and market prospects for their produce; more so in the early 1600s than a century later, landowners – even those above the rank of laird, bonnet laird or feuar – managed farming operations in person, and if they were absent their wives often took over.[5]

With Scotland's apparent relative economic decline in the second half of the seventeenth century, penurious yet socially ambitious men of high rank jostled with each other in what by the century's end had become an unseemly scrum for royal favour from a monarch since 1603 based in London. Their hope was that by obtaining government employment (not necessarily the same thing as work, particularly where sinecures were landed), they could tap into a more secure revenue stream.[6] After the Union of 1707, for many thousands of Scots, it was patronage that levered them into work, in the army and navy, the judiciary, the church, the universities – as well as a host of posts, some comparatively low-ranking, in customs and excise collection.[7] In an age of acute uncertainty about how ends could be made to meet, knowledge of the availability of even less prestigious positions that paid a regular income, no matter how small – as a menial town officer, for instance, invariably resulted in a small torrent of petitions; an added attraction was that those in these positions were usually provided with clothing and shoes. Applicants for such posts, where a degree of reliability and perhaps literacy were required, were often from 'respectable' citizens who had fallen on hard times, as in the case of Perth's Thomas Lawrence in 1784, a maltman burgess whose horse had died, and so was no longer able to sell ale, and who was trying to support his wife and child as a day labourer.[8]

While much changed, there were continuities – not least in the skills and knacks and the sheer amount of human physical strength required to carry out certain tasks, supplemented in some processes by animal power, and later by the use of water, wind and, fractionally, steam. An example is coal hewing, where the tools (picks, wedges, mells or hammers and shovels) and basic requirements of the job (physical strength allied to acute mental alertness and knowledge of the dangers of underground working) were little different in 1800 than they had been in 1600. The same was true of most mason work. Although the longwall method of coal extraction was introduced from England around 1760, its application was far from universal, and the traditional 'pillar and stall' or 'stoop and room' system survived long into the nineteenth century. Paid by the piece in order to encourage maximum effort – close supervision was virtually impossible – coal miners continued to work in their separate 'places', lit only by a candle, as they had for centuries.[9]

Other factors that determined what work would be undertaken included sex and age. During the period from 1600 to 1800, the gendering of work – although nothing new – became a more rather than a less obvious feature of the occupational matrix. It was the young who were often at the sharp edge of the workplace revolution that occurred in the last decades of the eighteenth century, although there were earlier outliers. Older people necessarily grasped at what opportunities for paid work they could find until they were physically incapable of doing so, at which time they were cast off to rely on, and contribute informally to, the support of family or the parish. Although a younger man, that 'he had no relation to rely upon' was the reason given by Gilbert Craigie in Orkney in 1791 for his having gone to plough Robert Stove's bear seed, and then to cut peat, even though he had previously agreed to enter with Andrew Dreaver as a kelper. Dreaver, however, had failed to pay him.[10] For those more fortunate – journeymen in the more affluent trades, for instance, who had contributed part of their income to their society's 'box', relief could be had from this source, as could many of the wives of their deceased husbands. A proportion though had to beg, and steal, even during what for most were periods of relative prosperity.

HUNGER, SUBSISTENCE AND THE SEARCH FOR WORK

Wanting employment was one thing; finding it was another. For centuries, more so than most other countries in Europe, Scots from all social backgrounds, but primarily those of the lower social orders, had been part of a national exodus in search of livelihoods abroad, mainly overseas – with England exerting a pull too, but of unknown force until the picture becomes less hazy in the nineteenth century. As many as a quarter of a million people may have left Scotland during the sixteenth and seventeenth centuries, with others following in the next century.[11] Those who left were mainly males under the age of thirty, one in five of whom might have left the country in the first half of the seventeenth century. The gender balance shifted between 1650 and 1700, when more families departed. Emigrants went as small tenant farmers to Ulster, as peddlers (and merchants and tradesmen) to Poland.

Not a few settled and became citizens of places such as Cracow, Posnan and Warsaw. Others became mercenary soldiers in the pay of Scandinavian monarchs, or served in the armies of France and the United Provinces, many losing their lives in the process. Growing numbers – in a series of waves – crossed the Atlantic to America and the West Indies, which, by the eighteenth century, were drawing disproportionate numbers of skilled and educated Scots from the Lowlands: merchants, managers, lawyers and doctors. Indentured servants were enticed from both Highland and Lowland Scotland, as were soldiers. Whatever their background was, Scots were considered to be industrious and adaptable workers.[12]

Within Scotland, there was constant movement in search of work, as is highlighted by Alastair Durie in Chapter 10, above. Although the numbers of the unemployed fluctuated in accordance with economic circumstances and the incidence of national and localised disasters like plague and harvest failures, what contemporaries termed the industrious and 'occasional' poor or, less kindly, as vagrants, were always present, although probably in smaller numbers by the end of the eighteenth century. With parish support geared to the needs of the 'regular' or 'deserving' poor, others had little choice but to get on the road in the hope of finding the means of sustenance, although among this group were to be found individuals who were sick, blind or mentally defective.[13] Otherwise the poor but mobile provided an invaluable source of cheap, flexible physical labour, which could be employed on urban building projects, excavating foundations, shifting earth and carrying materials; in the countryside they could clear land of stones and unwanted trees and bushes and lay roads and paths. But such opportunities were time-limited and presented themselves sporadically; underemployment and alongside it poverty, were endemic.

If, judging by contemporaries' accounts of the extent of vagrancy in Scotland, any expectations the poor had of lifting themselves out of the casual labour market usually ended in disappointment, there were patterns of work migration which were more fruitful. Young adult males had long moved to take up apprenticeships in the larger burghs. Females were no less mobile, so much so that at the end of the seventeenth century as many as one in ten Scottish girls between the ages of fifteen and twenty-four may have been employed as a domestic servant in the four biggest Scottish towns.[14]

Differential wage levels had long encouraged labour mobility on a local level, but the widening gap between wages in the Highlands and the Lowlands as the revolution in agriculture got under way from around 1760, intensified the southwards flow of female hands. In part this was seasonal, with those moving drawn to the Lowland harvest. The temporary surge in demand for labour this created had been exploited by those seeking work as harvesters – termed 'huikis' or 'hooks' – from 1600 at least.[15] Over time in the Lowlands the year-round pool of labour provided by sub-tenants and cottar families was drained in the process of rural economic rationalisation. Population growth and the subsequent pressure on resources in the western Highlands and Islands acted as a further spur to movement outwards.

But whether young women journeyed far or remained at home – more likely in the case of the daughters of the better off tenant farmers than cottar offspring – adolescence spent at work in either domestic or farm service was the norm for most single females in Scotland for much of the period covered in this chapter. The setting up of female-only households was frowned upon by the kirk, however. Young women who lived alone or without older males to supervise them, as fathers or masters, were viewed as purveyors of vice, as happened in Dumfries in 1704, during what for the whole of the country was a period of intensified moral fervour. The town council noted with some alarm, how 'many loose women do designe yet to Shake themselves free from service', opting instead, to 'keep chambers to ye Scandall of the place'.[16] Yet with market forces creating a sufficient demand for their services, single women did frequently live and work outside the family home, and were in a town like Edinburgh able from the seventeenth century to obtain some formal education, as well as training in specialist skills that assisted them in maintaining their independent status.[17]

Time spent in service was for most females a temporary if crucial formative phase of their lives, with the normal pattern being for those employed to return to their home parishes just prior to or at marriage, usually in their mid-twenties, as happened elsewhere in north-western Europe.

Even more short-lived was the period of engagement of both unmarried men and women with any one master – other than for craft apprentices who tended to see out their agreed terms which could be as long as four and five years and in some cases six and seven years – with perhaps two of these being used to prove a man's worth as a 'sufficient' tradesman, before being admitted as a freeman of the particular craft.[18] Domestic and farm service engagements were for six months or a year, a restriction imposed in 1621 in what was only a partially successful attempt by parliament to stop servants driving up wages by engaging to work on a daily or weekly basis. While not everyone moved – usually short distances only, of a few miles – at the end of their term, farm servants could expect to find a new employer as their agreements expired, or within another year or two, more so females than males.[19] Less often servants were dismissed, when a girl became pregnant, for example, or for thieving, or disobedience or insubordination; thus, even for workers on longer contracts, unemployment was 'only an indiscretion away'.[20] Servants who left their employer without permission, on the other hand, could expect to be searched for, brought back and fined or imprisoned. This kind of constraint apart, the picture created here, of considerable labour mobility, is reinforced by what is known of the work practices of country tradesmen who, when employed at their own craft, such as shoemaking or tailoring, operated on a peripatetic basis, visiting the homes of their customers, if then they executed the orders on their own premises.[21]

The situation tended to be different in the towns – although sick-nurses, wet-nurses and midwives left their own homes to work where they were wanted, in the first two instances for days, weeks and perhaps even months; washerwomen and seamstresses, on the other hand, collected work and orders and executed these elsewhere, at their own lodgings or in rented premises. Artisans, too, had their workshops and in some trades clustered together in particular districts. For fairly obvious reasons fleshers, tanners, candlemakers and dyers tended to be closely concentrated, as in Edinburgh were the goldsmiths and over time the main brewers. Most shops and stalls – operated by women as well as male traders – were also to be found clustered in particular parts of the town, as well being scattered in closes, stairs and houses.[22] Bakers were distributed more evenly through the community, along with weavers, tailors and cordiners (shoemakers) who chose to live in closer proximity to those who bought their services, by ordering a piece of cloth or clothing or a pair of shoes.[23]

The pattern whereby seekers after work moved to find it, carried on into the early years of industrialisation. In one sense those concerned had little option, with the above-mentioned process of consolidation of farms on improving estates and the silent but ruthless dispersal of cot-towns (a hamlet comprising mainly cottars and their families) and other clusters of sub-tenants gathering pace: the so-called Lowland Clearances.[24] Technological advances hastened the process, with the spread after 1763 of James Small's horse-drawn plough replacing the more cumbersome and labour-heavy ox-ploughs, so reducing the numbers of animals and men required.[25] Former country dwellers were drawn by the pull of employment opportunities and the financial rewards that went with these – along with the opportunities in towns for consumption and 'carnal joys'. Not only was there an expansion in the number of hands wanted in established trades like hand-loom weaving, shoemaking and tailoring, which in many places were being organised on factory lines, in workshops under a single roof. Urban expansion also heightened demand for domestic servants, but in the country as well as the towns few persons of substance were without at least one female servant; overall, female servants were many times more numerous than men.[26]

Altogether new occupational designations also came into being: tobacconists, confectioners and wigmakers, for instance, appear in poll tax lists in Edinburgh for the 1690s, but not earlier. Wigmaker apprentices initially were barbers, whose services as peri-wigmakers and hair cutters (especially if they could advertise themselves as 'from London'), became indispensable for the better off fashion-conscious inhabitants of the larger burghs in the eighteenth century. Printing expanded, too, but bookbinding as a craft was largely a post-1780 development, while a host of long-established occupations were sub-divided by specialization: wrights continued to do joinery work, but not cabinet-making, chair-making or upholstery.[27] Other previously unknown jobs were created as new kinds of manufacturing emerged and as specialist tasks were created through the division of labour, including in the textile trades carder, comber, reeler, piecer, bleacher, thread-mill driver (especially common in and around Paisley) and cotton spinner. In the countryside, too, new categories of worker were created: hedgers, ditchers and thatchers, for example, as opposed simply to day labourers, particular skills resulting from the waves of enclosing that swept Lowland Scotland in the 1760s and 1770s and again in the 1790s. In Scotland the saddler was increasingly common also, with the growing use of horses in farming, and the first ploughing matches – along with races – where prizes could be awarded for lavishly-decorated, well-made saddles; skills – of saddler and ploughman and his horsemanship – celebrated.[28] Others – the 'tasker' who thrashed grain with the hand-held flail – tended to disappear, in this instance with the advent of Andrew Meikle's horse-driven threshing mill.

By the end of the eighteenth century, it was in and around the burghs that most work in manufacturing was to be found, as well as in the rural mills, bleachfields and other works that sprang up alongside rivers and streams mainly in the low-lying lands of southern, central and eastern Scotland. By 1800 there were some sixty cotton mills, mainly powered by water. Flax spinning mills appeared from 1787, although in woollens and framework knitting the move to centralised production was slower. The earlier move outwards into what would later be thought of as peripheral locations – for spinning as well as bleaching and to a lesser extent iron manufacturing – was reversed, as proprietors concentrated their resources and management efforts on larger works usually in or on the margins of the central belt of Scotland, and reaped the advantages of economies of scale.[29] While the labour of part-time domestic spinners was cheap, as William Lindsay and other putting-out merchants in Orkney discovered, the downside was poor quality yarn, theft of flax and under-sized reels – and verbal abuse and even threats of violence on the part of those accused of such practices.[30]

Growth in manufacturing capacity – and the labour to support this – was most marked in Renfrewshire, the booming centre of Scottish textile production where between 1755 and the 1790s the population rose – largely through in-migration – by an unprecedented 135 per cent. This was in west-central Scotland, the engine-room of the industrialising economy where population expansion was greatest over the course of the eighteenth century.[31] By and large, the places that were growing fastest were those where things were mined or made.

Even so, employers in some sectors had been prepared to take work to where labour could be found. Central to this process were the activities of the Board of Trustees for Manufactures, established in 1727 as part of government efforts to quell unrest in Scotland arising from the damaging impact of the Union of 1707, which had aided the Jacobites and resulted in widespread civil disorder in 1724 when the malt tax was imposed. One of the Board's aims was to create employment through support for the linen industry, by improving quality at all stages of manufacture, but also by encouraging flax growing and setting up spinning schools and distributing spinning wheels in those parts of the country where unemployment, underemployment and poverty were fostering political disaffection. Domestically-based textile production had long been carried out in rural Scotland, more so where pastoral and subsistence farming was predominant. Most of this appears to have been in the hands of the producers themselves, and in this respect was uncoordinated. Most of the work was part-time and seasonal. The Board, however, allied to the activities of merchant manufacturers, landowners and the British Linen Company, founded in 1746, all of which put out dressed flax to be spun by domestic spinners, took employment in manufacturing into Argyll as far west as Iona and northwards through Ross, Sutherland and Caithness and across the Pentland Firth to Orkney.[32] Literally thousands of females were thereby drawn into the market economy for the first time.

In their homes, in addition to a plethora of household tasks, women spent long hours preparing and spinning either wool or linen yarn, on their feet if they used the ubiquitous drop spindle, or muckle or walking wheel. This was prior to the introduction in the eighteenth century of the treadle-driven spinning wheel, which allowed the spinner to sit.[33] Wool-spinning on the other hand, done on larger wheels, was 'more severe', and to impart twist to the thread required women to walk several paces from the wheel, a process that could add up to twenty or thirty miles of walking a day, all for 4d. in the 1790s.[34] At its peak in the third quarter of the eighteenth century, domestic spinning, by this time largely for the market, employed four out of five females in Scotland. Woollens, however, received little in the way of state support. Even so, the existence of low-cost female labour from poor rural households with time on their hands that could be devoted to income-generating activity provided the basis for a mushrooming in outworking in Aberdeenshire in the eighteenth century, when Aberdeen merchant-hosiers gained control of a scattered army of some 30,000 part-time mainly female stocking knitters, who collectively by 1793 were turning out 900,000 pairs.[35]

WORK AND ITS REWARDS

At the beginning of the seventeenth century, work for most Scots was subsistence-driven. This was most evident in the countryside, where around nine out of ten Scots were to be found in 1639. Even in 1801 almost two-thirds of the nation's people were still country dwellers, or residents of villages and hamlets of 2,000 or fewer inhabitants.[36] In the towns, where to some degree the link with the land – and self-sufficiency – had been broken (although the extent was variable and in some places as much as 40 per cent of the urban male population could be classified as 'agricultural'), money earnings were more important. This was true whether for skilled artisans and their journeymen, the growing number of workmen and day labourers of various descriptions, or the many townswomen who in the medieval and early modern periods brewed and sold ale, or who prepared other foodstuffs for sale, mainly on an intermittent basis but occasionally full-time.[37]

Scottish rural society was complex in its structure and exhibited significant regional and even estate-by-estate variations which make generalisations difficult. Put simply, at the top were the major landowners and lairds, beneath them was a complex array of tenants, below which were numerous sub-tenants and cottars. With most members of these largely self-sufficient, peasant households which lay at the broad base of the social structure of rural Scotland labouring to subsist and organised for the most part on a communal basis, links with the monetised economy were few. Anything akin to a consumer revolution was barely visible until the last three or four decades of the eighteenth century. Salt and perhaps some small pieces of iron – for implements and cooking utensils – were all most people had to purchase, although chapmen took out into the country districts other wares, such as thimbles, needles, bone combs, garters, silks and ribbons.[38] Otherwise specialist services were provided as and when required on a barter, non-market basis by the afore-mentioned tradesmen who were scattered among the cot-towns and on the larger estates. Millers and smiths were particularly important, but few worked wholly at a single occupation. Making a living demanded adaptability – a preparedness for men and women to turn their hands to virtually any task that was required. Dual- and multi-occupations were commonplace, as at St Madoes in Perthshire where the tradesmen were employed at salmon fishing during the summer. Conversely, inhabitants of the fishing villages which lined the coasts of Angus, Aberdeenshire and Banffshire, were frequently crofters and part-time farmers as well as fishermen long into the eighteenth century.[39] The same was true of the towns, where single occupations were far from being the norm until well into the eighteenth century – including for those in higher status occupations such as Edinburgh physicians and advocates.[40] Self-sufficiency was important in town as well as country: in the substantial burgh of Perth in the mid-eighteenth century, most families were still spinning wool and flax for their own needs, although weaving and dyeing were carried out by specialists.[41]

In the countryside, scanty sales of far from regular surpluses of agricultural produce provided virtually the sole source of coin in the seventeenth century. The greatest proportion of agricultural rents was commonly paid in kind, as well as in forms of labour service. In the western Highlands and the Islands, even at the end of the eighteenth century, farming for most inhabitants was geared toward subsistence; reports from the Hebrides suggest that in some places, under the sway of commercially-oriented landlords, the demands of labour service were more rather than less onerous: making kelp, tanning leather, peat digging, gathering and shearing sheep, spinning wool and harvesting.[42]

However, as the evidence of county justices of the peace lists of prices makes clear, there were waged employees in the countryside in the early 1600s – although sometimes fees were prescribed in the form of kindly payments, most notably in Midlothian where, uniquely, 'hinds' and 'half-hinds' were paid in the form of a cottage, a kailyard (kitchen garden), a portion of ground for growing grain and grazing, and some basic foodstuffs. Shoes and clothing – or an ell of linen from which a shirt or dress could be made – were sometimes included too, although not only in Midlothian. There and elsewhere farm servants hired by the year and half-year at fee-ing fairs, were paid only in part in money – not necessarily a disadvantage as kindly payments of items like milk, meal and potatoes sheltered workers from the sharp edge of rapid price increases, as occurred during the inflationary 1790s. Many were expected to bring with them a wife or other female whose labour would be called upon on a casual, usually seasonal basis to serve the needs of eastern Lowland Scotland's mixed agricultural system: sowing; weeding; thinning and harvesting crops – although if the fields were 'male' space and females entering it subordinate (other than at harvest time), within the home it was the womenfolk who were dominant.[43] Other country dwellers, including craftsmen such as weavers, wrights, thatchers and shoemakers, and day labourers, were paid either by the piece or by the day. Their wage could also include meal, meat and ale and 'aquavitae' (whisky), although few made a living by using their craft skills alone.[44]

But virtually everywhere, there was an integral role for the labour of rural women and children; the quern – for grinding grain by hand – was pretty well universal in country districts, and food preparation a critical if easily overlooked element in keeping the labouring household going. But for paid work, women rarely received more than half the male rate, other than during the harvest when demand for labour intensified, and there was no improvement in their relative position as the eighteenth century progressed, other than for those females who were drawn into more or less full-time work as hand-spinners or as muslin sewers in the countryside.

Towards the end of the seventeenth century, the cash nexus was becoming increasingly prevalent in the Highlands as well as the Lowlands.[45] This is well-illustrated in north and eastern Perthshire, where flax growing and part-time spinning and linen weaving became widespread. Exports surged from the 1680s, the greatest part of which was taken south to England overland by a small and expanding army of what around 1700 comprised some 1,000 peddlers and hawkers – 'the great transporters & vendors of our Linen Manufacture', according to the magistrates of Glasgow in 1730; these 'petty chapmen' went round the summertime linen fairs and purchased with 'ready money' small quantities of cloth produced for sale by country weavers, thereby enabling them to 'pay their rents & provide themselves in their other necessarys'.[46] Some households turned to brewing, especially in the vicinity of the buoyant Edinburgh market, and in the remote townships of the Hebrides to whisky distilling as a means of adding value to their grain crops.

More so than formerly, earnings from manufacturing in the countryside were the means by which those concerned paid their rents.[47] Indeed, in the more advanced agricultural regions like Strathmore, cottars and servants had by the end of the seventeenth century managed to accumulate cash and other material assets of one sort and other, and some were even in a position to act as small-scale creditors; formerly such signs of relative affluence had been largely confined to lairds and bigger tenant-farmers.[48] Yet there were swathes of the Scottish countryside where the lot of the small sub-tenant and cottar were desperate; many had difficulty finding the cash portion of their rent, even in war and famine-free years.[49] During a particularly severe period of the Little Ice Age – from around 1670 and up to the early 1700s – tenants on several Highland estates were simply unable to pay their rents, forcing many to abandon their holdings to become landless seekers of employment or other means of support.[50] But even a century later, harvest-related distress in the Lochaber district sent 1,500 females on a desperate search for lint to spin.

Indeed, until the final third of the eighteenth century, the impression is of a society where paid employment on a regular basis was not easy to find. In an economy long dependent upon the export of raw materials and low-grade semi-manufactures, serious skill bottlenecks emerged, but these were overcome by enticing workers from England, Ireland and the continent of Europe, as appropriate; in the eighteenth century glass-making, pottery manufacture, iron making, bleaching and dyeing all had resort to imported labour.[51] At particular times and places demand for unskilled workers could also be acute, above all for the harvest. Even so, visitors frequently commented on the alleged 'indolence' of the Scots (although the accusation was levelled against the labouring poor in England too), which the more perceptive recognised not to be a national character failing, but instead a rational response to the facts of under- and unemployment, and rates of pay which offered little incentive to work harder; more often the prescription was to combine low wages with moral reform.[52]

By 1800 the vast majority of rural dwellers were either rent-paying farm tenants, or paid employees, that is, servants of various designations and day labourers. Indeed, the bulk of the rural labour force now comprised an army of largely landless labourers – rural proletarians. This was despite the marked regional variations there were in the ratios of wage-earners to single tenant farmers, 10:1 at one extreme. This was in the Lothians, where single-tenant farms had since the fifteenth century begun to replace most multiple tenancies; a similar situation prevailed in the counties immediately to the south and across the river Forth to the north. In Ayrshire and the south-west smaller family-run farms were usual. Despite the predominance of one-plough or one-pair horse farms in the north-east, even there wage-earners outnumbered independent farmers almost three to one. In Ayrshire, however, they were more likely than elsewhere to be living under the same roof and eating meals with their employer. But indoor farm servants were to be found outside East Lothian well into the nineteenth century.[53]

Others combined their roles as subsistence farmers and employees, constructing a living from multiple by-employments. Estate workers and cottars might be paid an annual fee from which their employer deducted sums for the portion of land they held for grazing a cow, housing and any food from his table. Often crucial was the matter of whether the contract would include an allowance for clothing and shoes.[54] But the pace of the process of Lowland clearance just described was far from uniform, and on some estates substantial numbers of cottars remained. Indeed, in low-lying Shetland in the far north, through the eighteenth century, 'scattald' or common land continued to be held by a rapidly growing population of tenants who, in return for their landholdings, paid their rents in the form of the (entire) proceeds of their summer fishing, along with some butter, oil or animals.[55]

In the second half of the eighteenth century, however, there was a more marked presence of artisans, increasingly working full-time at their trades (other than in winter, when outside working could be curtailed), who were now housed in newly-constructed villages: tradesmen like masons, slaters and carpenters who were employed in building projects; dykers, hedgers and drainers who helped shape the improved landscape; and smiths and wrights who made and repaired farm implements. Few places were without a sizeable cluster of hand-loom weavers, and others with smallholdings who worked mainly for the aforementioned town- and village-based merchant-organisers of domestic production.

The difference now was that they were more or less full-time and employed at a single occupation rather than taking on a range of tasks which meant that none was performed particularly well.[56] A few butchers and bakers even found employment, their services in demand as rural incomes rose.[57] Similar tendencies were visible in the north-east by the end of the eighteenth century, as fishing there became increasingly commercialised. A gendered division of roles was clear too: only men and boys went to sea; women – and children – baited lines and dealt with the catch, although the sight of Newhaven fishwives selling their wares in Edinburgh from baskets on their backs had long been a familiar one; until the end of the eighteenth century it was on the backs of women that most of the vegetables, salt and sand (for washing floors) were transported. Similarly, in rural districts the carrying tasks – of seaweed for manure or of peats from the moorland cuttings – were usually allotted to women, a double burden given that invariably these were in addition to child-care and other home-based demands.[58]

None the less, by and large, and not neglecting the evidence there is of weeks, months and sometimes a year or more of severe difficulty, as a whole rural dwellers were less often living on the margins of subsistence. In the early 1700s contemporaries noted how hard winters were for the families of the labouring poor. In the Highlands around Inverness, households were described as having neither had work 'nor diversions to amuse them', and sitting 'brooding' over their fires, although such a portrayal neglects the evidence that a range of tasks were carried out in the countryside during the winter months: the feeding of animals now sharing the same roof; mending tools and equipment; making baskets, rope and yarn; and threshing and seed preparation, but within the home and in barns, kilns and mills.[59] But within such communities most individuals would engage in short bursts of paid employment only, and for wages that remained more or less static for the best part of a hundred years from the mid-seventeenth century, and for many may even have fallen.[60]

From around 1760, however, and by the end of the eighteenth century, skilled workers in both town and country were more obviously enjoying the material benefits of the market economy, even if their participation in this phase of comparative good fortune would prove to be short-lived and was, as ever, subject to dislocation. The weakening of the craft incorporations' hold over entry to their trades meant that labour markets could quickly become overcrowded, with the resultant insecurity of employment. Nevertheless, in central Scotland in the decades up to 1793 the coincidence of rapid economic growth in both town and country that generated an intensifying demand for labour, and population expansion that was largely dependent on natural increase, had the effect of pushing up income levels to unprecedented heights for many households.[61] Consequently, diets became more varied, household furnishings might include a clock and a kettle, and the dress of better-off labouring people incorporated some fashionable touches, such as pearl necklaces.[62] But such a conclusion masks the striking variations in wages and earnings within trades and occupations, between them, between individuals doing the same job (but at varying levels of intensity) and between regions and districts.

Combinations of workers in a number of trades flared into being to press home the advantages that favourable market conditions created; an early example (from 1674) involved coal miners who demanded not only 'exorbitant' wages but also a four-day week.[63] On more than one occasion in the eighteenth century, the tailors in Edinburgh used the favourable market conditions of a monarch's death and the surge in demand for black mourning dress to demand higher wages and better conditions, although more often collective action in this trade which was relatively easily picked up by incomers was defensive. But combinations became more common in a range of occupations as workers, less likely than formerly to rise to the rank of master, organised to provide security for themselves in sickness and old age. They sought, too, to defend their privileges, to resist employers' attempts to cut wages and where they could, to improve their rates of pay. But collective action was not confined to industrial workers. Also able to drive a hard bargain were farm servants, particularly in the south-east, where demand for their services was strong, and also those in the west in the vicinity of mills or ironworks, which competed for scarce labour. There could be a distinction between males and females though, the former being at a premium in and around Muirkirk in south Ayrshire, where iron-making was flourishing owing to the French wars.[64] Particular skills were also in demand, shearers, for example, employed for the duration of the harvest. Even if conditions were such as to delay harvesting operations, by the 1790s farmers in some localities were obliged to look after those they had taken on, the alternative being desertion and an uncut crop.

Yet life was no idyll, either in the towns or the country, and while working conditions varied, whether in a town workshop or loom-shed, a country mill or on a bleachfield, there was little concern for comfort or safety; work-related disabilities and illnesses were rife, and sharply reduced life expectancy – although for the population as a whole over the period, mortality (especially infant mortality) declined.[65] Living standards for the bulk of the common people outside the central belt appear not to have risen at all.[66] In Edinburgh, the nation's capital, well into the eighteenth century even in middling rank households the wives of professionals such as ministers, writers and teachers, as well as of craftsmen, had necessarily to seek employment on their own account in order to maintain an acceptable level of household income. Grave-clothes-making, mantua-making, shopkeeping and rouping were among the occupations they engaged in.[67] As late as the 1790s in the households of most day labourers it was a struggle to make ends meet, especially if the winter was harsh and work hard to find; periodic sharp downturns in economic activity could throw thousands out of work for a few weeks, months or even longer, or force down wages and earnings to levels that made it hard for households to get by.[68] A run of poor harvests and economic depression from 1800 and up to and including 1802 combined to raise the prices of foodstuffs and reduce the availability of employment even at minimal wages. In Perthshire there were reports of labourers collapsing from hunger in the fields where they worked. In the Highlands and the islands of the north and west, the continuing paucity of opportunities for work (other than via migration, either permanent or temporary) or for generating a cash income, drove many in poorer seasons to search for sustenance that included a range of sea-fish, shell-fish, birds and an even wider array of weeds[69]

And even while wage levels in and around the manufacturing centres and the rural hinterlands of the larger towns did rise, it was the waged work carried out by previously under-employed (in the market sense) female and child members of families that accounted for a large chunk of the living standard increases observable in many households – as much as 45 per cent in some cases. In Renfrewshire half of the county's female and child population may have been employed outside the home by 1780, in thread mills, on bleachfields and in other processing and finishing processes.[70] But most of the new openings into paid employment for females were sharply circumscribed, by being limited to repetitive tasks and subordinate positions, often on a casual basis, and always at lower rates than their nearest male equivalents.[71] As with males, there were enormous variations in the 1790s from the lower rates of around 3s. or 3s. 6d. a day earned by stocking knitters in the north-east, to the 15s. that was achievable by Kirriemuir flax spinners.[72]

TASKS, TIME AND PASTIMES

In some respects the nature of work was transformed over the period covered in this chapter. Edward Thompson's characterisation of pre-industrialised work as task-oriented still has much to commend it. According to Thompson, workers engaged in bouts of intense activity interspersed with periods of idleness. Tasks were largely determined by the seasonal calendar and custom: the discipline of clock-time lay in the future.[73] Labouring people set their own pace of work, and devoted time to crop- and animal-tending, searching for fuel and engaging in other activities that indicated a considerable degree of self-sufficiency.

Thompson, however, has his critics, and the case for an eighteenth-century watershed in attitudes to and in the nature of work can be overstated.[74] Clock-time mattered even in pre-industrialised Scotland, determining when meetings were to be held and certain goods sold at market. In the burghs the inhabitants were roused by a town drummer or sometimes a piper, or in Glasgow from 1678 by a trumpeter, with the onset of evening being announced in the same manner; a town's bells could serve a similar purpose.[75] There were good reasons for marking time in this way: although the length of the working days of apprentices and journeymen varied between trades and from place to place – and over time – twelve and up to fourteen hours were the range within which most urban tradesmen seem to have laboured, starting at 5 or 6 am and finishing at either 6 or 8 pm, although summer and winter times differed and an allowance should be made for meal times. When the ill-fated Company of Scotland trading to Africa and the Indies began business in 1696 the accountants, cashiers, clerks and other employees worked regular office hours from 8 am to 6 pm, with a two-hour break at midday. In the countryside, too, where labourers and others were more likely to be employed by the day, it was commonly understood that this meant twelve hours of effort. Less was paid if the full complement of hours was not met.[76] The same appears to have applied to coal miners, although in some cases they began work earlier (around 4 am), and what mattered more than hours worked was the quantity of coal put out; it was this that determined how much they would be paid, a concept miners referred to as the 'darg'.[77] But burgh rules and Justice of the peace's price lists and declarations about hours to be worked are one thing; more problematic

Figure 11.1 *Town piper and drummer, Haddington, late eighteenth century. Town officers like James Livingstone and Andrew Simpson (pictured) paraded the streets of their burghs to announce the start and end of the day. Apart from creating a structure of clock time in the towns, they also heralded proclamations to be made by the provost and magistrates. Source: East Lothian District Council (www.scran.ac.uk).*

is ascertaining how rigidly rule books were applied or how closely work was monitored. The indications are that apart from the vagaries in work patterns caused by inclement weather and seasonal variations in demand for certain kinds of employment, there was much less of the regularity of work, under close supervision (other than for apprentices, whose performance as well as their behaviour was strictly monitored, usually under their masters' roofs) than would come later. Even so, it appears that in 1800 the hours of attendance expected of some craftsmen were fewer than they had been in the seventeenth century.[78]

Except during periods of dearth and where individual circumstances, such as illness prevented it, labouring people in Scotland appear to have been physically capable of putting in long hours. Over the course of the early modern period the diets of the lower orders became increasingly dependent upon oats, supplemented by small quantities of milk, but also fish, meat, eggs, butter, cheese and vegetables when available; its plainness notwithstanding, oatmeal provided the basis for an 'uncommonly healthy' diet and one which, conceivably, contributed to the peculiar strength and endurance which contemporaries noted not only among Scottish males, but females too – although this was toward the end of the period rather than for the bulk of it, when the range of available foodstuffs was not only restricted, but the quantities were often meagre too. Foodstuffs of these basic kinds were cheap, however, and recognising the advantages of a fit and physically strong labour force, by the turn of the nineteenth centuries, farmers did not stint in making available ample energy-giving fuel to their servants. The greater ubiquity of the potato from the early decades of the eighteenth century provided another source of calories and other nutrients essential for health and physical exertion.[79]

What is reasonably clear, too, is that to an extent that would diminish in the nineteenth century, work and leisure – and pleasure – intermingled, as in the central Highlands in May and June when whole townships or the greater part of their inhabitants celebrated their departure for the upland shielings – the summer grazings, a sign that summer had arrived, a period of replenishment for humans and livestock alike.[80] In the towns also certain civic occasions provided opportunities for urban elites as well as the lower orders to break with the routines of everyday life and enjoy spectacle, music, noise, feasting and inebriation. The annual riding of the burghs' marches (or boundaries) was one of these – in which the trade and craft guilds featured prominently.[81] Another was the monarch's birthday, celebrated with increasing regularity in many places from the time of the restoration of King Charles II. Some traditional events stretching deep into the past survived the kirk's post-Reformation assault on religious festivity and carried on in new guises. Arguably the most notable was 'Fastren's E'en', associated with Lent but which was marked in the eighteenth century by well-attended cock-fights and ball games with large teams that could be formed on the basis of neighbourhood, age or marital status. At Fisherrow, near Musselburgh married fish-wives were matched against their unmarried counterparts. Involving careful preparation, great anticipation and much collateral damage before the winners were decided after a contest that could last for hours, such occasions acted as a communal safety valve.[82] Lammas was also the occasion of fairs, although these were held on other days throughout the year too, and provided not only a distraction from work but also the opportunity to buy essential items, such as livestock, along with trinkets of various sorts and cheap dress accessories.[83] For the unattached, hiring fairs were places for finding a new master, but fairs also provided an opportunity to seek out a partner, either for a temporary or a more permanent coupling; friends and relatives intermingled too, and shared news – and a bottle. Many towns held horse races which drew large crowds, and the welcome spending of cash by visitors alongside the ubiquitous brawling and frequent bouts of debauchery. Shows and trades processions also enlivened urban society. In

Perth, the former were largely confined to Fridays and commenced around midday, thereby bringing the working week for many hundreds to a colourful conclusion.[84]

There were also occasions where earning a living appears to have taken second place, indicative perhaps of a 'leisure preference' among at least some communities of working people in early modern Scotland. The working week for coal miners in Fife was punctuated by irregular absences taken to attend weddings, baptisms, funerals and wakes, although some men worked for the full six days decreed by law in 1647. Country weddings usually took place on Fridays, although ceremonials connected with the nuptials could begin a day or two earlier. As far as can be ascertained, for most paid employees, work ceased at Yule and also around Handsel Monday, at new year, the so-called 'daft days' which in much of Scotland comprised a period of drink-infused festivity. Tradesmen expected to be paid for their time off. But as in pre-industrial England, in addition to the annual cycle of holidays and festive events, there were what have been called 'everyday forms of refreshment and diversion', routine relaxations as simple as chatting, gossiping, or story-telling which relieved monotony and fatigue.[85] Drink was more than an annual treat, and in some occupations was a regular feature of the work routine, along with time off for breakfast and dinner. Masons in Perth, paid on a daily basis, were said to have taken 'especial care not to hurry the job', and insisted on being supplied with a mid-morning dram; block-print workers near Glasgow sent for whisky every midday.[86] This, however, was unusual; ale was the standard drink offered to the labouring classes, although with growing reluctance on the part of most employers.

Much more common was the expectation that workers would be rewarded with a quantity of whisky or ale on agreement of a new hiring or completion of a particular contracted task. Throughout much of Scotland the end of the harvest – symbolised by the last 'rip' or cut of standing corn – was marked in a similar fashion, if with greater spectacle, and often with dinner, music and dancing, inspired by relief that the harvest was in and rejoicing that it had been a good one.[87]

Miners and others, including hand-loom weavers and shoemakers, also tended to work less hard on Mondays (some not at all), but stepped up their efforts towards Saturday – to complete contracts and maximise earnings.[88] Even though earnings for both males and females on some Highland estates were miserly in the early 1700s, a labour force could still be marshalled, with harvest work being orchestrated by a piper and maintained by communal singing, and perhaps the promise of some whisky at the end of the day. The harvest, the crowning moment of the agricultural year, was not only critical in itself but it also had a ritualistic function, as a means of generating 'psychic satisfaction'.[89] With the spread of hand-spinning in the countryside, groups of female spinners organised 'rockings', gatherings which combined work with entertainment in the form of song, story-telling, laughter and games, although moralists noted disapprovingly that by the later eighteenth century these had become the locus of drinking and dancing and promiscuous acts by young people. In the north-west and the Hebrides, too, teams of women sang rhythmic songs as they waulked cloth.[90] Such customs, habits and attitudes were carried on into the first phase of industrialisation. Skilled workers like hand-loom weavers in the 1790s and beyond and whose earnings were sufficient to allow them to indulge their passion for poetry writing and reading, and singing, participated in sports such as bowling and curling, and diversions including fishing and berry picking – although often these were evening diversions.[91]

But the search for profits in an era of increasingly internationalised markets forced employers to pay closer attention to production costs. Capitalist farming too – and the simple act of paying someone to carry out a particular job – led landlords and tenant farmers to look for returns commensurate with their outlay, and to monitor working practices more closely. 'To make the greatest improvement at the Smalest Expense' is the 'great Secret of Farming' wrote one estate factor in 1767 – words backed by action as he reduced the number of shearers and binders hired for the harvest.[92]

The proportion of time spent in paid employment also increased. Prior to the middle of the eighteenth century, it was only a minority of cottars, day labourers or rural craftsmen who were able to find paid work for as many as 220 days per annum, the equivalent of around four days a week. Employment was irregular; much time was spent in idleness, a nagging hunger and at certain times of the year, in conditions that were bone-chillingly cold, and damp.

In the second half of the eighteenth century though, the indications are that 300 or more days were being worked each year by larger numbers of Scots, formerly something that had probably applied only in the urban craft sector.[93] The five- and even the six-day week were becoming the norm. Not only did the working week lengthen, so too for many did the intensity of the effort required. Hand-powered thread mills are a case in point: introduced into Renfrewshire from Holland around 1722, over time they became bigger, as did the effort required to turn the crank so that by 1780 there were 120 such machines in Paisley factories – powered by shifts of Highland males.[94] As this suggests, it was the textile industries that were in the vanguard as the demands of paid work became more onerous; as early as 1737, at the spinning and weaving village of Ormiston, all children were reported as being occupied, and restricted to one hour of play each day.[95] By the second half of the eighteenth century, the repertoire of songs sung by domestic spinners included titles such as 'The Weary Pound of Tow', with the lines, 'The spinning, the spinning, it gars my heart sob / When I think upon the beginning o't', offering vivid testimony of how gruelling what was once a part-time activity had become for many thousands of females.[96] In some cotton mills, the machines were kept running for twenty-four hours a day, in two shifts. Weaving was the single biggest employer of (mainly) male labour in manufacturing in 1800; not only was this work more regular and almost exclusively full-time compared with a century earlier, it was all hand- and foot-powered. But the seasons continued to pulse through this and other occupations, with weavers leaving their looms at seed-time and for the harvest well into the next century. The bleachfields that were laid out in many Lowland parishes demanded more or less continuous working when they were in operation, that is, during the brighter days from April to October. Many employed only the male master bleacher and a handful of his assistants throughout the year. Even the water-powered cotton mills could be stopped during dry weather, a hard frost – which could last for weeks – or an excess of rain that could swamp the water-wheel.[97]

There had long been employers who had sought to exert their authority over their workers. Sir John Clerk's ceaseless (but largely unsuccessful) attempts to inculcate regular habits in his coal mines are one example from the seventeenth century; another is the managers of the cloth manufactory at Newmills in Haddington, formed in 1681, who struggled for decades to recruit and retain the labour they required, and resorted to a mix of paternalist strategies which included inducements and punishments – physical as well as monetary – to encourage their employees to work hard and without embezzling materials or removing themselves and seeking better paid and perhaps easier work elsewhere.[98]

Over the course of the eighteenth century, however, such approaches became more widespread. Under assault were customary practices – the aim being to create an army of workers whose sole source of support was the wage earned in return for a given amount of regular labour. To stamp out the freer and easier attitudes to work inherent in pre-industrial society, where possible, workpeople were cut off from their families, friends and neighbours – and drink. At the revolutionary Carron Iron Works near Falkirk – situated in a 'country of Idleness', according to the company's directors – walls were erected and gatekeepers appointed to monitor time-keeping, prevent embezzlement and to keep out undesirables. A challenge for many employers was to recruit middle managers – supervisors who would exercise day-to-day control over operations, although it could be difficult to find men who were prepared to distance themselves from the value systems of the communities from which they were drawn and to adopt the harder-edged attitudes to work of their masters. Accordingly, a high proportion of the workforce in the first mills and factories were vagabonds, the unemployed and desperate and those without friends or family, although there were some rural mill-owners who deliberately recruited families for the range of labour requirements these self-regulating units conveniently satisfied.[99] Neither in the countryside was the new regime welcomed, loosening as it did the older bonds of paternalism. At the heart of the greater rationality that was being applied to labour matters was the afore-mentioned concept of the division of labour; it was in parts of the country like the Hebrides, where the impact of industrialisation was indirect, where multi-tasking was more likely to survive among the adult male population; it had long been the lot of women.[100]

The watchwords were 'order and economy', and they were applied more or less universally. Edinburgh bookbinders, for instance, complained that the lighter parts of the process were being done by boys and girls, whereas the efforts of the skilled journeymen were being concentrated on the heavier work, upon which they had to labour solidly for eleven hours or so, in contrast to their previous 'inconstant' pattern of working.[101] Master glovers in Perth had frowned on card and dice playing by their servants and apprentices from the early seventeenth century, but in 1784 they made it clear that it was when these games – and quoits – were played 'during . . . ordinarie working hours', that the most severe punishments would follow.[102] The same forces were evident in the countryside. James Boswell, proprietor of the improving estate of Auchinleck in Ayrshire declared in 1793 that 'no estate can flourish where the tenants are not kept to steady order and regularity'. Accordingly, perquisites like gleaning rights and even the liberty of keeping of a milk cow were subject to attack. Workmen were to be accustomed to buy milk from their waged work.[103]

Initially at least, and where those concerned were able to find alternative ways of making a living, attempts to impose new working regimes found little favour. At most of the new centralised workplaces – from Newmills in the 1680s through to the New Lanark cotton mills a century later – employees who stayed for more than a year were probably in the minority.[104]

We can question, however, the degree to which everyday experience for most adult males changed, certainly in comparison with many women and children. As far as everyday life in Scotland's first industrial revolution was concerned, it was several thousand of those aged between six and seven and up to the age of around sixteen, who experienced most intensely the regularity, monotony and close supervision of the new age; it was the young along with sizeable numbers of largely adolescent females who were the shock troops of the emergent industrial army.[105] The scale of employment of children in the new workplaces was in some instances phenomenal: in Renfrewshire they accounted for more than 80 per cent of mill employees in 1809. Around the same time, 62 per cent of Scotland's manufacturing workforce comprised females, youths and children.[106]

Yet even within textiles the picture was far from universal; in 1812 most of the 150,000 people the industry was thought to have employed still worked at home, alone or with family members and perhaps one or two others. This was the situation that prevailed in most other sectors too.

But for most of the seventeenth and eighteenth centuries, however many days were spent at work, there was one – the Sabbath – where little or no labour was expended. In the seventeenth century church attendance was the normal expectation even within a large town like Edinburgh.[107] Even in Glasgow, at the start of the nineteenth century the Sabbath was fairly strictly observed: with the streets, according to one visitor, resembling 'a City of the Dead' during divine service.[108] One Ayrshire minister recalled the late-eighteenth-century Sabbath's 'solemn stillness', with the only sound being the chime of parish church bells.[109] Admittedly his reference point was rural Ayrshire, but within Scottish society generally the concept of the Sabbath as a holy day was deeply internalised, even if for many by the later eighteenth century it was at rest, or in the pursuit of leisure and drink-induced pleasures that the day was spent – increasingly so the urban working classes, for whom there were few pews in the overcrowded churches even though a substantial proportion of them were of a pious inclination.[110] Nor were labouring people and their families always welcomed, other than at special services, or at the civic Sundays schools opened from the mid-1780s in a bid to stem the tide of 'licentiousness' among the young.[111] There were those, however, who did break with church strictures about working on the Sabbath: examples include sellers of milk and drawers of water in Edinburgh and Dundee and Tay ferrymen; countless others appear in kirk session minute books, with those accused of Sabbath breach being keen to prove that they had worked out of necessity, as in harvesting grain on the first dry day following several days of rain; harvesters as a body were notorious Sabbath-breachers, certainly in the seventeenth century.[112] Some simply defied the kirk, like the salt workers of Dysart who, for a time in the first half of the eighteenth century, continued to tend their pans on Sundays.[113] But there was considerable enthusiasm for religion among working people in Scotland, no more so than the hand-loom weavers for whom, during their so-called 'golden age' toward the end of the eighteenth century, Sunday was a day of devotion.[114]

WORK, STATUS AND IDENTITIES

Cultural historians have contested the Marx-derived notion that labour was 'the defining human activity and the bedrock of culture', arguing instead that this was simply one of the 'bundles of association' that formed an individual's social identity.[115] In early modern Scotland, loyalties, identities and status were determined by a series of concentric but interlocking bonds, the elements of which changed according to circumstances and over time. Place, neighbourhood, religion, values, family, kin and gender all mattered, as at times did the antiquity of Scottish nationhood, and nation – especially in opposition to England: a visitor to Edinburgh in 1705 observed that even 'the children, which can just speak, seem to have a naturall Antipathy to the English'.[116] But for many, occupation was more simply than a means of making a living, important as that was. It was a 'badge of social acknowledgement';[117] it also conferred a degree of status – not only for observers but for working people too.

The importance of occupation in this respect is more easily documented in the towns than the countryside. The merchant guildry and craft brethren

Figure 11.2 *Weaver's headstone, Kilspindie Parish Church graveyard, Perthshire. This headstone, dating from 1786, upon which are also carved a handloom and shuttle, illustrates two important points: craft pride and the relatively high standing of handloom weavers within their communities in the seventeenth and eighteenth centuries. Source: Christopher A. Whatley.*

of the trade incorporations founded in previous centuries were dominant forces within burgh society, and often sat on town councils and kirk sessions. The various trades guilds, associations and incorporations jealously protected their members from the incursions of strangers – 'unfreemen' and unqualified men – who sought to undercut the prices of burgesses and freemen who had served craft apprenticeships. Often (but not always) they were wealthy, with members contributing to common funds, or a 'box', for the support of aged members of the craft and their dependants. The Sea Box Society – for seamen – was the most affluent organisation in the burgh of Bo'ness at the end of the seventeenth century.[118] Admission to the incorporations was prized and certain standards of behaviour could, therefore, be expected, with those offending society rules risking expulsion. There were also strict rules for dress – another distinguishing mark.[119] Occupation was also a determinant of what place was allotted during civic rituals – one of the most public in the burghs being the annual or bi-annual ridings of the town's marches or boundaries. At Dundee in 1709 it was decreed that in the first rank of perambulators would be the magistrates and town council, but following them were to be the merchants, seamen and maltsters. The trades were in third place, followed by 'the small branches of the gildrie'. To be at the rear implied inferior status, and squabbles and even fights could break out if members of a particular trade felt that their dignity was being offended, as at Musselburgh in 1732 when the weavers found themselves placed behind the tailors. Nor were they inclined to march near the butchers, whom they described as 'Men of Blood'.[120]

The elevated status the trades sought and obtained within their communities was reflected in the special pews, galleries, boxes and lofts in the towns' churches for which they paid rent and then let to their members.[121] Traces of this long-standing tradition survive in the panelling in Burntisland parish church, upon which are depicted the various crafts' insignia. Not surprisingly for a maritime burgh, ships, shipmasters and seamen are prominent.[122] Masters and journeyman (and their womenfolk and families if there was room), and apprentices, sat together as a body, although the first-named had the best seats. That the seventeenth and eighteenth centuries comprised a period in which craft status was of particular importance is to be seen in the many headstones of deceased masters and journeymen that survive in greater numbers from the early 1600s, on to which are carved the distinctive tools and other once easily recognised emblems of their trades.[123] Epitaphs in praise of particular trades further emphasised the place of occupation as a marker of social worth, reinforced in appropriate cases where the moral attributes of the deceased were recorded too, such as truthfulness and honest dealing, piety, kindness or bravery. Yet funerary monuments of this kind which celebrated a man's lifetime's work were by no means confined to the towns: the survivors of farmers, gardeners, foresters, colliers and others also erected gravestones depicting these occupations.

The status of occupations was not fixed, but altered over time; Edinburgh over the course of the seventeenth century saw the number and material circumstances of the fleshers drop, while the position of apothecaries improved markedly.[124] By the end of the eighteenth century the weaving craft in some cloths had lost much of its former esteem, with the length of apprenticeships in linen for instance having been reduced severely – to months in some areas, where women were picking up the trade.[125] Shoemaking, too, was under threat; even though in 1763 the deacon and masters of the incorporation of shoemakers in Kirkwall could claim that their rules had 'subsisted past memory', there was little they could do to resist the encroachment into the burgh of outsiders, or even the town's piper from setting up as a shoemakers.[126] In the manufacturing heartlands of Scotland in the second half of the eighteenth century, a series of employers, operating in defiance of the vested interests of the guilds – and sometimes from within – exercised their right to employ what workers they wanted, regardless of whether those they employed had satisfied the craft courts. Nor were they concerned if those they employed worked outside the burgh boundaries.

Without clear occupational designation, craft pride and the sense of unity and collective concern this created, a man's – or a woman's – position within society was much less certain; those without a craft or other 'skill' were more likely to be poor, dependent upon the kirk and the charity of individual benefactors for relief. It was presumably the knowledge that this could be their fate that caused females to resist where they could the consequences of the strengthening male-driven conceptualisation of the worlds of business, commerce and crafts as masculine realms. They did so by gaining equal entry as masters in some trades – to the glovers' incorporation in Dundee in the early years of the seventeenth century, for example, and to the tailors in Glasgow from the 1730s as mantua-makers; by working independently or alongside their husbands as equal partners in others; and by carrying on the businesses of deceased husbands who had been merchants or master craftsmen.[127]

The occupational associations referred to so far comprised primarily masters, although journeymen were also admitted. In some trades, however, journeymen – along with apprentices and servants – formed their own associations, the main function of which was to create their own relief funds. As observed already they also began to mount challenges against their employers, over wages, hours and working conditions. With regular meetings and sharing joint concerns a collective consciousness within particular employments emerged, which by the end of the eighteenth century showed signs of widening into a consciousness of class and an interest in radical politics. But identification with, and pride in, craft skills also played their part in maintaining workers' identities. In several places journeymen cordiners paraded each year on 25 October, St Crispin's day, their patron saint. In many trades apprenticeship regulations were enforced, the occasion of their completion often marked by a brothering ceremony, usually involving copious quantities of liquor.[128] While acknowledging that the workplace had long been a place that had the potential for conflict, by the end of the eighteenth century, for more Scots than ever before, the workplace was becoming something of a battleground.[129]

Notes

1. For a fuller account of labour market conditions see K. Wrightson, *Earthly Necessities: Economic Lives in Early Modern Britain* (New Haven, CT, 2000), p. 308.

2. T. C. Smout, *Scottish Trade on the Eve of the Union, 1660–1707* (Edinburgh, 1963), pp. 47–80.

3. R. S. Craig and A. Laing, *The Hawick Tradition of 1514* (Hawick, 1898), pp. 18–39.

4. National Archives of Scotland (NAS), Marchmont Papers, GD 158/965, ff. 279–80, earl of Marchmont to King William, 19 July 1700.

5. M. B. Sanderson, *Scottish Rural Society in the 16th Century* (Edinburgh, 1982), pp. 170–1.

6. L. Colley, *Britons: Forging the Nation 1707–1837* (New Haven, CT, 1992), pp. 125–32.

7. R. Sunter, *Patronage and Politics in Scotland, 1707–1832* (Edinburgh, 1986), pp. 22–76.

8. Perth and Kinross Council Archives (PKCA), Perth Burgh Records, B59/24/11/222/1, A List of Persons applying for the Office of Town Serjand, April 1784.

9. B. F. Duckham, *A History of the Scottish Coal Industry, Vol I :1700–1800* (Newton Abbot, 1970), pp. 66–72; A. B. Campbell, *The Lanarkshire Miners: A Social History of their Trade Unions, 1775–1874* (Edinburgh, 1979), pp. 26–48.

10. Orkney Archives (OA), Kirkwall, SC 11/5/1791/16, Answers to the petition of Andrew Dreaver, 6 July 1791.

11. Anon., *The Present State of Scotland Considered* (Edinburgh, 1745), p. 22.

12. T. C. Smout, N. C. Landsman and T. M. Devine, 'Scottish emigration in the seventeenth and eighteenth centuries', in N. Canny (ed.), *Europeans on the Move: Studies on European Migration, 1500–1800* (Oxford, 1994), pp. 76–111; A. I. Macinnes, M.-A. Harper and L. G. Fryer (eds), *Scotland and the Americas, c. 1650–c. 1939: A Documentary Source Book* (Edinburgh, 2002), pp. 8–26; D. Ditchburn and M. Harper, 'Aberdeen and the outside world', in E. P. Dennison, D. Ditchburn and M. Lynch (eds), *Aberdeen Before 1800: A New History* (East Linton, 2002), p. 395.

13. R. Mitchison, 'Who were the poor in Scotland, 1690–1830?', in R. Mitchison and P. Roebuck (eds), *Economy and Society in Scotland and Ireland 1500–1939* (Edinburgh, 1988), pp. 142–4.

14. I. D. and K. Whyte, 'The geographical mobility of women in early modern Scotland', in L. Leneman (ed.), *Perspectives in Scottish Social History* (Aberdeen, 1988), p. 97.

15. W. Howatson, 'The Scottish hairst and seasonal labour 1600–1870', *Scottish Studies*, 26 (1982), 15–18.

16. Dumfries Archive Centre, Dumfries Council Minutes, A2/8, 6 March 1704.

17. E. C. Sanderson, *Women and Work in Eighteenth-Century Edinburgh* (Houndmills, 1996), pp. 74–107.

18. A. M. Smith, *The Nine Trades of Dundee* (Dundee, 1995), pp. 33–4.

19. R. A. Houston, 'The demographic regime', in T. M. Devine and R. Mitchison (eds), *People and Society in Scotland, Volume 1, 1760–1830* (Edinburgh, 1988), pp. 20–1.

20. J. Aitchison, *Servants in Ayrshire, 1750–1914* (Ayr, 2001), pp. 43–5; T. Barry and D. Hall, *Spottiswoode: Life and Labour on a Berwickshire Estate, 1752–1793* (East Linton, 1999), pp. 136–7; A. J. S. Gibson and T. C. Smout, *Prices, Food and Wages in Scotland, 1550–1780* (Cambridge, 1995), p. 284.

21. D. Buchan, *The Ballad and the Folk* ([1972], 1997 East Linton, edn), p. 25.

22. Sanderson, *Women and Work*, pp. 16–22.

23. W. Makey, 'Edinburgh in mid-seventeenth century', in M. Lynch (ed.), *The Early Modern Town in Scotland* (London, 1987), pp. 205–16.

24. See P. Aitchison and A. Cassell, *The Lowland Clearances: Scotland's Silent Revolution 1760–1830* (East Linton, 2003).

25. A. Fenton, *Scottish Country Life* (East Linton, 1999 edn), p. 227.
26. See Aitchison, *Servants*, pp. 128–33.
27. W. H. Fraser, *Conflict and Class: Scottish Workers 1700–1838* (Edinburgh, 1988), pp. 28, 30.
28. J. J. Wilson, *Annals of Penicuik* (Edinburgh, 1891), p. 187.
29. C. A. Whatley, *Scottish Society, 1707–1830: beyond Jacobitism, towards Industrialisation* (Manchester, 2000), pp. 227–33.
30. OA, Kirkwall, SC 11/5/1764/28, Petition of William Lindsay, 16 April 1764.
31. T. M. Devine, 'Urbanisation', in Devine and Mitchison, *People and Society*, pp. 28–9, 35.
32. J. S. Shaw, *The Management of Scottish Society, 1707–1764* (Edinburgh, 1983), pp. 124–43; A. J. Durie (ed.), *The British Linen Company, 1745–1775* (Edinburgh, 1996); Whatley, *Scottish Society*, p. 131.
33. I. Mackay, 'Spinning & spinning wheels in the National Museums of Scotland', *History Scotland*, 7:2 (March/April 2007), pp. 22–7.
34. D. McClure (ed.), *Ayrshire in the Age of Improvement* (Ayr, 2002), p. 129.
35. R. E. Tyson, 'The rise and fall of manufacturing in rural Aberdeenshire', in J. S. Smith and D. Stevenson (eds), *Fermfolk & Fisherfolk: Rural Life in Northern Scotland in the Eighteenth and Nineteenth Centuries* (Aberdeen, 1989), pp. 68–71, 76–8.
36. I. D. Whyte, 'Scottish and Irish urbanisation in the seventeenth and eighteenth centuries: a comparative perspective', in S. J. Connolly, R. A. Houston and R. J. Morris (eds), *Conflict, Identity and Economic Development: Ireland and Scotland, 1600–1939* (Preston, 1995), pp. 17–18.
37. I. D. Whyte, 'The occupational structure of the Scottish burghs in the late seventeenth century', in Lynch (ed.), *Early Modern Town*, pp. 222–233; E. Ewen, '"For whatever ales ye": women as consumers and producers in late medieval Scottish towns', in E. Ewen and M. Meikle (eds), *Women in Scotland c. 1100–c. 1750* (East Linton, 1999), pp. 129–32; R. E. Tyson, 'People in the two towns', in E. P. Dennison, D. Ditchburn and M. Lynch (eds), *Aberdeen Before 1800: A New History* (East Linton, 2002), p. 123.
38. A. Fenton, 'The people below: Dougal Graham's chapbooks as a mirror of the lower classes in eighteenth-century Scotland', in A. Gerdner-Medwin and J. H. Williams (eds), *A Day Festivall* (Aberdeen, 1990), p. 75.
39. J. R. Coull, 'The fisherfolk and fishing settlements of the Grampian region', in J. S. Smith and D. Stevenson (eds), *Fermfolk & Fisherfolk* (Aberdeen, 1989), p. 37; Buchanan, *Travels*, p. 36.
40. Dingwall, *Late 17th Century Edinburgh*, pp. 128–31.
41. J. Penny, *Traditions of Perth* (Perth, 1836), pp. 243–4.
42. Revd J. L. Buchanan, *Travels to the Western Hebrides from 1782 to 1790* (Waternish, 1997 edn), pp. 22–3, 67.
43. D. Simonton, 'Work, trade and commerce', in L. Abrams, E. Gordon, D. Simonton and E. J. Yeo (eds), *Gender in Scottish History since 1707* (Edinburgh, 2006), p. 201.
44. Gibson and Smout, *Prices*, pp. 264–9, 289–91; C. Young, 'Rural independent

artisan production in the east central Lowlands of Scotland, c. 1600–c. 1850', *Scottish Economic & Social History*, 16 (1996), 19–23, 31–3.

45. Leneman, *Atholl*, pp. 19–20; R. A. Dodgshon, *From Chiefs to Landlords: Social and Economic Change in the Western Highlands and Islands, c. 1493–1820* (Edinburgh, 1998), pp. 109–10, 237–9.

46. PKCA, Perth Burgh Records, B59/24/8/12, Memorial, March 1730.

47. M. Young, 'Rural society in Scotland from the Restoration to the Union: challenge and response in the Carse of Gowrie, c. 1660–1707', unpublished Ph.D. thesis (University of Dundee, 2004), pp. 280–302.

48. Sanderson, *Scottish Rural Society*, pp. 171–6.

49. I. D. and K. A. Whyte, 'Debt and credit, poverty and prosperity in a seventeenth-century Scottish rural community', in R. Mitchison and P. Roebuck (eds), *Economy and Society in Scotland and Ireland 1500–1939* (Edinburgh, 1988), pp. 70–80; I. B. Inglis, 'Scottish testamentary inventories: a neglected source for the study of Scottish agriculture – Dunblane, 1660–1740', *Scottish Archives*, 10 (2004), 62–3.

50. R. A. Dodgshon, 'The Little Ice Age in the Scottish Highlands and islands: documenting its human impact', *Scottish Geographical Journal*, 121:4 (2006), 328–33.

51. Whatley, *Scottish Society*, pp. 80–1.

52. *Present State of Scotland Considered*, pp. 19–20; Wrightson, *Earthly Necessities*, p. 321.

53. M. Gray, 'The social impact of agrarian change in the rural Lowlands', in Devine and Mitchison, *People and Society*, p. 60; A. Orr, 'Farm servants and farm labour in the Forth valley and south-east Lothians', in T. M. Devine (ed.), *Farm Servants and Labour in Lowland Scotland, 1770–1914* (Edinburgh, 1984), p. 30.

54. Gibson and Smout, *Prices*, p. 263; see also Barry and Hall, *Spottiswoode*, chs. 12 and 13; Aitchison, *Servants*, pp. 62–3.

55. B. Smith, *Toons and Tenants: Settlement and Society in Shetland, 1299–1899* (Lerwick, 2000), pp. 65–76.

56. Young, 'Rural independent artisan production', pp. 27–35; J. Mitchell, 'Memories of Ayrshire about 1780', in W. K. Dickson (ed.), *Miscellany* (Scottish History Society, Edinburgh, 1939), pp. 266–7.

57. G. Sprott, 'The country tradesman', in Devine, *Farm Servants*, p. 149.

58. J. R. Coull, 'The fisherfolk and fishing settlements of the Grampian region', in J. S. Smith and D. Stevenson (eds), *Fermfolk & Fisherfolk* (Aberdeen, 1989), pp. 38–41; Simonton, 'Work', p. 205; D. A. Symonds, *Weep Not for Me: Women, Ballads and Infanticide in Early Modern Scotland* (University Park, PA, 1997), p. 121; McClure, *Ayrshire*, p. 16.

59. *Burt's Letters from the North of Scotland* (Edinburgh, 1998 edn), p. 207; W. S. Hewison (ed.), *The Diary of Patrick Fea of Stove, Orkney, 1766–96* (East Linton, 1997), pp. 27–8.

60. Gibson and Smout, *Prices*, ch. 8.

61. J. Treble, 'The standard of living of the working classes', in Devine and Mitchison, *People and Society*, pp. 194–200.

62. Whatley, *Scottish Society*, p. 223.

63. Fraser, *Conflict and Class*, p. 39.
64. Aitchison, *Servants*, p. 48.
65. R. E. Tyson, 'Contrasting regimes: population growth in Ireland and Scotland during the eighteenth century', in S. J. Connolly, R. A. Houston and R. J. Morris (eds), *Conflict, Identity and Economic Development: Ireland and Scotland, 1600–1939* (Preston, 1995), p. 69.
66. Gibson and Smout, *Prices*, pp. 338–9.
67. Sanderson, *Women and Work*, pp. 108–35.
68. Gibson and Smout, *Prices*, p. 350; Penny, *Traditions*, pp. 138–43; see also C. A. Whatley, 'Roots of 1790s radicalism: reviewing the economic and social background', in Bob Harris (ed.), *Scotland in the Age of the French Revolution* (Edinburgh, 2005), pp. 23–48.
69. R. A. Dodgshon, 'Coping with risk: subsistence crises in the Scottish Highlands and islands, 1600–1800', *Rural History*, 15 (2004), 16–17.
70. S. Nisbet, 'The rise of the cotton factory in eighteenth-century Renfrewshire', unpublished Ph.D. (University of Paisley, 2003), p. 125.
71. C. A. Whatley, 'Labour in the industrialising city', in T. M. Devine and G. Jackson (eds), *Glasgow, Volume I: Beginnings to 1830* (Manchester, 1995), pp. 370–2.
72. Gibson and Smout, *Prices*, p. 354.
73. E. P. Thompson, *Customs in Common* (1991), pp. 361–82.
74. See H. J. Voth, *Time and Work in England 1750–1830* (Oxford, 2000).
75. Whatley, 'Labour', p. 362.
76. D. Watt, *The Price of Scotland: Darien, Union and the Wealth of Nations* (Edinburgh, 2007), p. 75; Gibson and Smout, *Prices*, pp. 280–1.
77. J. Hatcher, *The History of the British Coal Industry, Volume 1, Before 1700* (Oxford, 1993), p. 386.
78. Fraser, *Conflict and Class*, p. 34.
79. A. Gibson and T. C. Smout, 'Scottish food and Scottish history', in R. A. Houston and I. D. Whyte (eds), *Scottish Society 1500–1800* (Cambridge, 1989), pp. 73–4; Whatley, *Scottish Society*, p. 227; L. A. Clarkson and E. M. Crawford, 'Dietary directions: a topographical survey of Irish diet, 1836', in Mitchison and Roebuck, *Economy and Society*, p. 190; Aitchison, *Servants*, pp. 56–9.
80. Bil, *The Shieling*, p. 174.
81. Bogle, *Common Ridings*, pp. 87–90.
82. R. S. Fittis, *Sport and Pastimes of Scotland* (London, 1891), pp. 158–70; see also, R. I. M. Black, 'Scottish fairs and fair names', *Scottish Studies*, 33 (1999), 1–64.
83. J. Morris, 'The Scottish fair as seen in eighteenth and nineteenth century sources', *Scottish Studies*, 33 (1999), 89.
84. Penny, *Traditions*, pp. 122–3.
85. R. W. Malcolmson, *Popular Recreation in English Society, 1700–1850* (Cambridge, 1973), p. 15.
86. A. Thomson, *Maryhill, 1750–1894* (Glasgow, 1895), p. 17; Penny, *Traditions*, p. 245.
87. Fenton, *Scottish Country Life*, p. 72; see also A. Philip, *The Parish of Longforgan: A Sketch of its Church and People* (Edinburgh, 1985), pp. 234–5.

88. C. A. Whatley, 'A caste apart? Scottish colliers, work, community and culture in the era of "Serfdom", c. 1606–1799', *Journal of the Scottish Labour History Society*, 26 (1991), 9–10; Penny, *Traditions*, pp. 40–1, 133–8; Fraser, *Conflict and Class*, p. 27.

89. *Burt's Letters*, p. 213; Thompson, *Customs*, p. 361; Buchan, *Ballad*, p. 23.

90. Aitchison, *Servants*, p. 101; Buchanan, *Travels*, p. 36; Mitchell, 'Memories', p. 288.

91. N. Murray, *The Scottish Hand Loom Weavers, 1790–1850; A Social History* (Edinburgh, 1979), p. 172.

92. Whatley, *Scottish Society*, p. 125.

93. Gibson and Smout, *Prices*, pp. 280–5.

94. Nisbet, 'Rise of the cotton factory', p. 69.

95. Whatley, *Scottish Society*, p. 264.

96. C. A. Whatley, 'Sound and song in the ritual of popular protest: continuity and the Glasgow "Nob Songs" of 1825', in E. J. Cowan (ed.), *The Ballad in Scottish History* (East Linton, 2000), p. 155.

97. A. J. Durie, 'Saltoun Bleachfield 1746–1773', *Transactions of the East Lothian Antiquarian and Field Naturalists Society*, 15 (1976), 63; Nisbet, 'Rise of the cotton factory', pp. 165–6.

98. G. Marshall, *Presbyteries and Profits: Calvinism and the Development of Capitalism in Scotland 1560–1707* (Edinburgh, 1980), pp. 176–97, 235–47.

99. C. A. Whatley, 'The experience of work', in T. M. Devine and R. Mitchison (eds), *People and Society in Scotland, Vol. 1, 1760–1830* (Edinburgh, 1988), pp. 234–39; Nisbet, 'Rise of the cotton factory', p. 237.

100. Buchanan, *Travels*, p. 36; Simonton, 'Work, trade and commerce', p. 203.

101. Whatley, *Scottish Society*, pp. 266–7.

102. PKCA, PE 67/22, Glovers Incorporation of Perth, Index, p. 7.

103. N. P. Hankins and J. Strawhorn (eds), *The Correspondence of James Boswell with James Bruce and Andrew Gibb, Overseers of the Auchinleck Estate* (Edinburgh, 1998), pp. 124, 194.

104. Marshall, *Presbyteries and Profits*, p. 185; Butt, 'Labour relations', p. 144; Whatley, *Scottish Society*, p. 264.

105. Whatley, 'Experience of work', p. 244.

106. C. A. Whatley, 'Women and the economic transformation of Scotland, c. 1740–1830', *Scottish Economic and Social History*, 14 (1994), 29.

107. Houston, *Social Change*, pp. 185–6.

108. W. Ruddick (ed.), *John Gibson Lockhart. Peters Letters to his Kinsfolks* (Edinburgh, 1977), p. 168.

109. Mitchell, *Memories*, pp. 297–8; Buchanan, *Travels*, p. 3.

110. Whatley, 'Labour', pp. 385–6.

111. C. G. Brown, *Religion and Society in Scotland since 1707* (Edinburgh, 1997), pp. 95–8.

112. R. Mitchison and L. Leneman, *Sin in the City: Sexuality and Social Control in Urban Scotland 1660–1780* (Edinburgh, 1998), pp. 40–9; Howatson, 'Scottish hairst', p. 17.

113. R. Mitchison and L. Leneman, *Girls in Trouble: Sexuality and Social Control in Rural Scotland 1660–1780* (Edinburgh, 1998), p. 115.

114. Murray, *Scottish Hand Loom Weavers*, p. 165.

115. G. Crossick, 'Past masters: in search of the artisan in European history', in G Crossick (ed.), *The Artisan and the European Town, 1500–1900* (Aldershot, 1997), pp. 4–15; in the same volume see also J. R. Farr, 'Cultural analysis and early modern artisans', pp. 56–74.

116. J. Taylor, *A Journey to Edenborough in Scotland* (Edinburgh, 1903), pp. 126, 132–3.

117. P. Corfield, quoted in Dingwall, *Late 17th Century Edinburgh*, p. 130.

118. P. Cadell, 'The Reverend John Brand and the Bo'ness of the 1690s', in G. Cruickshank (ed.), *A Sense of Place: Studies in Scottish Local History* (Edinburgh, 1988), p. 9.

119. Smith, *Nine Trades*, p. 16.

120. City of Dundee Record and Archive Centre, Council Book, Dundee, vol. VIII, 1704–1715, 21 June 1709; K. R. Bogle, *Scotland's Common Ridings* (Stroud, 2004), p. 88.

121. Smith, *Three United Trades*, pp. 23–5.

122. I. Somerville, *Burntisland: Port of Grace* (Burntisland, 2004), pp. 93–9.

123. B. Wilsher, *Understanding Scottish Graveyards* (Edinburgh, 1985), pp. 31–6; B. Wilsher and D. Hunter, *Stones: A Guide to Some Remarkable Eighteenth Century Gravestones* (Edinburgh, 1978), pp. 62–120.

124. Dingwall, *Late 17th Century Edinburgh*, pp. 160–1.

125. Whatley, 'Labour', pp. 362–3; Buchanan, *Travels*, p. 35.

126. OA, K7/19, Representation of the Deacon and Masters of the Incorporation of Shoemakers, 9 September 1763.

127. Smith, *Nine Trades*, p. 20; Simonton, 'Work, trade and commerce', pp. 206–11.

128. Houston, *Social Change*, p. 225; Campbell, *Lanarkshire Miners*, pp. 41–2; Thompson, *Maryhill*, p. 12.

129. Whatley, 'Labour', pp. 375–6, 386–7; Fraser, *Conflict*, pp. 81–99.

Annotated Bibliography

CHAPTER 1: EVERYDAY STRUCTURES, RHYTHMS AND SPACES OF THE SCOTTISH COUNTRYSIDE

How the Scottish countryside changed between 1600 and 1800, now boasts a considerable literature. Among the earlier substantive studies, J. E. Handley's *Scottish Farming in the Eighteenth Century* (London, 1953) account of change can still be read profitably, but its treatment is wholly focused on change as an eighteenth-century affair and on technical aspects of farming change. Subsequent studies have been more concerned to show how key aspects of change were rooted in the seventeenth century and how change transformed the rural community no less than its field economy. Following A. Fenton and T. C. Smout's, 'Scottish agriculture before the improvers – an exploration', *Agricultural History Review*, 13 (1965), 73–93 suggestive review of possible changes in farm output during the seventeenth century, I. D. Whyte's *Agriculture and Society in Seventeenth-Century Scotland* (Edinburgh, 1979) substantially reworked our understanding of this neglected century, at least for Lowland areas. As well as highlighting changes in the nature of farming and the strides made towards specialisation, his book does much to define the changing character of the everyday rural community at this stage. His systematic analysis of data is matched by Tom Devine's *The Transformation of Rural Scotland: Social Change and Agrarian Economy 1660–1815* (Edinburgh, 1994). Devine's book is the most searching study to date of how change affected the nature of the rural community during the seventeenth and eighteenth centuries. It not only provides a valuable survey of how processes like tenant reduction changed the character of the farm community across the Lowlands, but also casts a revealing light on the nature and timing of farm improvement and how the wider rural community changed between 1660 and 1815.

From M. Gray's still valuable *The Highland Economy 1750–1850* (Edinburgh, 1955) onwards, the Highlands and Islands are also well served by studies of the rural community and its economy from 1600 to 1800. F. J. Shaw's *The Northern and Western Islands of Scotland: Their Economy and Society in the Seventeenth Century* (Edinburgh, 1980), A. I. MacInnes' *Clanship, Commerce and the House of Stuart 1603–1766* (East Linton, 1996) and R. A. Dodgshon's *From Chiefs to Landlords* (Edinburgh, 1998) all provide surveys dealing with the countryside, but from different perspectives. On more specialist topics, E. Cregeen's 'Tacksmen and their successors: a study of tenurial reorganisations in Mull, Morvern and Tiree in the early eighteenth century', *Scottish Studies*, 13 (1969), 93–144 affords a well-researched analysis of how the structure of the Highland rural community was changing by the early eighteenth century, while E. Richards' *History of the Highland Clearances: Agrarian Transformations and the Evictions, 1746–1886* (London, 1982) remains the most comprehensive analysis of the social and agrarian changes wrought by the spread of sheep and deer.

CHAPTER 2: IMPROVEMENT AND MODERNISATION IN EVERYDAY ENLIGHTENMENT SCOTLAND

This chapter deals with the interrelationship between people's lives and the houses they inhabited prior to 1800, and the bibliography falls into four sections. The first addresses how people built if left to themselves, or vernacular architecture. Ronald Brunskill is the veteran vernacularist of Britain, albeit principally of England, to which *Traditional Buildings of Britain: An Introduction* (London, 1992) is an excellent window. In Scottish terms, there is Bruce Walker and Alexander Fenton's *The Rural Architecture of Scotland* (Edinburgh, 1981), Geoffrey Stell and Anne Riches (eds), *Materials and Tradition in Scottish Building* (1992), Elizabeth Beaton's *Scotland's Traditional Houses* (Edinburgh, 1997), Robert Naismith's *Buildings of the Scottish Countryside* (London, 1985), Historic Scotland's series of *Technical Advice Notes* (or TANS) and the publications of the Scottish Vernacular Building Group – see their *Bibliography Vols 1 &2* (Edinburgh, 1987). Much relevant information is contained in the *Compendium of Scottish Ethnology* series – particularly vol. III – *Scotland's Buildings* (2003). Less has been written about the improved landscape – certainly from the humbler perspective, although Alan Tait's *The Landscape Garden in Scotland, 1735–1835* (Edinburgh, 1980), Robert Naismith's *Buildings in the Scottish Countryside* (London, 1984) and Tim Buxbaum's *Scottish Garden Buildings – from Food to Folly* (Edinburgh, 1989) are useful. Literature on house interiors is not extensive, and Annette Carruthers' edited *The Scottish Home* (Edinburgh, 1996) is only a start. The best covered area is urban change during the Enlightenment, led by Alexander Youngson's *The Making of Classical Edinburgh* (Edinburgh, 1966), Tom Markus's *Order in Space and Society – Architectural Form and its Context in the Scottish Enlightenment* (Edinburgh, 1982), Colin McWilliam's *Scottish Townscape* (London, 1975), and Charles McKean's revisionist 'Twinning cities – modernisation versus improvement in the two towns of Edinburgh', in B. Edwards and P. Jenkins (eds), *Edinburgh – the Making of a Capital City* (Edinburgh, 2005), Bill Brogden (ed.), *The Neo-Classical Town: Scottish Contributions to Urban Design since 1750* (Edinburgh, 1996), and John Frew and David Jones (eds), *The New Town Phenomenon – The Second Generation* (Edinburgh, 2000). David Daiches, *The Scottish Enlightenment: A Hotbed of Genius* (Edinburgh, 1986) is a good introduction to a very wide field, as is Nicholas Philipson and Rosalind Mitchison's *Scotland in the Age of Improvement* (Edinburgh, 1996). Scotland is also well served with two complementary architectural inventories: The *RIAS/Landmark Trust Illustrated Architectural Guides to Scotland* (1982ff: twenty-seven volumes published to date) and the *Buildings of Scotland* (1984ff.) which are both geographically organised. Their interpretations differ. Finally, this chapter has depended heavily upon contemporary writings: for every one published, many more remain in archives throughout the land, but the key ones have been Edmund Burt's *Letters from the North of Scotland* (1734), Thomas Pennant's two *Tours in Scotland* (1772 and 1776), Francis Grose's *The Antiquities of Scotland* (1797), Robert Heron's *Scotland Delineated 1799*, Thomas Garnett's *Tour through The Highlands* (1800), Dorothy Wordsworth's *Recollections of a Tour made in Scotland AD 1803*, Alexander Campbell's *Journey from Edinburgh through Parts of North Britain* (1803), Robert Forsyth's five-volumed, *Beauties of Scotland* (1805–8) and Robert Southey's *Journal of a Tour through Scotland in 1819*.

CHAPTER 3: DEATH, BIRTH AND MARRIAGE IN EARLY MODERN SCOTLAND

Early modern Scottish demography relies on drawing inferences from a range of erratically surviving sources, and so requires a breadth of knowledge about the workings of Scots society. The obvious sources are James Gray Kyd (ed.), *Scottish Population Statistics including Webster's Analysis of Population 1755* (Edinburgh, 1975) for Webster's figures; records of the church, including parish registers of baptisms, marriages and deaths, and the minutes of kirk session meetings, which are indirect but sometimes remarkably informative on population, illness, marriage and more, available through the National Archives of Scotland, at www.nas.gov.uk; and the *Old Statistical Accounts*, useful for the late eighteenth century, at http://edina.ac.uk/stat-acc-scot. For secondary reading on population, see Michael Flinn, Judith Gillespie, Nancy Hill, Ailsa Maxwell, Rosalind Mitchison and Christopher Smout, *Scottish Population History* (Cambridge, 1977) and A. J. Youngson, 'Alexander Webster and his "Account of the number of people in Scotland in the year 1755"', *Population Studies*, 15:2 (1961); Helen M. Dingwall, *Late 17th-Century Edinburgh: A Demographic Study* (Aldershot, 1994) and Maisie Steven, *Parish Life in Eighteenth-century Scotland: A Review of the Old Statistical Account* (Aberdeen, 1995). More recently, see R. E. Tyson, 'Population patterns', in M. Lynch (ed.), *The Oxford Companion to Scottish History* (New York, 2001), pp. 487–489; and his 'Contrasting regimes: population growth in Ireland and Scotland during the eighteenth century', in S. J. Connolly, R. A. Houston and R. J. Morris (eds), *Conflict, Identity, and Economic Development: Ireland and Scotland, 1600–1939* (Preston, 1995). On famines and the great famine of the late seventeenth century, see Ian Whyte, *Agriculture and Society in Seventeenth-Century Scotland* (Edinburgh, 1979); and Laura Stewart, 'Poor relief in Edinburgh and the famine of 1621–24', *International Review of Scottish Studies*, 30 (2005).

As guardians of village morals, overseers of courtship and marriage and as agents of relief to the poor, local ministers and elders of the kirk, as well as ministers' and elders' wives, figured in virtually all facets of birth and death in the village; see the Revd James Anderson, *The Ladies of the Covenant, Memoirs of Distinguished Female Characters, Embracing the Period of the Covenant and Persecution* (New York, 1880); and on marriage and marriage law, see T. C. Smout, 'Scottish marriage, regular and irregular, 1500–1940', in R. B. Outhwaite (ed.), *Marriage and Society: Studies in the Social History of Marriage* (London, 1981), pp. 204–36; A. E. Anton, '"Handfasting" in Scotland', *The Scottish Historical Review*, 37:124 (October 1958) 89–102; W. D. H. Sellar, 'Marriage by cohabitation with habit and repute: review and requiem?', in D. L. Carey Miller and D. W. Meyers (eds), *Comparative and Historical Essays in Scots Law: A Tribute to Professor Sir Thomas Smith QC* (Edinburgh, 1992), pp. 117–36 and A. D. M. Forte, 'Some aspects of the law of marriage in Scotland: 1500–1700', in Elizabeth Craik, (ed.), *Marriage and Property: Women and Marital Customs in History* (Aberdeen, 1984), pp. 104–18; Leah Leneman, *Alienated Affections: The Scottish Experience of Divorce and Separation, 1684–1830* (Edinburgh, 1998) and Rosalind K. Marshall, 'The wearing of wedding rings in Scotland', *Review of Scottish Culture*, 2 (1985), 1–12 and Bruce Seton, 'The distaff side: a study in matrimonial adventure in the fifteenth and sixteenth centuries', *Scottish Historical Review*, 17 (1920), 272–86.

On children, illegitimate births, infanticide and the Old Poor Law, see Rosalind K. Marshall, 'Wet-nursing in Scotland: 1500–1800', *Review of Scottish Culture*, 1 (1984), 43–51; Rosalind Mitchison, *The Old Poor Law in Scotland. The Experience of Poverty, 1574–1845* (Edinburgh, 2000) and with Leah Leneman, *Girls in Trouble* (Edinburgh, 1998); *Sexuality and Social Control: Scotland 1660–1780* (New York, 1989) and 'Scottish illegitimacy ratios in the early modern period', *Economic History Review*, 2d series, 40:1 (1987), 41–63; Deborah A. Symonds, *Weep Not for Me: Women, Ballads, and Infanticide in Early Modern Scotland* (University Park, PA, 1997) and Anne-Marie Kilday, 'Maternal monsters: murdering mothers in south-west Scotland', in Yvonne Galloway Brown and Rona Ferguson (eds), *Twisted Sisters: Women, Crime and Deviance in Scotland since 1400* (East Linton, 2002).

CHAPTER 4: ILLNESS, DISEASE AND PAIN

The topic of illness, disease and pain covers a wide spectrum of factors and influences. Primary sources are relatively sparse, particularly for the earlier part of the period, and comprise mainly institutional records, personal letters and recipes, local council records and publications by physicians or surgeons. The secondary historiography is limited, but expanding. General histories of medicine usually afford Scotland scant attention, but works such as R. Porter, *The Greatest Benefit to Mankind: A Medical History of Humanity from Antiquity to the Present* (London, 1997) are still useful in elucidating the development of Western medicine, which was at the core of Scottish healing. The three main histories of Scottish medicine are J. D. Comrie, *History of Scottish Medicine* (London, 1932), D. Hamilton, *The Healers: A History of Medicine in Scotland* (Edinburgh, 1981) and H. M. Dingwall, *A History of Scottish Medicine: Themes and Influences* (Edinburgh, 2003). They take different approaches but complement each other. An excellent source for study of the medicalisation of hospitals is G. Risse, *Mending Bodies, Saving Souls. A History of Hospitals* (Oxford, 1999) and histories of individual hospitals include J. L. M. Jenkinson, M. S. Moss and I. F. Russell, *The Royal. The History of the Glasgow Royal Infirmary 1794–1994* (Glasgow, 1994). The rise of 'professional' medicine is covered in recent institutional histories: J. Geyer-Kordesch and F. Macdonald, *Physicians and Surgeons in Glasgow. The History of the Royal College of Physicians and Surgeons of Glasgow 1599–1858* (Oxford, 1999), and H. M. Dingwall, *A Famous and Flourishing Society. The History of the Royal College of Surgeons of Edinburgh, 1505–2005* (Edinburgh, 2005). Dynastic features of medicine in the Highlands are well demonstrated in J. Bannerman, *The Beatons. A Medical Kindred in the Classic Gaelic Tradition* (Edinburgh, 1986). A key feature of early modern medicine is the importance of folk healing in all areas, urban and rural, rich and poor. Regional variations are explored in M. Beith, *Healing Threads. Traditional Medicines of the Highlands and Islands* (Edinburgh, 1998) and D. Buchan (ed.), *The Writings of David Rorie* (Edinburgh, 1994), while the essentially herbal nature of treatment is covered in T. Darwin, *The Scots Herbal. The Plant Lore of Scotland* (Edinburgh, 1997). Also of interest here is R. Porter and M Teich (eds), *Drugs and Narcotics in History* (Cambridge, 1995). Closely allied to folk medicine was witchcraft, and the more non-political aspects of the witchcraft phenomenon are explored in J. Miller, 'Devices and directions. Folk healing aspects of witchcraft practice in seventeenth-century Scotland', in J. Goodare (ed.), *The Scottish Witch-Hunt in Context* (Manchester, 2002). The beginnings of the separation of physical and mental illness are illustrated in R. A. Houston, *Madness and Society in Eighteenth Century Scotland* (Oxford, 2000). There is much scope for ongoing research into all of these aspects of illness and healing.

CHAPTER 5: NECESSITIES: FOOD AND CLOTHING IN THE LONG EIGHTEENTH CENTURY

Scottish food and clothing have generated many published commentaries over the years, mostly focused on the so-called 'traditional' or nationally distinctive, ranging from tartan through to porridge and whisky. Yet scholarly discussions within a sustained historical framework have been thin on the ground. A recent study of oats, G. Wallace Lockhart, *The Scots and their Oats* (Edinburgh, 1997) along with the classic economic history of the milling industry, Enid Gauldie, *The Scottish Country Miller, 1700–1900: a History of Water Powered Meal Milling in Scotland* (Edinburgh, 1981) go some way towards a foundation for understanding the basic foodstuff of most eighteenth-century Scots. The economic history is further advanced in A. J. S. Gibson, and T. C. Smout, *Prices, Food and Wages in Scotland, 1550–1780* (Cambridge, 1995), which also deals with changing nutritional standards. But to form a deeper appreciation of what food meant within the cultural context in which it was prepared and consumed, the historian can easily exploit the tools of the anthropologist alongside contemporary commentary, as represented, for instance, in the considerable scholarship of Mary Douglas. See, for an introduction, Mary Douglas (ed.), *Constructive Drinking: Perspectives on Drink from Anthropology* (Cambridge, 1987). Studies of food and drink in England help us to understand some of the similar conditions that prevailed in Scotland. So Peter Clark, *The English Alehouse: A Social History, 1200–1830* (London, 1983) describes a phenomenon that most Scots would have found familiar. And there is much useful information to be gleaned from such publications as *The Cambridge World History of Food*, edited by Kenneth F. Kiple *et al.* (Cambridge, 2000). For the impact of food on the well-being of the population see the pioneering statistical study, R. Floud, K. Wachter and A. Gregory, *Height, Health and History; Nutritional Status in the United Kingdom, 1750–1890* (Cambridge, 1990).

The history of tartan textiles and clothing is well served by such classic accounts as John Telfer Dunbar, *A History of Highland Dress* (Edinburgh, 1962) and my own recent study of the Highland gentry, which takes an anthropological approach to material culture, has much to say about textiles and clothing among an elite group – see Stana Nenadic, *Lairds and Luxury: the Highland Gentry in Eighteenth-Century Scotland* (Edinburgh, 2007). There are a few focused articles on aspects of clothing in Scotland, including E. C. Sanderson, 'Nearly new: the second-hand clothing trade in eighteenth-century Edinburgh', *Costume*, 31 (1997). But again we can turn to some of the classic accounts of clothing cultures in other countries to better understand the similar developments in Scotland, particularly those from France such as Daniel Roche, *The Culture of Clothing: Dress and Fashion in the Ancien Regime* (Cambridge, 1994). Britain as a whole has been well-served by the recent scholarship of Beverly Lemire on the cotton industry and ready-made clothing – see her essay, 'Developing consumerism and ready-made clothing in Britain, 1750–1800', *Textile History*, 15:1 (1984), 21–44 along with Beverly Lemire, *Fashion's Favourite: the Cotton Trade and the Consumer in Britain, 1660–1800* (Oxford, 1991). And John Styles, 'Clothing the North: the supply of non-elite clothing in the eighteenth-century North of England',

Textile History, 25:2 (1994), 139–66, along with John Styles, 'Custom or consumption? Plebeian fashion in eighteenth-century England', in Maxine Berg and Elizabeth Eger (eds), *Luxury in the Eighteenth Century: Debates, Desires and Delectable Goods* (Basingstoke, 2003), 103–18, and *The Dress of the People: Everyday Fashion in Eighteenth Century England* (London, 2007) offer many useful parallels with similar trends in Scotland. Other recent studies of clothing that offer useful insights include David Kuchta, *The Three Piece Suit and Modern Masculinity* (Berkeley, CA, 2002) and Georgio Riello, *A Foot in the Past: Consumers, Producers and Footwear in the Long Eighteenth Century* (Oxford, 2006). And finally, for an excellent introduction to the anthropology of clothing see, Amy de la Haye and Elizabeth Wilson, (eds), *Defining Dress: Dress as Object, Meaning and Identity* (Manchester, 1999).

CHAPTER 6: COMMUNICATING

Inevitably perhaps for a topic as capacious as the one covered by this chapter, published work is in some areas extensive, but in others almost non-existent. For the role of language in binding and dividing communities and as an aspect of social and indeed political identity, the best starting points are probably Charles James and Wilson McLeod, 'Standards and differences: languages in Scotland 1707–1918', in *The Edinburgh History of Scottish Literature, Vol. Two: Enlightenment, Britain and Empire*, Ian Brown *et al.* (eds) (Edinburgh, 2007) and Charles Withers, *Gaelic in Scotland, 1698–1981: The Geographical History of a Language* (Edinburgh, 1984). A stimulating European perspective is provided by Peter Burke in his *Languages and Communities in Early Modern Europe* (Cambridge, 2004). R. A. Houston's study, *Scottish Literacy and Scottish Identity: Illiteracy and Society in Scotland and Northern England 1600–1800* (Cambridge, 1983) is essential reading on the shifting contours of literate and oral cultures, but should be read alongside T. C. Smout, 'Born again at Cambuslang: new evidence on popular religion and literacy in eighteenth-century Scotland', *Past and Present*, 97 (1982). See, too, for the centrality of oral culture in the Highlands, Allan Macinnes, 'Gaelic culture in the seventeenth century: polarization and assimilation', in Steven G. Ellis and Sarah Barber (eds) *Conquest and Union: Fashioning a British State, 1485–1725*, (London, 1995). A convenient summary of developments in education is provided by R. D. Anderson in his *Scottish Education Since the Reformation* (Dundee, 1997), although there is very little in print on the actual experience of education and, more oddly, on informal ways of learning. The importance of the latter has not yet been fully grasped. Work on books and reading is similarly patchy, partly because historians of the Scottish Enlightenment have been so singularly obsessed with the producers rather than reception of ideas. This is beginning to change, however, and current research by Mark Towsey, formerly of the University of St

Andrews, and Vivienne Dunstan of the University of Dundee, promises to fill some of the gaps. Meanwhile, consult Houston's book listed above. The broader culture of print – newspapers, printed ballads and chapbooks – as well as the growing significance of letter writing also lack systematic modern studies. For the former, there is, however, an abundance of readily available primary material, much of it in electronic form, for which go initially to the National Library of Scotland website. Bernard Capp's *When Gossips Meet: Women, Family and Neighbourhood in Early Modern England* (Oxford, 2003) shows how illuminating a study of talk can be, although there is no equivalent for Scotland. However, there is much of interest in Leah Leneman, 'Defamation in Scotland 1750–1800', *Continuity and Change*, 15 (2000). Travel journals, diaries and journals provide some of the most stimulating sources for the study of this topic, although inevitably the view they create is one very largely from above. A personal favourite is James Boswell's journals, if only because he fashioned his identity in such a self-conscious way from literary sources and agonised so much about matters of language and communication. A readily available, and affordable, edition is *Boswell's Edinburgh Journals 1767–1786*, Hugh M. Milne (ed.) (Edinburgh, 2003). The entries in the *Statistical Account* contain much of relevance, not least because they were written at a moment when the political consequences of literacy and reading were pressing very hard on the minds of contemporaries.

CHAPTER 7: ORDER AND DISORDER

As with so many topics in Scottish social history, the best starting guide to the ordering structures of early modern Scotland is T. C. Smout's *History of the Scottish People, 1560–1830* (London, 1969). This can be supplemented by the editors' 'Introduction', in R. A. Houston and I. D. Whyte (eds), *Scottish Society, 1500–1800* (Cambridge, 1989), and, for the forces that maintained order in the countryside, T. M. Devine's chapter, 'Social responses to agrarian "improvement": the Highland and Lowland clearances in Scotland', in the same volume. On the role of the kirk more specifically, see the late R. M. Mitchison's and L. Leneman's *Sexuality and Social Control: Scotland, 1660–1780* (Oxford, 1989), and, broader in its scope, M. Todd, *The Culture of Protestantism in Early Modern Scotland* (New Haven, CT, 2002). Of seminal importance in causing historians to re-think their understanding of accounts of social order built around the concept of paternalism is E. P. Thompson. See in particular his 'The patricians and the plebs', in E. P. Thompson (ed.), *Customs in Common* (London, 1991). For the application of the ideas of Thompson and other challenges to the 'orthodoxy of passivity' in Scottish society see R. A. Houston, 'Coal, class and culture: labour relations in a Scottish mining community, 1650–1750', *Social History*, 8 (1983), 1–18 and C. A. Whatley, 'How tame were the Scottish Lowlanders during the eighteenth century?', in T. M. Devine (ed.), *Conflict and Stability in Scottish Society, 1700–1850* (Edinburgh, 1990), pp. 1–30. Varieties of protest and disorder are explored in greater detail in C. A. Whatley, *Scottish Society, 1707–1830: beyond Jacobitism, towards Industrialisation* (Manchester, 2000). For disorderliness on an everyday level, often the best sources, paradoxically, are kirk session minutes; the ubiquity of the disobedience they reveal is partly captured in L. Leneman and R. Mitchison, *Sin in the City: Sexuality and Social Control in Urban Scotland, 1660–1780* (Edinburgh, 1998), the coverage of which is wider than is suggested in the title.

CHAPTER 8: SENSORY EXPERIENCES: SMELLS, SOUNDS AND TOUCH

This chapter is the first focused study of the senses in Scotland during this period, and as such it is necessary to resort to works by historians examining smells, sounds and touch in other geographical settings for further reading. Their work can provide ideas of the kinds of sources and methods that prove fruitful for research into the sensory past, and their arguments about the development and meanings of sensory experiences gives the historiographical context to this chapter. The pioneering studies of the history of smell were C. Classen, D. Howes and A. Synnott, *Aroma: The Cultural History of Smell* (London, 1984) and A. Corbin, *The Foul and the Fragrant: Odor and the French Imagination* (Cambridge, MA, 1986). Since then, Constance Classen has published *Worlds of Sense: Exploring the Senses in History and Across Cultures* (London, 1993) and Emily Cockayne has written *Hubbub: Filth, Noise and Stench in England 1600–1770* (New Haven, CT, 2007). Cockayne's chapter 5 on noise is especially inspiring, although her study mainly focuses on urban areas, and London in particular. Mark S. R. Jenner's work on smells has been very influential, and includes 'Civilization and deodorization? Smell in early modern English culture', in P. Burke, B. Harrison and P. Slack (eds), *Civil Histories: Essays Presented to Sir Keith Thomas* (Oxford, 2000), pp. 127–44. For introductions to the history of sound in this period, see, B. R. Smith, *The Acoustic World of Early Modern England: Attending to the O-Factor* (Chicago, 1999) and D. Garrioch, 'Sounds of the city: the soundscape of early modern European towns', *Urban History* 30:1 (2003), 5–25. Touch is the sense probably least explored by early modern historians, although the exploration of the significance of one form of touch in K. Harvey (ed.), *The Kiss in History* (Manchester, 2005), will hopefully inspire future research. The collection of essays in E. D. Harvey (ed.), *Sensible Flesh: On Touch in Early Modern Culture* (Philadelphia, PA, 2003) and especially the Introduction by the editor, may provoke ideas. Possibly the most useful source of primary material for this chapter was travellers' accounts. A good printed collection of these is found in P. Hume Brown (ed.), *Early Travellers in Scotland* (Edinburgh, 1891).

CHAPTER 9: BELIEFS, RELIGIONS, FEARS AND NEUROSES

This chapter examines a range of fears – general and specific – that were experienced during this period and draws on a selection of material which covers both the social and economic history, and the history of the church, in Scotland. Works about the church include M. Lee, *The Road to Revolution: Scotland under Charles I, 1625–37* (Urbana, IL, 1985); D. Mullan, *Scottish Puritanism, 1590–1638* (Oxford, 1998); D. Stevenson, *The Scottish Revolution, 1637–44* and *Revolution and Counter-Revolution, 1644–51* (Edinburgh, 2003). M. Todd's *The Culture of Protestantism and Early-Modern Scotland* (New Haven, CT, 2002) and M. Graham's *The Uses of Reform: 'Godly Discipline' and Popular Behavior in Scotland and Beyond, 1560–1610* (Leiden, 1996) both cover the church and its influence on popular behaviour and practice. For works related to European belief and witchcraft S. Clark, *Thinking with Demons: The Idea of Witchcraft in Early Modern Europe* (Oxford, 1997) is extremely valuable and thought provoking and K. Thomas, *Religion and the Decline of Magic* (London, 1971), although somewhat older, is still useful. S. Wilson, *The Magical Universe: Everyday Ritual and Magic in Pre-Modern Europe* (London, 2002) provides an extensive range of comparative material about the magical universe inhabited by European society and the beliefs and rituals which were used as a means to control it. The collection of essays in J. Goodare (ed.), *The Scottish Witch-Hunt in Context* (Manchester, 2002) and, particularly, J. Goodare, L. Martin and J. Miller (eds), *Witchcraft and Belief in Early-Modern Scotland* (Basingstoke, 2008) offer a number of new theories and interpretation about witchcraft and its practice in Scotland. As this chapter is primarily about fear, the essays in W. Naphy and P. Roberts (eds), *Fear in Early Modern Society* (Manchester, 1997) provide interesting discussions about different manifestations and causes of anxieties.

CHAPTER 10: MOVEMENT, TRANSPORT AND TRAVEL

Movement is such a pervasive element to life and living that it is difficult to find any work relating to this period where it does not feature either directly or indirectly as a main theme or as a backcloth. The difficulties of travel within Scotland have long been taken as given, thanks in no small measure to the contributors in the late eighteenth century to Sir John Sinclair's *Statistical Account of Scotland*, and the county *General Surveys of Agriculture*, anxious to highlight both what was being done and what needed to be done. There is much of great eyewitness value in these accounts. But work such as John G. Harrison's, 'Improving the roads and bridges of the Stirling area *c.* 1660–1706', *Proceedings of the Society of Antiquaries*, 135 (2005), on the situation in the Stirling area has provided a valuable corrective to the assumed picture of a system which was unimproved and a failure. Local and regional historians have, in fact, regularly taken up the challenge of exploring transport change at the local level, as with John Patrick's pamphlet on *The Coming of Turnpikes to Aberdeenshire* (Aberdeen, 1985). There are the topical enthusiasts for Highland bridges (Gillian Nelson), or ferries (Linda Chapman), or canals: see, for example, the recent study of Len Paterson, *From Sea to Sea, The History of the Scottish Lowland and Highland Canals* (Glasgow 2006). The older work of A. R. B. Haldane on the *Drove Roads of Scotland* (1968) and the *Scottish Posts* (1971) is still worth respect and consideration. A helpful synthesis which brought together in accessible form writing on transport in Scotland was Anne Gordon's, *To Move with the Times* (Aberdeen, 1988); a new and updated edition would be welcome.

Since the 1970s, transport history as such has rather fallen out of favour within the academic community, though not with the wider historical community, but important work has been done on the flows of migration for work and, indeed, for pleasure. Ian D. Whyte's study of population mobility in early modern Scotland is valuable in highlighting the extent to which people did move. Emigration has, of course, always been in the spotlight, and both it and migration understandably feature to effect in the pioneering, if now dated, opus edited by Michael Finn and others, *Scottish Population History* (Cambridge 1977). Travellers' accounts, of which there are many, are vital in opening a window on the realities of travel, though they can be treated with too much respect. John Allan's journeying in the 1690s, as caught in his diary through John Barrett's transcription (Kinloss, 2004) is particularly valuable in terms of place, time of year and experience, made all the more significant in that he wrote only for himself and not for a wider audience. A good taster is P. Hume Brown (ed.), *Early Travellers in Scotland* (Edinburgh 1891, Edinburgh 1978). But there are many others.

CHAPTER 11: WORK, TIME AND PASTIMES

The classic account of the transition from pre-industrial work to the work regime that accompanied the Industrial Revolution is E. P. Thompson's 'Time, work-discipline and industrial capitalism', first published in 1967 and reprinted in his *Customs in Common* (London, 1991). Other seminal works that contain little or no Scottish material but which provide essential background for anyone wishing to explore the nature of work and worker attitudes generally, include C. R. Dobson, *Masters and Journeymen: A Prehistory of Industrial Relations 1717–1800* (London, 1980) and J. Rule, *The Experience of Labour in Eighteenth-Century Industry* (London, 1981). A splendid Scottish equivalent is W. H. Fraser, *Conflict and Class: Scottish Workers 1700–1838* (Edinburgh, 1988). An invaluable source on working hours, and the irregularity of work – and pay – not only for the eighteenth century but earlier too (about which much less is known), see A. J. S. Gibson and T. C. Smout, *Prices, Food and Wages in Scotland, 1550–1780* (Cambridge,1995). Specifically on women, see E. Sanderson, *Women and Work in Eighteenth-*

Century Edinburgh (Houndmills, 1996), and C. A. Whatley, 'Women and the economic transformation of Scotland, c. 1730–1830', *Scottish Economic & Social History*, 14 (1994), 19–40. For a gendered approach to the subject, which covers a longer period, see D. Simonton, 'Work, trade and commerce', in L. Abrams, E. Gordon, D. Simonton and E. J. Yeo (eds), *Gender in Scottish History since 1700* (Edinburgh, 2006), pp. 199–234. Some of the challenges for Scottish employers in moulding an army of obedient, sober, regularly attending, workers are highlighted in R. A. Houston's seminal 'Coal, class and culture: labour relations in a Scottish mining community, 1650–1750', *Social History*, 8:1 (1983), 1–18. In the English context the assault on leisure and the impact of this on the experience of work is systematically examined in H.-J. Voth, *Time and Work in England 1750–1830* (Oxford, 2000). On aspects of leisure activity in the period 1600–1800, a good start can be made in J. Burnett, *Riot, Revelry and Rout: Sport in Lowland Scotland before 1860* (East Linton, 2000).

Notes on the Contributors

Helen M. Dingwall is an Honorary Lecturer (formerly Senior Lecturer) in the Department of History, University of Stirling. She is author of *Late-Seventeenth Century Edinburgh: A Demographic Study* (Aldershot, 1994); *Physicians, Surgeons and Apothecaries: Medical Practice in Seventeenth-Century Edinburgh* (East Linton, 1995); *A History of Scottish Medicine: Themes and Influences* (Edinburgh, 2003) and *A Famous and Flourishing Society: History of the Royal College of Surgeons of Edinburgh 1505–2005* (Edinburgh, 2005).

Robert Dodgshon was Gregynog Professor of Human Geography in the Institute of Geography and Earth Science at the University of Wales, Aberystwyth until his retirement in 2008. Between 1998 and 2003, he served as Director of the Institute. In 2002, he was elected a Fellow of the British Academy. He has researched extensively on the history of the Scottish countryside, producing books that include *Land and Society in Early Scotland* (Oxford, 1981) and *From Chiefs to Landlords* (Edinburgh, 1998). Currently, he is preparing a text on the history of landscape in the Highlands and Islands for publication and is working on a Leverhulme-funded project on European mountain communities, 1500–1900.

Alastair Durie, formerly of Glasgow University, is now a part-time teaching fellow at the University of Stirling, with continuing research and publication activity in the fields of tourism, medical and sports history, dealing with such topics as the spas and the seaside, golf and grouse. Among his publications is *Scotland for the Holidays. Tourism in Scotland 1780–1939* (East Linton, 2003), to which he is currently writing a sequel on tourism from 1939 to 2000.

Elizabeth Foyster is a Senior College Lecturer in History and Fellow of Clare College, Cambridge. She is the author of *Manhood in Early Modern England: Honour, Sex and Marriage* (Harlow, 1999), and *Marital Violence: An English Family History 1660–1857* (Cambridge, 2005). She is the editor, with Helen Berry, of *The Family in Early Modern England* (Cambridge, 2007), and is the editor, with James Marten, of the forthcoming series for Berg, *A Cultural History of Childhood and Family*.

Bob Harris is a Fellow in History of Worcester College, Oxford. His main publications include *Politics and the Rise of the Press: Britain and France*

1620–1800 (London, 1996), *Politics and the Nation: Britain in the Mid Eighteenth Century* (Oxford, 2002) and *The Scottish People and the French Revolution* (2008). He is currently working (with Christopher Whatley and Charles McKean) on an AHRC-funded project on smaller Scottish towns in the age of the Enlightenment, as well as on a social and cultural history of gambling in the British Isles and British empire in the 'long eighteenth century'.

Charles McKean is Professor of Scottish Architectural History, Department of History, University of Dundee. He is a frequent consultant on historic buildings and towns, and is a member of two of Historic Scotland's Burgh Survey teams. He has published over fifty articles and chapters in books, many on the architecture, gardens, culture and conservation of the Scottish Renaissance, and his twenty-two books include *Fight Blight* (London, 1977), *The Scottish Thirties* (Edinburgh, 1987), *Edinburgh – Portrait of a City* (London, 1992), *The Making of the Museum of Scotland* (Edinburgh, 2000), *The Scottish Château* (Stroud, 2001) and *Battle for the North* (London, 2006). With Bob Harris and Christopher Whatley, he is currently working on the AHRC–funded project studying the smaller Scottish town in the Age of the Enlightenment.

Joyce Miller completed her Ph.D. at the University of Stirling in 1999, and was then a Research Fellow for the Survey of Scottish Witchcraft based at the University of Edinburgh. She has written several popular books on Scottish history and magic and belief, including *Magic and Witchcraft in Scotland* (Musselburgh, 2004), and a number of articles on magical healing practices associated with witchcraft and the appearance of the devil in witchcraft narrative. She currently teaches a number of courses at the universities of Stirling and Edinburgh, and is an historical researcher for an Edinburgh-based oral history/reminiscence organisation.

Stana Nenadic is Senior Lecturer in Social History at the University of Edinburgh. Her research is mainly concerned with the middle classes and elites in Britain in the eighteenth and nineteenth centuries. She also has an interest in material culture. She is the author of *Lairds and Luxury: the Highland Gentry in Eighteenth Century Scotland* (Edinburgh, 2007) and was the editor of *Scottish Economic and Social History* from 1998 to 2002. Her current project is concerned with professionals in London and Edinburgh, 1750–1800.

Deborah A. Symonds is Professor of History at Drake University, where she teaches European, women's and world history. She has written *Weep Not for Me: Women, Ballads, and Infanticide in Early Modern Scotland* (University Park, PA, 1997) and *Notorious Murders, Black Lanterns, and Moveable Goods:*

The Transformation of Edinburgh's Underworld in the Early Nineteenth Century (Akron, OH, 2007). She prefers to work from the records of Scotland's High Court of Justiciary when possible, although she is currently editing some of the unpublished work of her mentor, Elizabeth Fox-Genovese.

Christopher A. Whatley is Professor of Scottish History at the University of Dundee, where he is also Vice Principal and Head of the College of Arts and Social Sciences. He is a Fellow of the Royal Historical Society and a Fellow of the Royal Society of Edinburgh. His main publications include *The Scots and the Union* (Edinburgh, 2006, 2007), *Scottish Society, 1707–1830: Beyond Jacobitism, towards Industrialisation* (Manchester, 2000), and *The Industrial Revolution in Scotland* (Cambridge, 1997). He is currently working (with Bob Harris and Charles McKean) on an AHRC-funded research project into the smaller Scottish towns during the Age of the Enlightenment.

Index